Handbook of International Financial Management

Handbook of International Financial Management

EDITED BY ALLEN SWEENY
AND ROBERT RACHLIN

McGraw-Hill Book Company

New York   St. Louis   San Francisco   Auckland   Bogotá   Hamburg

Johannesburg   London   Madrid   Mexico   Montreal   New Delhi   Panama

Paris   São Paulo   Singapore   Sydney   Tokyo   Toronto

Library of Congress Cataloging in Publication Data
Main entry under title:

Handbook of international financial management.

Includes index.
1. International business enterprises—Finance—
Handbooks, manuals, etc.   I. Sweeny, Allen.
II. Rachlin, Robert, Date.
HG4027.5.H36   1984   658.1'599   83-25581
ISBN 0-07-062578-6

1234567890   DOC/DOC   8987654

ISBN 0-07-062578-6

The editors for this book were William A. Sabin, Chet Gottfried, and Kate
Scheinman, the designer was Al Cetta, and the production supervisor was Sally L.
Fliess. It was set in Times Roman by Bi-Comp, Incorporated.

Printed and bound by R. R. Donnelley & Sons Company.

Contents

Gerald Kramer
Senior Management Partner
The Globecon Group Ltd.

Rodrigo K. Briones
Senior Associate Partner
The Globecon Group, Ltd.

Hing Q. Lum
Director, Corporate Finance
Warner-Lambert Company
and
Pearson Graham
Director of Operating Investments
TRW, Inc.

James M. Needham
Partner
Arthur Young & Company

Robert M. Donnelly
President and CEO
El-o-matic USA

Shiva C. Vohra
Vice President and Manager
Directorate of International Corporate Finance
Algemene Bank Nederland N.V.

Chapter 11
Financing Foreign Investments—
The International Capital Markets 11-1

George T. Cassidy
Treasurer
International Operations Group
St. Regis Corporation

Chapter 12
International Banking Relationship Management 12-1

Ronald J. Rogala
Senior Vice President
Central National Bank of New York

Chapter 13
International Cash Management

 13-1

Fred L. Cohen
Manager, Financial Institutions Consulting Group
Peat, Marwick, Mitchell & Co.

Chapter 14
Accounting in the International Arena

14-1

J. Kenneth Hickman
Partner
Arthur Andersen & Co.

Chapter 15
Auditing in the International Arena

 15-1

John Franklin
Partner-in-Charge
International Desk
Peat, Marwick, Mitchell & Co.

Chapter 16
Budgeting for International Operations 16-1

Gerald F. Lewis
Controller
Mobil Corporation

About the Editors

ALLEN SWEENY is currently vice president for planning and development for International Nabisco Brands. Prior to holding that position, he was vice president of finance and planning for International Standard Brands, where he was responsible for the accounting and financial affairs of some thirty-five foreign subsidiaries. Before joining Standard Brands, Mr. Sweeny held various positions with Exxon Corporation; during most of his career with that company he lived in Colombia and Argentina.

Mr. Sweeny received a B.S. from the University of Kansas and an M.B.A. from Harvard Graduate School of Business.

He has contributed to various professional journals and is the author of *Accounting Fundamentals for Nonfinancial Executives* and *R.O.I. Basics for Nonfinancial Executives*. He also coauthored *Budgeting Fundamentals for Nonfinancial Executives* and, most recently, coedited the *Handbook of Budgeting* published by John Wiley & Sons.

Mr. Sweeny now resides in Manhattan but continues to travel extensively abroad.

ROBERT RACHLIN is president, Robert Rachlin Associates, Plainview, New York, and is an internationally known lecturer, author, and consultant in the areas of financial management.

His associations with major corporations and his numerous clients both in the United States and internationally bring him a reputation among business professionals. He has lectured around the world in such countries as Venezuela, Brazil, Belgium, Mexico, England, Italy, Malaysia, Switzerland, Israel, Canada, Guatemala, Singapore, Nigeria, and Australia.

His books include *How to Use Return on Investment as a Management Tool*, *Return on Investment—Strategies for Profit*, *Profit Strategies for Business*, *Successful Techniques for Higher Profit*, and *Managing Cash Flow and Capital During Inflation*. He is a coeditor of the *Handbook of Budgeting* and a contributor to magazines and to the *Controller's Handbook*. Four of his books have been chosen as main selections by The Executive Program, a Macmillan Book Club.

Mr. Rachlin received a B.B.A. from Pace University in accounting and an M.B.A. from St. John's University in management and economics.

He is a frequent lecturer to professional groups, companies, universities, and practicing professionals. He is also the recipient of the "Fellow" award for outstanding service to the planning profession by the Planning Executives Institute, and served as New York Chapter president for this organization.

Preface

The growth of international business, and the attendant rise of the multinational firm, has been one of the most significant business developments since the end of World War II. The *Handbook of International Financial Management* is concerned with the specific skills, concepts, and techniques that must be employed by those who are or will be charged with the financial management of these ever-increasing global enterprises.

It has been written *by* practicing professionals for practitioners. It has been written *about* all aspects of the unique and critical role that the international financial function plays in the overall success of an international business.

The nineteen chapters that follow draw on the expertise of senior executives, consultants, bankers, and other experts from a variety of prominent multinational institutions. They discuss such topics as:

- Organizing the international financial function
- Understanding, forecasting, and reporting exchange exposure
- Managing and minimizing exchange loss
- Political and economic risk analysis of foreign investments
- Capital budget analysis of foreign investments
- Analysis of foreign acquisitions and mergers
- Foreign licensing as an alternative to direct investment
- International banking and cash management
- Accounting and auditing in the international arena
- Budgeting and control for international operations
- International tax planning and execution

Our very special thanks to the twenty-one authors of this handbook who found time in their already busy schedules to contribute so significantly to this project. We are also particularly grateful to Ines Botero H. for her invaluable administrative assistance and to Bill Sabin and his competent staff at McGraw-Hill for their guidance and support.

Robert Rachlin
Allen Sweeny

Handbook of International Financial Management

One:
The Size, Scope, and Significance of International Business

JAMES BURTLE

James Burtle is professor of economics at Iona College in New Rochelle, New York. Mr. Burtle previously was managing editor of *The International Country Risk Guide*, published by International Reports; vice president in the economics department of W. R. Grace & Company, responsible for exchange rate forecasting and advising on foreign exchange management; and staff member of the International Labor Office in Geneva, Switzerland. He has written numerous articles on international economics and finance and has coauthored *The Great Wheel, The International Monetary System*, with the late Sidney Rolfe. He has served as a member of the Advisory Committee to the U.S. Office of Management and the Budget on the presentation of the U.S. balance of payments and has testified before the Senate Banking Committee on international monetary reform and the operation of foreign exchange markets. Mr. Burtle earned both his B.A. and M.A. degrees from the University of Chicago.

Today most major companies have a key officer who is exclusively concerned with international finance; typically, he or she heads a staff of significant size. This is a relatively recent development—twenty years ago international finance usually was one of the many responsibilities of the corporate treasurer or chief financial officer, since international finance rarely required separate company personnel.

International finance management has gained in importance in most businesses for several reasons. Overall, financial management, domestic and international, has become more complicated and professionalized. Money management is more difficult in a world of floating exchange rates than in one of fixed exchange rates. Finally, and probably most important, international business has grown much more rapidly than business in general. Some writers now estimate that about one-third of the world's gross national product (GNP) is produced under the management of international businesses; a more precise estimate is impossible, because accurate figures are not available for either world output or output of international businesses.[1] International businesses certainly have gained enormously in significance. Moreover, the organization of international business has been almost totally transformed.

Before World War I, most international investment was portfolio—for the purchase of bonds and stocks of companies over which the purchaser has no significant control. Direct investment—over which the parent company exercises control—was less important. In the 1920s, direct investment became more significant, rising to about 25 percent of lending abroad. In the 1930s, portfolio investment declined, and direct investment showed only small increases. After World War II and particularly after the establishment of currency convertibility in Europe in 1958, there was a surge in foreign investment; however, unlike investment in the pre-1914 era, the surge was mainly in direct investment.

It is important, however, to keep in perspective the relative importance of direct and portfolio investment compared with overseas lending by banks. Data for the United States—from which there is the best information on international capital—indicate that bank capital has risen more rapidly than direct investment and that, as a source of U.S. capital abroad, bank capital has become almost as important as direct investment. As shown in Exhibit 1-1, the net U.S. position abroad in the private sector increased from $49.3 billion in 1960 to $516.6 billion in 1980. In the same period, direct investment abroad increased 6.8-fold from $31.9 billion to $215.6 billion, while bank loans outstanding showed a 38.5-fold increase from $5.3 billion to $203.9 billion. There were also rapid increases in nonbank loans, and portfolio investment—as indicated by privately held foreign securities—increased at about the same rate as direct investment, although from a smaller base. It should be stressed, however, that a substantial part of the lending abroad of U.S. banks might not have taken place if there had not been a jump in direct investment abroad. (The data in Exhibit 1-1 indicate book values for direct investments.) In addition, the multinational corporations borrow heavily abroad. As shown in Exhibit 1-2, based on a survey by the U.S. Department of Commerce, assets of U.S. companies abroad in 1977 were

EXHIBIT 1-1   U.S. Investment Position Abroad, Private Sector
($ Billions)

	(1) Direct investment	(2) Foreign securities, privately held	(3) Outstanding nonbank loans	(4) Outstanding bank loans	(5) Total
1960	31.9	9.6	2.6	5.3	49.3
1965	49.5	15.2	4.8	12.0	81.5
1970	75.5	21.0	8.6	13.8	118.8
1971	83.0	23.5	9.6	16.9	133.1
1972	89.9	27.6	11.4	20.7	149.7
1973	101.3	27.4	13.8	26.7	169.2
1974	110.1	28.2	17.0	46.2	201.5
1975	124.1	34.9	18.3	59.8	237.1
1976	136.8	44.2	20.3	81.1	282.4
1977	146.0	49.4	22.3	92.6	310.2
1978	162.7	53.4	28.1	130.8	375.0
1979	187.9	56.8	31.5	157.0	433.2
1980	215.6	62.5	34.7	203.9	516.6

Note: Investment positions are book values, thus excluding borrowings for U.S. businesses abroad.

SOURCE: U.S. Department of Commerce, *Survey of Current Business*, August 1982, p. 45; August 1981, p. 56; August 1978, p. 57; October 1977, p. 23; August 1976, p. 32; October 1975, p. 32; August 1974, p. 5; October 1972, p. 21.

EXHIBIT 1-2   Assets
Abroad of U.S. Companies,
Direct Investments, 1977
($ Billions)

Mining	4
Petroleum	136
Manufacturing	259
Trade	19
Finance[a]	44
Other	28
Total	490

[a] Excludes banking.
SOURCE: U.S. Department of Commerce, *Survey of Current Business*, October 1981, p. 40.

$490 billion. These U.S. companies abroad in 1977 had a book value of $146 billion (Exhibit 1-1) but had borrowed $344 billion to bring their total assets up to $490 billion. A significant part of the $344 billion in estimated borrowings undoubtedly came from the U.S. bank loans outstanding abroad at $92.6 billion in 1977. (See Exhibit 1-1, column 4).

Although data on foreign direct investment positions are less readily available for countries other than the United States, other developed countries are not unimportant in the direct investment scene. Exhibit 1-3 shows

EXHIBIT 1-3   Direct Investment Positions Abroad, Major Developed Countries
(End of Year, $ Billions)

	1967	1971	1973	1975	1976
United States	56.6	83.0	101.3	124.1	136.8
United Kingdom	17.5	23.7	26.9	30.8	32.1
West Germany	3.0	7.3	11.9	16.0	19.9
Japan (fiscal years)	1.5	4.4	10.3	15.9	19.4
Switzerland	5.0	9.5	11.1	16.9	18.6
France	6.0	7.3	8.8	11.1	11.9
Canada	3.7	6.5	7.8	10.5	11.1
Netherlands	2.2	4.0	5.5	8.5	9.8
Sweden	1.7	2.4	3.0	4.4	5.0
Belgium-Luxembourg	2.0	2.4	2.7	3.2	3.6
Italy	2.1	3.0	3.2	3.3	2.9
All other (estimate)	4.0	5.1	6.3	15.1	16.8
Total	105.3	158.6	198.8	259.8	287.9

SOURCE: Organization for Economic Cooperation and Development, *International Investment and Multinational Enterprises*, Paris, 1981, p. 39.

direct investment positions abroad for major countries for 1967, 1971, 1973, 1975, and 1976. Although these statistics are somewhat out of date and may present some problems in comparability between countries, it is safe to conclude that the United States supplies roughly 50 percent of the total foreign direct investment position. The actual data show a small decline in U.S. relative importance from 53.8 percent in 1967 to 47.5 percent in 1976. As indicated in Exhibit 1-4, the host countries of direct investment outflows in 1971 and 1976 were mainly developed countries. Japan was, however, an exception—its percentage of investment in developing countries was roughly half the total. In most cases, companies abroad are affiliates of the parent company. Affiliates are incorporated under the laws of the host country, but a controlling interest in affiliates is held by the parent company. A relatively small proportion of businesses abroad are branches—simple extensions of the parent company not incorporated abroad. In 1980, for exam-

EXHIBIT 1-4   Direct Investment Positions in Developed and Developing Countries, 1971 and 1976

	Investment position		Percent of total	
	1971	1976	1971	1976
United States ($ billions):				
Developed	62.0	107.4[a]	74.7	78.5
Developing	21.0	29.4	25.3	21.5
Total	83.0	136.8	100.0	100.0
United Kingdom (£ billions):				
Developed[b]	4.8	8.5	71.6	75.9
Developing[b]	1.9	2.7	28.4	24.1
Total[b]	6.7	11.2	100.0	100.0
Germany (DM billions):				
Developed	17.1	32.8	71.8	69.8
Developing	6.7	14.2	28.2	30.2
Total	23.8	47.0	100.0	100.0
Japan ($ billions):				
Developed[c]	1.8	7.3	50.0	47.4
Developing[c]	1.8	8.1	50.0	52.6
Total[c]	3.6	15.4[d]	100.0	100.0

[a] Includes $6.2 billion in unallocated investments.
[b] 1975 data used in place of 1976 data; excludes oil.
[c] Fiscal years.
[d] Excludes $500 million unallocated.
SOURCE: Organization for Economic Cooperation and Development, *International Investment and Multinational Enterprises*, Paris, 1981, p. 47.

ple, of about $215 billion in U.S. direct investment abroad, about $33 billion was in branches and $182 billion in affiliates.[2]

The book value position of affiliates depends on two sources of funds. As indicated in Exhibit 1-5, there are outflows of capital from the parent company and income earned by the overseas affiliate that is plowed back into the business. In addition, in calculating the total book value position of the affiliate, there are valuation adjustments (usually small) reflecting the sale or other changes in the values of assets abroad. In 1979, for example, Exhibit 1-5 indicates that the U.S. investment abroad increased to $187.9 billion from $162.7 billion in 1978. This change of $25.2 billion came from $6.3 billion capital outflow from the United States, $19 billion in reinvested earnings of affiliates, and $100 million negative valuation adjustment.

Exhibit 1-6 indicates the relative significance of U.S. direct investment abroad compared with U.S. domestic operations. It is clear that U.S. multinational operations overseas are important compared with their total operations: In 1977, assets of foreign operations of 3425 multinationals were $490 billion or 24.1 percent of these companies' aggregate assets, both foreign and domestic, at $2033 billion. Sales of foreign operations in 1977 at $648 billion were 31.5 percent of total sales, both foreign and domestic, at $2060 billion. Employment of affiliates of businesses abroad in 1977 (7.197 million) was 27.6 percent of total employment in these companies. More up-to-date data are available on capital expenditures of affiliates of U.S. companies. As indicated in Exhibit 1-6, in 1980 foreign affiliates of U.S. companies had capital expenditures (financed by both equity and borrowing) of $42.4 billion. This was 12.5 percent of total U.S. expenditure for plant and equipment ($338.4 billion).[3]

EXHIBIT 1-5 Formation of the U.S. Direct Investment Position, 1950–1980 ($ Billions)

	Capital outflow	Reinvested earnings	Valuation adjustments	Change in position	Total position
1950	0.6	0.5	0.0	1.1	11.8
1960	1.7	1.3	−0.9	2.0	31.9
1965	3.5	1.5	−0.1	5.0	49.5
1970	4.4	3.2	−0.2	7.4	75.5
1975	6.2	8.0	−0.3	14.0	124.1
1976	4.3	7.7	0.8	12.8	136.8
1977	5.5	6.4	−2.7	9.2	146.0
1978	4.7	11.3	0.7	16.7	162.7
1979	6.3	19.0	−0.1	25.2	187.9
1980	2.2	17.0	8.5[a]	27.7	215.6

[a] Reflects a transfer of assets of a U.S. company to a host government.
SOURCE: U.S. Department of Commerce, *Survey of Current Business*, various issues.

THE HEYDAY OF DIRECT INVESTMENT, 1960–1973

Direct investment outflows from 1960 to 1973 increased in the overall Organization for Economic Cooperation and Development (OECD) area at a 12 percent per year rate, about 50 percent greater than the growth rate in current dollars in gross domestic product (GDP) for the area. Since inflation was about 4 percent per year in this period, real growth in direct investment outflows was about 8 percent per year. In the last half of the 1970s, the share of foreign-owned companies in total production in manufacturing was 51 percent in Canada (1974), 28 percent in France (1975), 22 percent in Germany (1976), 24 percent in Italy (1977), and 19 percent in the United Kingdom (1975).[4]

In the early 1970s more than half of direct investment abroad was from U.S. companies. This was all the more striking because exports of U.S. capital were restricted between February 1965 and January 1974 on a voluntary and then mandatory basis (after 1967) to reduce the balance-of-payments deficit. But the contribution of other countries to direct investment was by no means insignificant. Between 1967 (when data on the stock of direct investment abroad are more readily available for major countries) and 1976, as indicated in Exhibit 1-3, the total stock of direct investment abroad jumped from $105.3 billion to $287.9 billion. Of this amount, the United States' share was 53.8 percent in 1967 and 47.5 percent in 1976.

DIRECT INVESTMENT ABROAD SINCE THE MID-1970S

Between 1973 and 1979 direct investment abroad, in real terms adjusted for inflation, slowed to approximately 3 percent per year growth compared with about 8.5 percent from 1960 to 1973.[5] To a large extent this reflects a slower rate of growth in world trade and in output and investment. Moreover, most investment opportunities, particularly in Europe, may already have been tapped.

EXHIBIT 1-6 Indicators of the Relative Importance of U.S. Multinationals, 1977

	U.S. parent	Affiliates abroad	Total	% Affiliates abroad
Assets ($ billions)	1543.0	490.0	2033.0	24.1
Sales ($ billions)	1412.0	648.0	2060.0	31.5
Employment (thousands)	18,885.0	7197.0	26,082.0	27.6
Plant and equipment expenditure, 1980 ($ billions)	296.0	42.4	338.4	12.5

SOURCE: U.S. Department of Commerce, Survey of Current Business, July 1981, p. 63, and October 1981, pp. 11, 40.

The exaggerated idea of U.S. companies taking over most of Europe, presented very eloquently in Jean-Jacques Servan-Schreiber's *The American Challenge*, was replaced in some circles by the view that European businesses would become very influential in the United States.[6] From 1968 to 1973 the United States accounted for 45.8 percent of outward investment flows, but from 1974 to 1979 this share had fallen to 29.3 percent. (See

EXHIBIT 1-7 Inward and Outward Direct Investment Flows, 1961–1978
(Percentage Distributions among Thirteen Countries)

	1961–1967	1968–1973	1974–1978
Inward direct investment flows			
Canada	16.2	12.1	3.2
United States	2.6	11.4	26.7
Japan	2.0	1.7	1.2
Australia	15.6	12.9	9.5[a]
Belgium	4.5[b]	6.1	9.4
France	8.2	8.2	15.2
Germany	21.3	16.4	14.7
Italy	11.5	8.3	5.0
Netherlands	4.7	8.5	6.0[c]
Sweden	2.4	1.7	0.5[d]
United Kingdom	9.7	7.4	6.1
Spain	2.7	3.7	3.7
Norway	0.8	1.4	4.1
Outward direct investment flows			
Canada	2.3	4.5	6.2
United States	61.1	45.8	29.3
Japan	2.4	6.7	13.0
Australia	0.7	1.4	1.6[a]
Belgium	0.3[b]	1.4	2.5
France	6.9	5.2	7.8
Germany	7.2	12.5	17.0
Italy	3.6	3.3	2.0
Netherlands	4.4	6.8	9.6[c]
Sweden	2.0	2.4	3.7[d]
United Kingdom	8.7	9.1	9.2
Spain	0	0.3	0.6
Norway	0	0.3	0.9

[a] From 1974 to 1976.
[b] From 1965.
[c] From 1974 to 1978.
[d] From 1974 to 1977.
SOURCE: Organization for Economic Cooperation and Development, *International Investment and Multinational Enterprises*, Paris, 1981, pp. 40 and 41.

Exhibit 1-7). In part this reflects overseas firms' catching up with U.S. technology and establishing affiliates in the United States to maintain their gains. The process whereby the United States led direct investment overseas in the late 1960s and early 1970s appears to have reversed itself. As indicated in Exhibit 1-7, another striking feature of the 1970s was the sharp drop of investment inflows into Canada. These dropped from 12.1 percent of total inflows in the period 1968–1973 to 3.2 percent from 1974 to 1978.

It is also striking that in the period after 1973 flows of direct investment to developing countries tended to accelerate. In current dollars the rate of increase was 7 percent from 1960 to 1968, 9.2 percent from 1968 to 1973, and 19.4 percent from 1973 to 1978.[7] About 50 percent of this outflow appears to have been from the United States.[8] Currently about 45 percent of exports of developing countries are from foreign affiliates of overseas companies. As indicated in Exhibit 1-8, about half of the stock of direct invest-

---

EXHIBIT 1-8   Stock of Private Direct Investment of Major Developed Countries, by Host Countries[a]
(End of 1978, $ Millions)

Europe		Central America	
Cyprus	90	Bahamas[c]	2,060
Gibraltar	30	Barbados[c]	180
Greece	1,050	Belize	75
Malta	120	Bermuda[c]	4,300
Portugal	560	Costa Rica	290
Spain	5,700	Dominican Rep.	390
Turkey	450	El Salvador	150
Yugoslavia	170	Guadeloupe	55
Total (9%)	8,170	Guatemala	290
Africa, North of Sahara		Haiti	80
Algeria[b]	385	Honduras	270
Libya[b]	660	Jamaica	900
Morocco	350	Mexico	6,000
Tunisia	280	Neth. Antilles	2,500
Egypt	245	Nicaragua	(90)
Total (2%)	1,920	Panama[c]	3,140
Africa, South of Sahara		Trinidad and Tobago	1,300
Angolia	(100)	West Indies (Br.)	970
Benin	34	Total (26%)	22,860
Botswana	57	South America	
Burundi	26	Argentina	3,340
Cameroon	370	Bolivia	140
Central African Empire	(70)	Brazil	13,520
Chad	(26)	Chile	1,440
Congo (P.D.)	170	Colombia	1,510
Ethiopia	(100)	Ecuador[b]	660
Gabon[b]	780	Guyana	230
Gambia	15	Paraguay	110
Ghana	280	Peru	2,150
Guinea	200	Surinam	420

(Exhibit continues)

EXHIBIT 1-8 Stock of Private Direct Investment of Major Developed Countries, by Host Countries *(Continued)*

Guinea (Eq.)	20	Uruguay	330
Ivory Coast	530	Venezuela[b]	3,620
Kenya	520	Total (31%)	27,470
Lesotho	4	Middle East	
Liberia[c]	1,230	Bahrain[c]	210
Malawi	100	Iran[b]	(1,000)
Mali	10	Iraq[b]	150
Mauritania	25	Israel	1,000
Mauritius	24	Jordan	70
Mozambique	(100)	Kuwait[b]	180
Niger	100	Lebanon	(100)
Nigeria[b]	1,130	Oman[b]	50
Rhodesia	(400)	Qatar[b]	150
Rwanda	25	Saudi Arabia[b]	250
Senegal	340	Syria	70
Seychelles	12	United Arab Emirates[b]	190
Sierra Leone	82	Total (1%)	1,220
Somalia	(100)	Asia (including Oceania)	
Sudan	60	Afghanistan	(20)
Swaziland	50	Bangladesh	(80)
Tanzania	170	Brunei	300
Djibouti	10	Burma	65
Togo	100	Fiji Isl.	220
Uganda	(10)	Fr. Polynesia	45
Upper Volta	20	Hong Kong[c]	2,100
Zaire	(1,250)	India	2,500
Zambia	330	Indonesia[b]	5,760
Total (5%)	4,668	Korea (Rep. of)	1,500
		Malaysia	2,680
		Nepal	10
		New Caledonia	145
		New Hebrides	40
		Pakistan	790
		Papua-New Guinea	860
		Philippines	1,820
		Singapore[c]	1,900
		Sri Lanka	70
		Taiwan	1,850
		Thailand	445
		Total (26%)	23,000
		Grand total (100%)	89,308

[a] Includes Development Assistance Committee (DAC) Secretariat estimates for reinvested earnings.
[b] OPEC Member.
[c] Offshore banking center.
Note: Stock figures represent estimated book values.
SOURCE: Organization for Economic Cooperation and Development, *International Investment and Multinational Enterprises*, Paris, 1981, p. 46.

ment in non-OPEC LDCs (less developed countries) is in thirteen countries: Brazil, Mexico, Argentina, Peru, Colombia, India, Malaysia, Taiwan, Hong Kong, Philippines, Singapore, South Korea, and Zaire. In other developing areas, direct investment has grown much more slowly. This seems to indicate that a "takeoff" point has to be achieved before an LDC can become a significant absorber of direct investment. Although data are not readily available, it appears that the OPEC countries are relatively small both for inflows and outflows of direct investment. These countries have preferred portfolio-type investments for capital outflows and have financed most of their development with their own capital. This situation may change, however, because the decline in oil prices has led to shortages of capital, particularly in Nigeria, Indonesia, Algeria, and Venezuela.

FOREIGN DIRECT INVESTMENT IN THE UNITED STATES

As the growth of U.S. direct investment abroad has slowed, foreign direct investment has picked up in the United States, as shown in Exhibit 1-9. The foreign direct investment position in the United States more than doubled from $30.8 billion in 1976 to $65.5 billion in 1980. It has been financed to a significant extent by reinvested earnings. For example, in 1979, of the $12 billion rise in the foreign direct investment position in the United States, $4 billion was in reinvested earnings. As indicated in Exhibit 1-10, the largest part of the direct investment inflows into the United States came from Europe; those from the United Kingdom were especially significant.

Probably as Europe and Japan caught up with the United States, many of the same opportunities that had appeared abroad appeared in the United States. However, as discussed in the next section, it is not always clear why

EXHIBIT 1-9 Formation of Foreign Direct Investment in the United States,
1970–1980
($ Billions)

	Capital inflows	Reinvested earnings	Valuation adjustments	Change in position	Total position
1970	1.0	0.4	0.1	1.5	13.3
1975	1.4	1.2	−0.1	2.5	27.7
1976	2.7	1.7	−1.2	3.1	30.8
1977	2.1	1.6	0.1	3.8	34.6
1978	5.3	2.6	0.0	7.9	42.5
1979	7.9	4.0	0.1	12.0	54.5
1980	4.7	6.2	0.2	11.0	65.5

SOURCE: U.S. Department of Commerce, *Survey of Current Business*, August 1981, p. 41; August 1980, p. 38; August 1979, p. 39; August 1978, p. 40; October 1977, p. 27; and August 1973, p. 50.

investors choose the direct investment form of business organization for overseas investment.

MOTIVATIONS FOR INVESTMENT ABROAD

The rise of the multinational company engaged in managing direct investment abroad has been a challenge to theorists attempting to develop a meaningful overall view of the world economy. Most early theories of the international economy were developed with emphasis on trade rather than investment. Adam Smith, in 1776, advanced the then-revolutionary idea that every nation would be better off if each specialized in what it could do best. Such specialization would emerge from a world of free trade in contrast to the mercantilist view that each nation should apply trade restrictions to maximize its balance-of-payments surplus. Ricardo showed that Adam Smith's theory applied even to poor countries that had no absolute trade advantages—they would almost always have comparative advantages in some product. Over more than 150 years, Ricardo's theory of international trade was subjected to a series of extensive refinements, mainly to take into account the impact on trade of situations of diverse factors of production and differences in demand conditions in different countries. In the most modern theory of international trade—the Heckscher-Ohlin model—each country under free trade produces what is best adapted to its factor endowments. Free trade tends to equalize wage rates and interest rates, although obviously this is a very slow process. But even in their more elaborate formulations, the earlier international economists had relatively little to say about international investment and almost nothing to say about direct investment. When international investment was considered, it was usually in the form of portfolio investment with the rather simplistic assumption that capital would move to areas where rates of return were high-

EXHIBIT 1-10 Foreign Direct Investment Position in the United States, by Country of Ownership, 1975–1980
($ Billions)

	Canada	U.K.	Other Europe	Japan	All other	Total
1975	5.4	6.3	12.3	0.6	3.1	27.7
1976	5.9	5.8	14.4	1.2	3.5	30.8
1977	5.6	6.4	17.4	1.8	3.4	34.6
1978	6.2	7.6	21.5	2.7	4.4	42.5
1979	7.2	9.8	27.6	3.5	6.4	54.5
1980	9.8	11.3	32.1	4.2	8.0	65.5

SOURCE: U.S. Department of Commerce, *Survey of Current Business*, August 1981, p. 41; August 1980, p. 38; August 1979, p. 39; August 1978, p. 40; and October 1977, p. 27.

est. There was no formal conception of an investment abroad that would move *both* money and management overseas.

The classical explanation for movements of capital in terms of differences in rates of return on investment is not strongly supported by available data. As shown in Exhibit 1-11, the evidence is less than compelling that the movement of capital abroad is simply a matter of the pull of higher rates of return. Data on rates of return in petroleum are not comparable between the United States and overseas because of wide differences in calculating special oil payments such as depletion. The "other" category, mainly services, is too much of a mixed bag to compare between areas. A more coterminous but nevertheless very imperfect comparison is between rates of return on book value reported by U.S. affiliates abroad (Exhibit 1-11) and rates of return on equity of U.S. domestic manufactures as reported by the Federal Trade Commission. Between 1970 and 1980 the average rate of return on U.S. investment abroad in manufacturing was 13.6 percent compared with 13 percent earned in the United States in the same period. However, in the 1970 to 1975 period, the differential was somewhat wider at 13 percent on foreign direct investment in manufacturing compared with 11.5 percent on U.S. manufacturing.

These data on comparative rates of return are not strictly comparable in all cases. The data for U.S. rates of return are on an aftertax basis. Foreign

EXHIBIT 1-11 Rates of Return on Book Value in Manufacturing of U.S. Affiliates Abroad and on Equity in U.S. Domestic Manufactures, 1970–1980

	Return to manufactures in the United States	Return to U.S. affiliates abroad in manufacturing	
		Overall	LDCs
1970	9.3%	11.4%	11.9%
1971	9.7	11.3	10.8
1972	10.6	13.9	12.4
1973	12.8	16.5	13.3
1974	14.9	14.0	13.9
1975	11.6	11.1	13.5
1976	14.0	12.5	11.3
1977	14.2	11.8	11.6
1978	15.0	15.6	14.7
1979	16.5	18.4	14.3
1980	14.0	12.7	16.5

SOURCES: Federal Trade Commission, Division of Financial Statistics, *Quarterly Financial Report for Manufacturing Corporations,* Fourth Quarter, 1980, p. 16, and U.S. Department of Commerce: *Survey of Current Business,* various issues.

rates of return are also on an aftertax basis except that income remitted to the United States, after payment of foreign income and remittance taxes, may still be subject to U.S. taxes if overall foreign tax rates are lower than in the United States. Moreover, by sales of materials, equipment, technology, patent rights, and licensing fees, the U.S. company may boost its rate of return even though the benefit does not usually show explicitly in profit and loss statements. As shown in Exhibit 1-12, receipts of U.S. companies' remittances of royalties and fees from affiliates in 1980 were $5.7 billion—15.5 percent of profit remittances ($36.8 billion).

From 1970 to 1980, the average rate of return in manufacturing in developing countries was 13.1 percent; this figure is not significantly different from the rate in developed countries, but it is likely that rates of return do not reflect the costs of executive time in the supervision of the overseas business. Management problems overseas are likely to be very great.[9] Aside from the risk of some form of expropriation, operating a business in an LDC may involve conflict with governments that do not respect human rights or international boycotts. Distinguishing between legitimate payments and bribes and dealing with labor relations in different countries can also be difficult. Some of these problems are discussed in more detail in Chapter 6.

It is of course true that marginal rather than average rates of return are relevant to a company's choice of an investment area. Data for marginal rates of return are not available, but it seems doubtful that marginal rates would have been enough different from average rates of return to account for the large outflow of direct investment.

Another theory suggested to account for the surge in U.S. direct investment abroad in the 1970s is that the dollar in the 1970s was overvalued. Therefore U.S. companies, according to this view, purchased lower-cost plants and equipment abroad. However, this line of argument is valid only when the foreign affiliate is a supplier to the parent company. Otherwise, an undervalued foreign exchange rate affects both the earnings and the value of the investment so that the exchange rate has no effect on the rate of return. In some cases investments may have been made in the expectation of a higher exchange rate, but such anticipations do not appear sufficiently widespread to account for the rapid growth of foreign direct investment. On the contrary, uncertainties in the outlook for exchange rates that emerged in the late 1960s were a marginal deterrent to investment abroad.

WHY DIRECT INVESTMENTS?

Since patterns in rates of return and exchange rates fail to explain direct investment abroad, why direct investment has been undertaken and why it has been preferred to portfolio investment become key questions. These questions provide more than academic interest—they are of vital concern to company financial officers who share in the decision making for new external investments. Decision makers must ask over and over: Is there something special about this kind of investment that will make it ultimately more advantageous than other investments? Are we following some wrong principle into a project that will be more difficult to manage and will involve greater risks? Because of the lack of information in many cases, the danger of being railroaded into a wrong foreign investment is probably greater than on the domestic scene.

One of the more recent works on international investment by Rugman makes the convincing point that most direct investment arises from imperfections in the market.[10] Otherwise, as stated by Stephen Hymer, a company would never want to take on management responsibilities overseas.[11] There are two main sources of market imperfection. First, the company may have certain competitive advantages that it cannot expand at home but wants to push overseas. Longer-term gains are predicted from a rising market share even though returns overseas may not immediately appear greater than at home. The second reason for going overseas is to overcome imperfections in foreign markets. An important example is the jumping of tariff walls by establishing plants abroad. Also important is the greater proximity to operations abroad often in both markets and supplies. Finally, the company may have a technology that is too sensitive to license or sell abroad. It must be produced under the company's own management.

One general view of this process of expansion abroad is found in Raymond Vernon's theory of the product cycle.[12] The theory begins with the development of a new product. As was true of the auto and radio industries, in the beginning a relatively large number of firms in the industry offer a variety of designs and styles, but only some of the firms succeed. Thus a smaller number of companies emerge after an initial shakedown. These surviving companies take advantage of their larger scale and begin exporting. As companies increase their exports abroad, they become concerned that the governments of their customers will apply tariffs and restrictions on imports. The enterprising multinational corporation will attempt to overcome these restrictions by establishing itself in the importing country. In some cases actual tariff barriers may not exist, but foreign competitors may become more adept in imitating the product. A direct investment abroad may protect the product's competitive position because of the advantages of proximity, possible easier access to suppliers, and on-the-spot marketing advantages. When considering this theory, note that the great 1960–1973 surge in direct investment coincided with an even more rapid growth in world trade at about 14 percent per year. However, insofar as the theory implies a jumping over of trade barriers, were these restrictions, especially in developed countries, really important enough to produce the great outflows of direct investment?

Much of the direct investment discussed in product cycle theories is horizontal—a company attempts to produce the same product as at home. This type of investment should be distinguished from vertical and conglomerate types of investment. When a company undertakes a vertical type of investment, it adds a new stage to its production process, for example, when a steel company invests in an iron ore mining company abroad. In a conglomerate investment, a company takes on a business abroad that has no connection with its other lines of business.

Fred Knickerbocker has developed a theory of direct investment that considers this movement of capital abroad as mainly the result of oligopoly.[13] Firms invest abroad to gain advantages in market share over their competitors, even though the operation may not be particularly profitable in the short run. Oligopolistic firms may simply copy each other's actions in building new plants and expanding operations abroad. This tendency is even stronger when the oligopolistic firm has special advantages such as R&D, patents, access to capital, and marketing skills that smaller firms may not possess. In some cases in the United States, firms may have gone overseas to expand by mergers without violating U.S. antitrust laws. In terms of vertical integration, oligopolistic firms will strive to get sources of supply, since they greatly fear having to depend on their competitors for raw materials.

Another view sees direct investment arising not so much from imperfections in product markets as from imperfections in security markets. In many countries security markets are poorly organized and often manipulated. Against this background, it would be naive to expect that a company could get the same benefits of foreign direct investment simply by buying foreign securities. However, this explanation of direct investment fails in countries like Canada and Great Britain where security markets are well organized but where there have nevertheless been very large inflows of direct investment.

Some direct investment abroad may be explained by companies diversifying their sources of income. Portfolio theory, increasingly emphasized in business schools, has taught that losses will be reduced in any particular year if a firm is in different activities. Investment in a number of countries would protect against recessions or political upsets in any one country—all the eggs would not be in one basket. One may question, however, whether there are not diversification opportunities enough within major countries without encountering the great uncertainties of going abroad.

Finally, note that the basic idea that a firm is trying to maximize its return on investment—even over a long-term perspective—has been challenged by Richard Cyert and James March.[14] They argue that each division in a company acts to maximize its benefits—in bonuses, salaries, staff size, and pride of accomplishments—without regard to overall company results. Overseas investment plans become elements of intracompany conflicts. Control over offshore affiliates becomes part of the spoils of an endless intramanagement game for position and power. Economically rational decisions may be given relatively low priority, especially by a weak top management who wants a quiet life free of pressures from the barons in charge of different branches of the company. Decisions will be made on a compromise "meat-ax" basis. For example, one-half of retained earnings in the home business may be invested overseas regardless of actual opportunities abroad. Such compromises easily become precedents that have almost the force of law in the company mores. This kind of behavior, without really careful advance planning, is a trap that sophisticated financial officers should avoid.

OBJECTIONS TO MULTINATIONALS FROM THE DOMESTIC ECONOMY

As multinational corporations have expanded abroad, a minor industry has developed for the evaluation of their alleged benefits and harm to both the parent economies and the economies of the host countries. These critical evaluations are reviewed here because financial officers, in deciding on investment policies, should be aware of the criticism that the company will face almost inevitably as its relative position overseas becomes greater.

Multinational firms are accused of weakening the parent country's balance of payments by exporting capital, of causing unemployment by diverting jobs abroad, of facilitating tax avoidance, and of encouraging monopolies. Two lines of argument point to damage to the country's balance of payments by multinational firms. The first argument is that the outflow of capital is a minus item in the country's balance of payments. This was the motivation for the voluntary and mandatory U.S. controls on capital outflows between 1965 and 1974. However, the negative effect of capital outflow has usually been offset by profit remittances and fees and royalty payments. As indicated in Exhibit 1-12, in 1960 outflows of direct investment (defined to include reinvested earnings) ($2.9 billion) were in the same order of magnitude as income on direct investment ($3.6 billion). By 1980, however, income on direct investment ($36.8 billion) was almost double the direct investment outflow ($18.5 billion). In addition, fees and royalty payments from affiliated companies abroad were $5.7 billion. Also note that in 1980 the U.S. trade deficit at $25.3 billion was more than offset by the $36.8

**EXHIBIT 1-12   Selected Items in the U.S. Balance of Payments, 1960–1980
($ Billions)**

	Merchandise exports	Merchandise trade balance	Fees and royalty income from U.S. affiliates abroad	Income from direct investment abroad	Direct investment outflows, including reinvested earnings	Reinvested earnings
1960	19.7	4.9	0.6	3.6	−2.9	−1.3
1965	26.5	5.0	1.2	5.5	−5.0	−1.5
1970	42.5	2.6	1.8	8.2	−7.6	−3.2
1971	43.3	−2.3	1.9	9.2	−7.6	−3.2
1972	49.4	−6.4	2.1	10.9	−7.7	−4.5
1973	71.4	0.9	2.5	16.5	−11.4	−8.2
1974	98.3	−5.3	3.1	19.2	−9.1	−7.8
1975	107.1	9.0	3.5	16.6	−14.2	−8.0
1976	114.7	−9.3	3.5	19.0	−11.9	−7.7
1977	120.8	−30.9	3.9	19.7	−11.9	−6.4
1978	142.1	−33.8	4.7	25.5	−16.1	−11.3
1979	184.5	−27.3	5.0	38.3	−23.9	−19.0
1980	224.0	−25.3	5.7	36.8	−18.5	−17.0

SOURCE: U.S. Department of Commerce, *Survey of Current Business*, June 1981, pp. 38–39.

billion in income on direct investment. Of course, in the short run a bulge in investment outflows may be temporarily disadvantageous to the balance of payments, but unless the country simply cannot wait for the counterflow of remitted earnings and royalty payments, the net effect is likely to be favorable if the investment outflow is directed to reasonably profitable investments.

Of perhaps greater concern is the possibility that exports will suffer because products formerly exported from the parent country will be produced abroad. A rebuttal argument is that the setting up of a facility overseas will stimulate demand for exports of machinery and equipment and for raw materials. This is a mitigating but probably not a total offset to the loss of exports. Statistical evidence indicates that investment overseas first raises exports but that this tendency may reverse itself later.[15] However, even if exports decline, the controversy is not settled because the exports lost to a home-based multinational might otherwise have been lost to a foreign competitor. Against this background, failure to invest abroad would have led to a loss of potential remittances on income earned abroad as well as a loss of exports.

A second line of argument against the multinational firm from its home base, frequently used by trade unions, is that foreign investment diverts capital abroad and thus causes a loss of jobs or wages or both. Professor Peggy Musgrave has argued that if an estimated $90 billion in capital invested abroad in 1974 had been invested in the United States, labor's share of U.S. income would have been 79.4 percent instead of 72.2 percent.[16] In other words, capital would have been relatively more plentiful, but its earnings in profits and interest would have been relatively lower and the earnings of labor would have been relatively higher. Of course, no one knows for sure what marginal productivities attach to relatively more capital employed and relatively less labor employed. In particular it is uncertain whether the United States would have been harmed by less transfer of technology abroad, since it often has to be accompanied by a transfer of capital. That technology was already in use in the United States, and a loss might have resulted from an inability to sell more of it abroad. However, there is the argument that the United States, by transferring its technology abroad—even to U.S. affiliates—is building up future competition. The rejoinder is that technology can be kept away from foreign countries for only a relatively short time in any case.

A more fundamental question is whether the trade union movement in any country should attempt to restrict the outflow of capital even if this outflow is adverse to its share of national income. Insofar as the outflow of capital hurts U.S. workers, it results in gains to foreign workers. Implicit in the argument is the assumption that benefits to workers in a particular country are more important than benefits to workers in some other country. Theoretically, in a free capital market the overall world income is higher. There is, however, as already discussed, the problem that some capital flows designed to defend oligopoly advantages—as in Knickerbocker's case where companies simply copy each other—may earn less abroad than at home and may not be really optimal. However, it would be an awesome task to decide which capital flows are optimal and which nonoptimal in view of limited statistical data and the uncertainties ahead for all investments.

The third argument against multinational companies is that they are used basically as a tax dodge. Taxes on earnings abroad are deferred so that, in effect, the multinational company gets an interest-free loan for the period between when profits are earned and when they are remitted. Moreover, there are criticisms that overhead costs and transfer prices are shifted in such a way that incomes are moved into areas of lower tax rates. Some of these issues are discussed in Chapter 18; at this juncture, however, it is worth noting that many tax loopholes have been closed and in any case, there are now limited advantages resulting from switching incomes between the parent company and affiliates, since tax rates abroad are now ordinarily not much lower than in the United States.

OBJECTIONS FROM THE HOST COUNTRIES

As multinationals, especially in the late 1970s, came under attack from the home economies, criticisms were probably even greater in the host countries. Multinationals are widely criticized in host countries on both political and economic grounds; often very little attention is given the benefits they may provide in capital, employment, training, and technology. In recent months, however, a significant cooling of this criticism has occurred, particularly in LDCs seriously in need of foreign capital and overextended in bank borrowing. Moreover, there is growing recognition that foreign direct investment is about the only way to gain the benefits of modern technology. Although basic principles can be learned in foreign universities or acquired through the purchase of patents or licensing, the actual application of technology in most cases can be effective only if there is "learning by doing" in a multinational enterprise that already has the technology. There is, however, a cost to the host country of becoming "modern": a significant part of its industry may become controlled by multinationals. In a realistic appraisal, this would be a small price to pay for gains in technology; inevitably, however, foreign investment raises nationalistic objections. Such objections are by no means confined to LDCs. For example, foreign investment in the United States, although usually of much less overall significance, has met resistance, particularly with respect to foreign purchases of farm land.

The multinational is frequently charged with interfering in politics in host countries. This criticism can be answered by company policies to prohibit strictly any political activities in the host country by nationals of the country of the parent company. Such prohibition is not feasible, however, for nationals of the host country who are employed by the firm. In fact, a sophisticated criticism of multinational companies by Albert Hirschman is that they politically neutralize the bourgeoisie that in European countries was the vanguard of political movements for desirable social changes.[17] No such pressures exist when this group is dominated by foreigners who do not want to become involved in politics.

Some criticisms of multinationals in host countries are essentially the same as the sometimes valid criticisms of business generally. They may sacrifice resources and the environment for immediate profit objectives. They may ignore standards of health and safety. They may strengthen monopolies. Among socialists, multinationals are, of course, subject to the same criticisms as private industry in general.

In addition to the criticisms that may apply to businesses in general, host countries have special criticisms that apply directly to multinational companies. Like all employers, they may be accused of paying wages that are too low, but a more sophisticated criticism is that they pay wages that are too high to a small group that becomes an enclave separate from the rest of the country. A dual economy is thus created. This criticism relates to another sophisticated argument that multinationals tend to adopt technologies used in the parent country—technologies that are often too capital intensive for countries with widespread unemployment and underemployment. The result is that too few jobs are created.

Multinational firms are also accused of shaking up the culture of a country by replacing a traditional culture with an alien business culture. Even though incomes may rise in a statistical sense, overall happiness and the quality of life decline.

Finally, multinational businesses are accused of disrupting the foreign exchange system of a host country by excessive profit remittances and capital repatriations. Measures taken by multinational companies to avoid foreign exchange losses by borrowing and remitting the borrowed funds abroad tend, it is alleged, to promote the very currency weaknesses that multinational businesses try to protect themselves from.

SUMMARY

Financial officers in major companies must be prepared for the special problems that arise from foreign direct investment. This is a relatively new form of international investment and a special challenge to international financial managers because it requires much greater day-to-day operational responsibility compared with the two other major forms of international capital movement (portfolio investment and bank lending).

Most direct investments abroad are affiliates; i.e., they are incorporated in the host country with the parent company holding a controlling interest. A minority of direct investments are branches which are simply extensions of the parent company without being incorporated abroad. Typically, there are three sources of financing for foreign direct investments. First, the company receives injections of funds from the parent company, either as an investment or as an intracompany loan. Second, the company abroad reinvests part of its earnings; in the typical case, not all earnings are remitted to the parent. These two sources of financing provide the company book value—also known as its "position" or equity. A third source of funds is external borrowing by the affiliate company (but not intracompany borrowing, which, in most statistical presentations of investment abroad, is considered part of the affiliate's equity). Overall, the affiliate company's assets are defined as its equity (arising from inflows from abroad plus retained earnings) plus its external liabilities.

Despite the great importance of direct investment abroad, there is no agreement on why direct investment takes place. Rates of return on book value for direct investments in manufacturing overseas, at least for U.S. data, are not substantially higher than comparable earnings on home investment. Purchasing foreign securities, it is sometimes argued, might have achieved the same result without the added management responsibilities of direct investment.

Exchange rate changes do not appear to be an explanation for direct investment. Both earnings and the base (i.e., book value) on which rates of return are calculated are affected to the same extent by currency devaluations and revaluations.

Most theories explaining direct investment are based on a perception that markets are oligopolistic and/or certainly highly imperfect. Against this background, companies go abroad to protect positions that they have gained in these imperfect markets. They act, for example, to protect R&D advances that often cannot be marketed without losses of proprietary advantages, to jump over trade barriers raised by foreign governments, and to fight for market shares against competition, even though in the short run such strategies may have limited rate of return advantages. In the longer run, however, expansion overseas may become the main earnings base for a company after markets at home have become saturated and suffer from severe competitive pressure.

Regardless of its motivation, foreign investment clearly showed a remarkable rate of growth, particularly in the period from 1960 to 1973. It increased by 12 percent per year or, in real terms, by about twice the rate of increase in real GDP in the OECD area. Since the mid-1970s, however, in real terms direct investment abroad has slowed, especially from the United States. However, between 1976 and 1980, foreign direct investment in the United States has more than doubled from $30.8 billion to $65.5 billion.

As multinational companies have increased in importance in international business, they have come under widespread criticism both by countries of the parent companies and by host countries. In parent company countries they are charged with weakening the balance of payments by promoting the outflow of capital. This may be a short-run problem, but in the long run the inflow of remittances from direct investments abroad usually will exceed outflows of capital.

It is also claimed that multinationals export jobs. Although there may be some statistical evidence for this tendency in some industries, in many cases foreign competition would have had an even more serious effect on employment if the parent company had not moved aggressively to protect its interests overseas. Another argument against multinational business from the home side is that it is used for a tax dodge. This criticism was once stronger than it is now. Currently, differences in tax rates are seldom enough, except possibly in some LDCs, to give the foreign affiliate any special advantage.

In host countries, multinational businesses have been accused of owning a disproportionate amount of local industry, of interfering in politics, of not creating enough jobs because their operations are too capital intensive, and of disrupting the host country's foreign exchange system by excessive currency remittances. Many of these criticisms of multinationals differ little from radical criticisms of business in general. These criticisms ignore the difficulties involved in getting the benefits of high technology without a significant level of foreign investment, especially in LDCs. In most cases, the know-how of actually applying modern technology cannot be learned from university courses. To use modern technology also requires on-the-job experience that is usually available only in firms with prior experience. Thus host countries have increasingly realized that moves to destroy a foreign business are usually counterproductive.

NOTES

1. Orville Freeman, *The Multinational Company*, Praeger, New York, 1981, p. 2.
2. U.S. Department of Commerce, *Survey of Current Business*, August 1982, p. 22.
3. U.S. Department of Commerce, *Survey of Current Business*, July 1981 and October 1981.
4. Organization for Economic Cooperation and Development (OECD), *International Investment and Multinational Enterprises, Recent International Investment Trends*, Paris, 1981, p. 38.
5. Ibid, pp. 11–12.
6. London, Hamish Hamilton, 1968.
7. OECD, *International Investment*, p. 43.
8. Ibid., p. 44.
9. See Thomas N. Gladwin and Ingo Walter, *Multinationals under Fire: Lessons in the Management of Conflict*, Wiley, New York, 1980.
10. Alan M. Rugman, *Inside the Multinational*, Columbia University Press, New York, 1981, especially chap. 2, pp. 38–51.
11. Stephen Hymer, *The International Operations of National Firms: A Study of Direct Foreign Investment*, MIT Press, Cambridge, Mass., 1976.
12. "International Investment and International Trade in the Product Cycle," *Quarterly Journal of Economics*, May 1966, pp. 190–207.
13. *Oligopolistic Reaction and the Multinational Enterprise*, Harvard Graduate School of Business Administration, Boston, 1973.
14. *A Behavioral Theory of the Firm*, Prentice-Hall, Englewood Cliffs, N.J., 1963.
15. C. Fred Bergsten, Thomas Hart, and Theodore H. Moran, *American Multinationals and American Interests*, Brookings, Washington, 1978, pp. 97–98.

16. *Direct Investment and the Multinationals: Effects on the United States Economy,* Subcommittee on Multinationals, Senate Foreign Relations Committee, 1975, p. 97.
17. *How to Divest in Latin America and Why,* Princeton University International Finance Section, no. 76, 1969, especially pp. 7–8.

REFERENCES

Adler, F. Michael, and Gary C. Hufbauer: *Overseas Manufacturing Investment and the Balance of Payments,* Tax Policy Research Study, no. 1, U.S. Treasury, 1968.

Bergsten, C. Fred, Thomas Hart, and Theodore H. Moran: *American Multinationals and American Interests,* Brookings, Washington, 1978.

Cohen, Benjamin J.: *The Question of Imperialism: The Political Economy of Dominance and Dependence,* Basic Books, New York, 1973.

Cyert, Richard, and James March: *A Behavioral Theory of the Firm,* Prentice-Hall, Englewood Cliffs, N.J., 1963.

Dunning, John (ed.): *International Investment,* Penguin, Harmodsworth, United Kingdom, 1972.

Freeman, Orville: *The Multinational Company,* Praeger, New York, 1981.

Gladwin, Thomas N., and Ingo Walter: *Multinationals under Fire: Lessons in the Management of Conflict,* Wiley, New York, 1980.

Helleiner, Gerald K. (ed.): *The World Divided, the Less Developed Countries in the International Economy,* Cambridge University Press, London, 1976.

Hirschman, Albert: *How to Divest in Latin America and Why,* Princeton University International Finance Section, no. 76, 1969.

Hymer, Stephen: *The International Operations of National Firms: A Study of Direct Foreign Investment,* MIT Press, Cambridge, Mass., 1976.

Kindleberger, Charles P.: *American Business Abroad,* Yale University Press, New Haven, Conn., 1969.

––––– (ed.): *The International Corporation,* MIT Press, Cambridge, Mass., 1970.

Musgrave, Peggy B.: *Direct Investment and the Multinationals: Effects on the United States Economy,* Subcommittee on Multinationals, Senate Foreign Relations Committee, 1975.

Organization for Economic Cooperation and Development, *International Investment and Multinational Enterprises,* Paris, 1981.

Perkins, J. O. N., S. J. Potter, W. B. Reddaway, and C. T. Taylor: *Effects of U.K. Direct Investment Overseas,* Cambridge University Press, London, 1967.

Rugman, Alan M.: *Inside the Multinational,* Columbia University Press, New York, 1981.

Salera, Vergil: *Multinational Business,* Houghton Mifflin, Boston, 1969.

Servan-Schreiber, J. J.: *The American Challenge,* Hamish Hamilton, London, 1968.

United Nations: *Transnational Corporations in World Development,* New York, 1978.

U.S. Department of Commerce: *Survey of Current Business,* 1972–1981.

U.S. Federal Trade Commission, Division of Financial Statistics: *Quarterly Financial Report for Manufacturing Corporations,* Fourth Quarter, 1980.

Vernon, Raymond: "International Investment and International Trade in the Product Cycle," *Quarterly Journal of Economics,* May 1966, pp. 190–207.

––––––: *Sovereignty at Bay,* Basic Books, New York, 1971.

Two: Organizing the International Financial Function

DONALD E. GARRETSON

CHRISTINA M. TEMPERANTE

Donald E. Garretson is a vice president of 3M and president of the 3M Foundation, a corporate philanthropic organization. He has served 3M in many capacities, including treasurer and financial vice president. He earned his A.B. degree and Phi Beta Kappa honors from Washington and Lee University and an M.B.A. from the Harvard Graduate School of Business Administration.

Christina M. Temperante is currency manager in 3M's financial services department. She is responsible for anticipating changes in international currency exchange rates and for cross-currency transactions. Ms. Temperante has served 3M in many financial capacities, including senior accountant and financial analyst in the international operations. She earned a B.A. degree in accounting and business administration from Westminster College and an M.B.A. degree in finance from St. Thomas College.

EFFECTS OF THE BUSINESS CLIMATE

The most important concept in any international financial function must be flexibility. Changes in the corporate product line, in sourcing, in corporate structure, or in the outside operating environment demand quick adjustments within the organization. A financial organization which is firmly and permanently established will not be able to adjust to rapid changes.

Over the past twenty-five years, the business climate, changing national regulations, volatile exchange rates, and worldwide financial crises have made rapid change a way of life for the multinational corporation. In the 1960s, interest rates were very high, and, with many controls on U.S. investment overseas, many U.S. corporations began to borrow abroad to expand their international business base. Because funding was so crucial, the management of international cash was often centralized. Great emphasis was placed on the fast collection of funds, and excess funds were moved around the subsidiary network to reduce total borrowing.

In the 1970s, firms continued to expand overseas, and many corporations' international sales approached one-third to one-half of their total sales. At the same time, interest rates and inflation continued to rise, and floating exchange rates changed everyone's outlook. The issuance of Financial Accounting Standard (FAS) 8 meant that exchange gains and losses would go directly to the income statement, and suddenly the financial function within a multinational corporation received much greater attention. Financial considerations became the deciding factor in many corporate determinations. A move was made toward greater centralization, more specialization, and better expertise.

In the 1980s, the environment has changed again. The Financial Accounting Standards Board (FASB) issued FAS 52, which reverses much of the action of FAS 8. Now foreign exchange gains or losses related to balance sheet items are reported on the balance sheet rather than the income statement. Financial and political crises in many developing countries have made some U.S. corporations reconsider their plans for expansion. Volatile exchange rates have continued into the 1980s. However, on the positive side, the strides made in information technology have greatly improved the firm's ability to communicate on a worldwide basis, and the sheer size of international operations in many companies has forced the development of much greater expertise in the field of international finance, within both corporations and the banking world. This expertise will be increasingly important as we move to meet the challenges of the next decade.

CENTRALIZATION VERSUS DECENTRALIZATION

A definition of terms is necessary even to begin a discussion of the issue of centralization versus decentralization. A centralized international financial function has a strong staff at the parent company level which controls virtually all decision making and planning. The subsidiary financial staff only implements the decisions of the parent. International financial executives in such a case might report to the corporate financial function. In a decentralized function, the executives at the parent company issue a few guidelines, but a majority of the financial decisions and actions occur at the susidiary level, which sends back some reports to the parent. Typically, the international financial executives report to line executives at some lower level, possibly divisional or regional, and the parent or central office financial management deals primarily with policy matters.

Often the most important variable in choosing between a centralized or decentralized function is where the expertise exists. A very small company with very little international experience would probably centralize, keeping everything under tight control. On the other end of the spectrum, a company with a very strong, sophisticated staff at headquarters might also centralize, believing that it would be able to provide a global outlook which would best serve the total corporation. One must be careful that—where expertise is located within the corporation—too much specialization does not create a situation in which line and staff management is very dependent on the special knowledge of one function. The formal organization can become insignificant in this event.

The corporate structure will also be a variable in the degree of centralization in finance. A company with a strong international division at headquarters would invite the same centralized type of organization financially. A large percentage of financing transactions overseas would encourage centralization. The proportion of foreign sales in relation to the total sales is another variable. If an international presence has been built by acquisitions, decentralized relationships would probably continue, especially if the parent staff is less familiar with international problems.

Other considerations focus on the difference in operating environments of the subsidiaries. The number of locations, the exchange controls in the countries, and the degree of volatility of exchange rates could all be key issues. A special communications problem might also be a consideration in the centralization decision.

There are advantages to both centralization and decentralization. A centralized financial function allows close control of financial issues at headquarters. Decisions flow to the top of the financial organization. This process ensures that key issues will get the attention of top management. It also ensures consistency and compliance with the corporation's global policies. A decentralized company would argue that the above advantages could be disadvantages. Should all financial decisions be taken to the top? Not only can data collection costs be enormous, but also centralizing decision making at headquarters can stifle flexibility. Many opportunities may be lost because quick answers were not possible.

Evolutionary Phases?

In the early 1970s, Sidney Robbins and Robert Stobaugh examined three phases of financial organizations.[1] In the first phase, international sales are a very small percentage of the total. Consequently management does not believe that the international financial function needs special attention. Each subsidiary's financial staff is left to operate on its own.

In the second phase, international sales range from 15 percent to 30 percent of the total company. Top management, often because of some shock such as major losses or general displeasure with field management, becomes convinced that international finance needs separate attention. They may feel that larger sales justify a more centralized approach with a more specialized staff at headquarters. Final decisions are then made at headquarters with very little input from overseas management.[2]

In the final phase, a compromise is made, mixing centralization and decentralization. One could argue whether this is truly the last phase—perhaps firms keep their organizations swinging back and forth from a more centralized to a more decentralized form. As mentioned above, there are clear advantages and disadvantages of each type of organization, and, from time to time, firms may find the disadvantages of one form untenable and begin to move in the opposite direction. The argument could also be made that, once again, the environment may play just as important a role as the magnitude of international sales in determining the organizational form. For instance, the increased reliance on computers may encourage centralization.

As another example, many firms today establish centralized reinvoicing centers, in part because of the change in accounting standards, in an effort to optimize cash management. However, increased trade barriers in some countries could force a more decentralized approach.

Combining Centralization and Decentralization

Most firms will try to build a financial organization that incorporates the best aspects of centralization and decentralization. The number of financial options and their complexity makes it unmanageable to make all decisions at headquarters, yet there is a need for a broad set of guidelines for all subsidiaries to follow. This usually takes the general form of a strong headquarters staff to set policies and strategies and a financially sophisticated staff at the local level to act within a set of guidelines. Results are regularly monitored at headquarters. This approach depends heavily on the expertise of subsidiary financial management to maximize cash resources and to identify credit sources. The goal is to encourage the local initiative and to have the local management bring innovative proposals up the line for review and discussion at headquarters. Close two-way communication between the subsidiaries and headquarters is also essential.

Many companies use some sort of rule book to centralize policies and procedures. Headquarters issues the rule book to show standards for various financial decisions such as borrowing and investing or terms of payment on intercompany accounts. It would also set out required reporting procedures. Subsidiary financial management is free to work within these rules. Anything unusual would be referred to headquarters.

Other firms use a regional group to bridge the gap between headquarters and overseas locations. The regional function is a vehicle to facilitate communications both with subsidiaries and with foreign financial information sources. Some decisions are made at the regional level, which avoids having all questions outside of the guidelines referred to head office. This regional group attempts to capitalize on intraregional overlaps such as cross-border funding, centralization of cash resources, and areawide financial strategies. They have close relationships with subsidiary management, both financial and nonfinancial, and with the local financial community. The reporting lines vary, depending on the general corporate structure (which will be discussed in depth later). Often the regional financial management has to report both to regional line management and to the corporate finance group.

A typical mix of centralization and decentralization might split decision making in the following manner: The local financial manager would be responsible for implementing corporate financial programs, recommending strategies, performing international cash management and foreign exchange management functions, and borrowing and repayment of borrowing within certain limits. At corporate headquarters, responsibilities would include setting dividend policies; making debt guarantees and approving borrowing above the subsidiary limits; handling intercompany flows, capitalizations, and acquisitions; managing foreign exchange exposures not hedged at the subsidiary level; and approving long-term investments. Committees are also used to make key decisions in some firms; these combine aspects of centralization and decentralization, depending on the makeup of the committee and the types of decisions made.

Another major responsibility of headquarters staff is the continual monitoring of the subsidiary financial management. This can be done informally through personal contacts, frequent conversations, and visits or more formally by the use of reports, planning processes, and periodic formal reviews. The informal communication is crucial even if formal systems are used. One of the dangers of a formal reporting system is the proliferation of highly structured reports, leading subsidiary personnel to feel that the headquarters staff is demanding lots of meaningless data. Reporting should be continually reviewed for its validity and actual utility in making important decisions. This is important in any corporate environment, but it is especially important in international activities where language and cultural differences increase the possibility of misunderstanding or frustration with the reporting workload. Formal reviews require corporate-level approval of plans for the following period. This again allows headquarters to make major decisions but gives subsidiaries the flexibility to work within those decisions.

It is often necessary to look past the organizational structure to determine the degree of centralization. An informal organization frequently is a mix of centralization and decentralization based on individual personalities or issues, although the formal organization may not fully reveal these aspects.

Centralizing the Cash Function

Centralization or decentralization may not be applied uniformly across all financial functions. The most common financial function to be centralized, even without other centralization, is cash management. The organization could take many forms, but in the most extreme case, all cash worldwide is centralized either at headquarters or in a special subsidiary. Other subsidiaries hold only petty cash.

There are more obvious advantages to cash centralization than to other financial centralizations. Bringing cash resources together globally allows a firm to use cash from one subsidiary to avoid borrowing somewhere else. The information flow encourages better forecasting of cash flows and helps in exposure management by facilitating cash movement to avoid depreciating currencies.

There are also problems in cash pooling. The biggest obstacles are tax regulations and exchange controls which could prohibit cash movements. The Internal Revenue Service (IRS) in the United States may consider some cash transfers as dividends. Sophisticated and often expensive communication systems are essential to use the cash effectively. Besides getting information on cash balances, banking and money market information is also needed. One of the drawbacks to a centralized cash function can be that the subsidiaries do so little investing or borrowing locally that close banking relationships cannot develop, making that source of local financial information of negligible help.

In some companies, a cash-pooling system is simulated but rarely actually done, due to concerns about IRS rulings. In these companies, regular cash reports are received at headquarters, and the staff there is responsible for analyzing arbitrage opportunities. Decisions are centralized, but the actual cash is not.

Other firms have several pools of cash located in various nations where the absence of exchange controls facilitates cash management. These centers are still under the control of the parent company. Subsidiaries repatriate excess funds or channel them into these pools wherever possible considering exchange and tax regulations.

Banks play a major role in some global cash systems. Funds are located in one international bank, often in Switzerland, and the bank handles all services, paying interest on some accounts and frequently handling foreign exchange and netting operations.

Many companies work within a corporate bank structure. The parent company acts as the central banker, and any excess funds go to the parent. There is an attempt usually to keep some decentralization within this structure. Local financial managers can deposit, invest, or borrow at their own discretion. However, forecasting by the subsidiaries is very important so that parent companies can plan their investments and hedging operations.

CORPORATE STRUCTURE

The organization of the financial staff is most directly influenced by factors within the corporation itself. The type of product sold, the number of subsidiary locations, the main competitors—these variables greatly affect the organization of the financial function. But the single most important influence is usually the structure of the rest of the corporation.

Multinational corporations tend to be organized in one of three general forms:

1. International division
2. Worldwide product structure
3. Functional organization

International Division Structure

The most common multinational organization breaks down the total corporation into two parts: domestic and international. The separation is usually made at the very top levels of management. Other than a few specialized staff groups that cut across the corporation, all functions are split between domestic and international operations.

As with any organization, there are both problems and benefits to an international division structure. Often in a large multinational company, domestic issues take precedence over international problems for a number of reasons: Most companies started out as domestic only, the proximity of domestic executives lends more emphasis to the solution of domestic problems, and domestic problems are often less complex and more familiar to the average employee. By setting up an international division, a corporation demonstrates the importance of foreign business. International executives are located at headquarters to ensure that international perspectives are considered in top management decisions. International expertise can be developed as a criterion for top executive positions. A general strategy can be established for all the international operations.

The same factors that create a positive international attitude can also cause some disadvantages. Splitting the company at the very top may cause a competitive situation which can develop into a "we-they" attitude that can be counterproductive. By separating the domestic divisions from direct interplay with the subsidiaries, lower-level division management may lose an important input. In some cases a separate international group becomes another layer of management and slows down the decision-making process. Therefore international managers must develop excellent relationships with domestic managers for ease of communications.

For the financial function, a corporate international division structure leaves a large question. Is finance one of those functions which needs a separate organization to serve both international and domestic divisions, or should international financial executives report to the head of international with a parallel organization in domestic? As in the above discussion of centralization and decentralization, corporations swing from one side to the other. In recent years, the trend has been toward a corporate financial function combining domestic and international divisions.

When local financial directors report to the corporate financial function, they are better able to alert the subsidiary general manager to corporate problems and strategies. They are more like independent advisers to the general manager and are more free to voice a conflicting viewpoint. This type of structure prevents a situation in which the subsidiary financial results can be affected by biased decisions of a strong subsidiary manager. At the same time, this organization could result in an alienation of the subsidiary director and the subsidiary financial director. The financial director might fail to take full advantage of the special issues within the local company.

XYZ Company is an example of a firm which has all its financial staff within corporate finance. Exhibit 2-1 shows a chart of its financial organization. The vice president of finance reports through an administrative vice president to the chair of the board. The financial function is divided into a controller's division and a treasury division. Controller functions include internal auditing, global taxes, financial systems, accounting, and the international controller function, which is further subdivided into reporting, accounting, operations analysis, and planning. XYZ Company also has some regional staffs. The reports group collects information from subsidiaries and regions by product and assembles it into regular reports or special reports on significant problems. The operations analysis group looks at major investment questions, especially those relating to manufacturing facilities.

Responsibilities of the XYZ Company treasurer include insurance, credit, cash management, benefits, and international finance. The international treasurer's function is organized by region with another manager specifically for international credit. The international treasurer is in charge of foreign exchange, international finance, international cash management, international credit, and banking relations. When setting up relations with new banks, local financial managers recommend any new accounts or banking relationships under their local criteria, but the international treasurer makes the final decision.

In general, the local financial managers implement corporate policies and make recommendations. They are evaluated by both the corporate financial manager and the subsidiary managing director. Corporate treasurers are evaluated by their impact on interest income or expense and exchange gains or losses.

When the financial function is centralized within the international division, the subsidiary financial manager reports to the managing director of the subsidiary. There may also be an international financial executive at headquarters reporting to the top international executive. At the local level, advantages are obvious. Local management is a much more unified team, and consequently local issues are often handled more quickly. The subsidi-

EXHIBIT 2-1   **Financial Organization of XYZ Company.**

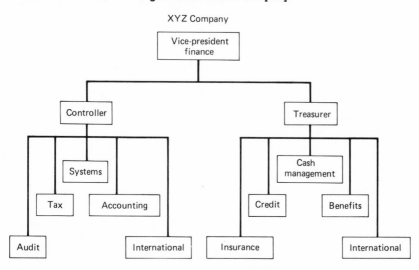

ary financial director in this organization is not viewed as an outsider, so operating decisions may get more financial input. This arrangement also contributes to the managing director's financial expertise.

However, in some cases the managing director may not be able to effectively manage a financial function. If there are problems, the strong local team concept may inhibit the seeking of outside or home office help; in fact, many issues may not be passed on to headquarters at all. Thus the broad corporate perspective may be somewhat lost.

ABC Company is organized in an international division structure, and the international finance function is located within the international division. Under the vice president of international is a director of international administration who has responsibility for exports, credit, legal affairs, control, and treasury. The financial directors in the subsidiaries report to their managing directors but have a "dotted-line" relationship with the international controller and treasurer. (Dotted-line relationship means that there is a strong influence but not day-to-day decision making as to methods, compensation, and evaluation.) There is also a regional organization. Financial directors for the regions report to the international financial executives.

There are rulebooks for accounting procedures to keep reports comparable and to set limits as to decision making. Foreign exchange decisions, for example, are made at various levels. Local payables may be hedged at the local financial manager's discretion. The international treasurer decides on hedges against dividend payments, and a foreign currency protection committee makes the decisions concerning balance sheet hedging. Only short-term financing decisions are made at the local level, and any other financing decisions are made by the international treasurer.

As in all organizational frameworks, an international division structure may lead to a form of financial function which is a hybrid. That is, some parts of the function report through corporate finance while others report through the international division. This is especially common when the international division is just getting established. In many corporations, accounting is often part of the corporate financial function, but all else is within the international division.

DEF Company has specific tasks performed at each level of the financial function. Subsidiary controllers prepare all financial reports, including forecasts, budgets, audit reports, and local tax returns. They also do the financial analysis for their subsidiaries. International controllers train the subsidiary controllers, setting up procedures for budgeting and analyzing the subsidiary's performance. International controllers are very much involved in pricing policies. Corporate controllers set the standards for reporting, accounting, auditing, and capital budgeting. For instance, they decide what public accounting firm to select for the subsidiary and choose the data processing equipment for the local company.

The treasury division of DEF is also split into three levels. The subsidiary treasurer has the responsibility for short-term financing, credit and collections, investing excess cash within a set of guidelines, local insurance, local currency exposure management, and cash forecasting. The international controller again trains the subsidiary treasurer and reviews forecasts and exposures, getting involved in some financing questions. At headquarters the corporate treasurer sets policies for the above functions and handles banking relationships and stockholder relations.

An international division structure for a corporation may weaken the corporate financial function. It puts blinders on the executives when international financial issues are not a consideration in total corporate finance. But such a structure does help to bring international finance into the international strategy. However, there is a more cohesive approach to international business.

Worldwide Product Structure

Under a worldwide product structure, the organization is subdivided by product group, each group having worldwide responsibility. This type of organization has recently grown more popular, especially among high-technology firms who need to coordinate their product knowledge worldwide.

For the financial function, there is a real benefit in involving everyone in global issues. International concerns receive general attention. Financial issues also are more likely to be incorporated into operating decisions than would be the case in a different organization. However, something is also lost in this structure. In an area organization, there is a group of people who specifically look at the special needs of that geographical area in terms of regulations, political climate, or corporate social responsibility. With no geographical breakdown of responsibility, the international specialist may disappear.

Corporations handle this problem in various ways. The most common is to develop some type of regional staff to link the financial concerns of the corporate financial staff with the operating and accounting concerns of the product division financial staffs.

GHI Company is organized into six separate operating units which have global responsibilities. Each unit is run as an independent business, determining its own internal organizational structure. There is also an international staff group that attempts to tie together the total international framework across all product lines.

Financially, there are various organizations within GHI Company. The international staff has a finance group which monitors global foreign currency exposures, prepares budgets, sets global accounting guidelines, and prepares subsidiary reports.

Within each product group, a controller reports to division management. The controller's responsibilities include cost accounting, general accounting, budgeting for the division, data processing, and financial analysis. Accountants for each product line are located in Brussels; plant accountants report to them on a dotted-line basis. The Brussels accountants gather performance information by product and report on divisional working capital.

The assistant treasurer for international is part of the corporate financial staff. She or he is responsible for borrowing forecasts, subsidiary financing, cash management, and foreign exchange management. The treasury function is structured geographically. Credit and collection are the primary product division financial responsibilities other than the reporting of results.

GHI Company has tried to bring a total corporate financial outlook to the global operating units by attempting to emphasize regional management, especially in treasury management. The European regional office is the strongest of the regions. Four of the largest subsidiaries have treasurers who report directly to the European treasurer, who in turn reports through corporate finance. GHI Company would like to continue to give more responsibility to this region. However, the decision-making structure outside of treasury works against strong regionalization. With all operating units located at the parent company, headquarters becomes the center for new financial proposals relating to investments or capital expenditures as well as for final decisions on existing issues.

In Latin America and Asia, the subsidiaries are still very small. A treasury staff exists in only a few locations, so the assistant international treasurer handles these problems directly. There are no regional headquarters yet.

Another disadvantage of GHI's worldwide product structure is duplicate reporting. Operating financial information is required by the product group management, since the divisions are run independently. But financial data must also be collected by subsidiary and by political entity and region. The international staff is responsible for the latter, and thus the financial staff at the local level must deal with a complex set of reporting techniques. Continued effort must be addressed to compatible, reconcilable data accumulation.

A corporate finance group at GHI Company is responsible for consolidations, external reporting, Securities Exchange Commission (SEC) regulations, and stockholder relations.

One of the obvious requirements of this type of organization is close communications. GHI Company tries to move personnel around the organization to help educate managers about total corporate needs. There is no formal structure to bring together financial expertise throughout the corporation, so that communication becomes vital. Dotted-line relationships must be very strong.

Some firms organized in this fashion are structured into product groups everywhere except in cash management, which is centralized. In some cases, the subsidiaries run with basically a working cash balance leaving the entire cash management responsibility in the hands of the headquarters staff and/or regional staff together with the headquarters staff.

Functional Organization

A functional organization is used mainly in companies with a very narrow product line. All functions report globally—there is a single corporate marketing function, financial function, personnel function, etc. The worldwide product line structure discussed above is often quite advantageous for the operating or line organization of the company, but it causes some large difficulties for the financial organization. The functional structure is just the opposite, and, because it does not maximize the operating benefits to numerous main product lines, it is not as common. But when financial considerations are perceived as crucial to the business, a functional organization works very well.

This type of organization lends itself easily to having treasury become a profit center. JKL Company, for instance, breaks their treasury group into three pieces. One assistant treasurer is responsible for systems and strategies, doing economic forecasting, coordinating global credit, and setting long-term strategies for foreign exchange exposure management, as well as designing systems for the treasury group as a whole. The second assistant treasurer deals with problems, such as capitalizations, acquisitions, long-term financing, and lease-or-buy decisions. The third assistant treasurer operates the corporate bank, a short-term vehicle which handles cash flows, investments, and foreign exchange. There are also regional treasurers to fill the gap between corporate finance and the local subsidiary.

MNO Company illustrates some of the typical advantages and disadvantages of a functional organization. The company is organized into three product divisions, a global manufacturing group, and legal, financial, and research groups; all report to the president.

MNO Company was recently reorganized. The company had been very product-oriented, with little consideration given to financial issues. When the company had some good growth years, management found itself with increased financial problems. In reassessing the organization, management apparently found that the financial staff could not handle its new problems. The staff had been reporting to division management, which was not able to challenge the staff properly, perhaps because these executives did not consider finance as important as other areas of concern. In addition, there had been a lot of turnover within the financial staff.

The reorganization was a drastic move for MNO Company. The financial staff is now apparently much stronger. There is much greater consistency in reporting. Financial issues now get a much higher priority than before. However, there are some problems. Following the reorganization, the division managers felt they had been stripped of much of their authority. They no longer had responsibility for finance, research, or manufacturing. Even now, relations among groups appear strained. Strict functionalization reduces interaction between line and staff groups, and people may become very specialized and biased toward their own function. MNO Company is now attempting to rotate its managers among functions to broaden their experience.

Internationally, the controllers group is the only part of the financial organization which is structured specifically to deal with the global business. Both regional and subsidiary controllers report to the international controller. The subsidiary controllers recommend pricing, set foreign exchange strategies, prepare budgets, and supervise data processing. The regional controller coordinates the subsidiaries' financial operations and helps to train and advise their staffs.

Other Corporate Structures

Regional financial organizations have been discussed within other structures, but there is also a regional corporate structure. In this organization, each geographical area is a separate unit reporting directly to the president. This structure emphasizes building regional expertise in all functions.

Financially, regional groups are created which closely parallel a corporate financial group with treasury, control, auditing, and sometimes tax responsibilities. The finance group often reports directly to the regional general manager.

The disadvantages here are obvious. Global strategies are very difficult to create or implement. There must still be a corporate financial function, which again may lead to duplicate reporting. Because specialists at each region are physically apart, the organization is not conducive to pooling knowledge from region to region. Committees are very common in this type of structure to share information and to ensure consistency of policy and practice. Rulebooks also become necessary to ensure global consistency in financial reporting.

But the organization does encourage close working relationships between subsidiaries and regional financial managers, and it allows the financial manager in the region to marry different financial functions together within the area, including exchange controls, economics, tax issues, and accounting. It offers advantages, of course, if the nature of the business and the political entities in one region are different from those of the other regions.

SPECIAL CONSIDERATIONS

The general goal of a financial organization is to provide some centralized coordination while allowing enough flexibility so that subsidiaries can take advantage of their own individual opportunities.

If centralization fits the organization well in all but a few cases, some firms go to a core group of subsidiaries or branches which are centralized; they then treat the other subsidiaries or branches separately. Often joint ventures are the special cases outside the centralized core. Separate handling may also be deemed necessary where nationalization worries are great.

In these separate cases the role of the treasurer changes somewhat. Treasurers become less concerned with financing and investment and shift their emphasis to projected flows from these subsidiaries in the form of dividends. They may also be involved in divestitures.

Growth by Acquisition

Specialized technical knowledge is often gained by acquiring a company with that know-how. Part of what is gained by acquisition is the expertise of the management. The acquiring company must be careful not to organize or reorganize in such a way as to lose the particular talent it was so anxious to get.

From a financial point of view, headquarters may want to be very involved in the new overseas company's financial concerns. But because frequent communication is necessary, there is often a move toward regionalization.

In one company, the parent company staff has the authority for any external long-term borrowing or for short-term borrowing which is done in a different currency. That staff establishes major banking relations and policies for exposure management. Regional managers may approve any hedging of transaction exposure, short-term investments, or short-term borrowing in the local currency; they also coordinate pricing procedures and intercompany flows.

Another company grew by international acquisitions. Corporate finance sets a broad policy. The vice president of finance has a controller and treasurer reporting to him or her. The controller's responsibilities include accounting, data processing, and auditing, and the treasurer handles credit, insurance, benefits, banking relations, and payroll. An international division president has a staff which includes foreign operations managers, a planning group, technical service, and regional directors. These regional directors handle many functions usually thought of as financial and work with the subsidiaries on their budgets, cash flow needs, and intercompany activity. They also analyze subsidiary information.

Developing Expertise

In mixing centralization and decentralization, the goal is to take the best in each organizational form to maximize financial expertise in both the parent company staff and the subsidiary staff and to address financial decisions at the lowest level to expedite them.

The functional organization form discussed in the previous section is probably the best for providing a good career path for financial managers. Their main contacts are financial, and they can move within the function to learn the specialized aspects of their technical field.

A firm has to decide, however, what type of financial executive they want. A functional organization may train a good finance manager who is too parochial to have a good understanding of the other facets of a business decision. An international division organization may offer the financial staff more interaction with line management and hence better understanding of the overall business.

Treasury as Profit Center

In some companies, the treasury group is implicitly held responsible for gains or losses on exchange or interest costs. But, when treasury is a profit center, there is a separate group of financial statements, and results are measured against some predetermined criteria. Although this concept can be used for one aspect of treasury such as foreign exchange, it is most often visualized in the form of a corporate internal bank, encompassing all the treasury functions.

Setting up a corporate bank emphasizes the attempt to attain the lowest possible *total* cost of funds, including all financial factors. It is clearly a move toward centralization, usually provoked by extreme volatility in both exchange and interest rates.

In its purest sense, the profit center concept centralizes all treasury activities. All intercorporate and international cash transactions, including all foreign exchange transactions, are controlled at the central location. All investing and borrowing is done there. Only the profit center management may open or close bank accounts.

A more relaxed form of profit center is seen at PQR Company. There is an international money management function within the corporate treasury group. This group handles all foreign exchange transactions for the parent company and any other foreign exchange transactions given to it. The group monitors through periodic reports all other foreign exchange positions and hedges. A subsidiary may ask the international money market group for an internal hedge. At that time, the treasury would take over the position and decide whether to hedge it. The group is very active in making hedging recommendations to the international treasurers, and it also establishes all banking relations, approves subsidiaries' financial plans, and approves all borrowings over one year.

A profit center could eventually affect cash management, transfer pricing, intercompany transactions, inventory management, and credit terms. The justification for profit center treasury management is that each entity acting independently may not look at the overall needs of the total corporation.

SPECIAL PROBLEMS IN FINANCIAL ORGANIZATIONS

Financial considerations cut across nearly all areas of a corporation, and thus the organization of the financial function is sometimes more difficult than that of other functions. One of the unique things about finance is that the performance of line managers is often significantly affected by financial decisions. Evaluation of management must reflect understanding of the financial organization and the organizational location for certain key financial decisions.

The evaluation of international performance may be done either in local currency or dollars. In either case there are further questions: Is the manager responsible for earnings before or after tax? Do earnings include foreign exchange or inflationary gains or losses? How are these gains or losses calculated? Is interest income or expense included? What are the terms of intercompany or interdivision transactions? All these issues are explored in greater detail in Chapter 17, but they are noted here because of their relevance to the structure of a financial organization and to this all-important question: Does management have authority over those things which significantly affect the results for which management is held accountable?

In evaluation reports or in any other report, one constant problem for the financial manager is that accounting results often do not reflect the reality desired by management. An accounting loss may not necessarily be a cash loss.

Accounting reports can also be very confusing, especially to nonfinancial managers. Professional standards or government regulations demand that results be reported in a form that is not always the most straightforward.

Inflation is another problem in international financial reporting. Accounting regulatory bodies have not yet, despite prolonged effort, developed a universally acceptable method for dealing with this problem internationally.

Because of all the above, it is the financial manager's challenge to interpret or even to restructure financial data and to present them in a form that can be used for decision making.

STRUCTURING THE ORGANIZATION

The first step in evaluating an international financial organization is to take inventory of where the function is at the present time. How is the corporation presently organized outside of finance? How important are international operations to the total corporation? How many international locations are there, and how widespread are they?

Next look at the type of market in which the company operates. Are other competitors local? Is the business capital intensive or labor intensive? If it is very capital intensive, centralization of locations may be logical due to the high investment required to do business there. A different style of asset management may be needed.

What about the financial function? There are many examples of issues which may be included in a financial function, such as pricing, compensation, credit, data processing, economic forecasting, and political risk. Someone must resolve which of these functions should be done and who is responsible. What type of financial expertise is the firm trying to build?

It is then necessary to review the present decision-making levels within the financial organization and their functions. What is done at the corporate level? Is the corporate staff simply a consolidating and coordinating group, or does it consist of the primary decision makers?

Is there an international division? Does it have its own financial staff, or does it use corporate finance? Does the international division need a different type of financial help? Is it a coordinating group, or are its members decision makers?

Do regional organizations exist? If so, are they worthwhile? What is gained by regionalizing the financial function? To whom does regional management report? Where are they located? What types of decisions are made at this level?

At the subsidiary level one of the biggest questions is the quality of the financial people, since the decision-making ability of each subsidiary may depend on the personnel. There may be a split in which larger subsidiaries have more responsibility than do smaller subsidiaries. Is there a treasurer and controller at each location? Who do they report to? How is this system working?

How do product groups interact with finance? Do they have their own staffs? What are their financial needs? What types of decisions are they making?

Next examine the financial aspects of the firm's international business. Is there substantial borrowing? Are cross-currency trade flows large? Are translation exposures large? Are transaction exposures large? How are intercompany prices set? Is there excess cash in some subsidiaries? What currency is used for billing?

What tools are presently available or being used by the corporation for international financial management? Is there an annual budget? Who is responsible for putting it together? Who must approve it? Who is measured against it? Is it a commitment or a forecast?

What reports are presently coming in from the subsidiaries? How good is the information? Who is responsible for errors? What reports go out from the financial group to management? How heavily are they used? Who does the forecasting?

How is the financial system reviewed? Is there significant planning done in the financial group? How are international financial managers evaluated? Is treasury a profit center?

Finally, there is the question of authority. Who sets policies? How often are they reviewed? Who sets procedures? Are they informal or written up as a rulebook? How much leeway is there within the procedures? Who can recommend? How much attention is given to recommendations from below?

To summarize, a great many questions must be asked when deciding how to organize an international financial organization. They fall into the following categories.

1. Corporate structure
2. Nature of the business
3. Definition of the financial function
4. Existing decision-making levels
5. Financial needs

6. Financial tools
7. Authority

SUMMARY

The financial goal of a company is liquidity and solvency. The challenge to the company is to find an international financial organization that will most easily accomplish this goal. Organizations range from centralized to decentralized; most are some mix of the two, and many are more centralized vis-à-vis treasury functions such as exposure management and cash management.

To a great degree the corporate structure will determine the financial organization. The most common structure is an international division structure, although worldwide product divisions are becoming more popular. The financial organization that fits with these structures must bring together local needs with corporate requirements.

There are special considerations in financial organizations, for instance, companies which grew by acquisition may need a different type of structure. In some companies, the treasury is a profit center. Thus, in evaluating an international financial organization, one must ask an endless string of questions to determine goals, authority levels, and available tools. There is no one right organizational form, and each individual situation requires analysis.

NOTES

1. *Money in the Multinational Enterprise*, Basic Books, New York, 1973, pp. 37–47.
2. Ibid.

Three: Fundamentals of Foreign Exchange

HANS P. BELCSAK

Hans P. Belcsak is president of S. J. Rundt & Associates, Inc. Mr. Belcsak's experience includes banking positions in Germany and Italy, the position of head of the World Trade and Transportation Department of the Toledo area Chamber of Commerce, and positions within the Rundt Organization that include research analyst, partner, senior partner, and then president. Mr. Belcsak was educated in Innsbruck, Austria, where he majored in commercial law and political economics and obtained the degree of Doctor of Jurisprudence. He is a frequent lecturer at many associations and has written many articles for major publications.

F oreign exchange has its roots, as an astute French economist once observed, in the coexistence between the internationalism of trade and the nationalism of currencies. In its narrowest sense, foreign exchange is the act of converting the currency of one nation into that of another. The need for such transactions arises when, for instance, the French importer of a German piece of machinery pays the producer in German marks (paid for with French francs), when a U.S. corporation repatriates a dividend from its Italian subsidiary (out of earnings in Italian lire), or when a Swedish bank decides to place excess funds, held in Swedish crowns, on deposit in the Eurodollar market. Thus it is already evident that the enormous increase in the volume of foreign exchange business done every day has gone hand in hand, over the past three decades, with an equally impressive expansion of world trade and, perhaps more important, with the mushrooming of corporations and banks that are active on an international scale, with a multitude of foreign branch operations and subsidiaries.

In a wider sense, the term "foreign exchange" also defines assets, or, more precisely, all claims to another nation's currency that are payable abroad, whether they consist of funds held in foreign monetary units with banks abroad, bills, checks, or other financial instruments.

Foreign exchange rates are the equalizing prices which link different currencies. For the rather limited number of units that are traded on open markets relatively unfettered by government controls, such prices are determined by supply and demand. In this respect currencies differ little from any other commodity. Keep in mind, however, that more or less stringent official restrictions prevent the free play of market forces for the great majority of the world's 150-odd monetary units.

Where government fiat decrees an exchange value (often artificially overpriced), the logical consequence is usually the emergence of a black (illegal) or gray (officially tolerated) "parallel" market, quoting far weaker rates for the unit in question. Banks and corporations will not, as a rule, deal in these markets but should monitor them regularly, since they often provide telling indicators of devaluation risks. Frequently, moreover, a government—finding its currency under irresistible pressure—will set up a multiple exchange-rate mechanism with different prices applicable to different, specified transactions. In such instances, there will usually be one rate that is permitted to float freely, and it, then, becomes the gauge of a currency's weakness.

Many currencies are subject not only to restrictions on rate fluctuations in response to supply and demand forces but also to limitations of their convertibility. These can range from minor encumbrances, preventing conversion for certain purposes (e.g., the remittance abroad of a dividend which lacks prior approval by the authorities) all the way to curbs reducing a unit to a nonconvertible "inland" currency.

Thus, for the purpose of this chapter, the emphasis is on the relatively few currencies (primarily those of Western Europe, North America, and a handful of areas elsewhere in the world) for which the market rather than some national authority effectively sets the exchange rate.

THE GOLD STANDARD FROM 1880 TO 1914

The business of changing money goes back a long way, tied up, as it is, with the very beginnings of banking. Before it could evolve in its present form, however, two preconditions had to be met: (1) The practice of crediting and debiting accounts without actual, physical transfers of funds had to become common; this, in turn, required a high degree of confidence between banks. (2) An efficient system of communications was needed, which became available with the introduction of the telegraph, telephone, and teleprinter for commercial use.

Thus foreign exchange business in today's sense of the word is a relatively recent development, dating back no further than about 1880. It began in the heyday of the gold standard, a monetary system that lasted until 1914. Under this standard, gold was full legal tender in domestic markets. It was also the internationally recognized vehicle for the settlement of obligations. For the yellow metal to fulfill these functions, the central banks involved had to guarantee that they would buy and sell gold in unlimited amounts at a fixed price. Moreover, holders of gold were free to melt down coins to put the metal to different use or to have coins struck from bullion at the state mint, so that there were only marginal price differences between coins and bullion. And, finally, there could be no restrictions on imports or exports of the metal.

Of course, many countries lacked the reserves of gold needed to support a full gold standard. Their answer to the problem was often the introduction of a so-called gold exchange standard, under which the money in circulation consisted partly or entirely of paper but could be, on demand, exchanged into gold at a fixed price guaranteed by the bank of issue. It was rightly assumed that only a fraction of the banknotes would ever be converted in this manner. Hence, the bank of issue did not need to hold full gold coverage for the money it printed, but it had to have enough to maintain confidence in its ability to make good on the exchange guarantee. Internationally, the countries on the gold exchange standard kept their reserves mainly in the currencies of nations that followed the full gold standard, monetary units which by definition were freely convertible into gold.

The system was inherently stable and liberal. It was devoid of exchange controls and had an automatic balancing function that worked roughly as follows. A country running persistent balance-of-payments deficits suffered growing losses of gold. Since there was a direct link between its holdings of yellow metal and the domestic money supply, the drain caused a contraction of internal liquidity, pushed up interest rates, depressed prices and wages, and eventually generated capital inflows as well as an improved international trade competitiveness. Conversely, a nation tolerating continual surpluses in the external accounts saw its gold reserves (and thus the domestic money supply) swell, interest rates fall, and inflation accelerate, until mounting capital outflows and a worsening foreign trade balance erased the black entries in the balance of payments. Such natural adjustments not only were accepted by the central banks but also were frequently reinforced through changes in discount rates and open market operations.

At the start of the twentieth century, this system of international finance was highly developed and functioned on a global scale. Due to its geographic location and Great Britain's far-flung net of trade and banking relations, London became the world's undisputed financial metropolis. Based on the gold standard, the British pound was used as the key means of payment in international commerce and most other cross-border transactions. British bankers financed the bulk of world trade. Sterling balances were held in London by foreign governments and central banks, because "the City" was the only center where such funds could be invested in virtually unlimited amounts in what was regarded, at the time, as the world's safest currency.

Rates of exchange between currencies could fluctuate only narrowly between limits known as the "gold points," beyond which either (on the upside) the debtor preferred to settle an obligation in gold, or (on the downside) the creditor would insist on payment in yellow metal.

Perhaps the most important drawback of the gold standard was that it required governments to subordinate domestic economic considerations to the ideal of balance in their countries' external accounts. The system was, thus, feasible only for nations with well-developed economies and internal sociopolitical stability. For it to be viable, wages as well as prices had to have downward flexibility. After World War I, these conditions ceased to exist even in the economically most advanced countries.

CHAOS BETWEEN THE WARS

World War I brought staggering financing needs for the combatants, which the respective governments could meet only by letting their banknote printing presses run wild. To avoid the deflationary hardships which the gold standard would, as a result, have imposed on their economies, they blocked the mechanism's normal functioning with arrays of exchange controls, starting with the imposition of mandatory artificial exchange rates for banknotes.

After the war, the economies of Europe lay in tatters, inflation was rampant in many lands, gold reserves had been lost, and most currencies were left absurdly overvalued. Central banks no longer considered themselves obliged to honor their paper with gold. Even if they had wanted to remain true to their commitment, the vast amounts of banknotes printed and spewed into circulation during the war years would have made this impossible, even with the help of massive devaluations.

Besides, the war had toppled ideas as well as institutions. People began to ask whether the orthodoxy of the gold standard was really worth the sacrifices that the stern regimen demanded, particularly in the form of deflation and unemployment. The restoration of an international bullion standard thus proved impossible. In 1931, even Britain turned away from the system that had served it so well in its role as the world's foremost trader and financier. In 1933, the United States followed, in the process devaluing the dollar piecemeal from $20.67 per fine troy ounce of gold to $35.00 per ounce. A last-ditch effort by a group of European nations (Belgium, Holland, France, Italy, and Switzerland) to set up a geographically limited gold bloc collapsed in 1936.

The foreign exchange markets, not surprisingly, went through wrenching upheavals during this period and were battered by waves of competitive devaluations. In some countries, the consequences were truly catastrophic, including the utter ruin of currencies such as the German mark, the Austrian crown, the Polish mark, and the Russian rouble. Exchange controls proliferated, and international trade and investment suffered grimly.

During World War II, to make sure that there would be peace on the monetary and economic fronts after the war in the battlefields, the leading nations of the free world decided to convene—in 1944, before the guns had been silenced—a conference at a sleepy New Hampshire resort town by the name of Bretton Woods. Born out of this gathering, and from the marriage, there, of the ideas of British economist John Maynard Keynes and his U.S. colleague Harry Dexter White, was a new monetary system. This system was based, in essence, on the gold exchange standard but with the U.S. dollar rather than the British pound as its lynchpin and with a newly created organization, the International Monetary Fund (IMF), as its supervisory agency.

THE BRETTON WOODS CURRENCY SYSTEM

The currencies of the countries that participated in the Bretton Woods arrangement had fixed parities in terms of both gold and the U.S. dollar. The dollar, for its part, not only had a fixed parity in terms of gold but was also freely convertible into bullion for official holders of greenbacks—governments, central banks, and certain international institutions—at the official selling price of $35 per fine troy ounce.

The central banks of participants undertook to maintain their monetary units between narrow fluctuation margins of +1 percent and −1 percent of their parities. To ensure that the currencies would not burst outside these bands, the monetary authorities were pledged to buy or sell U.S. dollars in unlimited amounts. If a central bank lacked sufficient dollars for such intervention, it could sell gold to the U.S. government or it could obtain funds from the IMF through its "drawing rights," supplemented by direct credits from, or reciprocal swap facilities with, other central banks. The United States was under no obligation to intervene on its currency's behalf, but Washington had a commitment to maintain the dollar's fixed rate convertibility into gold.

The Bretton Woods system worked very well for a number of years, during which parity changes (permitted under the agreement) were few and far between. Although the mechanism kept spot rates stable, it did allow for flexibility in forward rates, since central banks were not required to restrain their movement. The key to the system's smooth functioning in the 1950s and early 1960s was that the U.S. dollar entered the post-World War II period as the world's strongest currency—one that was globally scarce, to boot. With 75 percent of the tallied global gold reserves in its coffers, with its banking system in the most liquid condition since the founding of the Federal Reserve, and with a massive productive capacity waiting to be fully exploited, the United States, through its dollar, filled the vacuum created by the collapse of the pound sterling in the 1930s and became the world's banker.

THE COLLAPSE OF BRETTON WOODS AND THE DEMONETIZATION OF GOLD

The dollar's position did not remain unchallenged for very long, however. In 1950, the U.S. balance of payments shifted from surplus into deficit, and, with the exception of a fluke surplus in 1975, it remained in the red every year thereafter. Gradually at first and then with increasing velocity, the international dollar shortage turned to glut. The first crisis of confidence, triggered by the realization that U.S. gold supplies had shrunk to the point where they no longer covered short-term U.S. liabilities abroad, erupted as early as 1960. It was temporarily overcome with the creation, in 1961, of the so-called Gold Pool, whose purpose it was to spread the responsibility of safeguarding the dollar's bullion convertibility among several nations.

But the U.S. balance-of-payments deficits continued, as did, after a pause of not quite five years, the growth in the global demand for gold. In June of 1967, France withdrew from the Pool, and the devaluation of sterling in the same year reinforced the gathering flight from paper money into the yellow metal. In March of 1968, a new, full-blown crisis was at hand, the Gold Pool collapsed, and Washington, in a last, feeble attempt to control the price of gold, announced the establishment of a two-tier market, with an official, fixed price of $35 per ounce for dealings between central banks and a second, free-floating price for all private transactions.

The bilevel arrangement quickly proved unworkable. The pressures on the dollar continued to mount, and on August 15, 1971, after a massive flight from greenbacks into European currencies (forcing central banks to yield to the onslaught and suspend intervention on behalf of the dollar), Washington bowed to the inevitable. Acknowledging formally what in practice had already become a fait accompli, the administration of President Richard M. Nixon ended the U.S. dollar's convertibility into bullion.

This sounded the death knell for all official parities and intervention points. Most countries hastened to join Germany and Holland in letting their currencies float. But the sentiment among governments was still predominantly against freely fluctuating exchange rates, and, in December of 1971, when the U.S. declared its willingness to devalue the dollar by 7.9 percent to $38.00 per ounce of gold from $35.00, the road was clear for a return to fixed rates.

THE SMITHSONIAN AGREEMENT

At a monetary conference held on December 17 and 18 of 1971, at the Smithsonian Institution in Washington, new parities were set, and currencies were given wider fluctuation ranges from −2.25 percent to +2.25 percent of parity. Against the dollar, the various monetary units thus had total trading ranges of up to 4.5 percent, and against each other they could move by as much as 9 percent. Although the parities and intervention points set at the time are of little practical significance today, they are still used as reference points, for instance for the calculation of trade-weighted appreciation or depreciation rates. The Smithsonian ranges for some of the most important currencies are listed in Exhibit 3-1.

Perhaps the Smithsonian arrangement might have had some durability if it had included the restoration of the dollar's convertibility into gold. Since this was omitted (for very practical reasons, since the United States no longer owned the amount of bullion reserves it would have needed), the new pact merely papered over cracks in the system without repairing its basic frailty. Confidence was not restored. By late 1972, it was clear that a renewed breakdown could not be prevented.

THE ADVENT OF FLOATING EXCHANGE RATES

On February 13, 1973, the U.S. dollar was devalued a second time, by 10 percent, to $42.22 per ounce of gold from $38.00. Under the pressure of relentless, huge flows of funds from dollars into the strong currencies of Europe (especially the German mark, Dutch guilder, and Swiss franc) and the Japanese yen, the affected countries moved swiftly to abrogate their intervention commitment and let their units float against the greenback, this time without much hope that fixed rates would be restored.

The Jamaica Agreement of 1976 merely legalized, from the IMF's point of view, what had become an irreversibly established fact. It revised article IV of the Fund's statutes, allowing each country to chose whether it wants to adopt a fixed or flexible exchange rate system, either independently or in conjunction with other nations. An eventual return to "stable but adjustable" parities was in fact called for, but this phrase is nebulous enough to permit just about any interpretation; in reality a new international monetary system worthy of the name is nowhere in sight.

THE SITUATION TODAY

One vestige of the fixed rate era does survive to this day. The European Economic Community (EEC), in its attempts to make at least some modest progress toward the long-sought goal of monetary union, decided in principle well over a decade ago to keep the fluctuations among member curren-

---

EXHIBIT 3-1 Key Central Rates and Intervention Points under the Smithsonian Arrangement
(Expressed in Foreign Currency Units per U.S. $1)

Currency	Lower intervention point	Central rate	Upper intervention point
Austrian schilling	22.78	23.30	23.82
Belgian franc	43.8075	44.8159	45.8250
Danish crown	6.8230	6.9800	7.1370
French franc	5.0005	5.1157	5.2310
German mark	3.1500	3.2225	3.2950
Dutch florin	3.1718	3.2447	3.3175
Italian lira	568.40	581.50	594.60
Japanese yen	301.07	308.00	314.93
Norwegian crown	6.4950	6.6454	6.7950
Portuguese escudo	26.6368	27.2500	27.8631
Spanish peseta	63.0231	64.4737	65.9243
Swedish crown	4.7048	4.8129	4.9212
Swiss franc	3.7535	3.8400	3.9265
United Kingdom pound	2.6643	2.6057	2.5471

cies within narrower bands than would have resulted from those permitted against the U.S. dollar. The plan received added urgency when the dollar margins were more than doubled under the Smithsonian Agreement. Although the latter allowed maximum fluctuations versus the U.S. dollar of 4.5 percent from top to bottom and thus permitted cross-rate changes among nondollar currencies of up to 9 percent, the EEC nations, in April 1972, undertook to limit the latter to 4.5 percent, or 2.25 percent on either side of par.

Out of this special arrangement, which was soon called the "snake in the tunnel" (with member currencies forming the snake, and the dollar band the tunnel, because of their appearance when rate movements were charted), has developed today's European monetary system (EMS). It links the German mark, the Belgian and Luxembourg francs, the Dutch guilder, the French franc, the Italian lira, the Danish crown, and the Irish punt to one another through a complex cross-rate grid of parities, ceilings, and floors shown in Exhibit 3-2. Within the EMS, fluctuation limits must be strictly observed, and parity changes are permissible only with the consent of the other members.

Otherwise, central banks today have a wide variety of options from which to chose in their selection of the most suitable method of exchange rate management, as may be seen from the schematic description in Exhibit 3-3.

It is moot whether any fixed-exchange-rate system, even one with the Smithsonian's broad trading bands, would have been able to survive the turmoil of 1973–1974—the Yom Kippur war, the Arab oil embargo, the subsequent assertion by the Organization of Petroleum Exporting Countries (OPEC) of its power as a cartel, the staggering oil price hikes that followed, and the dramatic shifts in resources they entailed. However, it is indisputable that the world today is as far away from any return to the discipline of fixed rates as it was right after the old order disintegrated in 1973. Even the EMS, with its aspirations of providing an "island of stability" in a sea of currency volatility, is beset by centrifugal forces because the economies of its members simply do not march to the same drummer.

This does not mean, of course, that governments have wholeheartedly embraced the idea of freely floating exchange rates. Even for those who claim to have done so, the external valuation of their currencies is much too important to be left unprotected and fully exposed to market forces. Dirty floats, i.e., those where central banks intervene when they feel that exchange rates are becoming "economically unrealistic," abound. But this is not to say that intervention under present circumstances is an effective tool. Unless it is internationally coordinated (which happens only on rare occasions), it tends to be messy and—except for brief periods—futile.

THE FOREIGN EXCHANGE MARKET

The foreign exchange market, as it presents itself today, is not an organized trading place in the same sense as stock or commodity exchanges are. There

EXHIBIT 3-2 European Monetary System (Upper, Central, and Lower Limits). All rates effective from February 22, 1982.

	DM	Hfl	BFr	DKr	FFr	Punt	Lit	ECU
Per 1 DM		1.130500	18.9036	3.46141	2.7655	0.29044	573.07	0.413540
		1.105370	18.4837	3.38433	2.5662	0.28402	539.72	
		1.080775	18.0734	3.30915	2.5050	0.27770	508.39	
Per 1 Hfl	0.925250		17.1028	3.13136	2.37065	0.262778	518.47	0.374117
	0.904673		16.7217	3.06162	2.31788	0.256944	488.27	
	0.884550		16.3495	2.99356	2.26628	0.251225	459.88	
Per 100 BFr	5.53301	6.11639		18.7266	14.1774	1.57155	3100.29	0.022373
	5.41018	5.98027		18.3099	13.8616	1.53659	2920.00	
	5.28999	5.84700		17.9019	13.5525	1.50240	2750.00	
Per 1 DKr	0.302196	0.334050	5.58601		0.77423	0.085830	169.33	0.122192
	0.295480	0.326625	5.46154		0.75706	0.083921	159.48	
	0.288900	0.319350	5.34000		0.74025	0.082055	150.20	
Per 1 FFr	0.399202	0.441252	7.37880	1.35090		0.113375	223.66	0.161403
	0.390301	0.431429	7.21415	1.32090		0.110853	210.65	
	0.361598	0.421825	7.05350	1.29160		0.108387	198.22	
Per 1 Punt	3.60086	3.98044	66.5600	12.1870	9.22619		2017.76	1.45603
	3.52090	3.89189	65.0792	11.9159	9.02098		1900.31	
	3.44257	3.80531	63.6315	11.6509	8.82028		1789.71	
Per 1000 Lit	1.96699	2.19304	36.3650	6.65800	5.04489	5.58749		0.0007662
	1.85280	2.04616	34.2466	6.27050	4.74714	5.26229		
	1.74498	1.92875	32.2550	5.90565	4.47107	4.95599		
Per 1 ECU	2.41815	2.67296	44.6963	8.18382	6.19564	0.686799	1305.13	

is no single, physical site where buy and sell orders are executed. Rather, the exchange market consists of an enormous, highly sophisticated, and efficient global communications system in which most transactions are verbally arranged by two parties and executed by telephone or telex. In this market, the banks are the natural intermediaries between supply and demand. Their dealing activity tends to establish uniform price ranges for individual currencies throughout the financial centers of the world, since any deviation too far from the average in a given geographic location will quickly be eliminated by arbitrage.

The exchange market operates literally around the clock, twenty-four hours a day. After the European centers close, New York is still active for several hours. Via the trading rooms on the U.S. west coast, the business then shifts to Far East centers like Tokyo, Hong Kong, and Singapore. These locations have been growing rapidly in importance, with Singapore, for instance, presently reporting an average transaction volume of as much as $8.5 billion a day. From the Far East, activity moves on to the Middle East, e.g., Bahrain, and from there back to Europe. It is no longer unusual for a

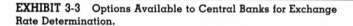

EXHIBIT 3-3   Options Available to Central Banks for Exchange
Rate Determination.

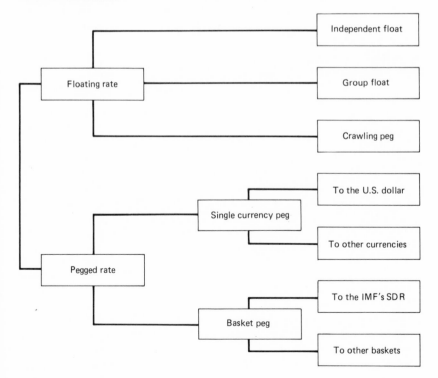

corporate treasurer in, say, New York, to get up at 2:00 a.m., eastern standard time, to call Hong Kong and arrange an urgent deal there. And banks with a well-placed international branch network will be quite prepared to accept stop-loss orders that will be taken around the globe, through the various time zones, to be executed wherever and whenever the stipulated exchange rate is reached.

The "depth" of the market fluctuates, of course, since it depends largely on the number of participants at a given moment. At times, reactions to reports coming over the wire services can have a strong influence, swelling the trading volume or drying it up. But, as a rule, the best markets with the greatest multitude of bids and offers are to be found between 9:00 a.m. and 12:00 noon eastern standard time, when Europe is still at work and New York is open as well. Trading activity tends to thin out after London closes, and it becomes even less lively toward the end of New York's business day.

The various centers do have certain peculiarities distinguishing them, but for the most part these are of little consequence for the corporate treasurer or exchange manager. Thus, in London, still the most important hub, the professional interbank market is conducted almost entirely over direct telephone lines connected to the offices of brokers, who report daily to the Bank of England. There are about 300 banks as active participants, who within the country do not deal directly with each other. In Switzerland, by contrast, the interbank market is bank to bank, without the intermission of brokers. New York traditionally has been a brokerage-oriented market, but some U.S. banks have always preferred to place their bids and offers directly with other banks. Of late, under the leadership of some of the bigger financial institutions, a general trend toward more direct dealing has developed.

In other major centers, e.g., Frankfurt, Brussels, and Paris, there exist meeting places, usually in stock exchange buildings, where foreign exchange business is transacted face to face at a set time, once or twice a day. At such sessions, called "fixings," rates are set for a number of major currencies against the national unit on the basis of bargains that are frequently struck with central bank participation. These rates can be used to execute orders previously placed with the banks. They often also serve as exchange prices for transactions (throughout the day) that are too small to be arranged through the open market, for government purposes such as the calculation of customs duties, and as statistical yardsticks. During the rest of the day, the centers operate much like other markets, and the fixings are, thus, in many ways quaintly anachronistic.

PARTICIPANTS IN THE EXCHANGE MARKET

Corporations are the real end-users of the market. They are the importers needing foreign currency to pay their suppliers or the exporters seeking to sell their exchange receipts. They are companies investing abroad, borrowing in capital markets around the world, repatriating profits and dividends from overseas subsidiaries, or receiving royalties and license fees. They are travel agencies, airlines, insurance agents, and shipping concerns covering foreign currency obligations or converting earnings. And they are multinationals seeking to hedge the "book exposure" that is created by the requirement that foreign assets and liabilities must be restated in consolidated form in the currency of the parent's country. Still, their transactions constitute, in terms of volume, a mere fraction of the total interbank market.

Individuals, like corporations, can be participants for a great variety of commercial and financial purposes. They can also use the market for purely speculative ends, in many parts of the world through the banking system, and in North America primarily through a special futures exchange, the so-called International Monetary Market (IMM). The IMM was originally established in Chicago as an adjunct to the commodity exchange, and it has a number of distinctive features which clearly set it apart from the bank exchange market. For instance, contracts must be for fixed amounts of currency or multiples thereof; there are no "odd-date" transactions, only deals for set maturities; contracts as a rule are "closed out" rather than paid out, i.e., profits and losses are booked but no foreign currency is actually delivered; the IMM has margin requirements; and there are limits on the fluctuation a currency is permitted per day—when the maximum is reached, trading stops. Arbitrage does take place between the IMM and the banks' market, however, and for this as well as psychological reasons the Chicago exchange can have a strong—at times even trend-setting—influence on interbank dealings.

Banks, particularly large commercial banks, are the dominant "players" in the market. They maintain dealing rooms both to trade for their own account and to service their corporate customers' needs. Among them, some are more pivotal than others. Not all banks are "market makers"—to attain this status, a financial institution must be a "good name," and this concept is usually associated with a large capital base as well as an international standing. Smaller banks are not necessarily excluded from the upper crust, but they may have to specialize in aspects of the market that their larger colleagues do not find sufficiently profitable, such as minor currencies or "broken" and "odd" maturities in the forward market.

Since banks act as principals in their buying and selling of foreign currencies, they must take some risks. If they wish to be prime operators, they must be competitive most of the time, and this means that they can rarely afford to match and cover every exposure, currency for currency, amount for amount, date for date. Still, there are marked differences in the attitudes of bank managements, ranging from the ultraconservative to the—at times—irresponsible. The collapse of Germany's Bankhaus Herstatt in 1974 was a classic case of a financial institution winding up in bankruptcy because of reckless overtrading. Since then, banks—both voluntarily and through regulations forced on them—have tightened the restrictions on their dealing rooms considerably, but such external and internal controls can only limit, not eradicate, the risks.

Central banks generally participate in the market either to stabilize exces-sively volatile exchange rate trends or to stop the depreciation or apprecia-tion of a currency believed to be moving too far away from an economically realistic external valuation. Since the abandonment of fixed parities and the adoption of floating exchange rates by most nations, the debate about the pros and cons of each system has never really stopped. Accordingly, govern-ments and their central banks over the years have blown hot and cold on the issue of intervention.

Official attempts to fight market trends may be in vain, because trading volume globally is now so large in the leading currencies that practically no central bank, on its own, has the financial firepower it would need to reverse a strong currency movement. Hence, unless and until central bank interven-tion becomes truly coordinated on an international scale, it will not produce the desired results except for short-lived intervals. National monetary au-thorities are also hemmed in by powerful domestic considerations, since large-scale intervention to support a falling currency contracts the domestic money supply, and efforts to rein in a rising exchange rate have an expan-sionary effect on local liquidity. In the first instance, the central bank must act as a seller of foreign exchange, buying its own currency; in the second instance, it is a seller of its currency and a buyer of foreign exchange.

However, the authorities the world over find the exchange rates of their currencies to be much too weighty influences on the well-being of their economies to be totally left to the vagaries of the market place. Thus there is today virtually no nation aside from the United States that practices a truly free, "clean" float. Although some central banks enter the markets only occasionally, others are constant participants—they do not always want their presence to be known and often operate, therefore, through commer-cial banks as intermediaries. As a rule, they will act in the spot markets; intervention in the forward markets is rare. In some countries, the central banks—for lack of other facilities—must provide the market in minor cur-rencies to allow commercial interests to cover their requirements. In others, exchange controls make the central bank the sole legal supplier of foreign exchange for a selected list or even the great majority of transactions.

Governments and their agencies have exchange needs of their own, for imports, remittances to cover a variety of expenses abroad (such as those of diplomatic and military personnel), payments of principal and interest on their foreign debt, and the buildup of international monetary reserves. They have exchange receipts to convert as well, from exports, investment yields, and interest earnings from foreign lendings.

Brokers are listed last in this lineup, because, in contrast to all the other participants, they are in the markets not as principals, trading for their own account and risk, but merely as agents with the task of pairing off buyers and sellers. They are not supposed to take currency positions of their own. Their role is strictly that of go-betweens and matchmakers working for commis-sions (or bank-paid salaries, as in the case of the Canadian brokers). Many bank dealers, particularly those in trading rooms which are not fully staffed, prefer the broking system, since it makes their work easier: instead of having to contact hundreds of banks, they can leave this chore to the broker, who must keep informed about the bids and offers that are in the market at any given time.

On the other hand, direct bank-to-bank dealing is less costly and allows for close (and valuable) person-to-person contacts between dealers. Also, there will be times when a broker cannot put a transaction together, while in direct trading the dealer called will almost always "make a market" in the spirit of reciprocity. But even the most outspoken opponents of the brokerage system concede that it contributes to the market's depth, since the brokers' interest in large transaction volumes encourages them to drum up deals that otherwise might not take place.

FOREIGN EXCHANGE TRADERS

The bank traders are the spotlighted actors in the exchange markets. Their stage is the trading room, a complex, state-of-the-art communications center with sophisticated arrays of direct telephone and telex links keeping them but a split second away from their counterparts in other banks and the brokers. Spot and forward rates are displayed on constantly updated video screens. There are printers of wire services like A. P., Dow Jones, and Reuters disgorging a steady stream of information on currency trends around the world and on the political and economic events that may affect these trends. Advanced electronic data processing equipment is employed to keep a running account of exchange positions and for the administrative handling of the business done.

What traders need to function effectively in this environment is, quite obviously, an exceptional ability to remain cool under pressure, a willingness to make instant decisions involving high stakes, and a terminology that allows them to compress sizable amounts of crucial information into a few, brief words. Dealers also have to have a high level of personal integrity, since contracts in the exchange market are normally concluded verbally, with written confirmations following only after the fait accompli. Not surprisingly, all this creates an atmosphere that fosters a unique cameraderie among traders, which, in turn, ensures that inevitably arising disputes are virtually always settled amicably. Bank traders see each other as competitors, but they are also keenly aware of their dependence on one another.

TRANSACTIONS

Spot Transactions

By definition, spot transactions are purchases or sales of foreign currency for "immediate" delivery, except that this exchange market expression in practice does not really mean immediate. In every exchange deal there are normally two key dates involved, the so-called *transaction date* on which the respective contract is concluded, and the *value date* on which settlement, i.e., the actual delivery of funds, must take place. Trading "spot" implies a value date that comes two good business days after the transaction date, with "good" (or "clear") meaning that the banks are open in both centers involved. For instance, a DM/U.S.$ spot deal concluded on a Monday would call for delivery the following Wednesday, assuming that Tuesday (and, of course, Wednesday) is not a holiday in either Germany or the United States. Likewise, a transaction on Thursday would be settled the following Monday, and one on Friday would have the next Tuesday as delivery date.

The objective of this arrangement is "compensated value," meaning that both parties to the deal should receive, and make, delivery on the same business day, so that neither loses out on the use of funds. Given the time differential between, say, Europe and the United States, compensated value could not be achieved with same-day delivery and often not even with next-day settlement. Thus, the two-day rule holds true for most currencies and markets, but not without exceptions.

There are some centers, especially in the Far East, which deal spot for delivery the following day, and some trade for "cash" settlement, meaning settlement on the same day. In New York, currencies within the same time zones (the Canadian dollar and the Mexican peso) are normally traded for next-day delivery. Even in other currencies and markets, cash or value the same day or next day is usually feasible as a contract condition, but the party initiating the deal must make its preference clearly known in advance and will be charged one or two days' interest, which will be built into the quoted exchange rate.

Spot is, thus, the all-important rate. It forms the basis for all other exchange transactions, and quotations for delivery or settlement on any other than the spot date will be calculated from this rate. If a customer contacts a bank with the expressed wish to buy or sell currency without specifying the delivery date, it is automatically assumed that he or she wants to deal spot.

Exhibit 3-4 shows some typical examples of spot rates for major currencies against the U.S. dollar. From these it will be seen that in most cases the "direct" quotation is used, which indicates how many units of a given currency are equivalent to one U.S. dollar. At one time, exchange traders in the United States used the "indirect" method of quoting, which expresses the U.S. dollar equivalent of one unit of another currency. While U.S. $1.00 = DM 2.5280 is the direct quotation, for instance, DM 1.00 = U.S. $0.3956 would be the indirect one.

Today, U.S. traders also quote direct, but there are exceptions to the rule. For example, when Great Britain did not have a decimal system, it was traditionally easier to quote the value of the pound sterling in terms of the foreign currency (including the U.S. dollar), and this practice has been retained, although the United Kingdom now does employ the decimal system. Thus, Exhibit 3-4 shows how many U.S. dollars one pound will buy, not the other way around. The same holds true for a small number of other currencies, including the Australian dollar, the Irish pound, and the New Zealand dollar.

An exchange rate quotation normally has two sides, the "bid" and the "offer." Since a bank will, of course, always buy at the low price and sell at the high price, in the German mark example in Exhibit 3-4 the bid side of DM 2.5280 shows the rate at which the dealer will buy dollars (and sell marks), and the offer side of DM 2.5300 gives the rate at which he or she will sell dollars (and buy deutsche marks).

In professional foreign exchange dealing among banks, traders normally quote dollar rates for all currencies. Thus, if a French bank asks a German bank about its rates, the German dealers will not quote deutsche marks against Fr. francs but deutsche marks against U.S. dollars. This habit developed in the 1950s and has been preserved to this day. When banks deal nondollar currencies against each other, therefore, they must work out cross rates. This is done in the following manner, using middle rates from Exhibit 3-4 for the example:

$$DM\,2.5290 = U.S.\,\$1.00$$
$$U.S.\,\$1.00 = Fr.\,Fr\,7.1450$$
$$\text{hence}\quad DM\,100 = \frac{100 \times 7.1450}{2.5290} = Fr.\,Fr\,282.52$$

Once a transaction price (exchange rate) has been agreed on between buyer and seller for a specified amount of currency, which almost invariably is accomplished over the telephone or by telex, the contract is firm and generally irrevocable. The bank trader will then make out a voucher containing the essential information (counterpart in the transaction, amount, exchange rate, delivery day, and location) which serves as basis for the calculation of the bank's exchange positions, for internal accounting pur-

EXHIBIT 3-4 Selected New York Closing
Rates on Monday, September 28, 1982

	Bid	Offer
U.S. $/DM	2.5280	2.5300
U.S. $/Switz. Fr.	2.1670	2.1700
U.S. $/Neth. f	2.7685	2.7710
U.S. $/Fr. Fr.	7.1400	7.1500
U.S. $/It. L	1423.0	1426.0
U.S. $/Den. Kr	8.8300	8.8500
U.S. $/Sw. Kr	6.2700	6.2900
U.S. $/¥	268.60	268.80
U.K. £/U.S. $	1.7000	1.7020

poses, and for the dispatch of a formal, written confirmation to the other party.

Forward Transactions

Foreign exchange can be bought and sold not only on a spot or cash basis but also for delivery on a stipulated future date (beyond two days), and both the settlement date and the price are agreed on when the contract is made. Theoretically, the forward price for a currency can be identical with the spot price, and on very rare occasions this may, indeed, be the case. Almost always, though, the forward rate is either higher (premium) or lower (discount). These margins, contrary to a widely held notion, are not an indication as to where the exchange markets expect a particular currency to move over the indicated period; rather they are essentially a reflection of the differentials between interest rates prevailing in the two centers involved.

If, for instance, deutsche mark interest rates are lower than those for U.S. dollars, the exchange markets will quote forward marks at premiums. By contrast, if U.S. dollar interest rates are lower than those prevailing for British pounds, forward pounds will be quoted at discounts versus the U.S. dollar. Under ideal circumstances, if there are no inhibiting restraints at all on the cross-border movements of money, the forward margins will be virtually identical to the differences between interest rates. Since such ideal conditions prevail in the Eurocurrency markets, deposit rates there offer an excellent guide for the determination of forward exchange rates.

On occasion, to be sure, there will be other forces at play. One will find, for instance, that strong devaluation rumors surrounding a currency will produce discounts substantially exceeding what the so-called interest rate parity calculation would indicate. Relationships can also be distorted by exchange controls, taxation, reserve requirements, and other factors impeding the free operation of market forces. And the forwards of minor currencies, for which large, sophisticated external deposit and lending markets do not exist, as a rule will not conform with interest rate differentials. But the principle does, by and large, hold for the major monetary units.

Forward transactions can serve a number of different purposes. They can cover future foreign currency payables for importers or lock in a firm price for the exchange proceeds expected by an exporter. They can eliminate the exchange risk entailed by a temporary investment abroad, protect a company with foreign subsidiaries against translation losses, or be speculative in the true sense of the word, entered into merely in the hope that they will yield a profit. They can be limited to single transactions or combine two deals. A simple purchase or sale for future delivery is an *outright forward transaction*. A simultaneous purchase and sale of a specific amount of currency for two different delivery dates is known as a *swap transaction*. If the latter involves a spot purchase and forward sale (or spot sale and forward puchase), it constitutes a *spot-forward swap* (for an example, refer to Exhibit 3-6). If it consists of two forward deals, e.g., the buying of DM 1 million for delivery in two months and the concurrent selling of this amount for settlement in six months, it is termed a *forward-forward swap*.

Before discussing these transaction types further, let us take a look at how rates are expressed. Forward prices are not quoted as such; dealers work only with the differences between spot and forward rates, expressed in one-hundredths of a unit. These margins very often remain stable even when spot rates go through sizable fluctuations, and therefore quoting just premiums and discounts requires fewer changes during the course of a business day. In many transactions (such as swap deals) the spot and outright forward rates are of no particular significance.

A glance at Exhibit 3-5 will show how spot rates and forward differentials are cited. In direct quotations, premiums and discounts are always decimal points in the respective currency against the U.S. dollar. In indirect quotations (e.g., for the British pound) the reverse is true. One obtains the forward rate by adding premiums to and subtracting discounts from spot rates. Although the indicated forward "points" do not carry plus or minus signs, one can still recognize in an instant that in the given examples the dollar is traded at discounts against the deutsche mark and the Swiss franc but commands premiums versus the French franc. Simply, a dealer's buying price (spot or forward) must always be lower than the selling price, since her or his bank is not in the business to lose money. Thus, the figure on the buying side will be larger than that on the selling side in case of a discount and smaller in case of a premium.

For instance, Exhibit 3-5 shows spot U.S. $/DM at 2.5280–2.5300, and the discount on three-month forward dollars at 262–257. If one deducts the latter from the former, one arrives at a three-month outright rate of 2.5018–2.5043, which means that the bank buys dollars for delivery in ninety days against payment of DM 2.5018 per greenback and sells them at 2.5043. The exceptional indirect quotation makes the British sterling example look strange until one considers that in this case the bid is a buying rate for pounds and the offer is a selling rate for pounds. In other words, the pound is quoted at premiums against the U.S. $, and the bank, for three months out, buys U.K. 1.00 at U.S. $1.7042 while it sells at U.S. $1.7065.

EXHIBIT 3-5   Forward Quotations for Selected Currencies on Monday, September 28, 1982

	U.S. $/DM	U.S. $/Switz. Fr	U.S. $/Fr. Fr	U.K. £/U.S. $
Spot	2.5280–2.5300	2.1670–2.1700	7.1400–7.1500	1.7000–1.7020
1 month	79– 74	135– 125	380– 450	5– 7
2 months	172– 167	275– 265	825– 925	22– 25
3 months	262– 257	405– 395	1370– 1470	42– 45
6 months	520– 510	770– 750	2550– 2750	128– 133
1 year	1085– 1055	1530– 1480	4600– 5100	315– 325

Often, those engaged in foreign exchange activities, for comparison purposes, need to express premiums and discounts not in points but rather in percent per annum, particularly when forward margins are to be measured against interest rates. A simple formula accomplishes this:

$$\frac{(\text{Forward rate} - \text{spot rate}) \times 100}{\text{Spot rate}} \times \frac{360}{n} = \% \text{ per annum}$$

In Exhibit 3-5, the bid side of U.S.$/DM spot is 2.5280, the three-month forward rate is 2.5018, and the n for the equation would be 90 (days). Therefore:

$$\frac{(2.5018 - 2.5280) \times 100}{2.5280} \times \frac{360}{90} = -4.16\%$$

EXHIBIT 3-6 Example of a Swap Calculation.

Premise: A U.S. corporation has US$ 10 million in excess funds available for three months. It has the option of investing the money either in the United States, or in Canada. In the latter case, to avoid any exchange risk, it prefers to enter a swap deal, i.e., to buy the Canadian dollars spot and simultaneously sell them forward for three months, the time when the investment would mature.

Interest Rates:	three-month U.S. Treasury Bill rate:	7.41%
	three-month Canadian Treasury Bill rate:	13.40%
Exchange Rates:	C$ spot rate:	1.2330
	three-month forward rate:	1.2376

Calculation of percentage gain or loss on swap

$$\frac{1.2376 \text{ (Forward)} - 1.2330 \text{ (Spot)}}{1.2330 \text{ (Spot)}} \times \frac{360 \text{ (Days in Year)}}{90 \text{ (Days in Period)}} = 1.48\% \text{ p.a.}$$

Investment comparison

Canadian Investment:	Canadian T-Bill rate	13.40%
	Minus Swap Loss	1.48%
	Net Yield On Canadian Investment	11.92%
U.S. Investment:	U.S. T-Bill rate:	7.41%
Canadian Investment Advantage:		4.51%

Comment: Interest rates are usually given in per-annum terms. Therefore, the swap gain or loss must be calculated in percent per-annum as well. In the above example, since U.S. interest rates are lower than Canadian rates, the forward C$ is quoted at a discount, or, conversely, the forward US$ at a premium.

Investors buy Canadian dollars spot (for the purchase of Canadian T-Bills), receiving C$ 1.2330 for each US$. They sell, concurrently, Canadian dollars forward for three months (for repatriation to the U.S. when their investment matures), paying C$ 1.2376 for every US$. The swap, thus, involves a loss, or cost, which must be deducted from the Canadian investment yield. For simplicity's sake, the example ignores any tax considerations.

In other words, the dollar is quoted at a discount of 4.16 percent per annum against the mark.

It should be evident that the forward markets are divided into standard maturities of one, two, three, six, and twelve months. But this is not to say that contracts cannot be obtained for other periods, sometimes called "odd dates." If asked to quote a price for a nonstandard time span, such as six weeks, a dealer will simply interpolate between one-month and two-month quotations.

The procedure for fixing the value date for forward transactions is also quite simple, since most money centers apply the calendar month approach rather than an exact number of days. Thus, if the spot date for a U.S. $/DM transaction falls on the 5th of April, the one-month maturity will fall on the 5th of May, if this happens to be a clear business day in the United States as well as in Germany. If it is not, settlement will be on the first following business day.

International business creates the need for forward operations whenever the exchange risk is to be hedged. If a U.S. importer has bought a machine tool in Germany, payable in ninety days in German marks, buying these marks for three months forward will not only eliminate the risk of a perhaps very costly rise of the marks in the interim but will also give him or her the basis for an exact price calculation. Similarly a U.S. exporter of computer equipment invoicing a Swiss distributor in Swiss francs and expecting payment in two months can eradicate the exchange risk by selling the receivables sixty days forward. Doing nothing in both instances would be tantamount to speculating—betting on a fall of the deutsche mark in the first case and on a rise of the Swiss franc in the second.

Currency exposures, and thus the need to cover them, can of course also arise from all sorts of nontrade operations. Investments in securities abroad, money market deposits, loans extended to subsidiaries, and direct investments all can create foreign currency assets. The accompanying exchange risk can be hedged by selling the respective monetary units forward. Borrowings in capital markets abroad, if done in foreign currencies, create exchange liabilities. The inherent risk can be hedged through forward purchases of these currencies. Since the assets and liabilities of foreign subsidiaries must be periodically translated into a consolidated balance sheet denominated in the parent's accounting currency, they, too, constitute an exchange exposure. And this risk can also be hedged with forward exchange sales or purchases, even if no actual transfers of funds are planned.

To make it easier for corporate customers to match the tenors of hedges with those of the underlying transactions or risk periods, banks offer a number of special services. For instance, although for many currencies forward deals of more than one year remain difficult to arrange, two-year, three-year, and even five-year contracts for major units (such as the deutsche mark, the French franc, the British pound, or the Japanese yen) are no longer uncommon. Shorter forward transactions can, of course, be stretched through regular renewals. Should a hedge prove too long, it can always be closed out prematurely.

Should customers not know exactly when they will need the foreign currency they intend to buy or will receive the exchange payment they expect from abroad, banks can accommodate them with a so-called *option contract*. Such options, to be sure, are not like put and call options in stocks or shares, which need not be taken up. Foreign exchange options must be executed, whether or not the underlying transaction materializes. In this case what is optional is merely—within a set frame—the delivery date. (Genuine currency put and call options are presently in the experimental stage in a few major centers; they may become available with fewer restrictions in the not-too-distant future, but for the moment both the types of currencies and the amounts and maturities for which such transactions are possible are quite limited.) Suppose a British exporter is virtually certain that a customer will pay, in U.S. dollars, within five to six months after shipment. The exporter can sell the dollars forward for delivery to the bank some time between the five- and six-month date. One thing must be kept in mind, though: forward discounts and premiums as a rule become larger as the lifespan of a contract lengthens. Since the bank has no intention of losing money on the deal, it will quote the most unfavorable rate, from the customer's point of view, within the given period. Thus, if the U.S. dollar at the time commands premiums against the British pound, the dealer will apply the five-month forward rate, with the smaller agio. If the greenback trades at discounts, the bank will use the six-month rate, with the stiffer disagio. Thus, the shorter the option, the better it is for the party taking out the contract.

CRITICAL FACTORS INFLUENCING EXCHANGE RATES

If it is, in the ultimate effect, supply and demand that determine the prices (rates) of currencies, then the logical next question is what determines this supply and demand? Back in the early days of the Bretton Woods fixed-exchange-rate system, trade relations between countries were all-important in this respect. At that time, nations with comfortable surpluses in their external goods exchanges almost always had strong currencies, while those running hefty trade deficits had monetary units that were devaluation-prone. The trick, then, was simply to evaluate how strongly opposed a government was to a devaluation and how much time the deteriorating trade balance and the dwindling exchange reserves would give the respective central bank for defending the unit (the time-honored technique of weighing the "enemy's" intent and capabilities).

Since then, however, the commercial and financial relations between nations have become far more complex and, accordingly, the factors to be considered in the assessment of currency trends are much more plentiful. To make any serious attempt at enumerating all or even most of them, and to describe how their influence differs from currency to currency, would go well beyond the scope of this chapter. Hence the focus is put on the most important variables, those which tend to have a bearing on all currencies and need to be screened for even the most rudimentary forecasting approach.

Broadly, these factors can be grouped in three categories: fundamentals, technical factors, and psychological influences. As a rule, the fundamental factors will determine the longer-range movements of a monetary unit, but they can be overshadowed by the technical factors in any given short-term period. As for the psychological influences, they will often be the decisive force in an otherwise undecided market.

Fundamental Factors

Foreign Trade. Even in our day and age, a country's foreign trade balance tends to have a considerable effect on its currency. If imports soar while the volume of exports shrinks, the cause is frequently an overvalued exchange rate. Sooner or later, this will have to be corrected with a devaluation, especially since exports generate jobs and imports can kill them. A government viewing a currency downgrading as a political onus may try to postpone the inevitable for some time, and, if it is convinced that the valuation of the currency is not the culprit behind the problem, it may take other steps to improve the foreign trade balance (such as offering special export incentives, hiking import tariffs, or controlling exchange allocations for purchases abroad). But such palliatives usually cannot deal with a real trade disequilibrium for any length of time, and when a devaluation is decided on belatedly, it will often have to be much larger than would have been necessary at an earlier stage.

The markets, in any event, will view the currency of a country with large trade deficits with suspicion. Since they are anticipating trends and not just reviewing historical developments, they will pay special attention to world market conditions for goods and commodities that have a heavy weight in a country's trade ledger, such as oil or foodstuffs on the import side and manufactures or raw materials on the export side. Clearly, forecasting trade trends for nations like Mexico or Venezuela requires projecting international oil prices and demand. For a country like Ghana, the tendencies of the world cocoa markets are the key to realistic projections. And for Zaïre or Zambia, global copper needs are the pivot.

Balance of Payments. Some countries, with few or no natural resources of their own, have a balance of trade that is chronically in deficit, but they manage to bridge the gap regularly with income from "invisibles," such as tourism, banking, and other services, and perhaps homebound remittances of nationals working abroad. Since their current-account balance of payments is, thus, in equilibrium or even surplus, the trade deficit need not spell weakness for the currency. Switzerland has always been in this position, as is, at present, the United States.

Thus one must look beyond the trade in visible goods to the other key items in a balance of payments to get reliable indications of the forces affecting supply and demand for a currency. Moreover, the invisibles can be as much of a burden for a country as they can be of help. For instance, interest payments on foreign debt fall into this category of balance-of-payments accounts, and it has become quite clear, particularly in recent times, that such obligations can have an enormously powerful influence on exchange rates. Moreover, even the current account is not always the main determinant; there are also short-term capital flows to be considered, which at times—perhaps due to political uncertainties or fears of exchange controls—can become so dominant that they outweigh all other influences on an exchange rate. Indeed, some forecasters rely exclusively on their projections of non-trade-related short-term cross-border movements of funds to assess currency trends.

Long-term capital flows (e.g., for brick-and-mortar investments) are also not to be overlooked. For instance, much of the Canadian dollar's plunge against the U.S. dollar during 1981 and the early part of 1982 was attributable to the Trudeau administration's new, nationalist energy policy, which triggered a massive flight of investment funds from the Dominion and discouraged new commitments by foreign (primarily U.S.) interests. In sum, then, virtually every segment of a country's balance of payments can be important, even decisive, and needs to be evaluated separately.

Reserves. If the main measurements of the balance of payments—visible trade, current account, and overall account—are all negative, and if, therefore, the nation under review suffers continuous net outflows of currency, the next question will have to be "how long can the drainage be coped with?" One quick answer is provided by the central bank's official reserve position, its holdings of foreign exchange, gold, and other international monetary assets. The best source for this information, if it cannot be obtained directly from government departments, is the International Monetary Fund in Washington, which summarizes pertinent data in a widely distributed monthly publication.

Simply put, when a nation runs balance-of-payment deficits and is on the verge of running out of reserves as well, it usually has little choice but to devalue its currency. But there are problems in determining exactly when it will find its coffers totally depleted. Official statistics rarely show how much of a published reserve total is borrowed, and they do not disclose how much may be "hot" money, i.e., short-term foreign capital attracted, perhaps, by high interest rates yet ready to flee the country at the first sign of trouble.

A meaningful reserve analysis, therefore, requires a careful study of past as well as current trends, a knowledge of a given central bank's accounting practices, and usually some insider information. Above all, it must include a thorough assessment of the respective nation's foreign debt position, particularly of the obligations that fall due within a year. The towering U.S. interest rates of 1980, 1981, and 1982 have persuaded many governments to concentrate on short-term borrowings abroad rather than become locked into long-term deals. The main country risk of the 1980s, therefore, will be illiquidity.

Economic Cycles. Most economies have, at a given time, an ideal rate of growth. Anything less than that will raise unemployment, create social and political pressures for artificial stimulation, discourage foreign investment in local equity or securities, and make reasonable fiscal planning extremely difficult. Anything more will pump up inflation, boost imports while depressing exports, distort financial markets, and lead to borrowing excesses. Therefore the main economic indicators [real gross national product (GNP) growth, industrial production, capital investment, consumer spending, and the like] need to be closely scrutinized.

Again, as with all factors influencing exchange rates, what these gauges say about the past is less important than the direction in which they point for the future. Evaluating them properly requires a more-than-fleeting knowledge of the country in question, since the same factors do not always carry the same weight. Consumer spending in the United States is more important than, say, in Switzerland, where exports prop a much larger share of GNP. Industrial production in Germany must be accorded more attention than in Venezuela, where the main growth impetus comes from the oil sector. And the fate of the automotive industry will be more crucial in Japan than in Sweden.

Unemployment. The jobless rate should be singled out as an especially decisive economic indicator. Every nation has a "threshold of pain" when it comes to the number of its unemployed. Although this trigger point has, admittedly, risen sharply throughout the industrial world since the early 1970s, in recognition that for most countries the booming growth rates of the 1950s and the 1960s are no longer attainable, there are still enormous differences in national attitudes. To this day, the Swedes tend to look at full employment as something akin to an inalienable right. In Switzerland, joblessness of more than 1 percent to 2 percent of the labor force would be viewed as an unmitigated disaster. By contrast, no one would be very upset over a U.S. unemployment rate of 5 to 6 percent. From the point of view of exchange rate forecasting, these differences indicate the course likely to be adopted by the politicians in power. Once the threshold of pain is crossed, it is usually only a matter of time until the emphasis of economic policy changes drastically from fighting inflation to pumping up economic activity. In most instances, this type of shift has adverse consequences for a country's currency, both at home and abroad.

Inflation. The erosion of a monetary unit's domestic purchasing power is another indicator deserving special mention. Economic theory holds that rapid inflation—against the backdrop of an unaltered exchange rate—will, over time, price a country's exporters out of their markets abroad and make competition with imports increasingly difficult for local industry. Eventually, a devaluation will become unavoidable. Some currency analysts have become so fascinated by empirical evidence supporting this thesis, that they concentrate exclusively on inflation rate comparisons in their exchange rate projections.

Indeed, it seems that the assumption underlying the so-called purchasing power parity theory is a valid one, at least over the longer run, but there are three things that one should keep in mind. First, the differentials between various countries are significant, not absolute, inflation rates. If industrial wholesale prices (or whatever price index one cares to use) rise at a yearly clip of 7.5 percent in the United States and at a pace of 11.5 percent in neighboring Canada, the difference of 4 percentage points indicates the speed at which an unchanged Can. $/U.S. $ exchange rate would become overvalued.

Second, governments are well aware that devaluation can be an inflationary force, since it drives up import prices. Thus, they often postpone a downward adjustment of their currency and fight market pressures in the hope that they can put a brake on the wage-price spiral at home. This makes inflation differentials rather untrustworthy indicators for short-term exchange rate trends, despite their validity for long-range projections. Third, inflation rates must be viewed in the context of a government's fiscal and monetary policies. If these are restrictive, a presently fast pace of monetary erosion may not have grave implications for the exchange rate. After all, the markets are moved by expectation much more than history or current conditions.

Monetary Management. Monetary management brings a new element into the picture, that is, the thrust of a government's domestic liquidity management. In principle, a policy aimed at keeping liquidity high, credit conditions easy, and interest rates low will lead to outflows of currency and thus a weaker exchange rate, whereas tight and dear money attracts inflows of funds. The drastic shift in the Federal Reserve's approach to the control of the U.S. money supply in the fall of 1979 was undoubtedly responsible for ushering in a period of unprecedented, worldwide strength for the greenback. Conversely, an explosion of liquidity in South Africa during 1979 and 1980, caused in large part by sky-high international gold prices and insufficiently restrained by the authorities, contributed materially to the plunge of the rand's exchange value in the second half of 1981 and the first semester of 1982.

Political Stability. Although impossible to quantify or even define in any meaningful way, political stability, nevertheless, should occupy a central place in exchange rate analysis. Since it is the government that determines economic policy and (in the case of fixed rates) decides for or against devaluation or (with floating rates) instructs the central bank to step up or cease its market intervention, the future of the people in power cannot be ignored in any forecasting attempt. Moreover, short-term movements of funds from one currency into another are strongly influenced by political (in addition to interest rate) considerations, and capital flight triggered by fears of government changes, other political upheavals, or even war can put enormous pressure on a monetary unit.

Political instability in most of Latin America has long contributed to the vulnerability of the region's currencies. Lately, the Hong Kong dollar has been hard hit by uncertainties surrounding the colony's political future. The Australian dollar, off and on, is being hurt by the results of public opinion polls showing that the Labour Party might come back to power. Even the dollar suffered seriously, in the days of President Nixon's Watergate crisis, from the exchange market perception that the White House had become too preoccupied with its own troubles to pay much attention to the needs of the U.S. economy.

Labor Attitudes. In most major countries organized labor is a potent power. It can disrupt economic activity, cause a country's balance of payments to deteriorate, unleash a flight of capital, force governments to change their economic game plans, and at times even bring a cabinet to fall. What the unions do, or plan to do, can, therefore, have quite a bearing on exchange rates. But the leverage of labor can vary considerably within the same country, depending on other circumstances that must be screened as well. In the United Kingdom, for example, union powers at present—in the middle of a severe economic recession and under a Tory government—are not nearly what they would be under a Labour administration at a time of economic boom and low unemployment. In Argentina, organized labor had much more influence when the Peronistas ran the country than it did when under the boot of the military.

Sociopolitical Trends. Finally, attention must also be given to a nation's social climate, since the seeds of potential upsets often lie here, rather than in the political arena or with the workers. In the France of 1968, an anti-Gaullist student rebellion (eventually attracting labor and leftist political support) threw the country into economic paralysis and eventually led to the resignation of President Charles de Gaulle. The latter's successor, M. Pompidou, soon afterward devalued the franc in a bid to make room for more reflationary economic policies. In other words, the origins of this particular currency downgrading were in the universities and high schools of Paris rather than the headquarters of the main unions or the Elysée itself.

Technical Factors

Technical factors come in an enormous variety, and the strength of their impact on exchange rates—from currency to currency and from trading period to trading period—is subject to marked fluctuations. For a time, such influences can totally erase the effect of the underlying fundamentals, but the emphasis, here, must be on the phrase "for a time." Technical factors almost by definition are short-term influences. They are of utmost importance to the bank dealers, since they must concentrate on a somewhat myopic outlook, but they have relatively little relevance for a corporate treasurer attempting to set budget rates for a twelve-month period, let alone for a company's planning department pondering the establishment of a foreign subsidiary.

Interest Rates. As mentioned earlier, interest rates—more precisely interest rate differentials—not only influence but actually determine forward exchange rates. Their effect on spot rates is less direct but still considerable. Simply put, high interest rates, all else being equal, attract inflows of funds and thus strengthen a currency, and low rates trigger outflows softening an exchange rate. In real life, though, the relationships are a bit more complicated. For one thing, political considerations play a vital role in the decisions of individuals, banks, corporations, and government agencies (such as SAMA, the Saudi Arabian Monetary Agency) as to where they place their excess money. If a country's political stability is in doubt, that country can have staggeringly high interest rates and still be unable to lure in foreign funds.

Another real life consideration is that exchange controls may prevent the impact of interest rates from making itself fully felt. The more such obstacles to the free flow of capital are erected, the less yield changes will influence exchange values. Their effect tends to be very visible, however, where few or no impediments exist (e.g., between the United States and Canada).

Of late, moreover, the markets have come to look at interest rate differentials in relative rather than absolute terms. They habitually deduct from nominal yields the local rate of inflation, thus arriving at "real" interest rates which are said to be better guides for exchange rate forecasters. There is some doubt as to whether international investors—and thereby actual flows of money—are much concerned with this newly polished concept, but as long as the markets choose to believe in it, any currency analyst had better pay attention. To be watched are money market rates rather than central bank discount rates, since the latter in most countries are now following rather than leading the markets. In the case of currencies that are traded in the so-called Euromarkets, the deposit and lending rates prevailing there are of paramount importance.

Seasonal Factors. Many currencies are subject to seasonal fluctuations in strength. This is particularly true for the monetary units of countries depending on tourism for a good part of their foreign exchange earnings. The Italian lira for instance, is predictably firmer during the summer, Europe's main vacation period, than in the winter. The same holds true for the Spanish peseta and, to a degree, the Portuguese escudo. By contrast, for the deutsche mark the months from June to September tend to create seasonal softness. Most Germans—inveterate travellers—insist on going abroad for the holidays in good times and bad, and the Federal Republic's current account balance of payments unfailingly shows the adverse effects of the money they spend in foreign countries.

Seasonal effects can also be linked to the harvest times for important cash crops and the subsequent rise in inflows of export revenues. Or, as in the case of Canada in the fourth quarter of every year, they can consist of a bunching of outbound payments of interest on foreign debt and the remittances of profits and dividends by local subsidiaries to their foreign parents.

Key Dates. For virtually every currency, there exist key dates around which the unit can, as a rule, be expected to perform better or worse than at other times. In Western Europe, the monthly and quarterly window-dressing periods are very important, when corporations and banks must adjust their liquidity positions and balance sheets to meet minimum cash or deposit requirements. Hence, prior to the end of every month and quarter, demand for local currency increases markedly in nations like Switzerland, Germany, or Belgium. This has a beneficial (if temporary) effect on the respective currencies, unless central banks counteract the squeeze by injecting extra liquidity. Key dates can also include tax deadlines (creating heavy credit demands), the times when large borrowings abroad are either converted into local currency or come due for repayment, and the days on which a country's latest economic indicators are announced (such as inflation statistics, foreign trade figures, or balance-of-payments results).

Controls. Of course, exchange controls will usually have a major impact on a currency's external value, both when they are clamped on and when they are lifted. Such curbs exist in a great variety of forms and range from relatively mild ones to restrictions that are so tough that they literally turn the unit they "protect" into nonconvertible inland money. Controls can aim at the currency directly, as do limitations on spot and/or forward deals for defined purposes, special taxes on foreign exchange transactions, strict conversion rules, or the domination of all exchange dealings by the authorities. They can also seek to influence exchange rates indirectly, as do prior import deposit requirements, restraints on the leading (prepayment) and lagging (conversion delay) of commercial obligations and assets abroad, ceilings on capital repatriation by foreign investors, limits on the outbound remittance of royalties and dividends, and the barring of foreign-owned subsidiaries from local borrowings to force their parents abroad to supply them with working capital in foreign exchange.

One type of control that is finding favor with an increasing number of governments is the introduction of multiple exchange rates for different purposes. In its simplest form, this approach leads to the creation of a (usually controlled) "commercial" rate for imports, exports, and related services such as insurance and freight charges and a (generally uncontrolled) "financial" rate for all other transactions. Belgium presently has a two-tier market for its franc as does South Africa for the rand and Argentina for the peso. But central banks usually find that a bifurcated currency is not immune to market pressures, and their response, in such an event, is often to take recourse to a still more complicated system consisting of several different exchange rates for different types of transactions. In the fall of 1982, multiple rate arrangements were in force inter alia for the Costa Rican colon, the Ecuadoran sucre, and the Egyptian pound.

Intervention. As emphasized earlier, although the purpose of currency floating is obviously to relieve central banks from the obligation to intervene in the exchange markets, in reality such intervention remains widespread, ineffective as it may be. To be sure, most central banks claim that, as a matter of policy, they will step in only when this is deemed necessary to prevent "disorderly market conditions." But disorderly is a term subject to so widely varying interpretations that it is virtually meaningless.

At one time, many of the major central banks had the financial firepower to turn a currency trend around. Today, the international pool of foot-loose capital that can wander from units perceived to be overvalued to others viewed as undervalued is so gigantic that no central bank can fight such flows with any hope for lasting success. Still, for short periods official intervention can halt or at least slow down the depreciation or appreciation of a given currency, and thus it merits consideration as a technical market factor.

Profit Taking. Whenever a pronounced currency trend has attracted a wave of protective and speculative buying or selling, there will come a time when market participants conclude that the exchange rate move has gone as far as it can. Let us say, for argument's sake, that the Japanese yen has been under intense downward pressure for several days. There have been massive flows of funds from yen assets into other currencies; Japanese importers have hedged their near-term exchange commitments; and large, speculative short positions in yen have been built up. Sooner or later, a few big players in the market will decide that the time is ripe for a reversal of their positions, either because they expect the central bank to come to the yen's aid in a big way, or simply because their intuition tells them that the unit's plunge is about to bottom out.

Once the profit taking begins, it spreads rather quickly, and as the yen starts to react to the sudden appearance of large-scale buyers by accelerating its recovery, those who are caught short act promptly to cover their exposures, thereby reinforcing the unit's uptrend. Admittedly, when and at what level profit taking (or loss cutting) will set in is usually impossible to predict with any reliability, since both the timing and the turning point are generally set by nonquantifiable psychological forces. It is the "gut feeling" of the market that determines the reversal, and, although professional traders may be able to catch such turns with remarkable surefootedness, they will, for the most part, be unable to explain exactly on what their instincts were based.

Yet there are times when the onset of profit taking becomes quite easily predictable. EMS realignments, for instance, have regularly been preceeded by large moves out of the member currencies apt to be devalued (the Belgian franc, the Luxenbourg franc, the French franc, and the Italian lira) into units likely to be revalued (the deutsche mark and the Dutch florin). Once the realignment has taken place, market participants find it safe to assume that another parity adjustment will not take place for some time to come, and liquidity and interest rate considerations regain the upper hand. It has, thus, been a regular feature of such EMS revisions that the devalued currencies right after the event trade at or near the top of their new fluctuation ranges and the revalued units start out at the bottom.

Psychological Factors

The third and last group of influences affecting exchange rates are factors that cannot be measured, weighed, or fed into a computer for analysis, but they are just as real and powerful in their impact as are the quantifiable variables. What makes market participants feel good or bad about a currency often cannot even be defined in any meaningful way. For analysts preferring to deal in tangibles, the mood of the market will always remain elusive and mysterious, but bank traders tend to have a keen sense for changes in this mood, and they are the only dependable source of information on this subject.

They will know when the markets do or do not like a new government. They feel the bullishness surrounding a currency that can make the exchanges ignore an adverse news item, and they sense when markets are so bearish about a monetary unit that not even the announcement of a major balance-of-payments improvement can halt its decline. In exchange dealings, what people believe is often much more decisive than what actually is, and thus ignoring the psychology of the market risks painful losses.

There is a phenomenon in exchange trading known as the "bandwagon syndrome." It means that participants are driven by a herd instinct, with everyone tending to fall into line once a clear trend becomes established. Most bank dealers and corporate treasurers have had some bitter experiences with attempts to "outguess" the markets, to buck a trend. They are quick to jump on the bandwagon, and once this vehicle gets rolling, nobody wants to be left behind. This explains why, in today's floating rate environment, currency movements, even when based on sound economic reasoning, tend to grossly overshoot all the marks that might be deemed justified by fundamentals. It also helps to illustrate why rumors, no matter how far-fetched, can often have a dramatic effect.

In a well-known children's tale, Winnie the Pooh, a cute little bear, walks around a bush. As he completes his circle, he discovers tracks, not realizing that they are his own. Made curious, he follows them, and as he comes around the second time, he is delighted to find two sets of tracks. And so, the story goes, the bear marches around, and around, and around the bush, until he is convinced that he is on the tracks of "oodles and oodles of woozles and weasels." In the exchange markets, a rumor, an opinion, will be passed on from one participant to another. Eventually, the comment will be reported back to its originator. She or he may not recognize it but will, most likely, take it as confirmation. In this manner, the rumors become stronger and stronger as they make their rounds, until they have a powerful influence on the currency in question. The "Pooh syndrome" surely does not lend itself to scientific dissection. But it is real, and it does move markets.

PROJECTING RATES

Where does all this leave the exchange-rate forecaster? Clearly, the whole business of currency analysis has changed drastically with the collapse of the fixed rate system and the transition to floating in the early 1970s. As long as there were firmly set parities, currencies could—barring a formal revaluation or devaluation—not go beyond their predetermined upper and lower intervention points. Thus, the only real question in the 1950s and 1960s was whether a country was in such a precarious balance-of-payments situation that it might be forced to clip its coin or whether upward pressures on the currency of a surplus nation might grow to the point where the government would have no alternative to a revaluation.

Today, just about anything can influence an exchange rate. Economic factors are still of decisive importance, certainly over the longer run. Among them, foreign trade, current account, and overall balance-of-payments developments still carry the most weight. But the markets now tend to look much further ahead than they used to, discounting trends that have not even set in yet and may not show up in the balance of payments for many months to come. A high inflation rate is seen as reducing a nation's international competitiveness and becomes, thus, a force weakening the currency long before its effects on trade are felt. The overall state of an economy will be critically assessed as to its implications for probable government policy, and the result of this evaluation—often a purely instinctive one—becomes a weighty market factor.

Since an exchange rate is always the relationship between two currencies, the market logically measures the plus and minus points for one monetary unit against those for another. And in such comparisons of manifold variables, political and/or psychological influences can have a formidable bearing on exchange rate fluctuations. Noteworthy in this context is that many currencies have a certain image that tends to color the views of market participants. The Swiss franc, for instance, has long had part of its inherent strength attributed to its standing as hedge currency. Of late, the U.S. dollar has taken on a similar image. The Japanese yen, on the other hand, has become a unit liable to suffer whenever political trouble brews in the Middle East. And, in turbulent times, it is now often such an image, rather than solid reasoning, that prompts people to move from one currency to another.

Attempts to find a systematic approach incorporating all these factors into reliably accurate exchange rate forecasts have been plentiful since fixed parities became a thing of the past. Scores of econometric computer models have been developed, generally putting special emphasis on a select number of indicators such as purchasing power parities, short-term capital flows through the balance of payments, or interest rate comparisons in inflation-adjusted terms. For shorter-range projections, economists have set up momentum models, seeking, without regard for the underlying fundamentals, to pinpoint turns in rate movements. Sophisticated charting methods have been devised on the premise that currency markets in essence are just commodity markets of a sort and that trend lines for exchange rates can, therefore, be prognosticated in the same manner as those for soybean or cotton prices.

All these techniques have proven useful within limitations, but, alas, not one of them has turned out to be consistently reliable or even has guaranteed a good batting average. Given the complexity and imponderability of so many of the factors influencing exchange rates one must doubt, indeed, that a computer program will ever be devised that can infallibly predict currency movements. The best one can hope for are forecasting methods that manage to get the direction right and perhaps come within a few percentage points of the top or bottom of an actual currency move. Luckily, though, money can be made and effective hedge programs can be implemented even with imperfect exchange rate forecasts—as long as the user takes the projections for what they are: educated guesses, at best.

Four: Understanding, Forecasting, and Reporting Foreign Exchange

FRANÇOISE B. SOARES-KEMP

Françoise B. Soares-Kemp is vice president of the Corporate Foreign Exchange Advisory Service for Credit Lyonnais. Ms. Soares-Kemp has written many articles on the subject of foreign exchange, including "The Futures Market" in *American Banker* and "French Franc, Apocalypse Now?" in the *Financial Times* of London. She earned her M.A. degree in economics at New York University and is a lecturer at the same university on the subject of foreign exchange management.

UNDERSTANDING EXCHANGE EXPOSURE

Understanding exchange exposure is complicated by the multiplicity of definitions and interpretations of what constitutes foreign exchange risk for the corporation. For example, anticipated foreign exchange rate movements represent no risk since they can be embodied in the corporate budget. (As an example, most of the impact of the devaluation of the Brazilian cruzeiro can be anticipated and reflected in the corporate plan.) However, unanticipated currency changes are a source of risk, since they cannot be incorporated in the budget.

The distinction between economic and financial risk also is important in understanding exchange exposure. Economic exposure or risk is the danger that business expenses could become uncompetitive because the real purchasing power of a currency has risen to a point where competitors with costs in other currencies could gain a significant advantage. Clearly this has happened previously to U.S. companies and others because of fluctuation in the U.S. dollar.

All other exposure or risk is financial and can lead to losses realized in cash or unrealized losses, which show up in companies' balance sheets. The following is an illustration of the sources of currency gains and losses.

Sources of Currency Gains and Losses

Balance sheet	Income statement	Devaluation	Revaluation
Assets	Revenues	(Losses)	Gains
Liabilities	Expenses	Gains	(Losses)

4-2

Exhibit 4-1 illustrates a typical transaction exposure that reflects foreign exchange gains and/or losses.

Economic exposure management is part of the wider subjective corporate planning task which includes estimating future cash flows over an arbitrary time horizon, using economic analysis. The finance, marketing, production, and sourcing departments must all be involved in this exercise. These departments must all take a hard look at whether a sustained real rise of a currency against the currencies of competitors will adversely affect a corporation's competitive costs and, therefore, its sales, profit margins, and market share, which in turn will reduce the return on the capital and revenue investment previously sunk in its present commercial activity and the present value of that investment. This forces the corporation to focus continuously on the specific nature of the business of each individual overseas subsidiary and allows no sweeping generalizations.

Furthermore, focusing on economic exposures is consistent with the overall corporate goal of maximizing cash flows or profits over time. In considering strategies for hedging budgeted cash flows, a corporation's options include changing foreign currency product prices and entering into forward foreign exchange contracts.

An exchange rate change will affect the U.S. corporation's dollar-denominated cash flows through two channels. First, changes in the foreign exchange rate will affect the dollar value of all relevant foreign currency-denominated cash flows directly. For example, for a U.S. dollar-based corporation, the dollar value of future sales denominated in a foreign currency will decline when the currency depreciates against the U.S. dollar. Second, actions taken in response to changes in the exchange rate can affect the foreign currency value of these cash flows. These actions could take the

---

EXHIBIT 4-1   A Transaction Exposure

Assets	Liabilities and owner's equity
Accounts receivable DM 100,000, U.S. $42,000 Initially (DM = U.S. $0.42)	Owner's equity DM 100,000, U.S. $42,000

	DM	U.S. $
Increase A/R*	100,000	42,000
Increase R/E†	100,000	42,000
Three months later (DM = U.S. $0.45)		
Increase cash	100,000	45,000
Decrease A/R	100,000	42,000
Foreign exchange gain		3,000
Increase R/E		3,000
Increase taxes payable		1,440
Decrease R/E		1,440
Net of taxes, the realized foreign exchange gain is U.S. $1560.		

* A/R = Accounts receivable. † R/E = Related earnings.

form of changes in sales volume or sales prices. Foreign currency values of future sales would increase if (1) prices are raised to compensate for depreciation of the currency or (2) sales rise because of increased competitive advantage in the foreign market. In these instances there is an automatic hedging mechanism which would partially or totally eliminate the exposure. The combined impact of these two factors determines the ultimate overall impact of exchange rate changes on the dollar-denominated value of cash flows. When the two effects do not offset each other, the affected flows are said to be "exposed" to the particular foreign currency involved.

Forward market hedges are appropriate only when foreign currency prices cannot be changed immediately following a change in the exchange rate between the particular currency and the dollar. The forward market hedge thus provides protection against losses that occur between the time of the exchange rate change and the compensating price changes.

Price changing to compensate for exchange rate changes is a marketing issue, and pricing policy must consider many factors in addition to exchange rate movements. Also, any price increase must be considered in terms of the corporation's long-range marketing strategy. Furthermore, the ability to change prices without affecting market share depends on the nature of local competition.

Volatility of exchange rate movements is a major consideration in pricing changes (see Exhibits 4-2 and 4-3). If a depreciating currency begins to appreciate after prices have increased, the market share for that product could be threatened. Thus exchange rate changes are financial in nature and frequently bear little relation in the short term to the local business environment. Trying to change prices as fast as exchange rates change is not advisable, since in reality, raising prices that quickly is usually impossible. Forward market hedges can provide protection against losses while pricing decisions are evaluated and implemented. The ideal hedge considers the time each entity needs to effect these changes; only in this way can the maturity of the hedge be structured to maximize its benefits.

Having defined economic exchange exposure, we can go on to identify

EXHIBIT 4-2 Currency Risk Expressed as Probability
of Currency Moving to Certain Levels.

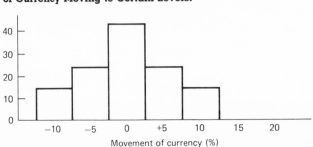

others. "Transaction exchange exposure" refers to gains and losses that arise from the settlement of transactions whose terms are stated in a foreign currency. Foreign exchange transactions may include (1) purchasing or selling on credit goods or services in foreign currencies, (2) borrowing or lending funds denominated in foreign currencies, (3) being a party to an unperformed forward foreign exchange contract, and (4) otherwise acquiring assets or incurring liabilities denominated in foreign currencies.

Translation exposure, often referred to as "accounting" or "FASB (Financial Accounting Standards Board) exposure," arises from the need to report consolidated worldwide operations according to predetermined accounting rules. Assets, liabilities, revenues, and expenses originally measured to a foreign currency must be restated in terms of a home currency to be consolidated with home currency accounts. There are three primary translation methods.

The current rate method (closing rate) translates all foreign currency items at the spot rate of exchange as of the balance sheet closing date. The current rate method became official U.S. practice in December 1981 with the issuance of FASB 52. FASB 52 replaced FASB 8 and requires current rate translation for all fiscal years beginning on or after December 15, 1982, and encourages earlier applications where possible. In the United States, under FASB 52, all assets and liabilities are translated at the current rate of exchange in effect on the balance sheet date. Income statement items, including depreciation and cost of goods sold, are translated at either the actual exchange rate on the dates the various revenues, expenses, gains and losses are incurred or at an appropriately weighted average exchange rate for the period. Dividends paid are translated at the exchange rate in effect on the payment date.

Existing equity accounts, such as common stock and paid-in capital, are translated at historical rates. Year-end retained earnings consist of the original year-beginning retained earnings plus or minus any income or loss for the year. However, gains or losses caused by translation adjustments are not included in the calculation of net income, and thus the change in retained

EXHIBIT 4-3　**The Wider the Range, the Riskier the Currency.**

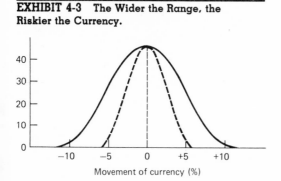

Movement of currency (%)

earnings does not reflect translation gains or losses. Translation gains or losses are reported separately and accumulated in a separate equity account with a title such as "equity adjustment from translation." Exhibits 4-4 and 4-5 show how calculations under FASB 8 (Exhibit 4-4) differ from those under FASB 52 (Exhibit 4-5) using the deutsche mark and the U.S. dollar.

There are other approaches to accounting for translation of foreign exchange gains and losses. The current/noncurrent (working capital) method is probably the oldest approach to accounting for foreign exchange gains and losses in some foreign countries, e.g., West Germany and South Africa. Under this method, all current assets and current liabilities of foreign subsidiaries are translated into the home currency at the current exchange rate. Noncurrent assets and liabilities are translated at historic rates, i.e., at the rates that were in existence on the date the assets were acquired or the liabilities were incurred. On the balance sheet, exposure to gains or losses from fluctuating currency values is determined by the net of current assets less current liabilities. Gains or losses on long-term assets and liabilities are not shown currently. Items in the income statement are generally translated at the average exchange rate for the period covered. Those items that relate to revenue or expense items associated with noncurrent assets (such as depreciation charges) or long-term liabilities (amortization of debt discount) are translated at the same rate as the corresponding balance sheet item. Exhibit 4-6 illustrates the current/noncurrent method.

Finally, under the monetary/nonmonetary method, monetary assets (including cash, marketable securities, accounts receivable, and long-term re-

---

EXHIBIT 4-4   FASB 8 Method

		Before depreciation		After depreciation	
	DM	**Rate**	**U.S. $**	**Rate**	**U.S. $**
Cash	1,000,000	.40	400,000	.35	350,000
A/R*	3,000,000	.40	1,200,000	.35	1,050,000
Inventory	2,000,000	.40	800,000	.40	800,000
Net property and equipment	4,000,000	.45	1,800,000	.45	1,800,000
Total assets	10,000,000		4,200,000		4,000,000
Accrued current liability	500,000	.40	200,000	.35	175,000
Bank loan (S/T)†	1,000,000	.40	400,000	.35	350,000
Long-term debt	2,000,000	.40	800,000	.35	700,000
Capital stock	2,500,000	.45	1,125,000	.45	1,125,000
Ret. earnings	4,000,000	Composite	1,675,000	Same	1,675,000
Translation loss	n/a				(25,000)
	10,000,000		4,200,000		4,000,000

* A/R = Accounts receivable. † S/T = Short-term.

EXHIBIT 4-5   FASB 52 Method

	DM	Before depreciation Rate	Before depreciation U.S. $	After depreciation Rate	After depreciation U.S. $
Cash	1,000,000	.40	400,000	.35	350,000
A/R*	3,000,000	.40	1,200,000	.35	1,050,000
Inventory	2,000,000	.40	800,000	.35	700,000
Net property and equipment	4,000,000	.40	1,600,000	.35	1,400,000
Total assets	10,000,000		4,000,000		3,500,000
Accrued current liability	500,000	.40	200,000	.35	175,000
Bank loan (S/T)†	1,000,000	.40	400,000	.35	350,000
Long-term debt	2,000,000	.40	800,000	.35	525,000
Capital stock	2,500,000	.45	1,125,000	.45	1,125,000
Ret. earnings	4,000,000	Composite	1,800,000	Same	1,800,000
Equity adjustment from translation	n/a		(325,000)		(475,000)
	10,000,000		4,000,000		3,500,000

* A/R = Accounts receivable. † S/T = Short-term.

EXHIBIT 4-6   Current/Noncurrent Method

	DM	Before depreciation Rate	Before depreciation U.S. $	After depreciation Rate	After depreciation U.S. $
Cash	1,000,000	.40	400,000	.35	350,000
A/R*	3,000,000	.40	1,200,000	.35	1,050,000
Inventory	2,000,000	.40	800,000	.35	700,000
Net property and equipment	4,000,000	.45	1,800,000	.45	1,800,000
Total assets	10,000,000		4,200,000		3,900,000
Accrued current liability	500,000	.40	200,000	.35	175,000
Bank loan (S/T)†	1,000,000	.40	400,000	.35	350,000
Long-term debt	2,000,000	.45	900,000	.45	900,000
Capital stock	2,500,000	.45	1,125,000	.45	1,125,000
Retained earnings	4,000,000	Composite	1,575,000	Same	1,575,000
Translation loss	n/a				(59,000)
	10,000,000		4,200,000		3,900,000

* A/R = Accounts receivable. † S/T = Short-term.

EXHIBIT 4-7 A Balance Sheet Hedge: Borrowing Foreign Currency When Interest Rates Are Equal

CASE A: Let's assume that one-year money is 8% in both the U.K. and the U.S. The hedge works as follows:

INITIALLY: Borrow £100,000 at 8% for one year, convert the proceeds at $2.00/£ ($200,000), and invest for one year in the U.S. at 8%.

ONE YEAR LATER:
1. Sell dollar security. Proceeds are
   ($200,000) + ($200,000 × 0.08) = $216,000
2. Convert proceeds into pounds
   $216,000 ÷ $1.80/£   = £120,000
3. Pay the loan in pounds
   (£100,000) + (£100,000 × 0.08) = <u>108,000</u>
4. Gain in pounds   = £12,000
5. Gain in dollars
   £12,000 × $1.80/£   = $21,600
6. Loss in exposed assets
   £100,000 × ($.20/£)   = ($20,000)
7. Net gain   = $1,600

In spite of the zero interest differential, there is a $1600 foreign exchange gain, because we save 0.20£ on every pound paid in interest (£8000 × 0.20/£ = $1600).

EXHIBIT 4-8 Borrowing a Foreign Currency with a 2 Percent Interest Differential

CASE B: Let's assume that interest rates are 10% in the U.K. and 8% in the U.S.

INITIALLY: Borrow £100,000 at 10% for one year, convert the proceeds at $2.00/£ ($200,000), and invest for one year in the U.S. at 8%.

ONE YEAR LATER:
1. Sell dollar security. Proceeds are
   ($200,000) + ($200,000 × 0.08) = $216,000
2. Convert proceeds into pounds
   $216,000 ÷ $1.80/£   = £120,000
3. Pay the loan in pounds
   (£100,000) + (£100,000 × 0.10) = <u>110,000</u>
4. Gain in pounds   = £10,000
5. Gain in dollars
   (£10,000 × $1.80/£)   = $18,000
6. Loss in exposed assets   = ($20,000)
7. Net loss   = ($2,000)

Because of the higher interest cost of borrowing (2%), the amount of the gain on the hedge does not entirely offset the loss.

ceivables) and monetary liabilities (current liabilities and long-term debt) are translated at current exchange rates, and all other assets and liabilities are translated at historical rates. Income statement items are translated at the average exchange rate for the period, except for those items such as depreciation and cost of goods sold that are directly associated with nonmonetary assets or liabilities; these are translated at their historic rates. This method is used in some European, Latin American, and Far Eastern countries, and it largely describes the method used by the U.S. corporations under FASB 8.

In summary, changes in foreign exchange rates may cause gains or losses on foreign exchange operations. Exhibits 4-7 through 4-15 summarize these effects, directing particular attention toward the difference between translation (accounting) methods and economic methods.

EXHIBIT 4-9   Increasing the Amount Borrowed to Offset the Interest Lost

The formula for fully offsetting the expected loss entails hedging a greater amount than the underlying exposure:

$$\text{Expected loss} = \text{Amount} (1 = i\text{U.S.}) - \text{Amount} [(1 + i\text{U.K.}) (1 + R)]$$
$$\$20,000 = \text{Amount} (1.08) - \text{Amount} [(1.10) (1 - 0.10)]$$
$$20,000 = \text{Amount} (1.08 - 0.99)$$

$$\text{Amount} = \frac{\$20,000}{0.09}$$
$$= \$222,222 = £111,111$$

Where iU.S. = interest rate in the U.S.
       iU.K. = interest rate in the U.K.
        R = change in currency value

EXHIBIT 4-10   The Impact on Profits If the Market Turns

CASE A: Interest rates are 8% in both the U.K. and the U.S., and the amount hedged is £100,000.

ONE YEAR LATER:

1. Sell dollar security. Proceeds are
($200,000) + ($200,000 × 0.08) = $216,000
2. Convert proceeds into pounds
$216,000 ÷ $2.10/£   = £102,857
3. Pay the loan in pounds
(£100,000) + (£100,000 × 0.08) = <u>108,000</u>
4. Loss in pounds   = (£5,143)
5. Loss in dollars
(£5,143) × $2.10/£   = ($10,800)
6. Gain on exposed assets
£100,000 × $0.10/£   = $10,000
7. Net loss   = ($800)

EXHIBIT 4-11   A Balance Sheet Hedge: Using the Forward When the Spot Rate Equals the Forward Rate

---

CASE A: The spot rate for sterling is $2.00, and the forward rate is at par, $2.00.

INITIALLY: Sell £100,000 forward one year at $2.00/£ = $200,000

ONE YEAR LATER:
1. Buy £100,000 on the spot market at $1.80 = ($180,000)
2. Deliver £100,000 on the forward contract = $200,000
3. Gain on forward contract   =   20,000
4. Loss on exposed assets   =   (20,000)

5. Net gain (loss)   =   0

The gain on the contract has exactly offset the loss on the exposed assets because the spot rate and the forward rate were equal. Usually, though, because of interest rate differentials, the forward rate will be at a premium or a discount to the spot rate.

EXHIBIT 4-12   Selling a Currency Forward at a Discount

CASE A: A 2% differential between U.K. and U.S. interest rates implies a one-year sterling rate of $1.96, a discount of 2% off the spot.

INITIALLY: Sell £100,000 forward one year at $1.96/£ = $196,000

ONE YEAR LATER:
1. Buy £100,000 on the spot market at $1.80 = ($180,000)
2. Deliver £100,000 on the forward contract = $196,000
3. Gain on forward contract   =   16,000
4. Loss on exposed assets   =   (20,000)

5. Net loss   =   ($4,000)

In this case, we have "locked in" an automatic loss due to the discount.

EXHIBIT 4-13   Increasing the Amount of the Forward Sale to Offset the Discount

---

To offset fully the expected loss entails hedging a greater amount than the exposure according to the formula:

Expected loss = Amount ($1.96) − Amount ($1.80)
    $20,000 = Amount (.16£)
Amount   = £125,000

INITIALLY: Sell £125,000 forward one year at $1.96/£ = $245,000

ONE YEAR LATER:
1. Buy £125,000 on the spot market at $1.80 = ($225,000)
2. Deliver £125,000 on the forward contract = $245,000
3. Gain on forward contract   =   20,000
4. Loss on exposed assets   =   ($20,000)

5. Net gain (loss)   =   0

EXHIBIT 4-14   The Impact on Profits If the Market Turns

CASE B1:

INITIALLY: Sell £100,000 forward one year at $1.96/£

ONE YEAR LATER:

1. Buy £100,000 on the spot market at $2.10/£	=	($210,000)
2. Deliver £100,000 on the forward contract	=	$196,000
3. Loss on forward contract	=	($14,000)
4. Gain on exposed assets	=	10,000
5. Net loss	=	($4,000)

CASE B2:

INITIALLY: Sell £125,000 forward one year at $1.96/£

ONE YEAR LATER:

1. Buy £125,000 on the spot market at $2.10/£	=	($262,500)
2. Deliver £125,000 on the forward market	=	$245,000
3. Loss on forward contract	=	($17,500)
4. Gain on exposed assets	=	10,000
5. Net loss	=	($7,500)

EXHIBIT 4-15   The Impact on Intercompany Exposures of Taxes

Suppose that when a loan is made, the following exchange rates prevail:

$$£1 = \$2.00$$
$$Fr.\,Fr1 = \$0.25$$
$$therefore \quad £1 = Fr.\,Fr8$$

The balance sheet (B/S) would show:

French Subsidiary				U.K. Subsidiary			
	Fr. Fr B/S	U.S. B/S			U.K. B/S		U.S. B/S
	Fr. Fr	$			£	Fr. Fr	$
Loan	400	100		Fixed assets	50		100
Equity	400	100		Loan	50	400	100
				Equity	0		0
					50		100

Now, what is the aftertax exposure?

Aftertax exposure = pretax exposure X (1 − tax rate).

(Exhibit continues)

EXHIBIT 4-15   The Impact on Intercompany Exposure of Taxes   (Continued)

Thus, from the parent's point of view:

	PT exp.*		$\times$ (1 − tax rate)	=	AT exp.†		Type
French sub	Fr. Fr	400	(1 − 0)	= Fr. Fr	400		Translation
U.K. sub	−£	50	(1 − 0)	= −£	50		Translation
U.K. sub	+£	50	(1 − 50)	= +£	25		Transaction
U.K. sub	−Fr. Fr	100	(1 − 50)	= −Fr. Fr	200		Transaction
Aftertax consolidated exposure				= Fr. Fr	200	($50)	
				= −£	25	(−$50)	

Let's assume the French franc declines by 20% against the dollar; sterling remains firm. The new exchange rates are:

$$£1 = \$2.00$$
$$Fr. Fr1 = \$0.20$$
$$£1 = Fr. Fr10$$

The parent will experience a translation loss on its French sub:

French Subsidiary

		Fr. Fr B/S	U.S. B/S
		Fr. Fr	$
Loan		400	100
Equity		400	100
R/E			(20)
		400	80

The loss, due entirely to translation, is $20.

In the U.K., the Fr. Fr400 loan, previously worth £50, is now worth £40, producing a taxable gain of £10. Thus, the balance sheet for the U.K. sub will appear as follows:

U.K. Subsidiary

	U.K. B/S		U.S. B/S
	Fr. Fr	£	$
Fixed assets		50	100
Taxes payable		5	10
Loan	400	40	80
Equity		0	0
R/E‡			
Transaction gain		5	10
		50	100

The aftertax gain for the U.K. is $10, due to the transaction. There is no translation gain or loss. The pound did not move.

The consolidated profit and loss is $10, composed of the $20 translation loss and the $10 transaction gain.

---

* PT exp. = Pretax exposure. † = AT exp. = Aftertax exposure. ‡ = Return on equity.

FORECASTING FOREIGN EXCHANGE RATES

Whether a corporation focuses on accounting or economic exposures, the stock market analysts seem to focus on the economic consequences of foreign exchange rate changes. Apparently this market reaction has been triggered by concerns over floating exchange rates, volatile foreign inflation rates, taxation of foreign source earnings, and the widespread political instability that has given rise to these conditions. An integral part of corporations' attempts to adjust to this volatile financial environment is the increased emphasis that they place on forecasting foreign exchange rate movements. Volumes of literature discuss the causes of these movements; in summary the main factors which make currencies move and influence the demand and supply of each currency in the markets are:

- Relative price levels and inflation rates
- Relative economic growth rates
- Relative interest rates, especially on the freely traded money markets like the Eurocurrency market
- Relative changes in the money supply in the currency areas concerned
- Investment or portfolio preferences of big international investors like the OPEC countries
- Bandwagon effects (if a currency seems to be on the way up, speculators may exaggerate the trend by buying in the hope of a quick profit)
- Intervention by central banks

The volatility of the foreign exchange and money markets of the late 1970s and, so far, the 1980s has caused corporations some great headaches. The rapid proliferation of forecasting services is a result of the corporate community's desire to get a better "handle" on the outlook in exchange and interest rates.

Regression analysis models are at the basis of many of these forecasting services, but the most impressive results have recently been obtained by market analysts called "chartists" who simply track price movements. Finally, some of the forecasters concentrate on so-called market psychology gleaned from the attitudes and statements of people with greatest direct influence on the supply and demand of currencies, such as the monetary authorities of the major reserve currencies and those responsible for administering the portfolios of the OPEC countries.

All three methods can be used simultaneously, since thus the many aspects of foreign exchange forecasting are all addressed.

It has been concluded in a foreign exchange survey of Euromoney that accurate forecasting is probably impossible in present conditions. All corporate foreign exchange managers are unavoidably in the business of forecasting, but they should restrict the field in which they have to forecast to the greatest extent possible.

There are several institutions that provide some form of advisory service in the area of foreign exchange. The following have formalized their consulting activities:

Business International Corp.
Chase Manhattan Bank
Chemical Bank
Citibank
Continental Bank
Data Resources Inc.
Forex
Manufacturers Hanover Trust
Marine Midland Bank
Morgan Guaranty Trust Co.
Multinational Computer Models, Inc.
Predex

IMPLEMENTING A FRAMEWORK FOR ANALYZING FOREIGN EXCHANGE RISK

Implementation of sound protective strategies means a planned and orderly approach to the foreign exchange problem, and a total program for a corporation should include the following steps.

First, decide exposure management goals. If the goal is to manage risks that may affect the currency gain/loss entry of the income statement, then FASB exposures are relevant. If the goal is to manage risks to cash flows or profits, then economic exposures are relevant. Senior management must address and specify this most fundamental issue in its goals. These goals should be clearly stated in writing and communicated to all units.

The next step is to centralize the management of foreign exchange at corporate headquarters. The foreign exchange manager should be responsible for formulating, coordinating, and implementing all foreign exchange exposure management functions. A foreign exchange committee should meet at least once a week to make policy decisions and review them occasionally.

Finally, a solid reporting system should be established. After the removal of subsidiary exchange risk from the individual subsidiary performance income budgets, these exposures are centralized along with FASB exposures at corporate headquarters. Then the following should happen: (1) Performance income budgets should be put together using rates available in forward foreign exchange market; (2) all performance income exposures should then be passed on to the corporate treasury department from each operating company; and (3) the treasury should net out offsetting performance income exposures and then hedge the rest in the forward market at the rates used in the budget.

Each month the variance from the budget is compensated by offsetting gains and losses in the treasury performance income-hedging portfolio. Treasury gains and losses on hedging performance income should be allocated to operating company performance income as a plug number to offset variances due to exchange rate changes. Any profits derived from managing these performance income exposures will remain in a profit center set up within the corporate treasury for this purpose. Internal reports for monitoring the company's exchange exposure will be necessary.

Each operating company should be responsible for providing estimated performance income exposures, by currency and by month, at the end of each year for the following year. As exposure forecasts change throughout the year, operating companies must make the treasury aware. Any losses or gains resulting from cancellation of forward cover will be passed through directly to operating companies. FASB exposures should be the responsibility of the corporate Treasury.

Responsibility for hedging decisions should be with the foreign exchange committee; the chair of the committee should be the treasurer, the vice chair could be the controller, and the remaining members should be the assistant treasurer international, assistant treasurer domestic, and the manager of foreign exchange. The manager of foreign exchange is responsible for assimilation of market information and distribution to committee members at the regular meetings.

Trading authority should be communicated from the finance committee with respect to the maximum limit of long or short positions by currency as well as the size of a permissible move by the foreign exchange manager without notification of the foreign exchange committee, the chief financial officer, or the chair of the finance committee.

The trading function should reside with the manager of foreign exchange. Documentation should be her or his responsibility as well, verified by the assistant treasurer international. The recordkeeping of exposures, positions, and the gains and losses should also be maintained by the foreign exchange manager.

Evaluation of the gains and losses on exposures and hedges should show results better than hedging everything. The results should be reported in the weekly foreign exchange review.

The accounting systems from the corporate controller's office should include: (1) allocating hedging gains and losses back to operating company performance income; (2) an audit trail for trading; and (3) monthly FASB and performance income gains and losses. The systems from the corporate treasurer's should include: (1) a monthly FASB exposure report and (2) a monthly update of performance income exposures based on input from operating companies. A monthly foreign exchange report from the corporate controller and a weekly foreign exchange review from the foreign exchange manager should be available.

A structured approach to the foreign exchange management function facilitates smooth functioning in an increasingly complex and crucial area. The ability to anticipate and prepare for events is critical in deciding whether a corporation can remain competitive in today's world.

REFERENCES

General

Aggarwal, Ray: *Financial Policies for the Multinational Company*, Praeger, New York, 1976.

Aggarwal, Ray and James C. Baker: "Using Foreign Subsidiary Accounting Data: A Dilemma for the Multinational Corporation," *Columbia Journal of World Business*, Fall 1975, pp. 83–92.

Ankrom, Robert K.: "Top-Level Approach to the Foreign Exchange Problem," *Harvard Business Review*, November 1976, pp. 79–90.

Corporate Exposure Management, First National City Bank, 1975.

Curtiss, Daniel W.: "Hedging Balance Sheet Exposure after Tax," *Euromoney*, April 1975, pp. 76–77.

Eiteman, David K. and Arthur P. Stonehill: *Multinational Business Finance*, Addison-Wesley, Reading, Mass., 1982.

Foreign Exchange Exposure Management, Chemical Bank, 1972.

Foreign Exchange Handbook, Brown Brothers Harriman, 1970.

George, Abraham M.: *Foreign Exchange Management and the Multinational Corporation*, Praeger, New York, 1978.

George, Abraham M. and Barry L. Klein: "Hedging Foreign Currency Exposure on an After-Tax Basis," *University of Michigan Business Review*, November 1976, pp. 12–18.

Hagemann, Helmut: "Anticipating Your Long-Term Foreign Exchange Risks," *Harvard Business Review*, March–April 1977, pp. 81–86.

Howlett, Keith: "Forward Hedging Does Pay, Because the Long Run Is Too Long," *Euromoney*, April 1977.

Kenyon, Alfred: *Currency Risk Management*, Wiley, New York, 1981.

Lietaer, Bernard A.: "Managing Risks in Foreign Exchange," *Harvard Business Review*, March–April 1970, pp. 127–138.

Mattlin, Everett: "How Corporations Are Playing the Currency Game," *Institutional Investor*, May 1976, pp. 25–33.

Prindl, Andreas R.: *Foreign Exchange Risk*, Wiley, New York, 1976.

Rodriguez, Rita M. and Eugene C. Carter: *International Finance Management*, Prentice-Hall, Englewood Cliffs, N.J., 1976.

Rosenwald, Roger W.: "How to Use the Various Definitions of Exposure," *Euromoney*, December 1976, pp. 101–110.

Solving International and Financial Problems, Business International, 1976.

Stobaugh, Robert B. and Sidney M. Robbins: *Money in the Multinational Enterprise*, Basic Books, New York, 1973.

Teck, Alan: "Control Your Exposure to Foreign Exchange," *Harvard Business Review*, January–February 1974, pp. 66–75.

Wasserman, Ulax J., Andreas R. Prindl, and Charles C. Townsend: *International Money Management*, Wiley, New York, 1974.

Windt, Stuart H. and Abraham M. George: "Multinationals Must Not Leave Local Taxes off the Books," *Euromoney*, April 1977.

Accounting

Financial Accounting Standards Board: "Statement of Financial Accounting Standards no. 8, Accounting for the Translation of Foreign Currency Transactions and Foreign Currency Financial Statements," October 1975.
Kemp, Donald S.: "The Attraction of Rule 52," Euromoney, November 1982.

Taxation

Costello, John J.: "Tax Consequences of Speculation and Hedging in Foreign Currency Futures," Tax Lawyer, vol. 28, no. 2.
Fuller, James P.: "Earnings and Profits," International Tax Institute Public Technical Meeting, March 1975.
Howard, Fred: "Overview of International Taxation," Columbia Journal of World Business, Summer 1975.

Economics

Dorfman, Robert: The Price System, Foundations of Modern Economics Series, Prentice-Hall, Englewood Cliffs, N.J., 1967.
Duesenberry, James S.: Money and Credit: Impact and Control, Foundations of Modern Economic Series, Prentice-Hall, Englewood Cliffs, N.J., 1967.
Eckstein, Otto: Public Finance, Foundations of Modern Economics Series, Prentice-Hall, Englewood Cliffs, N.J., 1967.
Kemp, Donald S.: A Monetary View of the Balance of Payments, Federal Reserve Bank of St. Louis, April 1975.
Kenen, Peter B. and Raymond Lubitz: International Economics, Foundation of Modern Economics Series, Prentice-Hall, Englewood Cliffs, N.J., 1967.
Officer, Lawrence H.: "The Purchasing-Power-Parity of Exchange Rate," IMF Staff Papers, March 1976, pp. 1–61.
Schultze, Charles L.: National Income Analysis, Foundations of Modern Economics Series, Prentice-Hall, Englewood Cliffs, N.J., 1967.

Foreign Exchange Background and History

Combs, Charles S.: The Arena of International Finance, Wiley, New York, 1976.
"Dollar Devaluation and International Monetary Reform," Harris Bank International Report, April 1973.
Foreign Exchange News, Union Bank of Switzerland, has published histories on the following currencies:

Austrian schilling	May 2, 1977
Belgian franc	November 29, 1976
Dutch guilder	September 27, 1976
French franc	June 28, 1976
German mark	July 26 and August 9, 1976
Pound sterling	April 12, 1976
Japanese yen	September 14, 1976
Canadian dollar	May 31, 1977
Danish crown	June 27, 1977

"From the End of Bretton Woods System to the Jamaica Agreement," *IMF Survey*, January 1976, pp. 22–29.

"Managing the World's Money," Schools Brief, *The Economist*, May 24, 1975, pp. 27–29.

Rolfe, Sidney E. and James L. Burtle: *The Great Wheel: The World Monetary System—A Reinterpretation*, McGraw-Hill, New York, 1975.

Solomon, Robert: *International Monetary System, 1945–1976, an Insider's View*, Harper & Row, New York, 1976.

"The European System of Narrower Exchange Rate Margins," *Monthly Report of Deutsche Bundesbank*, January 1976, pp. 22–29.

"The Snake Realignment—Much Ado about Nothing," *Foreign Exchange News*, Union Bank Switzerland, October 26, 1976.

Vries, Margaret Garritsen de: *International Monetary Fund 1966–1971: The System under Stress*, 2 vols., International Monetary Fund, Washington, D.C., 1976.

The following publications cover developments in foreign exchange markets:
  Quarterly Review, Federal Bank of New York
  World Financial Markets, Morgan Guaranty Trust
  International Currency Review (London)
  International Money Report, Business International
  The Economist (London)
  The Financial Times (London)
  Euromoney (London)
  Money Manager

Foreign Exchange Mechanisms

A Practical Guide to Foreign Exchange, Morgan Guaranty Trust, 1974.

An Inside View of the Foreign Exchange Market, Chase Manhattan Bank.

Financing Imports and Exports, Chemical Bank, 1976.

Hedging Guide, Merrill Lynch.

Holmes, Alan R. and Francis H. Schott: *The New York Foreign Exchange Market*, Federal Reserve Bank of New York, February 1965.

Mandich, D. R.: *Foreign Exchange Trading Techniques and Controls*, American Bankers Association, Washington, D.C., 1976.

Foreign Exchange Forecasting

Baschnagel, Hubert: "What to Expect from the Major Currencies," *Euromoney*, May 1977, pp. 49–51.

Best, Brinsley: "Looking Ahead Is Possible, But not More Than Five Years," *Euromoney*, July 1977, pp. 132–141.

Cernohous, Z.: "Problems of Forecasting Foreign Exchange Rates," *The Banker*, October 1976, pp. 1119–1122.

Donahue, Jeffrey C.: "Corporate Uses of Foreign Exchange Forecasts," *Euromoney*, July 1977, pp. 132–141.

"The Euro-dollar Market: Its Nature and Impact," *New England Economic Review*, Federal Reserve Bank of Boston, Boston, May–June 1975, pp. 3–31.

"The Euro-dollar Market: Some First Principles," *Morgan Guaranty Survey*, Morgan Guaranty Trust Company, New York, October 1969.

"The Financing of Business with Eurodollars," Morgan Guaranty Trust Company, New York.

Klopstock, Fred H.: "Money Creation in the Euro-Dollar Market—A Note on Professor Freidman's Views," *Monthly Review,* Federal Reserve Bank of New York, January 1970, pp. 12–15.

Murenbeld, Martin: "Economic Factors for Forecasting Foreign Exchange Rate Changes," *Columbia Journal of World Business,* Summer 1975.

"Some Questions and Brief Answers about the Eurodollar Market," *Joint Economic Committee Congress of United States,* Washington, D.C., 1977.

Five:
Management
of Foreign
Exchange Risk

GERALD KRAMER

Gerald Kramer is senior managing partner of the Globecon Group Ltd., a New York-based firm that specializes in international corporate treasury management consulting services. Mr. Kramer previously held the position of vice president of Chase Manhattan Bank and also worked at Texaco, Inc., and Business International Corporation, where he served as senior financial editor of *Business International* and as managing editor of *Financing Foreign Operations*. He earned his B.A. in economics and an M.B.A. in international finance and economics from City University of New York. He is a former adjunct professor of international business at Columbia University Graduate School of Business and is a frequent lecturer to professional and trade organization audiences.

F oreign exchange risk management is a complicated subject which involves all aspects of a multinational corporation's business dealings. It must
be approached systematically and with specific objectives in mind. Moreover, the approach to the management of foreign exchange risk must be
based on an understanding of what can and cannot be accomplished in
today's international economic environment.

Clearly, a thorough presentation of the subject is impossible in one chapter. What is possible, however, is a discussion of some basic premises,
financial theories, and responsibility assignments that are integral to the
management of foreign exchange risk. An appendix considers more practical ramifications of the approach suggested in the chapter.

BACKGROUND PREMISES

The basic premise of the management of foreign exchange is that a distinction must be made between two functional areas, that is, between the management of foreign exchange *uncertainty* and the management of foreign
exchange *risk*.

Foreign exchange uncertainty is the volatile impact that foreign exchange
movements have on *known cash flows, financial statement results, and
internal management performance evaluation criteria*. Its mitigation is a
function of sound financial management, whose primary objective is to
gauge the amount of unpredictability that is tolerable to senior management
and to control that uncertainty accordingly.

Foreign exchange risk is the impact that foreign exchange rate movements
have on *real underlying cash flows* (not the predictability of their collection,

but, rather, their inherent vulnerability to loss caused by an inability to price products as a U.S.-based company operating in foreign markets). Its control is an operational responsibility. How a firm prices its products and strategically views its markets will determine the effective management of that responsibility.

Thus the responsibilities of exposure management are divided as follows:

Foreign Exchange Uncertainty

Objective: Eliminate the unpredictable impact of foreign exchange rate movements on known cash flows (primarily booked receivables and payables) and reported financial results.

Responsibility: Largely a function of sound treasury management practices.

How Accomplished: By setting senior management tolerance points to this uncertainty and managing accordingly through an appropriate asset/liability management program.

Cost: The avoidance of unpredictability has attached to it some very predictable costs, e.g., interest expense and hedging discounts/or premiums. These costs must be incorporated into the analysis of each considered strategy.

Foreign Exchange Risk

Objective: Eliminate the real underlying impact that foreign exchange rate movements have on the parent currency value of overseas-generated cash flows.

Responsibility: Largely a function of operational policies as incorporated in product pricing, market strategies, and internal performance evaluation procedures.

How Accomplished: By developing pricing policies and evaluation techniques which are consistent with an objective of earning real returns in parent currency terms.

Cost: A real assessment of market opportunity—or lack thereof—must eventually emerge.

Intergrating Uncertainty Management with Risk Management: It is crucial to note that, although the above is presented as a segmented approach, these two important functions (namely, finance and operations) are not separate responsibilities when managing foreign exchange on a truly economic basis. In fact, a really economic approach to foreign exchange management requires that uncertainty and risk be managed both systematically and simultaneously. (See Exhibit 5-1.) Uncertainty is concerned with the predictability of cash flows and reported results and the market discounts for that uncertainty. Risk is concerned with real returns—and one cannot stay in business without them. Economics is concerned with the management and ascertainment of both. Furthermore, the truly international company is the one which has integrated these functions appropriately and

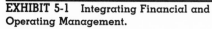

EXHIBIT 5-1   Integrating Financial and
Operating Management.

views roles and responsibilities accordingly. Unfortunately, there are still too many companies confusing these two functions, leading to a misunderstanding of what financial management can accomplish for the firm.

As a result, many corporations make treasury functions and financial management into profit centers attempting to offset operational losses by gains in foreign exchange transactions. This is a dangerous undertaking, since its effect is dubious at best and disastrous at worst. Financial management's only responsibilities are the elimination of uncertainty (as defined) and the identification of real aftertax arbitrage opportunities in the financial markets.

Financial Management: Concentrates on *known* cash flow exposure (where pricing cannot help) and seeks to insulate profit margins and reduce foreign exchange gain/loss visibility.

Operating Management: Concentrates on *projected* cash flows where pricing and market strategies can still be adjusted to eliminate real risk.

ECONOMIC RATIONALE FOR APPROACH

The following economic rationale must be understood for a full appreciation of the functions of exposure management. Although much of foreign exchange management (and senior executive attention) is primarily concerned with the short run, there are fundamental economic realities that are longer term in their evolution. But, since the long run is no more than the summation of short runs, in effect, these economic realities must be faced by each firm operating in today's international marketplace. Also, although these fundamental economic observations sometimes are called "theories," in actuality they embody the very essence and practices of international financial markets.

Purchasing Power Parity Theory

Of the three theories to be discussed, purchasing power parity theory (PPPT) is the best known. Essentially, the theory states that on average, and over time, relative differences in country inflation rates will ultimately be reflected in the exchange rate between two countries' currencies. For example,

P_{0f-1} = increase of 20%
P_{0d-1} = increase of 10%

where P_{0f-1} is price change in foreign country f from initial period P_0 to subsequent period P_1 and P_{0d-1} is price change domestically d from initial period P_0 to subsequent period P_1. If the initial rate for local currency is LC10 = $1.00, the new exchange rate will be

$$\frac{1.20}{1.10} = \frac{X_1}{10}$$
$$X_1 = 1.09 \times 10$$
$$= 10.9$$

The PPPT is well documented in economic literature and is thoroughly integrated into modern financial thought. For example, the fundamental acceptance of PPPT is one reason why fixed assets were translated at the historic exchange rate [under Financial Accounting Standard (FAS) 8]. The logic was that if a firm should translate its fixed assets each period at the current exchange rate (after writing them up for the local inflation rate), then over time, they would have the same U.S. dollar value as if they were always kept in historic U.S. dollar terms. In other words, the local inflationary effect on fixed assets was recognized as being directly offset by the external effect of devaluation. Thus, as a convenience, fixed assets were always translated at the historic exchange rate.

What is critical, however, is the recognition that relative differences in country inflation rates and subsequent exchange rate movements between two countries' exchange rates are immutably linked economic events. No one can say for sure when it will happen, but we do know that ultimately the value of one currency relative to another (which is no more than a reflection of relative purchasing powers) will be a result of inflation differences.

In some countries the link between inflation and currency change is dramatically apparent. Mexico, for example, has been experiencing accelerated inflation rates since 1971, and, as the acceleration has proceeded, so have the pressures on maintaining a fixed exchange rate for the peso. The 1976 devaluation, amounting to some 45 percent, was almost equal to the cumulative inflation differential Mexico had built up in the previous five years. The subsequent recent devaluations all have the same genesis. In essence, therefore, devaluations are external adjustments to internal inflation, and no amount of foreign exchange control short of international isolation can stop such adjustments from eventually taking place.

Even without delving into the relationship of this theory to ones to be discussed subsequently, it becomes obvious that a critical element in the economic analysis of the long-run profitability of the firm is the relationship between the prices of its products overseas (relative to local inflation rates) and to what degree this pricing is offset by subsequent exchange rate movements.

Interest Rate Parity Theory

Although the interest rate parity theory (IRPT) is not well known in its formal theoretical form, it is understood in practice by every international financial money manager. The IRPT states that the ratio of the forward and spot exchange rates between two countries' currencies will always equal the ratio of interest rates between those two countries. In other words, the discount or premium between two countries' currencies in the forward exchange market will always tend to equal the nominal interest rate differential between the two countries. For example,

$$R_{f0} = 12\%$$
$$R_{d0} = 8\%$$

where R_{f0} is the interest rate in a foreign country f at time R_0 and R_{d0} is the interest rate in the domestic country d at time R_0. Thus

$$X_1 = \frac{1 + R_{f0}}{1 + R_{d0}} \times X_0$$
$$= \frac{1.12}{1.08} \times 10 = 1.037 \times 10 = 10.37\,\text{LC}$$

where X_0 is the current exchange rate and X_1 is the forward exchange rate. Thus the local currency (LC) forward exchange rate will be $10.37\,\text{LC} = \text{U.S.}\$1.00$. Obviously, to compare interest rates in two different countries, similar factors must affect the determination of such rates. If two rates are to be accepted as interchangeable barring only that they apply to two different currencies, then, at the very least, their term and their risk must be viewed as the same. One-month money, for example, would have a different interest rate than one-year money, even if in the same currency. The same would hold true for corporate-issued monetary instruments compared to those issued by the government; the risk would be different. It should also be recognized that IRPT is effective all along the yield curve.

   This theory is important because it makes a critical link between country interest rate differentials and forward discounts and premiums. Indeed, it simply states that they are really no more than the same economic phenomenon. Yet frequently, in both accounting and taxation, they are treated as separate economic events, which leaves room for both opportunity and misunderstanding. Nevertheless, when looking at economic reality, this second link becomes critical for an understanding of foreign exchange management.

Fisher Effect

Perhaps the least well known of the three theories is the Fisher effect. First developed in the 1930s, the Fisher effect simply states that nominal interest rates rise to reflect anticipated levels of inflation. In other words, in addition to a risk-free return (government debt if so desired) plus a risk premium (for anything other than government debt), there is some level of return required by investors to compensate them for their expectations about future inflation. For example, nominal interest would be

$$Rn\,(1.08 \times 1.10) - 1 = 18.8\%$$

where anticipated inflation is 10 percent and R (real rate of interest) is 8 percent. If the nominal interest rate is 12 percent and anticipated inflation is 8 percent, then the real rate of interest is

$$R = 1.12 \times \frac{100}{108} - 1$$
$$= 1.037 - 1 = 0.037 = 3.7\%$$

The Fisher effect is possibly the most misunderstood of the long-run economic realities under discussion here. Confusion usually results from looking at short-term variables (prime rates, for example) in juxtaposition with announced inflation rates—often, they do not even approximate one another. However, the key rates to look at are long-term. Logically, no businessperson will loan long-term money at interest rates that do not compensate for inflation (or the reduction in purchasing power of the currency). Consequently, long-term rates build in inflation expectations. Thus there are numerous examples of the Fisher effect in the real world. Brazil, for example, has monetary correction which compensates asset holders through higher interest rates based on inflation developments. In addition, this inflation correction is also the basis for the minidevaluations of the cruzeiro. Another prime illustration was the long-term Swiss franc market during the mid-1970s, when the government managed through tight fiscal and monetary policies to reduce the rate of inflation to virtually zero. The long-term borrowing rate dropped to 3.75 percent, which is the general historical maximum potential real growth rate for any matured economy, and the assumed inflation expectation was zero.

Combining the Theories

PPPT states that relative differences in country inflation rates will ultimately be reflected in exchange rate differences; IRPT states that forward market discounts and premiums are no more than interest rate differentials; and FE states that interest rates embody inflationary expectations.

PPPT:

Inflation ————————————————————————→ Exchange rate changes

IRPT:

Discounts or premiums ——————————————→ Interest rate differentials

FE:

Inflation ————————————————————————→ Interest rates

What do these theories tell us about the management of foreign exchange on both short-term and longer-term economic bases?

1. If country interest rates embody inflationary expectations and relative differences in country inflation rates ultimately equal exchange rate differences, then it is true (but only over time) that the cost of hedging as embodied in discounts and premiums (which are interest rate differentials) approximates foreign exchange gains and losses.

2. If the above is true, then the very act of hedging is equal to the act of not hedging in its ultimate economic effect on the company. If the cost of the hedge can be equated to the exchange adjustment it is seeking to avoid, all other things being equal, the two decisions are the same.

3. A firm can therefore hedge nothing in the forward market or everything—economics would say they are exactly the same. However, corporate reality says that they are *not* equal. A hedge-everything policy seeks to eliminate all uncertainty that a no-hedge or even a selective-hedge policy cannot avoid, but this can be accomplished only by paying a very predictable cost. Also, most firms continue to selectively hedge on the basis that such a program can effectively outguess (or outperform) the forward exchange market. In other words, choosing when to take out hedges on the basis of forecasted currency movements will save money because the forward market rate is not a good predictor of the future spot exchange rate. Selective hedging, it is argued, can, therefore, minimize hedge costs or conversely result in net foreign exchange gains. This is a questionable assumption. It can, of course, be attempted if appropriate uncertainty tolerance points are established—and agreed on by senior management—beforehand.

4. If the theories are correct, then only operations can eliminate real risk, since the pricing and selling of a product (on an exante basis) is the only sure way to maintain protection from foreign exchange loss; i.e., over time a firm must price its products in local markets to compensate for subsequent exchange rate movements against the parent's home currency. (See Appendix 5B for more detailed discussion of this point.)

An explanation of the methods for pricing to compensate for exchange rate movements is beyond the scope of this discussion. *However, the crucial economic link between product pricing and foreign exchange loss cannot be avoided by any firm seeking to develop an economic approach to foreign exchange,* and financial management cannot make up this difference. This must be true if every financial action has associated with it a cost approximating the market's assessment of ultimate loss (risk). However, financial management provides a critical component in the economic approach, namely, the elimination of uncertainty in short-term financial results even when the firm is fully insulated from underlying risk. Thus, *the integration of risk management with uncertainty management is the only true economic approach to the management of foreign exchange.*

POLICY IMPLICATIONS

The policy implications of these three theories concern (1) the organization and implementation of an exchange risk management program, (2) the definitional base of exposure selected by the company, and (3) the methods used to evaluate and communicate the results of the program to the corporation's senior management.

Over time, foreign exchange gains and losses are embodied in the *cost of* "protection." (See Appendix 5A for a detailed discussion of this statement.) Consequently, financial management is concerned with gauging the degree of unpredictability the firm can tolerate and paying the predictable cost necessary to accomplish that level of senior management comfort. A forward contract (or any financial hedge) allows the firm to pay a predictable cost today to avoid an unpredictable cost (foreign exchange loss) tomorrow. To the extent that a firm selectively hedges it does so within the perimeters of acceptable uncertainty—too much uncertainty has a high economic cost and can have a very damaging impact on the credibility of treasury management.

These theories tell us that product pricing, and ultimately foreign exchange differences, must be viewed as critically linked economic events. This relationship may not be apparent in the short run due to the vagaries of the foreign exchange markets. However, an economic view of risk management must not be blinded by short-term views of the market or noneconomic measurement criteria, e.g., accounting approaches to viewing financial performance. The latter is not an obstacle easy to overcome for any firm seeking to manage its exposure on a longer-term economic basis.

Given that the cost of any financial hedge embodies the market's assessment of ultimate exchange gain or loss, the real role of financial management should be directed toward uncertainty management. *It must also identify, and act on, those nonmarket opportunities which can bring substantial bottom-line profitability to the firm without increasing financial uncertainty.* These opportunities are frequently found in arbitraging between country tax-laws (or even the same country's tax laws) and do not depend on outperforming the markets.

Finally, the ultimate policy implication of these theories is that the well-managed international company effectively integrates the role of uncertainty management with the role of risk management.

Policy Conflicts

In approaching the management of foreign exchange on an economic basis, there are numerous conflicts which may arise in both the communication and senior management's understanding of what precisely is being accomplished. This is true largely because most of the ways we have been educated to view performance have nothing to do with the economic relationships expressed above. Moreover, the senior management of most manufacturing companies do not have financial backgrounds, making it even more imperative that the economics of financial performance be carefully communicated before a program is implemented—the trade-offs must be clearly understood by all concerned.

Let us look at some of these conflicts.

1. An economic definition of exposure may have little to do with what accounting results show. The more a firm is embedded in accounting, the more difficulty it will have in managing economic results—senior management always believes in what is visibly reported, whereas much of what is really economics may not be seen until subsequent accounting periods and/or may never even be called foreign exchange gain/loss.

For example, foreign exchange adjustments are really no more than interest expense, discounts, or premiums, but senior management may not view foreign exchange adjustments as a normal cost of doing international business—even though interest expense is something every firm has! Further, much of what is considered foreign exchange loss may really be offset by the pricing of a firm's products (before an exchange adjustment, not after). Nevertheless, pricing offsets (or lack thereof) may never be seen as balancing those very visible exchange adjustments that must be explained to stockholders.

2. Economic management of foreign exchange requires more than treasury management cooperation. Treasury management must sell operations the idea that it too has a responsibility in the exposure management process. Specifically, foreign exchange risk management must be viewed as a proactive and strategic process with product pricing and sourcing strategies as an important element of that management. Frequently, operations will resist this process and responsibility, seeking to be evaluated only in local currency terms. The view that foreign exchange management is integrally linked to earning real returns in parent company currency terms is critical to the ultimate success of any economic approach to foreign exchange management.

3. The economic results of performance are always more difficult to ascertain than those of accounting. Also, senior management tends to gauge financial performance on a retroactive basis. However, financial and/or economic results cannot be correctly evaluated without drawing the proper link: (1) interest expense (discounts or premiums) relative to foreign exchange adjustments; (2) pretax results versus aftertax results; and (3) product-pricing strategies (and elasticities) versus foreign exchange adjustments. Only when these economic links are fully understood can we begin to appreciate the essence of what managing exposure on an economic basis really means. Financial results or economic performance cannot be viewed as an asymmetrical process. Foreign exchange movements occur because something has caused them. Financial results appear to be what they are because some price, somewhere, had to be paid. Bottom-line profitability is enhanced because treasury has properly identified certain nonmarket opportunities which have not increased the uncertainty faced by the firm.

Summary

First, financial practices should be driven by the need to manage—keep within identified tolerance points—the uncertainty faced by the firm. Second, financial management should be driven by the need to identify opportunities—where markets are temporarily inefficient or where there are nonmarket-created opportunities—which can contribute to the firm's bottom-line profitability without further increasing the firm's exposure to financial uncertainty. Third, financial management must remain firm in its position that it cannot accomplish the exposure management task alone. Product-pricing deficiencies must be seen as part of that process, with appropriate proactive involvement of operations in the product-pricing and sourcing strategy of the company. If anything, treasury-generated exchange gains (or avoided losses) should be considered gravy, never as a substitute for the business itself.

Appendix 5A
Protecting against
Exchange Rate Uncertainty:
Asset and Liability
Management Techniques

Asset and liability management simply involves offsetting a long (asset) position with a short (liability) position to achieve a "neutral" position to foreign exchange gain/loss, i.e., the gain/loss on long position equals the loss/gain on the short position. Thus, the firm is not exposed to the vagaries of exchange rates and their uncertain effects on cash flow or reported earnings.

There are numerous such techniques (see Exhibit 5-2) in asset and liability management; each has its own relative costs (see Exhibit 5-3). However, the primary strategies are as follows.

Forward Market Hedging. The offsetting of a long (short) position existing today with a short (long) position in the forward exchange market is known as "forward market hedging." The technique is usually extremely flexible as to timing, maturity, and amount and currency of denomination. Its cost is primarily embodied in the quoted discount or premium from the spot rate (today's rate for settlement two days forward). Most consider it the most versatile of all asset and liability matching techniques. Its main limitations are that it is sometimes viewed by senior management as too speculative

---

EXHIBIT 5-2 Basic Hedging Techniques

For Depreciating Currencies:
  Sell local currency forward
  Reduce levels of local currency cash
    and marketable securities
  Reduce local receivables by
    tightening credit
  Increase imports of hard currency
    goods
  Borrow locally
  Use leading and lagging of funds
    flows

and that exchange controls in many countries limit hedges to underlying commercial transactions.

Foreign Currency Borrowings. Foreign currency borrowings are the offsetting of a foreign currency asset position by either the parent or the local subsidiary. This technique has primarily been used for balance sheet hedging purposes, i.e., the elimination of translation adjustments to the parent company. This neutrality can be accomplished either by a local currency-denominated and -sourced loan or by a multicurrency facility with local currency options. In either case, the proceeds are placed in a nonexposed account, thus neutralizing the firm's long exposure to exchange gain or loss. The cost is the interest differential between borrowing in the currency of exposure versus the interest rate on comparable parent currency-denominated borrowings; excluding relative credit risks, it equates to the discount or premium on the two currencies in question. Its main limitations are credit limitation and less flexibility than forward transactions. Also, under FASB 52, translation accounting rules in the United States, the technique is ineffective at the local level because, as all assets are exposed, a local borrowing only serves to increase the firm's asset exposure by the same amount—assuming no subsequent dividend repatriation.

Leads and Lags. Using "leads" and "lags" means adjusting the timing of intercompany settlements to avoid or to take advantage of expected exchange rate changes. The matrix in Exhibit 5-4 highlights the fundamental workings of the technique. Essentially, using leads and lags seeks to take advantage of changes in currency values by maximizing receivable values and minimizing payable expenditures. The technique's success hinges on the accuracy of the firm's forecast, and its effectiveness is a function of the gain from timing adjustment relative to the cost of instituting that timing adjustment. For example, to speed up a receivable to avoid a depreciation

---

EXHIBIT 5-3   **The Cost of Protecting Exposure**

Depreciation strategies	Cost
Sell local currency forward	Discount and risk of currency moving in opposite direction
Reduce level of local currency cash and marketable securities	Operational problems, tax problems, opportunity cost (lower interest on hard currencies)
Reduce local receivables by tightening credit	Loss of business if credit terms are standard
Increase imports of hard currency goods	Interest costs for added funding
Use leading and lagging of funds flows	Interest costs or income lost

---

EXHIBIT 5-4 Leads and Lags Matrix

If have: If expect:	Receivable	Payable
Depreciation	Then lead	Then lag
Appreciation	Then lag	Then lead

means that a firm must either liquidate a monetary asset (which earns interest) or incur a liability (which bears interest). The movement of the exchange rate, *relative to this interest differential cost*, determines the success of the technique, assuming that visibility of exchange risk is weighed the same as the cost to eliminate it. Again, there is no free lunch—the technique has limited applicability to transactions between unrelated entities, there are numerous exchange controls, and many managements view the technique speculative or even as evidence of poor corporate behavior relative to preservation of national currency values. Also, any item subject to the technique must be carefully eliminated from any automatic clearing systems which may have been instituted.

CASE 1

The *first* example illustrates a firm which faced a loss of approximately $3.3 million on the 1976 devaluation of the Mexican peso. The firm had a *choice*. Should it cover in the forward market (i.e., sell pesos forward, at a discount, to cover its long position) or simply leave the position open and risk the possibility that the currency would not devalue and thus save the discount? The firm decided not to cover, since the cost to cover was too high and would put the firm's cash at unnecessary risk. As a result, the firm lost $3.3 million due to its uncovered asset position. Did treasury make the wrong decision? Did treasury fail to do its job? The answer requires some further thought and elaboration.

It is evident that the $3.3 million loss is almost equal (especially in present value terms) to the $3 million cost of covering the firm's exposure in each year since 1971 (see Exhibit 5-5). Thus, the so-called loss was no more than the market adjusting for the U.S./Mexican inflation differential which was fairly accurately reflected in the forward market's assessment of the cost of protection. By not hedging, the firm gained the use of cash, but it ultimately paid the price in reported earnings. Clearly, effectiveness can thus

EXHIBIT 5-5 Case 1: Aftertax Cost to
Hedge Mexican Exposure
($ Millions)

	Exposure	Hedge cost
1971	4.3	0.3
1972	4.5	0.3
1973	5.1	0.4
1974	5.6	0.5
1975	7.0	0.6
1976	8.8	0.9
Total cost		3.0

Estimated loss on 9/76 devaluation: 3.3

only be evaluated relative to what objective was sought. If increased cash flow was desired, an effective job was done. If the firm wanted earnings predictability, then it may have been better to pay the price. Thus policy objectives give the answer to the "good news" or "bad news" scenario.

Could the company have achieved both preservation of cash flow and earnings predictability? This is a question of timing, i.e., being on the right side of the market both times and requires a firm to forecast correctly and to act on such forecasts given the market's assimilation of market sentiment. Frequently, even if one can guess the correct timing, the cost of instituting the action quickly equals, if not exceeds, the pending adjustment. This was certainly true for the peso in 1976. Thus, accurate forecasting and market availability are prerequisites for a correct "both sides of the market" decision. The two events are not common occurrences. Also, each firm must search its capabilities to be in tune with market trends. Each decision to cover selectively means uncertainty for the firm, and uncertainty is clearly contradictory to the objectives of treasury management as originally set out in the beginning of this chapter.

CASE 2

Case 2 illustrates the same trade-offs as they apply to borrowing costs (see Exhibit 5-6). Again, the issue of reported-earnings uncertainty versus less visible interest expense is critical to the evaluation of the effectiveness of treasury's strategy choice. But remember that tax considerations can alter even the most perfect of correlations. For example, if exchange losses are not tax deductible but interest is, then strong-currency borrowings may be a poor strategy risk, even when markets are efficient. Thus, each country's tax treatment must be carefully integrated into any asset and liability management strategy.

EXHIBIT 5-6   Case 2: Three Methods of Financing the Same Transaction (Borrow $10 Million or Its Equivalent at No Exchange Risk) (Percent)

Options	Interest	Forward gain/loss	Net cost	Reaction
Borrow Eurodollars	7	0	7	Don't care
Borrow Euro Lira	20	+13	7	Happy
Borrow Swiss francs	3	−4	7	Upset

CASE 3

Case 3 illustrates essentially the same trade-offs as they apply to the lead/lag decision-making process (see Exhibit 5-7). In this case the firm had to decide whether to lead the lira-denominated receivable to Holland—thus incurring high interest cost—or to run the risk of lira depreciation relative to the florin. Because the Italian authorities generally lag their depreciation of the lira relative to market sentiment as embodied in Italian interest rates, the company requested normal payment terms and ran the risk of depreciation.

As a result, at the end of 1976, interest saved still far exceeded reported exchange losses. But what of losses for 1976 in isolation? For that year—the year of market adjustment—the company's reported losses were very visible and far in excess of the interest saved.

EXHIBIT 5-7   Case 3: Cumulative Effect of not Remitting $1000 of Lira to Holland

From 6/30/74 to	Aftertax Interest savings	Aftertax Exchange rate losses
9/30/74	$ 15	$ —
12/31/74	36	(30)
3/31/75	53	41
6/30/75	76	29
9/30/75	94	19
12/31/75	106	21
3/31/76	126	141
6/30/76	147	129
9/30/76	163	151
12/31/76	178	144

What really matters? Does a company care about interest opportunity cost saved (never even explicitly appearing in the financials) or its very visible reported exchange loss? More frequently than not, economics takes the back seat, and the treasurer is again at risk with regard to timing: Why could he or she not borrow up to the end of 1975 but be "smart" enough to lead in the first quarter of 1976? The same issue exists today for those firms questioning their borrowing of Argentine pesos at high interest rates, relative to dollar borrowings. The issue is one of timing and the role assigned to treasury relative to profit performance, earnings uncertainty, and so on.

Appendix 5B
Protection from
Underlying Exchange Risk

The goal of so-called proactive or ex ante strategies is to insulate the firm from real underlying economic risk, and thus such strategies are truly critical to the economic viability of the firm and its overseas operations. In using this strategy, the key is to view the firm's operations and marketing program as an integral part of the exchange rate protection program. Here opportunities to insulate the firm from real risk are to be found in:

1. Market choices
2. Pricing strategies
3. Choices of product
4. Alternatives in sourcing
5. Advertising campaigns
6. Market share orientation

A simple case illustrates the point. Increasingly, many firms are realizing that forward market costs are fairly accurate indicators of future exchange rate adjustments—given a reasonable time period. As a result, many of these firms are incorporating these market costs directly into their pricing policies or pricing evaluation processes.

For example, a major electronics firm now evaluates local pricing strategies by adding on local currency discounts (relative to the dollar) and deducting forward market premiums for the sale period in question. The idea is that, over a reasonable period of time, local prices must compensate the firm not only for adequate local profitability but also for any depreciation of that profit when brought back into U.S. dollar currency terms. Another variation on the theme is that many firms are using forward market rates in evaluating pro formas to actual operating results. In all cases, the key is pricing. If local prices keep pace with inflation differentials, and their ultimate embodiment in exchange rates, then exposure, in economic terms, may not even exist!

Thus it is the relationship of pricing to exchange rate adjustments which ultimately determines the firm's true exposure to exchange risk. Many firms are currently misstating their exchange risk to the extent that locally priced receivables may already compensate for subsequent devaluations. The concept of transaction exposure may not be as economic as it appears on the surface.

In summary, a firm's foreign exchange strategy must integrate both financial and operational considerations. If market costs ultimately equal exchange adjustments, then the elimination of uncertainty is what most techniques really seek. If a firm can price to compensate for real exchange loss, then true economic viability for the firm can be achieved.

ITEM CHARGED & DUE by

29998000471856
Graduate Student

12/31/2003 11:59 PM

International finance : cases and s
Carlson ... [et al.].

658.159 C 284

1
10001001590716

Six:
The Political and Economic Risk Analysis of Foreign Investment

RODRIGO K. BRIONES

Rodrigo K. Briones is a senior associate partner at The Globecon Group, Ltd., a New York-based international financial consulting firm, and is responsible for the company's Latin American financial services. He is also a special adviser to the Bank of Tokyo. He is an acknowledged expert on Latin America, having been an economist for Latin America at the Bank of America and a vice president and senior consultant for the Chase Manhattan Bank. In these positions he was responsible for foreign exchange advisory services, country risk assessment, foreign debt renegotiations, syndicated loans to Latin America, and consulting to major Latin American financial institutions, Central Banks, and multinational companies. In addition, he spent several years as a consultant with the United Nations in New York and Chile. Mr. Briones is also an associate professor of international business at the Graduate School of Business, New York University, and has taught at the Graduate School of Business, Pace University, and the University of Chile. He has published numerous articles on Latin America, and has participated in seminars sponsored by the IMF, Federal Reserve, United Nations, American Management Associations, World Trade Institute, Center for Latin American Monetary Studies, Council of the Americas, New York University, Business International, and Instituto Tecnologico de Monterrey.

Mr. Briones earned his B.A. and M.A. degrees in economics from the University of Chile. He also received an M.B.A. in international finance and economics from New York University.

F or the past sixty years, the world economy has become increasingly interdependent and trade has soared. Within this expanding environment, multinational companies have been actively deploying vast amounts of assets and assuming large liabilities overseas. Moreover, conducting business across national boundaries in nonstable political and economic environments has sometimes ended in unexpected business failures. The inability to assess the winds of change in some particular geographical areas has resulted in expropriations, nationalization, draconian foreign exchange controls, and other adverse managerial problems.

Undoubtedly, the challenges of the 1980s will place an increasing burden on multinational companies doing business abroad. Slow real economic growth in the third world, a direct consequence of explicit anti-inflationary policies in the industrialized countries, has resulted in unprecedented high unemployment levels. Although relatively more advanced developing countries may have the resilience to survive within a dynamic social environment, less developing countries do not. Slow rates of economic growth are building social tensions well beyond normal expectations; these tensions are shaking the very basis of the third world's current political-economic system. The current slow growth momentum has adversely affected the developing countries' export performance and the soundness of the international financial system. Debt-servicing problems will be the dominant issue in years to come, particularly in relation to the economic policies that third world borrowers ought to pursue to service their debt service commitments. Although the drastic slowdown in foreign exchange reserves accumulation by developing countries has been the dominant factor recently, high real interest rates have also had a negative impact on investment financing, adversely affecting overseas investment risk.

Hence multinational companies (MNCs) have become increasingly selective when allocating their resources abroad. As a matter of fact, the unprecedented high real yields in the United States had an adverse financial impact on developing countries, thereby increasing both local and external costs of financing. In most cases, returns on new investment projects by MNCs have been upgraded and the payback period has been shortened due to the uncertain future economic environment and costly financing. Likewise, MNCs have become increasingly selective when allocating financial resources overseas.

Foreign investment risk assessment, more commonly known as country risk, is not a newcomer in the field of social sciences. A clear example is the literature on the transfer problem (i.e., gift and reparation payments) and its implications in connection with war reparations, e.g., the Franco-Prussian War and Germany after World War I. Eminent economists such as J. M. Keynes, Bertil Ohlin, and Fritz Machlup, through empirical research and direct participation, tried to assess the capacity of a particular country to serve its international commitments, and more importantly, the set of economic policies that were supposed to be pursued by each debtor country.[1] Interestingly enough, during the discussions on Germany's World War I reparations, issues such as fixed versus flexible foreign exchange rate systems became quite popular in the economic literature. The main issue was related to the type of deflationary policy that Germany was supposed to pursue within a fixed exchange rate system. The adjustment process in the economy was supposed to be achieved through declining prices and wages, thereby reducing Germany's inflation below its main trading partners, theoretically improving both the allocation of domestic resources and export competitiveness. The latter would generate hard currency and save foreign exchange through a sharp decline in import demand, by which war payments could be met. Although the aggregate performance of some economic variables was assessed, e.g., balance-of-payment position and inflation and issues related to the economic effect of special economic policies, the resilience of a particular country relative to specific policies was also considered an essential component of the literature on the transfer problem.

In view of the world's current economic and political momentum, it is important to assess the recent evolution of country risk in the decision-making process of multinational companies. In the fifties and midsixties, the crucial issue in connection with country risk was associated with political risk, and the dominant players in the international arena were multinational companies looking for overseas business opportunities and continuous expansion of their subsidiaries. Within this context, the unanswered issue was how a particular host country would act against a certain multinational company with a large local physical presence (e.g., a plant facility). The main culprit was the existence of a political risk, and the worst outcome was nationalization. The political risk was translated as the probability associated with local political developments and their effects on the future profitability of a certain investment. Perhaps this emphasis on political risk was also a consequence of the behavior of North American multinationals that were active players in and followers of strategic areas of U.S. foreign policy. With a declining nationalistic mood in the early seventies, and the increasing role of commercial banks in the recycling of the petro dollars, the country risk assessment became relatively economic in nature, concentrating on the external capacity of a particular nation to service its external debt position.

Although political and social factors were included in the analysis, measurable economic variables were supposed to have the highest weight within different risk-rating systems. Political and social variables were also considered part of the judgmental process. In view of their increasing lending role, major international banks were able to develop sophisticated country evaluation models. In some instances judgmental components capable of assessing variables that were impossible to quantify (e.g., electoral possibilities for nationalistic political parties) were introduced. Nevertheless, at the end of the seventies, two countries with relatively strong economic performances and unalarming country risk ratings became major headaches for the international financial community. The first was Nicaragua. Although its overall economic performance was not as bad as other Central American and Caribbean countries (in terms of export outlook and industrial growth), there were major structural problems within its political-social infrastructure. In the case of Iran, a major OPEC producer, the evidence was perhaps more convincing in that economic ratings were not providing a clear warning in relation to domestic political developments with their adverse effects on foreign investment and private lending activities.

In the cases of Nicaragua and Iran, a thorough analysis of the political spectrum would have shown that radical political changes were the crucial factors to be considered in any risk assessment process. Consequently, those involved in country risk appraisal—above all, major commercial banks, which were the main leaders in the development of risk systems—reverted to pure political analysis and/or rating systems heavily biased toward political categories. Some established in-house political expertise; in a few instances, political analysis dominated the decision-making process associated with risk assessment.[2]

COUNTRY RISK EVALUATION

The process of evaluating the risks of doing business abroad for any firm involves judgmental factors as well as objective quantitative analysis. Under these circumstances different countries should be treated in a consistent fashion within a worldwide perspective. Whatever system is being used or developed to evaluate a particular country, this system should be completely objective; it should not be influenced by individual ties to a particular country and/or a biased judgmental approach.[3] Experience has shown that the assessment of some key variables can shed light on the country's future economic and sociopolitical performance. Corporate decision makers should be aware of past trends and future perspectives of domestic economic factors, such as rates of growth, inflation, and fiscal deficit. In addition, the composition of exports and their performance, the international reserve position, and the import coverage by international reserves, debt service payments, etc. are part of the vast array of variables related to the external liquidity of a particular nation. Moreover, attention should be devoted to the local economic structure, considering the different sectors in the economy, the relationship that exists within these sectors, the local infrastructure, etc. Finally, a complete country assessment should also include the sociopolitical categories (role of players, social unrest, etc.). As stated earlier, although these variables are difficult to assess, they are a major component of sound country risk assessment.

Most multinational companies do not have the in-house expertise to cope with assessing the variables mentioned. However, there are specialized consulting services covering these issues and offering specific advice on various countries.[4] In addition, multinational companies have a strong relationship with major commercial banks. The latter are heavily involved in country risk to minimize the risk associated with their overseas exposures and setting country limits. Commercial banks' increasing concern about the safety of their overseas loans has also been a major contributing factor to the development of country analysis. Consequently, in most instances a corporate decision maker might have access to a considerable wealth of information on the subject.[5]

The point of view of a private lender and its business risks may be different from that of a multinational company. For example, a bank could participate in a syndicated loan without having a branch and/or other type of physical presence (e.g., representative office) in a particular country. Undoubtedly, the developments in the local economy and the external sector will have a direct effect on the nation's capacity to serve its foreign debt. Although a multinational company may be operating through a particular license agreement and ultimately may be affected by the lack of hard currency, usually large multinationals do have a physical presence through manufacturing plants, joint ventures, and so on. Therefore, these companies' overseas business operations and profitability may be more vulnerable.

Considering these different points of view, a private lender's main concern is to assess all the factors that affect the generation of foreign exchange earnings by which debt service payments can be met. Ultimately, the private lender will try to minimize the transfer risk, that is, the convertibility of local currency into hard currency (dollar, deutschemark, British pound, etc.). The ultimate example is a developing country without any hard currency available which makes the sovereign decision of paying its foreign debt in local currency. Since most of the currencies of third world countries are not traded in major financial centers, the lender will be stuck with nontradable currency.

A multinational company is also concerned with transfer risk—when problems relating to debt service payments have occurred, multinationals have been severely affected. When Mexican banks were nationalized and foreign exchange controls implemented by the Lopez-Portillo government in September 1981, MNCs operating in Mexico got into a Kafkaesque operating environment.[6] Considering the volatility of the international economic environment, additional factors may exert adverse pressures on the profitability of a multinational's domestic operations. Of course, the most important component will be the availability of and accessibility to foreign exchange to remit profits, dividends, capital repatriation, and purchases of essential imports to maintain a workable domestic operation. The availability of foreign exchange is also crucial to the profitability of the subsidiary. The latter will be dominated by market performance, inflationary pressures, government regulations, etc. If an unprofitable operation develops and the access to hard currency is relatively expensive, the subsidiary may face an unbearable managerial problem. Furthermore, the possibility of nationalization and/or expropriation always exists should the domestic political spectrum shift into a nationalistic mood.

COUNTRY RISK: A MANAGERIAL PERSPECTIVE

Since the assessment of country risk involves the analysis of a vast array of categories, the exercise itself can be conceived as management process. To assess a particular foreign investment (and/or financing), some multinationals and financial institutions rely on standard credit analysis and/or simple capital budgeting. Although these tools may be appropriate from a purely technical perspective, the world's future uncertain business environment calls for additional supporting techniques.

For example, considering the kernel of foreign direct investment, a multinational company should take into account the political developments in a particular country. These developments could be associated with a dynamic game with different type of players. Within this environment, players such as foreign investors, local bankers, labor unions, and military establishment will be affected differently by the events occurring in that particular geographical environment. Rising interest rates, business deregulation, democratization process, legislation pertaining to possible nationalization, etc., will have a distinct impact on each of the players. Furthermore, each player will try to maximize current gains and minimize future losses through sound feasible strategies and coalitions with other game participants (e.g., foreign investors and local bankers, labor unions and the church). Consequently, those assessing overseas risks should consider this political game and, above all, should assess the strategies of the different players and the possibilities associated with specific workable coalitions. Once these strategies are assessed and the possible coalitions are identified, the analyst should consider the implications of the political game on the economic environment and its ultimate effect on the MNCs' future investment decision (and/or its current presence in a certain country). A good starting point is to assume that in any specific geographical time and space dimension all economic units (and/or players) operate within the same financial, social, and political environment. This special type of environment may be changed in view of the weight of each player (or coalition of players) within the country's decision-making process and its access to (and control of) political and economic categories.

In view of this example and the continuous instability in the third world economies (e.g., see-saw movements in prices of raw materials, fiscal restraint, foreign debt refinancing), MNCs increasingly need reliable information to assess country risk. Consequently, the process of investment risk analysis could be conceived as part of an entire corporate managerial task, and the staff or analysts involved should be more than strict economists and/or political scientists. Considering the magnitude of the world economic problems and their implication for future corporate policy, perhaps analysts with a Renaissance type of approach may be needed.[7] Nevertheless, in view of today's scientific specialization, it will be almost impossible to hire an analyst and virtuoso like Leonardo da Vinci with a thorough knowledge of social and exact sciences. Moreover, the applicability of theoretical principles and their interpretation will be a sine qua non condition. Nevertheless, there are alternative procedures outside the sphere of the Renaissance approach by which different variables can be assessed within the country evaluation spectrum.

A sound management decision will integrate risk evaluation within the corporate decision-making process. Although issues relating to the corporate decision-making process depend on the centralization or decentralization of a corporate management structure, the fact that a multinational subsidiary could be responsible for specific business objectives and investment targets may result in an active role in country risk. The relationship between the parent and the subsidiary will be enhanced, with the latter providing the information core. Hence this approach will result in an active participation of different corporate players, and their inputs would be considered within the global country risk approach. The country evaluation will be an important component of the short- and long-term objectives of a multinational company reflecting a prudent balance between profitability and risk.

In the short run, within this managerial concept of country risk, the subsidiary will be concerned with the profit maximization concept to make capital repatriations and remit dividends to the parent company. The fact that the subsidiary is actively communicating with the parent company in relation to country evaluation will establish the grounds for the long-run strategy of an MNC's entire worldwide operation. The establishment of a sound financial base across national boundaries, serving both the host country and the international markets, should be the core of any overseas investment decision that takes full advantage of the corporate resources available. By doing so, the MNC's shareholders' wealth will be maximized and the host country properly served. Consequently, country analysis is essential to assessing business strategies and overseas operations; country analysis is a major complement to the decision process without being a substitute for sound judgment. The integration of the decision-making process (subsidiary-parent company) should take into account the short- and long-run corporate objectives.

CORPORATE OBJECTIVES

Within the conceptual framework of country risk analysis, the operating and potential overseas business environment contains good and bad countries. Further, in each of these countries there are excellent and unacceptable business opportunities. Therefore, the risk-rating structure must be developed with a worldwide perspective. The structure, apart from evaluating risk, could also provide additional information on specific business opportunities that perhaps initially were discarded or plainly omitted. Since the risk evaluation system will have important policy implications for the corporate upper management, it is essential to maintain risk ratings and the country analysis on a timely basis. Sometimes there is an inclination in the corporate world to treat a country risk evaluation as an extension of a marketing proposal reviewing the MNC's operations or as part of a brief appendix in a new investment proposal. If this approach is followed, the risk evaluation process could become strictly judgmental in nature and therefore dominated by individual subjective factors. Therefore, initially the evaluation system should be completely independent of corporate market considerations.

For example, a multinational could have a large subsidiary in a particular country that faces an increasing number of problems such as high inflation, stiff foreign exchange controls, and inability to service its external liabilities. Considering the issues at stake and the ultimate potential response of the decision makers at the MNC's headquarters, the subsidiary might be exposed to a gradual reduction of operations. And ultimately, the subsidiary's fate could be associated with a gradual pullout process, a minor equity ownership in a joint venture with local investors, and/or license-patent type of agreements. These options do have a social cost in terms of local unemployment and overall corporate image, and therefore the decision makers may opt for the common wait-and-see attitude rather than make a drastic pullout decision. However, were personal judgmental values to become the dominant factors in deciding the MNC's future activities in that particular country, this type of decision-making process could have disastrous effects on the subsidiary's long-term performance and the MNC's overall image in a particular region.

MAJOR COUNTRY RISK COMPONENTS

A multinational company which has a global risk evaluation perspective theoretically would be operating within an optimal foreign direct investment portfolio minimizing its business risks. The MNC should constantly review its overseas exposures by country and should devote special emphasis to those investments that will be coming on stream in a particular period. Perhaps the latter could be associated with the economic value of the firm and the overall overseas risks involved. In the case of private lenders, for example, their balance sheets are constantly being reviewed both by country and by maturities due to the bank's concern regarding the safety of overseas loans. Federal regulatory agencies do play an important role, but the dynamics of international portfolio management in major financial institutions do show a specific need for country risk ratings and specific country lending limits. Once this process has been accomplished, country exposures will be monitored strictly on the basis of lending limits. This managerial process is also applicable to MNCs with large overseas exposures.

To accomplish the managerial objectives mentioned above, corporate analysts should have a thorough understanding of two country risk categories: the adaptability and the resilient concepts. The adaptability concept involves a set of economic variables that measures the capacity of a country to implement specific economic policies which are designed to restore, preserve, and/or enhance favorable trends within the local economy and its external accounts. Each government will have a set of instruments such as fiscal and monetary policies. Given a certain sociopolitical framework, a specific economic policy (depending upon the government's political philosophy, e.g., pure market approach, state capitalism, etc.) will be followed to obtain a desirable economic outcome and perhaps a special political arrangement. These instruments of economic policy will operate within a certain political and social environment. Under this set of circumstances, the country analyst will observe the past behavior and future outlook of a vast array of economic variables such as the rate of inflation, the level of economic activity (measured by real growth in gross domestic product), expansion in the money supply, unemployment levels, sectorial growth in agriculture, manufacturing, mining, and fiscal deficit. All these economic categories operate within a particular environmental framework characterized by a certain degree of historical, economic, and sociopolitical development of the society under study.

The resilience concept provides information about the capacity of a particular country to adjust its economy to exogenous shocks, that is, economic, political, and other type of shocks that lie outside the control of the local authorities. These exogenous shocks might have favorable (or unfavorable) effects on a country's external position and its local economy.

There are several tools to use in assessing the resilience of a country. Perhaps the most useful and feasible tool is historical approach based on the performance of the economy. The ultimate aim of this analysis is macro-economic aggregates, such as levels of economic activity and investment, inflation, and performance of different accounts in the balance of payment. Given the historical performance and a standard long-term forecast (e.g., at least five years), specific external shocks could be introduced, and the potential of a country to adjust its economy to different exogenous shocks observed. Resilience is almost impossible to measure by a single set of variables. Most likely a judgmental type of analysis will be used in assessing the ultimate effects of a drastic change in oil prices, the effects of civil war in a neighboring country, social unrest, etc. Perhaps a first stage in the analysis is to focus on the structure of the economy (e.g., relationship among different economic sectors) observing how this structure will react vis-à-vis an exogenous shock. Once this reaction has been evaluated, the second stage will be to concentrate on different expected scenarios, taking a short-, medium-, and long-term approach.

THE EMPIRICAL EVIDENCE

If a multinational company cannot develop its in-house expertise on risk assessment, there are several specialized services involved in country evaluation. Although some risk assessment systems do concentrate exclusively on political risk, others combine both political and economic analysis. Even though these risk systems tend not to be sophisticated, they do provide some guidance and assistance to a corporate decision maker. For example, *Institutional Investor* provides country risk ratings based on what could be defined as an opinion type of survey.[8] The sample is part of a large universe: the leading international banks. Each banker is supposed to grade a particular country within a scale of 0 to 100. Countries that approach the zero rating are associated with the lowest creditworthiness and the highest probability of default. Countries that are closer to the 100 rating have the relatively highest creditworthiness and the lowest probability of default. According to *Institutional Investor*, "The sample for the study, which is updated every six months, ranges from 75 to 100 banks, each of which provides its own ratings. All participants in the survey are assured that their responses and the fact of their participation are kept strictly confidential. Banks are not permitted to rate their home countries. The individual responses are weighted, using an Institutional Investor formula that properly gives more weight to responses from banks with the largest worldwide exposure and the most sophisticated country analysis system."[9]

Euromoney has developed an interesting risk evaluation system that takes into account the realities of the international capital market and the judgmental perception of international lenders.[10] This evaluation system relies on the actual loan spread paid by an individual borrower, that is, the premium that a major lender will charge on a particular loan relative to international yields. For example, a certain spread will be charged on U.S. prime rate and/or LIBOR (London Interbank Offered Rate). A higher spread over LIBOR will be associated with low creditworthiness and vice versa. Recently, *Euromoney* has extended its rating system to include for each borrowing nation "the terms it receives by taking into account each country's terms in all public international capital markets by its ease of access to each of those capital markets, and by its ability to use the innovations and borrowing options that are now a frequent occurrence."[11]

There are other country risk services that combine a judgmental type of approach with a scale-rating index based on different economic categories. These indexes refer to past economic performance and usually medium-term outlook (e.g., from one to three years). A thorough and monthly updated country risk analysis is available in the *International Country Risk Guide* published by International Reports.[12] The combination of indexes and judgmental analysis is reflected in more than seven indicators, such as inflation, foreign debt service ratio, international liquidity, foreign collection experience, external account performance, political stability, parallel market exchange rate, and business-government ethics. Assessment of each of these indicators is based on its historical and future performance and weighted on a scale from 0 to 100. Countries that fall below the 45 rating are considered extremely risky and relatively low in creditworthiness. A country that falls within the 45 to 75 range will be moderately risky; a rating above 75 is assumed to be slightly risky.

Finally, as mentioned earlier, multinational companies might be tempted to include country risk evaluation as an extension of their new marketing plans and/or directly within a capital-budgeting process. For example, expected net cash flows of a future project could depend on a certain country evaluation and the judgment of the financial analyst. The latter may be a byproduct of a particular scale risk-rating approach and judgmental factors. This, in turn, permits the buildup of alternative future scenarios that ultimately will be reflected in the expected net cash flows of a particular project. A further step in capital budgeting is to find the proper discount rate to obtain the internal rate of return. The discount factor should consider the risks inherent in a particular investment project and, therefore, will also reflect the analyst's perception in connection with a specific country. If the country under study has relatively high political and economic risk (low creditworthiness), the discount rate will be higher vis-à-vis the local prevailing opportunity cost of money measured by a combination of domestic interest rates.[13]

Capital budgeting in countries with relatively low political and economic risk (high creditworthiness) will use a discount factor similar to the prevailing local cost of money. Through the cash flows and the discount factor, country risk can be incorporated into the capital-budgeting process. Moreover, investment projects in high-risk countries will have a relatively higher discount factor and low cash flows when compared with a similar project in a less risky environment. Therefore, the particular yield of an investment project measured by the internal rate of return could be much lower than expected. Because of the investment risk assessment component, an attractive project for a multinational company might even be considered nonprofitable within its in-house financial guidelines (e.g., the funds will have higher investment yields in other countries or in certain local money market instruments).

These different risk-rating systems do have several limitations in relation to what they are supposed to assess and the different interpretations arising from each one. For example, a private lender may have other business concerns in a certain country rather than the loan that was used as a reference for the opinion survey and the spread approach on country risk. Moreover, perhaps that particular lender is willing to develop and sell other banking products to a certain country and/or might use the loan as its marketing penetrating strategy if there is no previous banking relationship. Consequently, that private lender may be more lenient in connection with the price of a loan, and, therefore, the spread over LIBOR may be much lower than what market conditions would indicate. Low-spread margins can be compensated by charging high commissions and/or, if applicable, can carry a special tax rebate on interest payments in the borrowing country. Furthermore, on the borrower side, a higher spread will be quite detrimental to future external borrowings. Therefore some countries would prefer to obtain low spreads and pay high frontal fees for their loans.

CONCLUSIONS

Is a multinational company capable of building a sophisticated overseas investment risk system? Will this system comply with the corporate objectives, thereby assisting the decision makers? These are some of the unanswered issues related to country risk evaluation. Several multinationals might be interested in developing risk-rating systems, but most MNCs would be unable to devote large financial and in-house human resources for the research, development, and implementation of sophisticated analytical risks models.

What should an advanced country risk rating system look like? A highly complex country risk system will rely on two basic concepts discussed earlier: the adaptability and resilience of an individual country. To assess these categories, a set of quantifiable economic variables must be identified and defined. Each must be observed through a particular period, and a medium- or long-term forecast (e.g., three to five years) is introduced. Each economic variable is assigned a particular weight within the overall rating index that the analyst intends to build.[14] For example, the adaptability index of Bank of America's country risk system will carry the following weights: per capital growth in real GNP (25 percent), inflation (20 percent), export earnings (15 percent), fuel and food imports (12.5 percent), export concentration (10 percent), and domestic savings (7.5 percent). The adjustment in the exchange rate and the nation's International Monetary Fund (IMF) position will each be assigned a 5 percent weight. On the other side, the external debt-servicing index includes debt-servicing capacity ratio (50 percent), months of imports covered by international reserves (20 percent), and external debt ratio as a percentage of GNP (20 percent). The compressibility index, that is, imports of food, fuels, and external debt service payments as a percentage of total export revenues will be assigned a 10 percent weight. These weights are obtained through different computer simulations and fine tuning of the historical information. Within the Bank of America's system, the analytical data matrix counts for two-thirds of the total rating, and the judgmental matrix counts for the remaining one-third. The analytical data matrix contains two components: the adaptability index, which assigns relative ratings from A (the highest) to E (the lowest), and the external debt-servicing index. The latter provides a relative rating that fluctuates from 1 (the highest) to 5 (the lowest). Therefore, the adaptability index furnishes a vast array of ratings. For example, the combination A-1 shows an outstanding creditworthiness, and E-4 represents a relatively high risk. The judgmental approach is introduced through the upgrading or downgrading of the ratings in the analytical data matrix. For example, after feeding the computer with the data of a particular country, a C-3 rating is obtained. The latter means that the index shows a relatively cautious creditworthiness. However, the local economic staff (e.g., perhaps a special country risk task force) is well aware that there are sociopolitical problems that would have to be solved in the near term. These problems might have an adverse effect on the country's future domestic economic performance. Furthermore, there could also be some clear indications of a poor export outlook due to a worldwide recession. In this case, there is an increasing probability of arrears in the nation's international payments, rollover in its short-term debt, and so on. Consequently, the C-3 rating may be downgraded into a D-4 based on judgmental considerations.

Judgmental analysis has become an increasingly important component of any sound country risk-rating system. As mentioned earlier, a country that can generate foreign exchange might, from the theoretical point of view, be able to satisfy its international commitments. However, the crucial issue lies in both the ability and the willingness of a particular nation to allocate foreign exchange by which debt service payments, dividends, profit repatriation, etc. can be made. Further, a great number of the political risk models tend to address the stability of a certain political environment and the specific actions that might be perpetrated against foreign investors. Some of them will also address indirectly the transfer risk and debt-servicing capacity of a particular country. Consequently, the ultimate judgment will rely on the user of the information. In doing so, the country analyst will take into account the managerial and exposure issues that an MNC would face in a specific geographical environment.

There are several judgmental and economic factors that a corporate risk analyst should not overlook.[15] The role of the government in the nation's economic environment, development and sectoral programs pertaining to the MNC's business environment, the local planning system, different procedures by which government resources are being allocated, etc., are extremely important. The participation of industry, agriculture, mining, and services in the local economic activity; the manner in which income is distributed by sectors and by income levels; different sets of regulations on domestic prices, foreign exchange, and trade controls are also useful. Within the area of economic policy, it is essential to understand the independence and degree of influence of the monetary authorities, the way that the government finances its deficits, and the availability and access to local funds by multinational companies.

As stated earlier, there is an increasing need to appreciate the sociopolitical and cultural factors. The political history of a particular nation can shed some light on past national-populist types of governments and their possible anticapitalistic roots. The role of the opposition parties and the military and the frequency of coups and related changes, the behavior of labor in urban and rural areas, social and ethnic group conflicts, etc. should also be assessed.

The depth and caliber of state management should also be analyzed, including the ability of a particular regime to live up to its philosophical and electoral commitments. Within the so-called legal factors, it is important to look at labor regulations, capital repatriation, licensing contracts, patents, trademark protection, domestic business law, taxation, and overall law enforcement. The participation in international organizations and regional integration schemes should also be analyzed.

There are several external factors that a judgmental approach should take into account. Perhaps the most important is socioeconomic dependence on other regional economies that ultimately will influence the levels of local economic activity and the political behavior of a number of players. This dependence could have a negative effect on a nation's political balance, thereby affecting the local attitude toward foreign investment. Additional external factors, such as the degree of regional military security and its dependence on particular power centers, should also be considered within a sound judgmental approach.

In view of the world's uncertain future economic environment, corporate managers will have to rely more on sound international risk evaluation systems. This task will be difficult if the subsidiary's earnings are not being repatriated, overseas suppliers are in arrears in connection with their hard currency liabilities, there are large unpaid intercompany accounts, domestic access to foreign currency to pay essential imports is impossible, etc. These and other issues previously discussed will continue to be the raison d'être for country risk appraisal. Since sophisticated technical risk systems are difficult to develop and implement, most multinational analysts will require astute and sound judgment. A variety of social disciplines, different information sources, and some of the analytic techniques developed in this chapter may be used.

Notes

1. J. M. Keynes, *The German Transfer Problem.* Bertil Ohlin, *The Reparation Problem: A Discussion.* Both articles were published by *The Economic Journal*, 1929. They are reprinted in *Readings in the Theory of International Trade*, selected by a committee of the American Economic Association; Howard S. Elis and Lloyd A. Metzler (eds.), Richard D. Irwin, Homewood, Ill., 1950. Professor Fritz Machlup's excellent review of the transfer problem is available in his *International Economics*, G. Allen, London, 1970. Part V contains a section on "Capital Movements and the Transfer Problem." For a classical and witty analysis on the subject, see "The Transfer Problem: Theme and Four Variations" (chap. 15) and "Foreign Debts, Reparations and the Transfer Problem" (chap. 16). Also a thorough discussion on the price and income effects are available in chapters 17 and 18.
2. "Meet the New Breed of Banker: The Political Risk Expert," *Euromoney*, July 1980, p. 9.
3. "Banks Revise Way of Making Foreign Loans," *Wall Street Journal*, February 18, 1983.
4. For example, see "Country Credit: The Grim Tidings," *Institutional Investor*, September 1982.
5. Most of the major commercial banks do not sell country risk services. Whatever country risk system is available, it is exclusively for internal use and is shared verbally (from time to time) with the bank's main customers.
6. In Mexico, after the nationalization of local banks and the introduction of stiff currency controls, a priority type of allocation for exchange purchases was established. Within this priority list, multinationals were granted a relatively low priority after payments of debt service by public sector agencies and financial institutions, essential imports, etc. This situation was reversed early in 1983, but the local cost of buying hard currency was exorbitant.
7. Ingo Walter, "Country Risk, Portfolio Decisions and Regulation in International Banking Lending," *Journal of Banking and Finance*, vol. 5, 1981, p. 85.
8. "Country Credit: The Grim Tidings," *Institutional Investor*, September 1982.
9. Ibid., p. 288.
10. *Euromoney Country Risk: How to Assess, Quantify, and Monitor It*, 1979. "The Country Risk League Table," *Euromoney*, February 1982.
11. "The Euromoney Country Risk Ratings," *Euromoney*, September 1982, p. 71.
12. International Reports, *International Country Risk Guide.* A thorough description of International Reports' rating system is also available in *Key to International Country Risk Guide.*
13. In most third world nations, capital markets are extremely thin and sometimes very unsophisticated when compared with their counterparts in industrialized nations. Further, these markets are under heavy government control. It is almost impossible to rely on market yields as a good proxy for the real cost of money if domestic interest rates are subject to ceilings and/or stiff credit control allocations. For further reference, see Rodrigo Briones, "Latin American Money Markets," in A. George and I. Giddy (eds.), *International Finance Handbook*, vol. 1, pt. 4, Wiley, New York, 1983.
14. A detailed description of Bank of America's country risk is available in Robert Heller, "Country Risk and International Portfolio Management." Paper presented to the Symposium on Managing Country Risk. New York. Jan. 24, 1980.
15. A detailed analysis of these issues is available in Rodrigo Briones, "Country Risk Evaluation: International and Social Context," in J. C. Garcia-Zamor and S. Sutin (eds.), *Financing Development in Latin America*, Praeger, New York, 1980.

Seven:
The Capital
Budget Analysis
of Foreign
Investments

HING Q. LUM

PEARSON GRAHAM

Hing Q. Lum is director of corporate finance at Warner-Lambert Company and responsible for reviewing capital spendings in both U.S. and foreign locations. Previously, Mr. Lum was manager of international financing at TRW Inc., where he was responsible for the financing of foreign operations and foreign currency exposures. Mr. Lum earned his Bachelor of Science degree in physics from The City College of New York and an M.B.A. degree in finance from The Bernard M. Baruch College.

Pearson Graham is director, operating investments, at TRW Inc. and responsible for the capital program and review of acquisitions. Mr. Graham earned B.S. and M.S. degrees in engineering from the University of Michigan and an M.A. degree in economics from Cleveland State University, where he was a lecturer in economics for seven years. He is also the coauthor, with Diran Bodenhorn, of *Managerial Economics*, Addison-Wesley, 1980.

Capital is usually invested to increase the value of the firm. This value may be increased by any of a number of strategies. For example, a firm may increase its value by reducing its costs of production or by providing additional facilities to produce a profitable good or service. The usual test for evaluating a capital investment is to estimate the incremental cash flows over time that result from making the investment and discounting the cash flows to present value. The two most commonly used measures of the value of an investment are net present value (NPV) and internal rate of return (IRR). Net present value is the value of cash flows discounted at the firm's cost of capital. Internal rate of return is the discount rate at which the net present value of discounted cash flows is equal to zero. An investment increases the value of the firm if the net present value is greater than zero or if the internal rate of return is greater than the firm's cost of capital.

Operating cash flows are often approximated by profit after tax plus depreciation. Other cash flows include the original investment in the asset and any tax credits or other incentives resulting from the investment plus required expenditures for additional assets to support the investment during the analysis period. Further, any residual retained by the asset at the end of the analysis period must be taken into account, since such value may be realized by sale of the asset or by its continued use. For example, a firm might invest $100,000 in an asset, depreciate the asset over five years according to a specified depreciation schedule, receive an investment tax credit equal to 8 percent of the investment, earn $30,000 per year for five years in additional aftertax earnings (PAT) from the goods produced by the asset, and estimate the worth of the asset at the end of five years to be $20,000. The internal rate of return of this investment is calculated to be 48.2 percent, as follows:

Year	Investment	PAT	Depreciation	Tax credit	Residual	Cash flow	Discounted at 48.2%
0	100,000			8,000		−92,000	−92,000
1		30,000	20,000			50,000	33,735
2		30,000	20,000			50,000	22,761
3		30,000	20,000			50,000	15,357
4		30,000	20,000			50,000	10,361
5		30,000	20,000		20,000	70,000	9,786
						Total	0

If the cost of capital of the firm is 20 percent, the internal rate of return indicates that making this investment will, if everything goes according to plan, increase the value of the firm. Alternatively, one can calculate the net present value of the investment to the firm by discounting cash flows at the firm's cost of capital, as follows:

Year	Investment	PAT	Depreciation	Tax credit	Residual	Cash flow	Discounted at 20%
0	100,000			8,000		−92,000	−92,000
1		30,000	20,000			50,000	41,667
2		30,000	20,000			50,000	34,722
3		30,000	20,000			50,000	28,935
4		30,000	20,000			50,000	24,113
5		30,000	20,000		20,000	70,000	28,131
						Total	65,568

The theory of investment briefly outlined here has been well developed over a period of many years.[1] William E. Fruham, Jr., provides case histories of a number of firms which, by means of effective strategies, have made investments that increased their value, in some cases in a spectacular way.[2]

International investment theory is not a subset of investment theory but is a combination of investment theory, international economic theory, international monetary theory, and risk. This combination is much less well developed than any of the individual theories. Further, some assumptions are typically made about cash flows and cost of capital; they are generally adequate for evaluating domestic investments but must be critically addressed when dealing with international investments. This chapter provides a method for analyzing foreign capital investments that relies on sound theories where they have been developed and raises issues to be dealt with by management judgment in the areas where theory is insufficiently developed. In the examples, we have usually assumed that a U.S. firm is investing outside the United States. Naturally, the principles apply equally to an international firm based outside the United States making investments outside its home country as well.

RISKS INHERENT IN FOREIGN INVESTMENTS

Most businesspersons consider foreign investments to be riskier than domestic investments. This is generally true. The risk of a foreign investment may be conveniently divided into three components. Business risk is associated with any investment, foreign or domestic. A new product may or may not be well accepted by the market, a new manufacturing process may be more or less costly than planned, or a competitor may or may not bring out a new superior competitive product. It can be argued that the business risk of a foreign investment is somewhat higher than that of a domestic one because, in many cases, the market, the culture, and the society all differ from those to which the executives of the firm are well accustomed. For a first order of approximation, however, it is probably reasonable to assume that business risk of a foreign investment is about the same as that for a similar domestic investment.

Political risk may exist for a domestic investment. A regulated industry may be deregulated, price controls may be established or lifted, or a more expensive component may have to be substituted for a substance made illegal. There are, however, more opportunities for political risk in foreign investment. For one thing, there are two national governments involved instead of one—the home country of the parent and the host country of the subsidiary. The objectives of the two countries may differ; tax laws may be changed; rights to repatriate capital may be revised; or, in an extreme situation, the asset may be expropriated by the host government.

Currency risk exists only for foreign investments and is greatest for investments in countries with run-away inflation whose governments have managed to maintain an appearance of a strong currency by not allowing exchange rates to drop. Currency risk may be overcome by hedging, maintaining a level of debt denominated in foreign currency offsetting the value of exposed assets. If the foreign investor senses a danger of devaluation, however, common financial markets are likely to do so as well, and foreign currency–denominated debt often becomes very expensive or unobtainable.

COST OF CAPITAL

Most capital investment analyses, whether using IRR or NPV, discount *incremental* cash flows using the firm's *average* cost of capital because there are ways of estimating average cost of capital, there are no good generally applicable ways of estimating incremental cost of capital, and because most investments reflect a continuation of the firm's existing investment policy so that the average cost of capital is probably a reasonable approximation of the incremental cost of capital.

The average cost of capital of a firm is generally agreed to be the weighted average cost of debt and equity. It is usually calculated on an aftertax basis, just as cash flows are calculated on an aftertax basis. The aftertax cost of debt is equal to the interest rate of funds available to the firm multiplied by 1 minus the tax rate expressed as a decimal.

There are two popular methods for calculating cost of equity. The fundamental valuation, based on work done by Miller and Modigliani[3] yields a cost of equity equal to

$$\frac{\text{Dividend}}{\text{Share price}} + \text{earnings growth rate}$$

A newer method, called the "capital asset pricing model" (CAPM), based on work done by Lintner and Sharpe, is based on the market rate for risk-free investments and a risk premium (Beta) for the equity.[4]

Cost of equity as calculated by CAPM is equal to:

$$R_i = R_f + B(R_m - R_f)$$

where R_i = return demanded by market on investment
(cost of capital)
R_f = return demanded on risk-free investment
B = relative riskiness of investment (Beta)
R_m = return on market portfolio of securities

Studies of financial markets have shown that share prices are largely determined by the future increase in wealth to be gained by owning the share, both through dividends and capital gains, discounted by a rate dependent on the real risk-free cost of capital, inflation, and risk.

Foreign investments are often made in countries with a high rate of inflation. Further, there are elements of risk in foreign investments that are probably of a greater magnitude than in comparable domestic investments. Since the firm's average cost of capital is based on its home currency and the average risk of its investments, it is clearly inappropriate to use the firm's average cost of capital in evaluating foreign investments unless the cash flows are translated into dollars and somehow are defined to include insurance against the greater risk of the investment.

Ways have been suggested by which a cost of capital may be estimated to take into account the local inflation rate and the higher risk of the investment. Although no single method is generally accepted, the cost of capital in foreign currencies may be approximated by a simple series of calculations based on local interest rates, local corporate income tax rates, the firm's cost of equity denominated in its home currency, a forecast of the anticipated devaluation rate, and a debt-to-equity ratio. If, for example, the local rate of inflation is so high that the interest rate in local currency is 140 percent and the corporate income tax is 40 percent, the aftertax cost of debt is calculated as follows:

(Interest rate) × (1 − tax rate) = aftertax cost of debt
140% × (1 − 0.40) = 84%

If the U.S. cost of equity is 20 percent and the local currency is expected to be devaluated by 100 percent annually (that is, the cost of dollars in local currency terms will double each year), the cost of equity may be calculated as follows:

$$100 \times \left[(1 + \text{devaluation}) \times \left(1 + \frac{\text{U.S. cost of equity}}{100}\right) - 1 \right]$$
$$= \text{cost of equity}$$
$$100 \times [(1 + 1.00) \times (1.20) - 1] = 140\%$$

A weighted cost of capital in local currency may then be calculated by multiplying the aftertax cost of debt and the cost of equity by the percentage of debt and percentage of equity respectively and adding the products. Thus, if the business is to be financed with 60 percent debt and 40 percent equity, the weighted cost of capital is calculated:

84% × 0.60 = 50%
140% × 0.40 = 56%
            106%

For convenience we will refer to this as the "local currency cost of capital." Note in this example that the financial markets are charging an interest rate that exceeds a combination of a reasonable real interest rate and the inflation rate. They are charging a premium for the risk that inflation will be even greater or for what we have earlier called "currency risk." This is common in hyperinflationary countries.

This calculation provides an approximation of the cost of capital denominated in a foreign currency, but it does not take into account the added political risk of a foreign investment. Because the evaluation of risk is subjective, no calculation to account for this element of added risk has gained widespread acceptance. One approach used by some firms is to evaluate specific countries in terms of risk. Countries may be grouped into risk categories and an arbitrary premium added to the calculated cost of capital to account for the added risk. For example, investments may be categorized as follows:

U.S. 0 percent risk premium.
Category 1. 2 percent risk premium. Prime credit country where political risk is minimal.

Category 2. 5 percent risk premium. Countries that are politically stable but not as solid as the prime credit countries. From time to time, foreign exchange restrictions may be imposed, such as earnings repatriation regulations that can hinder investors from obtaining returns from their investments.

Category 3. 9 percent risk premium. Countries usually classed as developing countries where the political climate is fairly stable but where the government tends to intervene in markets with abrupt changes in exchange rates, tax incentives, and price controls.

Category 4. 13 percent risk premium. Underdeveloped countries with generally unstable governments, lack of infrastructure, and a poor populace. Usually high financially leveraged and often with an unfavorable balance of payments.

Category 5. Determined on a case-by-case basis. Politically unstable and/or bankrupt governments, generally subject to revolutions and armed conflict resulting in an undesirable investment climate.

The risk premiums noted above are applied to dollar-denominated cost of capital. For convenience, we will refer to this as the risk-adjusted cost of capital.

STRATEGIES FOR INTERNATIONAL INVESTMENT

The following are four strategies a firm based in one country might use in making a capital investment in another country.

Comparative Advantage. The firm might want to produce its products in another country where factors of production such as labor and raw materials are more plentiful and cheaper than in its home country. The resulting products are typically exported. An example of this is the U.S. electronics firms that assemble products in some Asian countries where labor is plentiful and wages are low. The decision to produce in a foreign country depends on the mobility of the factors of production. Raw material is least mobile. Labor is somewhat mobile, but differences in language, social customs, and immigration quotas restrict movement of labor. Technology is somewhat more mobile than labor, since people can learn the technology without moving, provided that their training is adequate. Capital is quite mobile and typically flows to wherever there are returns. Thus, most investments based on comparative advantage are used to gain access to low-cost raw materials or labor. It is thus common to find a Swedish steel company in Africa for access to coal or a Japanese electronics firm in Korea for access to labor.

Learning Curve. The learning curve is a dynamic variant on comparative advantage; in a sense, it involves a shift from comparative advantage in labor to comparative advantage in technology. As the cumulative amount of a product ever produced increases by a given percent, the hours of labor required per unit decrease by some percent, and the rate at which this occurs remains relatively constant. This was originally observed in production of a product within a specific factory, but it also seems to apply in some degree to production of a product within a country. In a fundamental sense, it represents substitution of one factor of production—experience or learning—for another factor of production—hours of labor. Like production functions in general, there is no strong underlying theory to explain why the rate at which the substitution occurs should remain stable or why it should be applicable both within the walls of a factory and within the borders of a country. Although the theory may be weak, its application has resulted in major shifts in patterns of international trade. In the 1960s, when Japanese manufacturing technology was relatively primitive and labor was cheap, the Japanese automobile industry produced large volumes of automobiles for export and seized a significant market share. Using this volume to build experience, the Japanese were able to improve labor productivity more rapidly than wages (and the Japanese standard of living) increased, thereby reducing cost, increasing quality and features, increasing market share even more, and securing a strong market position in the world market. At present, Japanese manufacturing technology is among the highest in the world. The comparative advantage which Japan held with plentiful labor has now shifted to a comparative advantage held with plentiful technology. In common with other investments made as a result of comparative advantage, a significant share of the product is exported.

Market. A firm might want to produce for the local market in spite of a comparative disadvantage to overcome trade barriers such as shipping costs, tariffs, and prejudices among buyers against imported goods. Automobile manufacturers typically prefer to keep their supply lines short. Thus, if manufacturers of spark plugs, hydraulic brakes, and seat belts wish to sell their products to automobile manufacturers in another country, they must usually build a factory in or close to the same country in which the automobile is produced.

Portfolio Analysis. Markowitz's portfolio theory holds that the amount of risk which an investor must accept to receive a given return may be minimized by investing in a portfolio of securities. The logic is that unforeseen events cause returns on individual securities to fluctuate; by holding several securities simultaneously, the variation on return for a portfolio in total will be less than that for a single security of the same mean return since returns on one security probably will increase at the same time returns on another will decrease. This has been extended to ownership of physical wealth by a firm in the form of productive assets, thence to ownership of businesses producing and marketing various products by a conglomerate, and thence to ownership of assets in various countries by a multinational firm. The underlying theory is the same—that the ups and downs will tend to cancel each other out because business cycles in various countries are not perfectly synchronized. If this is true, we would expect the fluctuation in earnings of the total to be less than the fluctuation in earnings of operations in individual countries.

EVALUATING INTERNATIONAL INVESTMENTS

International investments are, by their nature, much more difficult to evaluate than domestic investments because at least two countries and economies are involved. Not only must one make and quantify operating assumptions for the investment, such as market share, revenue, cost structure, assets required, inflation and regulations, etc. in the host country, but also one needs to take a broader view by assessing how interactions between the countries and economies affect the investment's net return. One has to examine the political, economic, and financial factors affecting the valuation of one currency in terms of another as well as additional taxes, such as withholding taxes, affecting the return of profits to the investing country.

Exhibit 7-1 shows the conceptual framework used in capital budgeting analysis of international investments, where the different rings indicate additional factors which one must consider.

EXHIBIT 7-1   Conceptual Framework for Analysis of Foreign Investment.

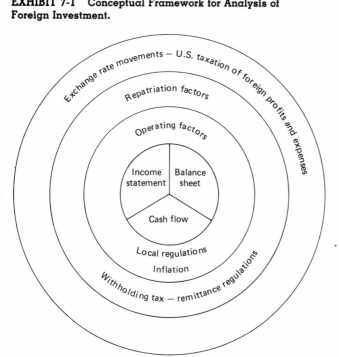

The core of any international investment analysis consists of the operating factors affecting the project, which in turn are quantified in an income statement, balance sheet, and ultimately in cash flow, which then will be discounted to generate a net present value for the project or used to calculate an internal rate of return. This is the basic local currency analysis.

When the basic elements are quantified, one needs to determine what the cash flow will be if profits are to be repatriated to the investors, because

EXHIBIT 7-2   International Profit Flows.

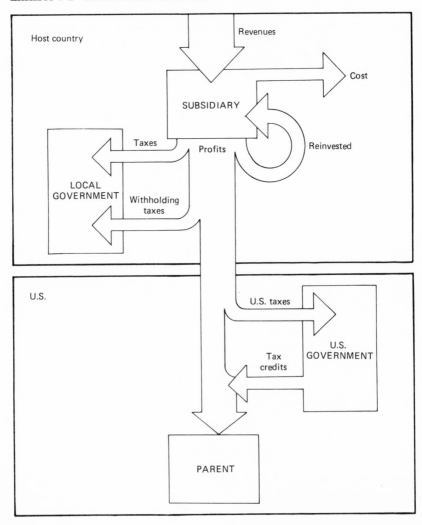

profits which are available for distribution are often not the same as profits which will end up in the hands of the investor (see Exhibit 7-2). Withholding taxes and remittance restriction are often imposed, which will sidetrack to the government's coffers some of the profits which are available for repatriation. Note that these additional taxes and charges are imposed on top of regular income and other taxes already imposed by local governmental authorities.

After repatriation and withholding taxes are considered one has to evaluate what these repatriated foreign profits are worth when converted into U.S. dollars from foreign currencies. This is fairly simple to do—just multiply the repatriated profits by the forecasted exchange rate. What is much more difficult to evaluate is the value of the profits and assets still remaining in the foreign country. This is a rather complex issue which will be covered in more detail below as we discuss each of these issues individually.

THE EFFECT OF EXCHANGE RATES ON FOREIGN INVESTMENTS

If a U.S. firm sends $900 of capital to the United Kingdom to buy £500 worth of assets at an exchange rate of £ = $1.80, and a year later returns £625 to the United States, equal to the original investment of £500 plus a 25 percent dividend of £125, at which time the dollar has been devalued and the exchange rate has become £ = $2.40, the U.S. firm has received $1500 or a 67 percent dividend on its investment in dollars of $900 as the result of changes in the exchange rate. If, on the other hand, the assets were purchased at £1 = $2.40, therefore costing $1200, and capital and dividends returned at £1 = $1.80 as a result of a pound devaluation, the U.S. firm would receive $1125 or $75 less than its original investment of $1200, even though the U.K. operation had paid a 25 percent dividend in pounds. In some countries, currency gains and losses can overshadow operating gains and losses.

The above example is fairly simple and straightforward. In real capital projects, however, assets invested in foreign countries are usually not liquidated at the end of each year and returned to the investor. Therefore, the value of the assets located in foreign countries in terms of the investor's currency cannot be determined exactly. Methods, however, have been developed to estimate the value of such assets. The generally accepted method currently in use is detailed in the Financial Accounting Standard Board (FASB) statement 52. Briefly, this statement calls for the classification of countries into two categories, hyperinflationary countries and nonhyperinflationary countries, where the hyperinflationary countries are those which had experienced inflation of 100 percent or more over a three-year period.

For the hyperinflationary countries, monetary assets such as receivables and payables are translated at the exchange rate in effect at the date of the financial statements. This is usually termed the current rate. Inventories and fixed assets are translated at rates in effect at the time the assets are acquired. This is usually termed the "historical" rate. For nonhyperinflationary countries, all assets and liabilities are translated at the rate in effect at the date financial statements are being prepared for.

In analyzing international investments, these methods of translation should be adhered to unless the economics of the situation dictate otherwise. For instance, one may translate inventory at the current rate in hyperinflationary countries because prices cannot be raised quickly enough to recover losses from exchange rate movements.

The above focuses on the valuation of foreign currency assets in terms of U.S. dollars, but it may not indicate the total impact of exchange on the investment overseas. Currency exchange can also affect the ability of a firm to compete in international markets. Purchasing power parity theory proposes that exchange rates will change to offset differences in inflation rates in different countries over the long run. In other words, the price of any moveable asset or commodity will be the same no matter where it is or what currency it is sold for, except for differentials due to transportations and tariffs. If this is not true at any point, assets will move to the place where prices are higher. For example, if a camera is sold for $300 in the United States and a comparable camera in Germany is sold for $200 and it costs $50 for freight and tariff to transport the camera to the United States, more cameras will move from Germany to the United States, thereby increasing the supply which will then cause the prices of the models to narrow. At the same time, there will be a greater demand for German marks, which will cause the exchange rate to appreciate, which will, in turn, make the dollar price of the cameras more comparable.

Purchasing power parity theory works in the long run, but one currency may be overvalued or undervalued in terms of another currency at any particular period; as the exchange rate changes, sales and profits of an international operation may be impacted by these changes. In the example above, if the deutsche, or German, mark is $0.40 and the camera is sold for DM500, more cameras will be exported to the United States. Therefore, sales and profits for the German camera plant will increase. However, if the exchange rate increases to $0.55, the all-in cost to import the German camera in the United States will be $325; therefore, the flow to the United States will stop, thereby reducing the sales and profits of the German camera plant. If U.S. investors own the camera plant in Germany, their return will be lowered. However, although the operation may have lower sales and profits in the deutsche mark, these German profits will be worth more in terms of U.S. dollars. The net result will, of course, depend on the exact economics of the situation.

Inflation differentials and purchasing power are but two of many factors which affect exchange rates. Some other prominent factors are political stability, interest rates, commodity prices, etc. Obviously, because these factors are out of the control of the investor, it is important to try to determine their trends and their impact on the direction of exchange movements to improve the probability that the project will achieve its projected return. Therefore, in analyzing international investments, it is not enough just to translate the profits and cash flows made in the foreign countries into U.S. dollars, one must also examine the total impact of exchange rates on the sales and profits of the foreign investment.

FOREIGN TAXATION OF INTERNATIONAL INVESTMENTS

Profits of an international investment are generally subject to several levels of taxation. First, they are taxed during the year by the host country's tax authorities. Then when investors wish to repatriate profits to their home country, profits are generally subject to a withholding or remittance tax. This is especially true with lesser developed countries which try to aid their balance of payments by imposing stiff taxes on repatriation, thereby discouraging the outflow of funds from the countries. Every country has its own form of regulations and restrictions. Some have a strict tax on dividends, such as 5 percent of gross amount, e.g., some western European countries. Some have graduated withholding tax rates, based on registered capital. The more earnings repatriated during a time span, the higher the level of withholding tax. Examples of these are generally found in Latin America. In rare instances, certain countries actually encourage the outflow of funds from their country, and they do this by lowering the tax rate on earnings repatriated. Germany and Japan are key examples of countries employing these techniques to achieve government goals. In any case, the cash flow that one sees from a purely local currency operations analysis is not what the investor will finally receive. Suppose that a foreign investment yields cash flow of $100 per annum, the exchange rate is constant, but there is a 20 percent withholding tax on dividends. If the shareholder desires to have a 50 percent payout rate on the investment, the cash flow would be only $40 to the parent and $50 will be kept at the foreign subsidiary. Thus, the total cash flow really is $90 instead of $100. Furthermore, if a higher dividend is paid, a larger portion of the cash flow will go to pay for taxes. This tends to decrease the real spendable return on the investment.

U.S. TAXATION OF FOREIGN PROFITS

To arrive at an accurate projection of a particular project's real return, one must analyze the impact of U.S. taxes on a project's profits. Some countries have income tax rates which are lower than the U.S. tax rate. For example, Hong Kong has a tax rate of 18 percent. Tax regulations in the United States require additional U.S. taxes to be paid on repatriated income to bring the effective tax rate to the U.S. rate of 46 percent. Furthermore, U.S. tax regulation also calls for portioning U.S. expenses, such as interest and overhead, to the foreign income under section 861. This tends to reduce the U.S. tax deduction for those expenses and, in many cases, to increase the overall taxes paid to the U.S. government. These regulations may greatly affect the expected return of a project. However, multinational companies which have international investments throughout the globe are allowed tax credits on profits earned in high tax countries to offset those earned in low tax countries. Therefore, it is not as essential for them to analyze the effect of U.S. taxation on a project-by-project basis as it is for companies with only a few international investments. The issue of U.S. taxes becomes an everyday tactical problem for multinational's tax accountants and lawyers to manage, rather than a long-term strategic issue for the particular project. By pulling proper amounts of dividends from each country and financing the subsidiaries correctly, multinational companies can minimize their worldwide taxes without tackling U.S. tax problems for each project.

ANALYZING CASH FLOW OF FOREIGN INVESTMENTS

There are essentially five different aspects of cash flow to focus on in analyzing foreign investments: (1) local currency cash flow of the investment; (2) the U.S. dollar cash flow derived by translating the local currency cash flow; (3) the U.S. dollar cash flow derived from translating the full balance sheet of the foreign investment; (4) the dividend flows of cash to the U.S. parent; and, finally, (5) a combination of dividend flows plus dollar value of cash flows remaining in the foreign country.

Local Currency Cash Flow

Focusing on local currency cash flow is the simplest way to analyze foreign investments and is equivalent to a U.S. investor analyzing a U.S. investment project. The essence of the measurement is profit after tax less changes in required investment or minimum net operating assets, or the minimal amount of assets needed to support the operation, including both working capital and fixed assets. By applying the concept of discounted cash flow, an internal rate of return can be calculated. This internal rate of return can then be compared with the local currency cost of capital, as described earlier, to determine whether it is attractive on the local level. Equally, this cash flow can be discounted by local currency cost of capital to see if the project will yield a positive net present value. This level of cash flow provides the greatest insight into the operating aspects of the investment. Although this analysis is worthwhile, it does not provide the U.S. investor with the full implication of the attractiveness of the investment.

U.S. Dollar Operating Cash Flow

By simply translating the local currency cash flows into U.S. dollars at the forecasted average or year-end exchange rates, we can arrive at a set of numbers which provide the U.S. investor with an indication of the operating cash flow of the investment. Again, these cash flows do not provide an overall view of the investment for the U.S. investor. The problem with looking at this set of cash flow numbers is that it does not properly take into account the value of the base investment. This is equivalent to evaluating an investment in stocks by focusing only on the dividend and forgetting about how the price of the stock is doing and what taxes will have to be paid on the dividends.

Fully Translated U.S. Dollar Cash Flow

To obtain a fuller picture of the investment, one needs to examine the investment base in dollars as well as the annual operating cash flow by translating into dollars the assets and liabilities of the operation. Although the FASB has dictated that U.S. corporations should use FAS 52 to translate the financial statements of foreign operations with current translation for nonhyperinflation countries and, basically, the FAS 8 method for hyperinflating economies, one needs to analyze the investment by translating the financial statements under the most economically appropriate method corresponding to the nature of the investment.

In making a dollar evaluation of the investment base located in a foreign country, a distinction must be drawn between the minimum net operation assets required to support the operation, which is the main focus of any capital budgeting analysis, and the balance sheet of the foreign operation, which is the main focus of the financial accountants. The minimum net operating assets are the operating cash, receivables, inventories, prepaid expenses less accounts payables, and accruals plus any fixed assets. The balance sheet consists of the above plus excess cash, marketable securities, and any debt. Unless the operation does not have any excess cash or debt, translating the balance sheet will produce different results from translating the minimum net operating assets. The latter will show up as the residual value and will not affect the interim dollar operating cash flows, whereas the former will affect the dollar annual cash flow.

As mentioned above, focusing on the minimum net operating assets and the operating cash flows will provide the most meaningful information on the investment's attractiveness in general. At times, it is important to focus on the dollar value of these nonoperating assets and liabilities as well as the operating assets, because they may affect the net return from the investment. For example, if a foreign operation has blocked profits and there are limited opportunities to redeploy them in the country, the value of these funds, which resulted from the investment project, may be continually eroded from the combined effects of inflation and devaluation so that what appear to be profits in one period actually disappear over time. Unless these effects are analyzed, a faulty picture may be presented.

Cash flow from operations as measured in local currency is a tangible item. That cash flow can be used to purchase assets, pay shareholders or debtors. Cash flow resulting from translation of local currency balance sheet to dollars may not be completely tangible, because it is an accounting concept, i.e., profits after taxes less change in assets and liabilities. Furthermore, full balance sheet translation is likely to intermix the investment decision with the financing decision, but it reveals what the books will show and, in limited cases, a more accurate view of the economics.

Dividend Cash Flows

The above analysis gives a fairly good idea of what the foreign investment will return in dollar terms, but it does not necessarily show what the U.S. shareholder will really receive. For a U.S. shareholder to receive full use of foreign profits, these profits must be repatriated in the form of dividends or branch remittances. Dividends paid by the foreign operation are usually reduced by local withholding or remittance taxes.

These dividend flows are further subject to U.S. taxes and corresponding credit allowances. One can use this stream of dividend flows plus an estimated residual value to generate an internal rate of return for an international investment based on the amount of funds which the investor has invested in the country. This method of analysis is especially appropriate for countries which have strict remittance regulations, such as the Ancom countries (Venezuela, Colombia, Peru, Ecuador, Uruguay). The equity built up in the foreign country can be and should be discounted to some value— perhaps the investor's registered capital—to be used as the residual value for the discounted cash flow analysis.

This type of analysis is very conservative, but it may be the best approach in these countries because profits which are blocked may never reach the investor. Currency devaluation, taxation, or expropriation can easily wipe out profits investors have retained in the country.

Combined Cash Flow

A combined cash flow analysis involves translating local currency financial statements into dollars reduced by the net amount of repatriation taxes, including both withholding and U.S. taxes. This method is a hybrid because it, in effect, incorporates the dividend flows with the retained flows. The cash flow may not be academically pure, but it reflects reality. The stock and credit markets appear to place full value on the retained profits overseas, even though they cannot be used to pay shareholders or U.S. creditors, and some additional expenses may be incurred if these funds are repatriated. Discounting this combined cash flow by the cost of capital will yield a fairly representative net present value, and, if an internal rate of return is calculated, it will also be fairly representative of the real return.

VALUATION OF PROFITS AND ASSETS RETAINED IN THE FOREIGN COUNTRY

Evaluating profits retained in the foreign country is one of the most perplexing issues in the analysis of international investment. Repatriated profits once converted into U.S. dollars and taxed by the U.S. government obviously are freely distributable to U.S. shareholders, and, therefore, there are no uncertainties regarding their value. A Canadian profit of Can. $1 million that is to be repatriated will yield a net of Can. $850,000 after Canadian withholding tax; if converted to U.S. dollars at an exchange rate of U.S. $0.80, it will yield U.S. $680,000. Furthermore, if no additional U.S. taxes are incurred because credit for taxes paid in Canada is substituted for taxes payable in the United States, then the U.S. parent company will have $680,000 which it can distribute to its shareholders or reinvest anywhere in the business. Suppose there remains another Can. $1 million of profit and cash flow reinvested in another project in the Canadian business. What value should one place on that money in U.S. dollars? Is it worth U.S. $800,000 (no withholding tax applied) or U.S. $680,000 (applying withholding tax in advance)? In other words, should potential withholding tax be deducted from profits which remain in the foreign country? Theoretically, it should be deducted, but since actual taxes are not accrued under U.S. (GAAP—Generally Accepted Accounting Principles) and creditors place nearly 100 percent value on these profits, one can follow the same practice in the investment analysis. However, one may want to increase the hurdle rate to account for this potential tax.

To complicate this issue further, suppose the profits are not repatriated at all because they are blocked under foreign government regulation. What value should one place on these profits in the calculation of an internal rate of return or net present value for the project? Even though U.S. GAAP and creditors give the firm full dollar value for these profits, prudence suggests that a discount be applied to these profits or the hurdle rate increased.

Mathematically, it is fairly easy to calculate a dollar value for the assets remaining in the foreign country for the purpose of arriving at a residual value for the IRR calculation. One can do this by applying FAS 52 for translation of foreign balance sheets into U.S. dollars or some other economically more appropriate translation method for that particular business. However, some of the assets which were built up in the foreign country may have been financed by retained earnings, which will be taxed if the assets are sold and the funds repatriated. Thus, the translated dollar value may not be an accurate representation of the actual amount which may be available to the investor, and some discounting of the residual value may be necessary to arrive at a more realistic return. To the extent that the investment project is for an extended time, this may not be a major problem because the residual value's impact on the internal rate of return or net present value calculation may be small.

INDEPENDENCE OF INVESTMENT AND FINANCING DECISIONS

In analyzing domestic investment, accepted theory and practice calls for the separation of the investment decision from the financing decision, usually by not including financing cost when calculating profits of the investment and using a weighted average cost of capital.

Although this separation can be achieved in an analysis of the operation in local currency terms, it is much more difficult to do when a full dollar evaluation is made. In preparing a dollar evaluation in which withholding tax is considered, net cash flow and, therefore, the project's return depends on the repatriation assumption, but the amount of dividend which can be paid at any time in turn depends on the available profits. However, profits are rarely identical to cash flow available for dividends. If dividends are greater than cash flow, one must consider financing for the dividends, thereby mixing financing with the investment analysis. Interest expense arising from these dividends will affect the next period's profits and dividends, which can be paid from those profits. Further, if dividends are less than available cash, a decision must be made as to the disposition of the excess cash. Should it be used to reduce debt, invested on productive assets, or on fixed assets? Furthermore, as financing is introduced, additional exchange gains or losses may result which will affect the return of the investment.

Aftertax financing expense can be added back to the profit after tax for the cash flow calculation, but separating the exchange and withholding tax effects of financing on the project's return is very difficult. For simplicity and pragmatic reasons, one shouldn't try to adjust for these effects, even though investment theory would like us to separate the financing decision from the investment decision process. For the certainty equivalent income statement, balance sheet, and cash flow, this is the best that can be done and still yield somewhat meaningful results.

AN EXAMPLE OF EVALUATING A FOREIGN INVESTMENT

The following example represents a pragmatic approach to analyzing a foreign investment. Although not every detail is dealt with in a theoretically pure way, it provides management with a way of considering foreign investments that is consistent with the way most companies analyze domestic investments and yields useful insights into the likely performance of the project in terms of adding value to the parent company.

ABC Corporation, a U.S.-based multinational, is considering applying to the Spanish government for approval to invest in a small assembly plant in Spain. Demand for the product in Spain is growing, and the 45 percent import duty on products imported into Spain has raised fears that a local entrepreneur will open a plant and preempt ABC from the Spanish market, which, it is believed, will eventually be an important one. ABC has a business strategy of maintaining its position as the lowest cost, highest market share producer, and it feels that if it does not maintain this position in Spain, its entire European position may become vulnerable in ten years or so.

ABC plans to limit the initial investment to locally purchased machinery with a value of 95 million pesetas—a peseta is a little less than one U.S. cent—to be installed in rented space in late 1983. The equipment will be depreciated on a straight-line basis over a period of eight years, starting in 1984. No royalties will be charged. Sales to the local market are forecast to be 75 million pesetas in 1984, with growth as shown in Exhibit 7-3. The pretax margin on sales is estimated to be 36 percent, except for 1984, when startup costs will hold it at 15 percent. The local tax rate on corporate earnings is 33 percent. For simplicity, the analysis will be made only through 1988, although a ten-year analysis period is more common.

No further fixed capital additions are anticipated, although this decision will be reevaluated in 1986, when output is expected to be constrained by capacity. Working capital requirements are estimated to be 20 percent of sales. The book value of the equipment at the end of 1988 will be 35,625,000 pesetas; its value to ABC at that time is estimated to be book value adjusted upward to account for Spanish inflation over the 1983–1988 period. This results in a residual fixed asset value of 66,444,000 pesetas, as well as 38 million pesetas of working capital.

ABC anticipates that the Spanish government will approve repatriation of 100 percent of earnings to the United States. Actual practice will be to repatriate the lesser of earnings (after payment of the 33 percent Spanish tax) or cash flow. That is, in years when cash flow is less than earnings, only the positive cash flow will be repatriated. Spain presently withholds a 15 percent tax on dividends as well as a 1.5 percent tax on remittance of income, for an effective tax rate of 16.5 percent tax on repatriated dividends. Although there have been rumors for some time of an increase in this tax rate, there is no good evidence that this will happen. Both the 33 percent tax on earnings and the 16.5 percent tax on dividends may be fully credited to U.S. taxes on repatriated earnings. Since the U.S. tax rate is 46 percent,

EXHIBIT 7-3   Spanish Investment Forecast (000s)

Year	Fixed capital requirements	Sales	Pre-tax margin on sales	Additions to working capital	Depreciation	Forecast GDP deflator	Forecast exch. rate Pta/$
1983	Pta 95,000	Pta —		Pta —	Pta —	348.4	114.93
1984	—	75,000	15%	15,000	11,875	389.2	105.95
1985	—	112,500	36	7,500	11,875	441.1	110.08
1986	—	150,000	36	7,500	11,875	512.6	116.29
1987	—	170,000	36	4,000	11,875	580.6	119.36
1988	—	190,000	36	4,000	11,875	649.8	124.11

additional taxes of 1.9 percent would have to be paid, since the effective tax rate on repatriated earnings is 44.1 percent (33 percent + 16.5 percent of 67 percent of pretax earnings). However, ABC is already in an excess foreign tax credit position, and such credits are therefore used to offset the additional taxes.

No tax credits or other investment incentives are available from the Spanish government for this investment. Spain is considered by ABC to fall in category 3, with respect to risk, demanding a 9 percent premium return.

ABC maintains a 20/80 debt/equity relationship and can borrow U.S. funds at 12 percent. It calculates its cost of equity at 18 percent, also dollar denominated, for a weighted average cost of capital of 16 percent. In summary, the data are as follows.

1. Estimated value of fixed asset at the end of 1988: Sp.Pta64,444,000
2. Estimated value of working capital at the end of 1988: Sp.Pta38,000,000
3. Local tax rate on earnings: 33 percent
4. Dividend policy: dividends equal to aftertax earnings or cash flow, whichever is less
5. Withholding tax rate on dividends: 16.5 percent
6. U.S. tax on repatriated earnings: 46 percent less credit for foreign taxes paid
7. Dollar-denominated pretax cost of borrowing: 12 percent
8. Dollar-denominated cost of equity: 18 percent
9. Weighted average dollar-denominated cost of capital: 16 percent
10. Risk premium for category 3 investment: 9 percent
11. Peseta-denominated pretax cost of local borrowing: 24 percent
12. Rate of Sp.Pta/U.S.$ devaluation (forecast): 2.3 percent per year (best-fit compounded growth rate of figures shown in Exhibit 7-3)

All the above information, estimates, and forecasts are needed to perform a total evaluation of a foreign investment. The first step is to evaluate operating cash flows in pesetas, using an estimated peseta-denominated cost of capital:

$$\text{Cost of debt} = 0.24(1 - 0.33) = 0.16$$
$$\text{Cost of equity} = (1.023 \times 1.18) - 1.00 = 0.21$$
$$\text{Weighted average} = 0.20 \times 0.16 + 0.80 \times 0.21 = 0.20$$

Thus, the weighted average peseta-denominated cost of capital is about 20 percent.

Cash flows to and from subsidiary in pesetas are calculated as follows. For convenience, cash outflows are shown as negative numbers and cash inflows as positive numbers.

Year	Fixed investment	PAT	Depreciation	Working capital	Residual	Cash flow
1983	−95,000,000					−95,000,000
1984		7,537,500	11,875,000	−15,000,000		4,412,500
1985		27,135,000	11,875,000	−7,500,000		31,510,000
1986		36,180,000	11,875,000	−7,500,000		40,555,000
1987		41,004,000	11,875,000	−4,000,000		48,879,000
1988		45,828,000	11,875,000	−4,000,000	102,444,000	156,147,000

Internal Rate of Return: 32 percent
Net Present Value at 20%: Sp. Pta40,352,382

The fixed investment is the 95 million pesetas for machinery. Profit after tax is equal to sales multiplied by the pretax margin on sales, less 33 percent tax. Depreciation each year is one-eighth of the machinery investment. Working capital requirements are equal to 20 percent of sales in the first year, with additional working capital requirements of 20 percent of the increase in sales each succeeding year. Residual value is the 64,444,000 pesetas it is judged the machinery will be worth plus the 38 million pesetas cumulative investment of working capital at book value. Cash flow is the algebraic sum of investments in fixed and working capital, aftertax profit, depreciation, and residual value. The calculation indicates that a local firm with a peseta-denominated cost of capital of 20 percent might expect to increase its value by more than 40 million pesetas by making this investment.

The next step is to calculate cash flows to and from the parent, translating cash flows into dollars, taking all taxes into account, and considering the risks of foreign investments. The initial investment in Spain is Sp. Pta95,000,000, which is equivalent to U.S. $826,600 when translated at the 1983 exchange rate of 114.93 pesetas per dollar. In this example, we have assumed that dividends will be paid by the Spanish subsidiary to the U.S. parent at a rate equal to the lesser of local profits after taxes or local cash flow. Exhibit 7-4 shows the amount of dividend to be paid. Column A shows the PAT and column B shows the cash flow. With the exception of 1984, when PAT exceeds cash flow, dividends are equal to PAT (see column C). Since Spain has in effect a withholding tax of 16.5 percent on dividends paid, actual dividends received will be smaller, as shown in column E. Converting the net dividends at the appropriate exchange rates, we arrive at the net dollar dividend to be received by the U.S. parent.

Although these dividends are taxed by Spain, they are still subject to U.S. taxation. Exhibit 7-5 shows the calculation of U.S. taxes payable, based on the tax rate of 46 percent. Since the effective Spanish tax rate is 44.1 percent (33 percent + 16.5 percent of 67 percent of pretax earnings), the U.S. parent has to pay additional taxes as shown in column D. However, since it is assumed that ABC is in an excess foreign tax credit situation (i.e., more taxes are paid overseas than can be used in the U.S.), U.S. taxes payable will be

EXHIBIT 7-4   Amount of Dividend to be Paid (000s)

	A. Earnings	B. Cash flow	C. Gross dividends (Lesser of A or B)	D. Withholding tax (16.5% × C)	E. Net dividends (C − D)	F. Exchange rate	G. Net dividends
1983	—	—	—	—	—	—	—
1984	7,538	4,413	4,413	728	3,685	105.95	$ 34.8
1985	27,135	31,510	27,135	4,477	22,658	110.08	205.8
1986	36,180	40,555	36,180	5,970	30,210	116.29	259.8
1987	41,004	48,879	41,004	6,766	34,238	119.36	286.8
1988	45,828	156,147	45,828	7,562	38,266	124.11	308.3

Columns (A)–(E) are in Spanish pesetas; column (G) is in U.S. dollars.

offset by excess foreign tax credits, so that aftertax cash flow (dividends) in the United States is equal to pretax cash flow.

This discussion covers only a part of the total project, i.e., flows to the United States. There remains some cash flow which is retained in Spain, the portion of which exceeds profit after taxes. These flows can be translated into dollars by simply dividing the appropriate exchange rates. Column C of Exhibit 7-6 shows the U.S. dollar equivalent amounts retained in Spain. In this analysis, it is assumed that the excess cash flow retained is employed at a rate equivalent to this project's internal rate of return, although many times there may not be such opportunities available—or even worse, the cash flow may be devalued over time, but this is considered to be a different issue. In discounted cash flow analysis, it is important to determine when and how much cash flows are available for redeployment or consumption by the investor, not how the cash will be used.

Finally, to complete the analysis, we need to focus on the residual value, i.e., the dollar value of the fixed assets of Sp. Pta64.4 million plus Pta38 m of working capital. We shall assume for simplicity that the whole amount will

EXHIBIT 7-5   Calculation of U.S. Taxes Payable (000s)

	A. Pre-U.S. tax dividend	B. Spanish taxes	C. U.S. taxes @ 46% on earnings (A + B)	D. U.S. taxes payable	E. Excess tax credits	F. U.S. taxes due
1984	$ 34.8	$ 27.4	$ 28.6	$ 1.2	$ (1.2)	—
1985	205.8	162.1	169.2	7.1	(7.1)	—
1986	259.8	204.6	213.6	9.0	(9.0)	—
1987	286.8	225.9	235.8	9.9	(9.9)	—
1988	308.3	242.8	253.5	10.7	(10.7)	—

EXHIBIT 7-6 Total Cash Flows

	A. Investment	B. U.S. net dividends received	C. (Spain) retained cash flow	D. (Spain) residual value	E. Net cash flow
1983	$826.6	—	—	—	$-826.6
1984		34.8	—	—	34.8
1985		205.8	39.7	—	245.5
1986		259.8	37.6	—	297.4
1987		286.8	66.0	—	352.8
1988		308.3	63.5	825.4	1,197.2

Internal Rate of Return: 26.8%
Net Present Value at 25%: $47.4

be available to the investor, even though, on liquidation or sale of the business, the investor may need to pay additional Spanish and U.S. taxes. This amount at the 1988 exchange rate is equivalent to U.S. $825.4. Summing up the first four columns in Exhibit 7-6, we arrive at the net cash flow in dollar terms after all relevant taxes are paid. Discounting this cash flow stream, an internal rate of return equal to 26.8 percent is found. Inversely, by discounting the cash flow stream by 25 percent, the U.S.-based multinational's risk adjusted cost of capital, it can be seen that this project will increase the firm's value by $47,400. Thus, based on NPV and IRR criteria established earlier, this project should be approved.

SUMMARY

Foreign investments are both risky and difficult to evaluate; their inherent risks include business risk, political risk, and currency risk. The difficulties of evaluating foreign investments using standard IRR and NPV techniques include establishing the cost of capital and defining cash flows.

There are four fundamental strategies that cause firms to make foreign investments in spite of these drawbacks. A firm might wish to achieve a comparative advantage in the cost of producing goods resulting from low-cost raw materials, labor, or other factors of production in a foreign country. It may want to take advantage of rapidly declining production costs due to accumulated production experience in a foreign country. It may need to gain access to foreign markets. Finally, it may wish to achieve a balanced portfolio for the purpose of reducing risk, although it would seem that the higher risk inherent in foreign investments would tend to minimize this advantage.

There are five aspects of cash flow which one can examine in making a complete analysis of the foreign investments. The first is discounting local currency cash flows. This is the simplest analysis and is the equivalent of a U.S. investor analyzing a U.S. investment. Only operating cash flows are considered, and a local currency cost of capital must be estimated for the discount rate. Second, U.S. dollar operating cash flows are discounted— these are simply the local currency cash flows translated to dollars. They can be discounted by an appropriate rate based on the firm's dollar cost of capital. Third, fully translated U.S. dollar cash flows are discounted. These take into account not only operating cash flows but also the effects of holding assets and liabilities denominated in a foreign currency. Fourth, dividend cash flows are discounted; these include only those cash flows repatriated to the United States net of both foreign and U.S. taxes. This is a very conservative approach and is particularly useful for investments in countries where remittances are closely controlled and may be blocked. Finally, combined cash flows are discounted. These take into account both dividends and retained earnings, as well as foreign and U.S. taxes. This is a hybrid calculation but seems to yield a result that best reflects the view of financial markets toward firms with foreign investments.

Particularly difficult problems of evaluating foreign investments include evaluating the risks inherent in new investments, valuing earnings retained in a foreign country, valuing the assets (residual value) in a foreign country, and separating the foreign investment decision from the financing decision. Methods are not available for dealing with all these problems in a theoretically pure way. Nevertheless, it is possible to deal with them on a judgmental basis to make a reasonable estimate of the value to the firm of a proposed foreign investment.

NOTES

1. Pearson Graham and Diran Bodenhorn, *Managerial Economics*, Addison-Wesley, Reading, Mass., 1980; James C. Van Horne, *Financial Management and Policy*, 5th ed., Prentice-Hall, Englewood Cliffs, N.J., 1980; Fred J. Weston and Eugene F. Brighan, Managerial Finance, 7th ed., Dryden, Hinsdale, Ill., 1981.
2. William E. Fruhan, Jr., *Financial Strategy: Studies in the Creation, Transfer, and Destruction of Shareholder Value*, Irwin, Homewood, Ill., 1979.
3. Merton H. Miller and Franco Modigliani, "Dividend Policy, Growth, and the Valuation of Shares," *The Journal of Business of the University of Chicago*, 1961, pp. 411–433.
4. John Lintner, "The Valuation of Risk Assets and the Selection of Risky Investments in Stock Portfolios and Capital Budgets," *Review of Economics and Statistics*, 1965, pp. 13–37 and William Sharpe, "Capital Asset Prices: A Theory of Market Equilibrium under Conditions of Risk," *Journal of Finance*, 1964, pp. 425–442.

REFERENCES

Carter, E. Eugene and Rita M. Rodriguez: *International Financial Management*, 2d ed., Prentice-Hall, Englewood Cliffs, N.J., 1979.

Eiteman, David K. and Arthur I. Stonehill: *Multinational Business Finance*, 2d ed., Addison-Wesley, Reading, Mass., 1979.

Graham, Pearson and Diran Bodenhorn: *Managerial Economics*, Addison-Wesley, Reading, Mass., 1980.

Wicks, Marie E.: *A Comparative Analysis of the Foreign Investment Evaluation Practices of U.S.-Based Multinational Companies*, McKinsey, New York.

Eight:
The Analysis
of Foreign
Acquisitions
and Mergers

JAMES M. NEEDHAM

James M. Needham is a certified public accountant and a partner and director of Mergers & Acquisitions Services at Arthur Young & Company, New York. His experience includes director of corporate development for a major international company and a management position on both the audit and the consulting staffs of another major international accounting firm. Mr. Needham has extensive experience in assisting both domestic and foreign-based clients in the full range of merger and acquisition activity, including the development and implementation of acquisition and divestiture programs, leveraged buyouts, and venture capital financing.

As the world economy becomes more integrated very few domestic acquisitions do not have some "foreign aspect" to them in the form of suppliers, customers, or competitors. The analysis of any acquisition is an attempt to assess the opportunities that a particular acquisition may offer versus possible investment risk. What is distinctive in a foreign acquisition is not the analysis of opportunity and risk but the *process* of analyzing the opportunity and risk, because the knowledge and perspective of the person making the analysis is substantially different in a foreign acquisition.

In domestic acquisitions, one makes implicit assumptions and judgments regarding areas of acquisition analysis which are close to one's level of knowledge and experience. An example would be the acquisition of a soft drink bottling company by a company already in the business. Clearly, most of the analysis will involve domestic considerations: national and regional demographics, market share, unit costs, etc. Very little attention will be paid to the global economy other than for the possible impact on the price of sugar and other ingredients. Judgments about the domestic and regional economy, industry structure, competitive position, capability of management, labor relations, etc. are more often the result of experience rather than of a process of explicit quantifications. However, the same acquisition made by a buyer not previously familiar with the bottling industry or a foreign buyer would entail much greater quantification and analysis, precisely because the "feel" of experience is missing.

ANALYSIS OF POLITICAL AND ECONOMIC ENVIRONMENT

To exercise prudent judgment regarding geopolitical and economic conditions of the target country the foreign buyer must understand or appreciate

8-2

the differences in local and regional cultures and business practices within the country. It should come as no surprise that, with the increase in global investment flows, a growing industry of professionals has been created to service precisely those needs of the foreign investor. These professionals include political advisors, economists, industry and market consultants, investment advisors, bankers, lawyers, accountants, and pension and labor consultants.

Thus one of the first visible differences between a domestic and foreign acquisition is that outside advisers are brought into the acquisition process at an earlier stage and that more outside advisers are used in a foreign acquisition.

Host-Country Analysis

The significant increase in global trading and the rapid transfers of currency have produced for many countries significant foreign trade imbalances and currency movement. In responding to these events, governments have resorted to a number of actions which may seriously jeopardize the investment of a foreign acquiror, including currency devaluation, inflation, currency controls, and tariff and import controls.

Since the actions of the host government can have a major impact on the stability and liquidity of a foreign acquiror's investment in the host country, the host country's political and economic stability and economic trends must be analyzed. Although it is highly unlikely that one can accurately predict the actions of one's own government, much less those of a foreign government, judgments about downside risk can still be made.

Government actions are often the results of forces at work in the political economy. If foreign investors analyze those forces, they may be better able to judge the possibilities of government actions which might jeopardize an otherwise successful acquisition.

One approach to host-country analysis involves using the same techniques that are used in analyzing a company. What are the host country's performance objectives (and are they being achieved) in gross national product (GNP) growth rate, employment levels, trade balances, demographic trends, wage and productivity trends, etc.? If the trends in these areas are not consistent with the government's performance objectives, then the foreign investor can expect a period of active government intervention in the economy. The pressures brought to bear on governments by international agencies such as the International Monetary Fund (IMF) have increased in recent years, increasing the chances of government corrective action.

That this analysis is difficult to perform in one's own country points out the difficulty that faces the foreign investor. Foreign investors must absorb much quantitative and subjective data which they can only hope to put into perspective by an on-site inspection of the host country. Foreign investors should be familiar with the views and incentives of the appropriate government and institutional leaders. They should establish contacts at various levels in the host country to judge the professional advice they receive and to compare that advice to their own first-hand experience.

It is precisely because host-country analysis is so difficult that there has been a significant increase in the use by foreign investors of joint ventures and local equity partners to help guide foreign investors through the maze and complexity of operating in a foreign environment. However, the use of these entities often creates its own set of operating problems. Among these operating problems are changes in objectives by one of the joint venture partners subsequent to the inception of the joint venture, disagreements relating to levels and timing of funding, allocation of management resources to the joint venture, and changes in perceived benefits as time passes.

Country analyses have often been applied only to less developed countries (LDCs), but actions by more developed countries in devaluations and increasing government control of domestic economies make it clear that an acquisition no longer can be considered without analyzing trends in the host country and that country's relationship to the global economy.

Cultural and Business Environment

If the quality, style, and incentives of management, employees, customers, and suppliers are important in a domestic acquisition, their importance to the success of a business increases as the distance between owner and site of operation increases. Failure to appreciate the differences between cultures and regions within countries may cause serious postacquisition problems, for example, incentives, work habits, undisclosed payments, kickbacks, and practices in the host country which are in conflict with the acquirors' codes of personal and business conduct.

Government and Regulatory Environment

Most countries have laws and regulations which apply specifically to foreign investors. They often govern how a foreign investor brings money into and out of a country and conditions for owning certain categories of investment. In the United States these restrictions apply to investments in such industries as radio and television stations, U.S. shipping, and companies deemed crucial to the national defense. Certain states restrict the acquisition of land by foreign investors. However, unlike most countries, foreign investments in the United States do not require government approval nor must an acquisition be financed with a foreign currency. Important as it is to review the laws and regulations at the national and local levels which apply to making an acquisition, it is just as important to review those laws and regulations which apply to closing or selling business and repatriation of funds. Most countries have regulations regarding corporate form, majority and minority stockholder rights, duties of directors, corporate and individual taxation, antitrust laws, environmental regulations, securities laws, labor laws, import-export restrictions, and social cost.

SETTING OBJECTIVES

Acquisition objectives are often similar in foreign acquisitions and domestic acquisitions. They include market extension, acquisition of technology, source of supply development, forward integration, threat from substitute products, etc. In a foreign acquisition, some additional considerations may include the moving of capital funds for either domestic or foreign political and economic reasons and/or the attempt to obtain a low-cost production and distribution advantage. Whatever the objective, it should be clearly stated and thought through in terms of commitment and what degree of risk the investor is willing to assume to achieve those objectives.

THE ACQUISITION PROGRAM

Acquiring an established business is frequently an easier and more timely approach to entering a market than is starting a new business. However, there are pitfalls in acquiring a company that can be avoided only by a thorough and systematic acquisition process. The process begins with establishing acquisition objectives and developing a program to implement those objectives. The acquisition program includes the selection of qualified professional advisors, the development of realistic acquisition criteria, a systematic candidate search and preacquisition investigation, the valuation of the acquisition target, etc.

There is more than one approach to finding an acquisition candidate in most countries, and the cost and time demands of each approach differ. The following list provides some recommendations for choosing the right approach.

- What industry should the acquisition candidate be chosen from, and how compatible should it be with existing operations? It has been my experience that the initial investment in a foreign country should be closely related to the acquiror's area of expertise to provide an operational frame of reference, notwithstanding that the foreign investor may still be operating in different markets with different production processes.
- What amount of equity money should be invested and what leverage is desired? What magnitude and timing of earnings and cash flow should the proposed acquisition provide? Many foreign investors want to acquire as small a company as possible for their first acquisition. "We just want to test the water and not make big mistakes" is a common phrase. My advice is to do just the opposite—buy the largest company you can afford. Smaller companies are usually owner-managed companies which may not have strong second-tier management that will stay with the company after the owner sells his or her interest. Smaller companies by nature of their size do not often develop strong middle management.

These are important considerations for an investor who will be located thousands of miles away from the operations.

- What unique strengths are desired, e.g., minimum market share, regional or national distribution, and management depth?

ACQUISITION SEARCH

Once a decision is reached about the broad acquisition goals, an acquisition plan should be prepared. In general, the plan should provide for internal acquisition search activities as well as the development of contacts with the professional firms involved in the merger and acquisition area.

In a domestic acquisition, a systematic search can often be enhanced through contracts with intermediaries who may be aware of companies actually for sale or who may be able to suggest companies that would be likely candidates. This is an opportunistic approach and often produces candidates which might not have been considered in a structured acquisition search. However, my experience is that domestic intermediaries rarely place foreign buyers at the top of their list of people to be contacted should they be representing a selling company. This is for a very good reason—an intermediary is paid when the client is sold, and the involvement of a foreign buyer generally requires longer to complete an acquisition. Accordingly, when a foreign buyer sees an acquisition opportunity from an intermediary, many domestic acquirors usually have already reviewed the situation. Foreign acquirors need to create their own opportunities, and this requires a disciplined acquisition search.

The internal acquisition search begins with the development of the acquisition criteria to be used in the search and then identifies industries and companies that meet the criteria. The search may be conducted by the company, by a professional firm, or, as is most common, by some combination of the two. At this stage, the search focuses on desirable companies rather than on those that may be for sale. In the United States, the search would typically be conducted using data available from the many specialized information services. Data may not be readily available for companies whose shares are not publicly traded, and special research will be necessary.

Except for a few large internationally known companies, many sellers of business likely to be acquired by a foreign buyer will not have had previous knowledge of the foreign buyer. Therefore it is a good idea to develop a compendium which describes the foreign buyer: description of business, some background on the principals, list of host country bank and professional references.

Identification of Industries

The availability and reliability of economic information varies from country to country. In the United States much information is available regarding prospects for various industries during the 1980s and 1990s. This information is produced by numerous economic research organizations. Although these economic organizations often disagree as to the relative performance of the various industries involved, they do provide useful background for the eventual selection process. When assessing macroinformation for various industries, remember that the companies within these industries often have significantly different growth rates and that market niches with different growth rates are often not identified at the macrolevel. Accordingly, the macroinformation is often more useful in identifying the industries to avoid. In addition, companies that stray from industries in which they are already knowledgeable often assume greater risk because they lack both the quantitative and the qualitative information needed to make investment decisions. The risks are compounded when one invests in both a foreign country and a foreign industry.

Once an industry has been identified, a structural analysis of that industry should be attempted: what types of companies are in that industry, what products comprise the industry, who is engaged in the manufacture of those various products, and what is the profitability within the manufacturing and the distribution cycle? In addition, possible substitute products, industry concentration, new entrants into the industry, exit barriers, and the role of suppliers and customers in imparting added value to the products should be considered. The assessment of market size by product segment and the competitive shares available is crucial to identifying market niches and competitive advantage.

Identification of Companies

The essence of any acquisition effort for either a domestic or foreign buyer is the identification of an acquisition candidate which meets most of the buyer's principal criteria—this rarely happens, but a disciplined acquisition search will increase the chances of finding an acquisition candidate which meets the essential elements of the buyer's criteria. Once a company has identified product categories within a selected industry, as well as the approximate size of the potential candidate, the acquisition search should be directed at the market leaders within those categories. What may be a market leader for one company may be a niche company for another. For example, a company seeking to become a market leader in an industry dominated by a few large producers will know that a substantial capital investment will be required. Accordingly, a company that is not prepared to make a substantial capital investment may seek to find a niche within that industry where the total market will be substantially smaller and where that buyer may be able to exercise a more prominent position. Only through an organized acquisition search can the acquiror obtain sufficient data to select the appropriate acquisition candidate. Many data bases in the United States and some other countries can provide information concerning companies within an industry, but the data bases are only a starting point; they are no substitute for direct contact with companies in the target industry or business segment. Domestic consultants often can help to develop profiles of companies in the target area. Once a sample group of acquisition candidates has been identified, the buyer should make direct contact with those companies to become familiar with the principals and the competitive dynamics within the industry and to assess the quality of the various management groups that she or he may acquire or face as competitors. Direct contact with a number of potential acquisition candidates is often difficult for many foreign buyers for two principal reasons: lack of time to invest in the courting and market research operation and, for many non-U.S. acquirors, a long tradition of confidentiality in domestic business relations that often conflicts with this hands-on research experience. However, I know no better way to gain some confidence in one's judgment than by making direct contact with acquisition candidates.

Contacting Acquisition Candidates

When approaching an acquisition candidate, the foreign buyer should seek the advice of local professionals associated with the merger and acquisition business. For example, in the United States it is not uncommon for an acquisition candidate to be contacted directly by a company or intermediary seeking to determine if the acquisition candidate would discuss the sale of a business. This direct approach often seems strange to many non-U.S. buyers. Consider using the services of organizations that provide professional services in the merger and acquisition field. They serve both large and small companies. The group includes:

- Investment bankers
- Large commercial banks
- Finders or brokers
- Major accounting firms, attorneys, and consultants
- Industry consultants

A company seeking to invest in a foreign country should carefully select a firm to work with. If confidentiality is important, the foreign investor may wish to use an independent third party to establish contacts. The fee or compensation arrangement should be settled at the beginning of the engagement and should be in writing. Fees may be charged on the basis of time spent, on a retainer basis, as a commission computed as a percentage of the purchase price, or on some combination of these methods.

It has been my experience that foreign buyers often have an advantage over domestic buyers because many sellers believe that a foreign buyer will allow management more autonomy; grow the business as an independent entity rather than combine it with an existing operation; depending on motivation and monetary exchange rates, be willing to pay more; be unencumbered by many of the reporting and accounting requirements, such as goodwill amortization, which face many U.S. public companies.

PRELIMINARY ANALYSIS

Essential to any negotiation is access to sufficient data and facts to make judgments and commitments during a negotiation process. Accordingly, the purpose of the initial acquisition review is to develop sufficient data. Some essential elements of this initial review include:

- Understanding the candidates' accounting policies and procedures— are they compatible with those of the buyer, such as basis for recognition of profit on sales, procedures used to record and control costs in operations and for inventory valuation, etc.
- Analysis of the business broken down into sales and gross products, by product lines if possible
- Analysis and description of the various assets and liabilities, including an analysis of tax accruals relating to the particular country and its taxation policies

These items highlight the areas for potential exposure in terms of potential liability or downside risk; they can also highlight possible areas for tax planning and restructuring of the acquisition agreement to provide maximum benefits in the contract. A review of prior financial statements and prior budget forecasts will help the buyer to assess the present forecast of future earnings and cash flows.

Often a definitive agreement requires that the seller satisfy a number of conditions, for example, by demonstrating in its audited financial statements that the seller's net equity and asset levels meet or exceed the minimum previously negotiated. The purpose of the audit is to assure the buyer that the seller's financial statements fairly reflect the financial aspects of the business. As is especially true for smaller businesses and divisions of larger entities, the process of audit verification often results in significant adjustments to the seller's financial statements and unfavorable disclosures which could affect the terms of the transaction. In addition, in the audit process the accounting firm generally learns a great deal about the operations of the seller, thereby permitting the firm to make recommendations as to the terms of the contract and approaches to strengthening the seller's internal procedures and organization in the postacquisition phase.

United States accounting and reporting rules are complex and the values reflected in financial statements can vary depending on a variety of factors. If the purchase price is based on net assets or future earnings, it is particularly worthwhile to commission an acquisition investigation or audit. The nature of the accountants' work can be tailored to the situation.

SIGNIFICANT U.S. ACCOUNTING PRINCIPLES AND PRACTICES

A useful tool for foreign investors to consider in terms of accounting issues, which may be distinctive from country to country, is to review some of the significant U.S. accounting principles and practices as a checklist for use in their own countries.

General Principles. The entity is a continuing operation. Assets are carried at the lower of historical cost or net realizable value. In accordance with the accrual method, revenues are recognized when earned, and expenses are accounted for when liabilities are incurred. Accounting policies are applied consistently from one period to another.

Consolidation and Equity Accounting. An interest of more than 50 percent in another company generally requires consolidation of the investee company's financial statements with those of the investor. An equity interest of 50 percent or less, which permits the investor to exercise "significant influence" over the investee, requires use of the equity method, under which the investor recognizes its proportionate share of the investee's net income in the investor's statement of income. Significant influence is generally presumed when 20 percent or more of the voting stock of an entity is owned by the reporting enterprise. Investments of 20 percent or less may be accounted for on the cost basis (historical cost adjusted for dividends received in excess of earnings subsequent to the date of investment).

Asset Valuation. Accounting principles in the United States generally do not permit a company to reflect in its basic financial statements appraisals or current market values that exceed the original cost to the company. Write-downs to market or net realizable value are required where the original cost of an asset will not be recovered through sale or use. Except for marketable equity securities, written-down amounts are carried forward to a subsequent period. Marketable equity securities are carried at the lower of aggregate cost or market, determined at each balance sheet date. An unrealized net loss resulting from the write-down to market will be included in net income for the period if the securities are classified as current assets. For those classified as noncurrent assets, the unrealized loss will be included in the equity section of the balance sheet.

Accounting for Business Combinations. Accounting principles in the United States provide two methods for accounting for business combinations: pooling of interests (merger) and purchase accounting (acquisition). These methods are not alternatives; the method used depends on the facts and circumstances of the acquisition.

In general, the pooling-of-interests method is used when the consideration exchanged to effect the combination is voting stock, although several other criteria must be met as well. Under the pooling-of-interests method, the recorded assets and liabilities of each company are normally carried forward by the combined enterprise at their previously recorded amounts. The purchase method contemplates a new basis of accounting for the assets and liabilities acquired that is equal to the purchase price. Goodwill is recorded when the purchase price exceeds the fair value of net assets acquired. Goodwill must be amortized over a period equal to its estimated life—a period not to exceed forty years. Other than amortization, goodwill cannot be written off partially or in full in any one period unless there is evidence that its carrying value has been diminished or no longer exists. In a purchase transaction, where the fair value of assets acquired and liabilities assumed exceeds the cost of acquisition (negative goodwill), the excess is applied as a reduction in the carrying value of noncurrent assets.

Inventory. Inventory comprises raw materials and purchased components, work in process, and finished products of merchandise held for sale in the ordinary course of business. These are accounted for at the lower of cost or market value. Cost includes both direct and indirect charges. Methods of determining the cost of inventory include average cost, "first-in, first-out" (FIFO), and "last-in, first-out" (LIFO) methods. Provisions are made for obsolete and slow-moving items in the inventory.

Property, Plant, and Equipment. Property, plant, and equipment assets are carried at historical cost less accumulated depreciation. Depreciation, depletion, and amortization are charged to income on a systematic and rational basis over the assets' estimated useful lives to the company. Straight-line depreciation, which allocates costs equally over the estimated useful life of the assets, is the method most frequently used. Depreciation methods which allocate greater portions of cost to the earlier years are also acceptable. The unit-of-production method is used for depletion of the cost of an investment in natural resources.

Reserves. Valuation reserves required to reduce the carrying amount of assets to their current realizable value are deducted from the appropriate asset on the balance sheet. Examples of such reserves are allowances for uncollectable receivables and for obsolete and/or slow-moving inventory. Reserves for contingent losses are not permitted unless it is probable, based on information available prior to issuance of the financial statements, that a loss has been incurred and that the amount can be reasonably estimated.

Capitalization of Interest. Interest costs are capitalized as part of the cost of acquiring or constructing certain assets that require a period to get them ready for their intended use. The capitalization period ends when the asset is ready for its intended use. The term "intended use" includes readiness both for use or for sale or lease. Assets that are constructed for sale or lease qualify for interest capitalization only if they are produced as discrete projects (for example, ships or real estate developments). Interest costs are not capitalized for inventories that are routinely manufactured in large quantities on a repetitive basis or for assets being held for future development of sale.

Accounting for Income Taxes. Comprehensive income tax allocation is required for all book/tax timing differences. The "deferral method" is followed and does not permit adjustment of accumulated balance sheet amounts for subsequent rate changes. Ultimate payment or collection of the tax related to the timing difference is not a factor in determining the current year's provision.

The tax effects of operating losses are not recognized in income unless realization (either as refunds of prior years' taxes due to carrybacks or as reductions of future income taxes due to carryforwards) is ensured beyond a doubt. Tax effects of operating loss carryforwards recognized subsequent to the loss year are shown as extraordinary items (not part of the results of ordinary operations) in the income statement.

Foreign Currency Translation. Different methods of accounting for foreign currency translation currently exist in the United States. Financial Accounting Standard (FAS) 8, which may be applied through fiscal periods ending in November 1983, requires the use of the temporal method of foreign currency translation. Under this method, items in the balance sheet carried at current prices (for example, cash, receivables, payables, long-term debt, and similar monetary-type items) are translated at current exchange rates. Items carried at historical prices (such as inventory, fixed assets, deferred income, capital stock, and similar nonmonetary items) are translated at historical exchange rates. Gains or losses that result from foreign currency translation are included in the income statement as they occur.

When exchange rates change, this approach to foreign currency translation has resulted in significant variations in reported earnings by multinational companies. This effect has been criticized by many in the U.S. business community, particularly since translation gains or losses recognized in the income statement are not necessarily indicative of future cash flow. Consequently, the Financial Accounting Standards Board (FASB) issued FAS 52 effective for fiscal years beginning on or after December 15, 1983.

Under FAS 52, foreign currency translation differs depending on the nature of the foreign operation. Assets and liabilities of operations that are self-contained and integrated within a foreign country are translated at the year-end exchange rate, and the translation adjustment is deferred in the balance sheet as part of the stockholders' equity. The income statement is translated at average exchange rates for the period. Foreign operations that are an extension of the parent's domestic operations are remeasured in dollars in a manner similar to FAS 8, and the resulting translation gains or losses are included in income.

Leases. Long-term leases that transfer essentially all the benefits and risks of ownership are accounted for as an acquisition of a capital asset by the lessee and as a sale or financing arrangement by the lessor.

Reporting the Effects of Inflation. Large public companies are required to report, as supplementary information, income from continuing operations that has been adjusted both for the effects of general inflation and for specific price changes. At a minimum, inventory, fixed assets, cost of goods sold, and depreciation, depletion, and amortization must be restated. Companies are free to restate whatever additional accounts they believe are necessary to disclose the impact of changing prices on the enterprise. The supplemental disclosures also include the purchasing power gain or loss on net monetary items, the current cost of inventory and fixed assets at the end of the year, and increases or decreases in such current costs expressed in constant dollars.

Related-Party Transactions. Companies are required to disclose the nature and financial impact of significant transactions, including those in the ordinary course of business, with a related party during an accounting period. The phrase "related party" includes a parent-affiliate relationship; principal owners, management, and members of their immediate families; and any other party with which the company may deal when one party has the ability to significantly influence the management or policies of the other, or another entity has the ability to significantly influence the management or operating policies of the transacting parties, to the extent that one of the parties might not fully pursue its separate interest.

Other Disclosures. Financial statements prepared in the United States contain many disclosures in the form of notes that are considered an integral part of the statements. These notes include a summary of significant accounting policies and detail information covering specific accounts and transactions in the financial statements. Many of these disclosures are required by generally accepted accounting principles and cover items such as research and development expenditures, details of income tax expense, long-term leases and other significant commitments, company pension plans, stock options, and contingent assets and liabilities. Other notes are intended to give the reader a clearer understanding of the business. For example, large public companies must provide segmented information, giving a breakdown of sales, operating income, and assets by industry segment and geographic area.

Audit Requirements. State laws do not generally require a corporation to appoint auditors to issue an opinion on its financial statements. Audited financial statements are also not required for federal or state income tax purposes. Audited financial statements are frequently required to comply with the provisions of debt agreements and other contractual obligations.

Companies that offer securities to the public or whose outstanding securities are traded publicly must file financial statements with the Securities and Exchange Commission (SEC) which have been audited by an independent public accountant. Stock exchanges also require that annual financial statements provided to stockholders be audited by independent accountants.

An auditor's report expresses an opinion as to the fairness of presentation of the company's financial statements in accordance with generally accepted accounting principles. The opinion also refers to the consistent application of generally accepted accounting principles. The auditor's report contains a separate scope paragraph, which refers to the application of generally accepted auditing standards in the conduct of the auditor's work.

Deviations from an unqualified opinion for matters other than an inconsistency in the application of accounting principles may have serious consequences. For example, stock exchanges and the SEC will not accept financial statement when the auditor's report contains qualifications for failure to follow generally accepted accounting principals or audit SCOPE restrictions.

The principal professional association of independent auditors in the United States is the American Institute of Certified Public Accountants, which issues pronouncements on generally accepted auditing standards, procedures, and professional ethics. One of the most important aspects of the Institute's code of ethics is that auditors must be independent of their clients. Consequently, a member is prohibited from becoming a director or employee of an audit client and from having a direct or indirect financial interest in an audit client.

Since every country has its own system of laws and regulations that affect accounting and taxation, the complexity of these laws and regulations should forewarn any potential investor in a foreign country to use the appropriate local professionals to put into perspective issues involved.

PERFORMING AN ACQUISITION INVESTIGATION

It is not uncommon for an acquisition to fail to provide the return on investment originally expected when the purchase was made. The frequency of divestitures in recent times is symptomatic of earlier, unsuccessful acquisitions. The best way to avoid an unsuccessful acquisition is to investigate the acquisition candidate as thoroughly as possible prior to making the acquisition. The nature and scope of the acquisition audit or review can vary substantially depending on the requirements of the specific situation. Often it is desirable to use an independent firm in conducting the investigation. Most commonly the investigation is undertaken by a team comprising the investor's operating personnel, an accounting firm, and an attorney and industry consultant.

Conducting a Preacquisition Review. The extent of the preacquisition review depends on whether one can access internal company data and how much data are publicly available. The degree to which the buyer can access internal data before finalizing the purchase is typically negotiated with the seller. The purpose of the review would include assessing the value of the acquisition candidate in terms of underlying asset values, future earnings, and their sensitivity to possible economic or competitive changes.

Review Tax Matters. In the United States, the tax structure of the acquisition typically has a greater financial impact on the seller than almost any other factor. For example, a cash purchase results in a taxable transaction for the seller, whereas a stock-for-stock exchange generally does not. Furthermore, whether the shareholder sells shares or has the company sell the assets can have a dramatically different result, for the seller and for the buyer as well. These and other tax factors should be reviewed by tax experts to prevent costly tax planning errors from being made. A U.S. seller would probably be reluctant to accept stock in a foreign company as part of the purchase consideration. Because of the complexity of the U.S. tax laws, it may be advisable to request a determination by the Internal Revenue Service (IRS) as to the tax consequences of the transaction prior to its consummation.

Pension Plans. Conduct an actuarial review of the company's pension plan to identify any unfunded or overfunded pension liabilities. Review legal and regulatory matters, employee benefit plans, and other legislated social cost change constantly; their potential cost can be assessed only through the use of qualified host country professionals.

VALUING AN ACQUISITION

The price on which the buyer and seller ultimately settle is a result of their negotiating skills, their eagerness to buy or sell, the existence of other opportunities, and the intrinsic value of the company being acquired. The valuation exercise should identify two things: (1) the price required to consummate the acquisition, which requires research into the seller's motivation for selling and prices paid for comparable companies, and (2) the highest price one can pay while still meeting goals for return on investment. This requires analyses of the company's earnings potential and associated business risk, future capital requirements, and other factors relevant to the buyer. Some of the major tasks in valuing a company are:

- Assessing management
- Understanding how companies are valued in the public and acquisition markets in the host country
- Forecasting future earnings and cash flow
- Deciding on a capitalization rate
- Performing the valuation

Assessing Management

Probably the most difficult task in the acquisition review is assessing management, since it is management and not the assets that produce the returns that the investor is seeking. Although personal chemistry is often difficult even for fellow nationals to assess, the differences of culture and the natural suspicions associated with foreign acquisitions make this assessment even more difficult. However, whether the buyer be domestic or foreign, the importance of personal chemistry cannot be discounted, and in fact it may play an inordinately prominent role in many buyer decisions. For example, the fact that a seller may have fluency in the acquiror's language may weigh more than it should in selecting an acquisition candidate. Again, as in so many instances, discreet use of professionals to determine the reputation of management of the selling company is crucial in assessing management, for after all, in this most intangible of assets, reputation among peers will be of great value in assessing quantitative aspects of the given management's performance.

Understanding How Comparable Companies Are Valued

Only a few countries have a public market for the foreign acquisition candidate's securities which will provide sufficient trading activity to determine comparable values. However, through the use of the appropriate professional advice, inquiries can be made of buyers of companies in the target industry as to how they approached the valuation in those industries. Each industry often develops its own rules of thumb for assessing those values generally expressed in terms of multiple of sales or book value or so much per unit of production or distribution. Whatever the industry rule-of-thumb value, it still comes down to assessing future earnings potential.

Forecasting Future Earnings and Cash Flow

When acquiring a company, one is buying future cash flows. Reviewing the reasonability of the cash flow forecasts is a critically important task. A useful starting point is to review the target company's performance over the previous five or more years to observe the company under various economic conditions. The review should cover not only the earnings and cash flow trends but also underlying relationships that can affect the forecasts, such as:

- Industry trends in financial performance
- Trends in market share among competition
- Gross profit margin trends
- Cost of goods sold and administrative expenses as percentages of sales
- Inventory and accounts receivable and payable turnover, to assess the adequacy of working capital
- Accounting practices that materially affect the reported profits–cash flow relationship
- Capital expenditure trends, to identify possible capital-spending requirements

Combining historical analyses such as these with industry comparisons is useful, and statistical services compile and publish industry averages and other financial statistics. A review of the forecast by an independent accountant is also useful. Such a review often introduces into the preparation of a cash flow forecast elements of discipline and thoroughness that might otherwise have been missing.

Analysis of prior trends and industry comparisons is a useful starting point for forecasting future earnings, but more fundamental analysis is required for a good understanding of the target company's business. Questions such as the following should be addressed.

- Are the product lines sufficiently competitive to position the company for future growth?
- How does current pricing compare to the competitors'; can it be maintained?
- Can the manufacturing capacity support the forecast sales growth?
- Is the company a low-cost producer in its industry?
- Are there opportunities for cost reduction?
- Is existing management capable of achieving required growth?

Following the analysis of the company's positioning within its industry, its resources, and its prior financial performance, future earnings and cash flow can be forecast.

Deciding on a Capitalization Rate

The capitalization rate should reflect the risk associated with the investment. For example, how has the acquisition candidate performed relative to its own industry, and how has its industry performed relative to a broad selection of industries? Have the acquisition candidate's earnings been volatile? Does the business depend on a few large customers? Are the products subject to rapid technological obsolescence? Foreign investors have to consider the currency risk. They may ultimately be interested in home country currency earnings and cash flow and thus must assess what risk premium has to be added to compensate for the fluctuations in the U.S. dollar currency exchange rate.

Making the Investment Decision

The final result of the feasibility study should be a financial evaluation of the projected return on investment. This would be based principally on projected cash flows in terms of discounted values to reflect inflation and the time value of money. All computations should take into consideration both U.S. and home country taxes. It is also useful to test the sensitivity of the cash flow projection to variations in key variables such as sales growth rates and gross profit margins. The investment can be made with greater confidence when one knows that the return on investment will be acceptable, even under conditions that are less favorable than expected. The cash flow forecast is also helpful for negotiating financing terms with banks and other sources of capital.

The forecast cash flows (over five to seven years) and the value of the investment at the end of the period should be discounted to a present value using the capitalization rate. The result will be the maximum purchase price one can pay and still receive an acceptable return on investment. However, the use of discounted cash flow analysis assumes that one understands how other companies in a given industry are valued and that sufficient judgment is brought to bear on the crucial factors of cash flows, time frame, and discount rates.

CONCLUSION

All the analysis used in assessing the potential rewards of a foreign acquisition and its downside risk end in the foreign buyers most important task—exercising prudent judgment by asking certain questions:

- Did I select the right country to invest in, the right industry, the right company?
- Did I pay a fair price for the best company I could afford, or did I try to find a bargain and end up paying more in future years to correct my bargain?
- Did I retain competent host-country professionals to assist me in the acquisition process and to monitor the investment after the acquisition?
- Have I provided sufficient incentives for the management in the host country to be consistent with their peers?

No one will be able to answer the above questions with absolute certitude, but a foreign buyer will be well on the way to exercising prudent judgment when approaching the foreign acquisition effort with the attitude of buying the best he or she can afford and remembering that often used but not as often practiced phrase, "You generally get what you pay for—maybe."

Nine: Licensing: An Alternative to Financial Risk

ROBERT M. DONNELLY

Robert M. Donnelly is president and chief executive officer of El-O-Matic USA, Inc., the U.S. subsidiary of a Dutch multinational organization. Mr. Donnelly's prior experience includes management positions with an international management and consulting company, QWIP Systems, division of Exxon Corporation, Memorial Sloan-Kettering Cancer Center, Pfizer, IBM, CBS, Lever Brothers, and the Equitable Life Assurance Society. Mr. Donnelly has been an active adjunct faculty member at the Graduate School of Business, Fairleigh Dickinson University, at Fordham University, and at New York University. He has developed and delivered professional seminars for major associations as well as companies. Mr. Donnelly is a member of the North American Society for Corporate Planning, the Planning Executives Institute, the Association for Corporate Growth, and the Forum for Corporate Responsibility. He has written, among other things, the *Guidebook to Planning: Strategic Planning and Budgeting for the Growing Firm*, to be published by Van Nostrand Reinhold Company, Inc.

T he transfer of technology has to continue if we are to survive in a world of decreasing natural resources. Technology transfer is also a continuing key ingredient in the worldwide balance of power. Licensing is an important technique that facilitates the transfer of technology on a global basis and sustains international competition.

Broadly stated, licensing is the vehicle that brings together companies that have common business interests but lack some resource to realize their plans. Licensing is a concept that allows the haves and have nots to negotiate a contractual agreement to their mutual benefit. Licensing can be the first step in the evolution of technological innovation and the optimization of research and development efforts.

However, like all aspects of good business, successful licensing requires management and planning. Unfortunately, there is no global clearinghouse for technology, nor will there probably ever be one. Consequently, the matching process represents a very complicated network that stretches around the world with a wide variety of intermediaries. The process is further complicated by worldwide politics, international laws, a variety of cultures, and global competitive secrecy.

Thus, although the concept of licensing is rather simple, the ways in which licensing agreements can be structured and the financial ramifications of those agreements can be very complicated. This chapter explores the key ingredients for success, the critical management aspects of licensing agreements, the financial structure and return expectations, and the function of licensing in the process of worldwide trade and multinational business development.

LICENSING AS A STRATEGY

Well-managed companies realize that long-term success requires good planning, which is why strategic planning has become their major management endeavor. Strategic planning includes identifying the organization's strengths and weaknesses, which, in most companies today, involves technology and maintaining the leading edge through constant emphasis on research and development (R&D).

Another aspect of strategic planning is portfolio analysis—the identification of the present and future profit potential of all of a company's products. This process of analyzing a company's position vis-à-vis its products and their respective markets leads to the natural question, "Where do we go from here?" The question, "What do we have to do to get there?" is even more important." To answer these questions requires some serious analysis, intuitive thinking, and conceptual planning. Every well-managed company is made up of businesses in different stages of their product life cycle. Each one of these businesses, or products, is a money machine of unique characteristics. The benefit of strategic planning is that it allows management to treat each business according to its respective role in the overall company portfolio, thereby producing the basis for considering licensing, in or out, as a strategy.

Strategic planning usually results in the following ongoing strategies that lend themselves to licensing opportunities:

1. We have existing products, technology, or know-how that is not compatible with our long-range strategic plan (e.g., Borden, Inc. sold its distribution rights to Jean Patou back to the French company because those products did not fit with their long-term strategy).
2. We need to acquire new technology to maintain our competitive position and to expand our business but we cannot take the time nor afford to acquire through grass roots efforts, to acquire a company with such technology, or to continue investment in R&D.
3. We have control of the channels of distribution, the financial resources, and the marketing know-how, but we do not have the products that we need to continue to capitalize on our unique market position.
4. We need to diversify outside of our saturated traditional geographic markets to survive.

In the first case, these products, technology, or know-how can be "licensed out"; some can be terminated. (This concept of licensing out will be discussed in combination with "licensing in" or "cross-licensing" as a strategy later in this chapter.) Licensing out can be a very viable strategy with attractive financial possibilities for the divesting of aspects of the existing business that do not fit with the future plans of management. Sometimes, this licensing-out activity can be a very interesting way to explore licensing-in opportunities, cross-licensing, or just gathering a lot of market intelligence for the future. It also allows management to become familiar with licensing and to make a lot of contacts in the process.

In the second case, we have the basic licensing scenario—a real need to acquire products or technology quickly without the financial commitment, time element, or risk associated with trying to do it ourselves. In this case we have the know-how, and we are looking for a partner with advanced technology that we can both grow into long-term profits.

In the third case, we have a similar situation but with an attractive market position that can be a key profit ingredient to a licensing partner. Sometimes it is difficult to differentiate between case 2 and 3, because some companies are in both situations.

The fourth scenario is also an attractive strategy for a foreign licensing partner, because it gives both parties an opportunity to explore new markets with equal risk. In most of these cases the partner with the technology knows the market but lacks the resources or desire to exploit it and the other partner has the resources and the need to expand into the market. This could be the other side of the first case.

WHY DOES LICENSING REMAIN SUCH A VIABLE TACTIC?

Historically, the combination of different organizations headquartered in different countries for the joint development and sharing of technological capabilities for their markets and other markets makes good business sense. These relations will continue to evolve out of a common desire of all managers to reduce the political and financial risks of beginning foreign operations by themselves. As all these managers will agree, partners can provide political awareness and cultural expertise that foreign managers would otherwise have to develop at considerable expense and time. The expansion of the worldwide market for automobiles is certainly a good example.

The other major incentive is the advantage any combination of technical and marketing know-how gives to the licensing partners over their respective competitors. Some companies view their licensing investments as an extension of their R&D capabilities without the considerable investment they would require if they did it by themselves or if their competitors tried to do it themselves.

Finally, licensing will remain a viable tactic for multinational businesses because, as inflation makes projects larger, technology more expensive, and the costs of failure too large to be borne alone, managers in many businesses will naturally seek out a less risky alternative. In addition, nationalist governments will continue to restrict autonomous foreign subsidiaries from operating within their borders, and licensing is still a relatively easy way to circumvent those restrictions.

Also, doing business outside of the industrially developed world carries with it any number of uncertainties: unstable governments and currencies, terrorism, transportation, distribution, communication, and social service infrastructures that threaten to collapse with each new domestic calamity. In these areas the level of risk almost precludes any direct investment and leaves licensing as a very viable way of doing business in these parts of the world.

MANAGEMENT AND LICENSING

As with all things in business a successful strategy has to be planned, agreed to by senior management, and assigned to a manager to implement. Some companies establish a licensing task force or committee, but the best tactic still seems to be to have one manager, or department, charged with executing the licensing strategy responsible to the executive committee.

Licensing Contract and Financial Commitments

The licensing agreement itself should be clear concerning the exclusiveness of the license in various geographic regions, sublicensing, expiration or termination of the contract, arbitration or litigation procedures in the case of dispute, disposition of products and/or special facilities at the end of the period of agreement, and surrender of trademark rights and other related illustrative data. If the agreement is written in more than one language, one of the languages should be established as the controlling text. In addition, a number of important financial points should be clearly included:

- During the period of the license, both licensee and licensor personnel will visit each other. Which party will bear the expense, approximately how often these visits will take place, and what kind of work will be accomplished during the visits must be understood.
- The royalty fee must be well defined, and, if based on a "sales price," all the components involved in arriving at that price should be clearly explained and their calculation illustrated.
- The currency in which the fees are to be paid, the timing of periodic payments, and the place of payment must be considered.
- Each royalty or license payment should be accompanied by a report outlining in detail the sales on which the payment is based.
- A thorough review of the tax implications of the licensing agreement by qualified international tax experts should be conducted.
- A provision should stipulate the negotiations, as need arises, of funding of special, additional research activities involved in maintenance of the advantages and opportunities that were initially perceived as the benefits of the association.

In joint ventures—and in some licensing agreements—the contribution of one partner may be technology and know-how, while the other partner puts up the capital. The supplier of technology can readily accept a one-time fee as compensation for its input and then might agree to accept a modest percentage of profits as a royalty to compensate its partner's capital investment. (A variety of conference board surveys of corporate policies on royalties, fees, and allocations, however, have not been able to establish a distinct pattern of payment for these kinds of agreements.)

The major managerial advantage of structuring an investment agreement so that payment to a joint venture or licensing partner can be made, in part, as a one-time payment for know-how, and, in part, as a continuing royalty is that it sets the stage for beginning the relationship in good faith and simultaneously offers an incentive to the technological partner to continue the basic research that first brought the parties together.

Organizational Structure and Job Responsibilities to Satisfy the Contract

To concentrate on this unique aspect of business management requires a clear understanding of the cooperative nature of licensing agreements. All licensing contracts are conceived in good faith; however, without a very clearly worded agreement as to who is to manage what and how that performance is to be measured, good faith can easily become questionable intent. This is especially true when the licensing agreement is between foreign companies.

Thus one of the most important items on the checklist during the licensing negotiations has to be the organizational responsibilities of both partners during and after implementation of the strategy. Because there are myriad combinations of licensing situations, it is impossible to address every possible contingency, but we can discuss some basic concepts of good organizational structure.

The first concept to consider is the structure of the executive committee—both partners should be represented in overseeing and guiding implementation of the strategy. The committee should have a chairperson with dual reporting responsibility to both partners and the authority to make certain decisions within the committee. This authority should be contained in the written charge to the committee or take the form of job descriptions for the chairperson and committee members. A periodic committee meeting schedule (*preferably at least quarterly*) should be set up and the minutes of such meetings delivered to each partner. The minutes should contain specific details on progress toward the strategic goals for that period, expenditures, any significant events that occurred since the last meeting, and any important problems or opportunities.

The committee members should be key working managers involved with the licensing strategy. In general, committee members are drawn from each functional area involved with making the licensing agreement work out as outlined in the contract. The time required to work on the strategy, participate in committee meetings, and write reports when necessary have to be agreed to by both partners when forming the committee.

The partners should have at least one annual meeting to discuss progress, make modifications, and maintain the spirit of the agreement. Good management requires teamwork, and successful licensing agreements have to have the same level of team involvement. Licensing agreement failures are usually a result of a breakdown in communications. Nothing stays the same, and the world does not stand still, and good management has to be flexible enough to modify licensing agreements when the conditions no longer fit the times.

Accounting and Control

Accounting and budgets are basic to business. The same holds true for licensing agreements. A budget or long-range operating plan for licensing agreements has to be developed just as you would develop and time the planned expenditures for any other strategy.

A particularly important aspect of the terms of the agreement address when and where the executive committee meets and how those expenses are to be shared. One must also consider how much is allocated to each subset of the project and the timing of those expenditures. Any major capital expenditures have to be detailed and put into the respective format to satisfy each company's capital expenditures policy. In addition, if there are to be shared expenses or machinery and equipment bought or exchanged between the partners, these expenses also have to be planned and budgeted.

This phase of planning for licensing contracts tends to be neglected or underestimated in most cases. The old adage that it will take longer and cost more is very applicable to licensing ventures. This is primarily because licensing relationships are long-term and in almost all cases some aspect of technology, competition, or the overall strategy of one of the partners changes during the life of the agreement.

Licensing strategies have to be reviewed and updated as part of the annual planning cycle like any other strategy. In this process their expenses and capital expenditures should be reviewed so they incorporate changes in the world as well as in the nature of the overall project. Accounting and control for licensing ventures is a lot like project control in a matrix management environment.

In general, the accounting aspect of these agreements is complicated by a variety of people involved from different functional areas doing different things related to the project at different times. The simplest accounting solution is to set-up a project number, or cost center, under which all expenses and capital expenditures are accumulated. These cost centers have budgeted expense categories and approved capital expenditure items. This facilitates the control aspect and allows for monthly, quarterly, and year-to-date reports to each partner's management to show their actual experience as compared to what was budgeted.

Licensing agreements require close monitoring; so many things are going on and can happen that are not easily allocable to the project because so many people are involved without the traditional direct-line reporting relationships. Another effective technique is to establish an approval process related to levels of expenditure. That way each responsible manager has to see and approve expenditures directly related to his or her involvement in the project. Although the subset-accounting technique is more onerous to administer it really contributes to better and closer monitoring of overall project expenses by each member of the licensing strategy team. It also allows the senior executive from each company better overall control of the project and the project team.

Another important aspect of budget control and the need to update the budget is that the amount of participation from each partner changes over time. Usually one partner will require the technical knowledge or marketing expertise of the other for a time but will learn enough so that the initial level of assistance will decline. This naturally causes changes to the budgeted resources of both partners.

THE MIX OF LICENSING AGREEMENTS

As was discussed at the beginning of this chapter, the decision-making process that leads companies to consider licensing as a strategy is a function of many variables in the history and nature of their business. In all cases the process is driven by technological innovation and competition in one way or another. Licensing tends to be a major strategy for most companies, and the organizational priority assigned to licensing usually guides its implementation.

Licensing as an Organizational Strategy

Licensing strategies are sometimes implemented as an organizational vehicle to change the overall domestic-international mix of the company's business as the management team looks to the future. Innovation and new product market development is the life blood of any company. However, in the natural life cycle of business, from time to time companies find themselves out of sync with the market place and are forced to react or go out of business. These situations also evolve out of a natural need to avoid risk, because, as projects get larger, technology more expensive, and the costs of failure too large to be borne by the organization, managers seek out licensing as a natural solution. As has been pointed out earlier, managers of international licensing agreements have to be sensitive to the organizational problems of communications between the partners because of language barriers, attitudes toward the urgency of time, the importance of job performance, financial resources, and the acceptance of change.

Licensing is a particularly good organizational strategy for ease of entry into a new foreign market, and many licensing managers find it easier, faster, and far less disruptive to accommodate foreign differences in style through licensing than through the confrontations that can develop with wholly owned subsidiaries. Planning may take longer, but implementation usually is quicker and smoother.

Licensing as a Multinational Vehicle

Companies look to foreign markets when they cannot achieve their strategic objectives in their home market. They become multinational primarily for one or more of the following reasons.

1. To earn incremental income on their existing technology and to find new technology
2. To expand their markets and to take advantage of foreign economies that grow faster than their own
3. To compete more effectively with foreign companies that are threatening their home markets
4. To keep up with their domestic competitors who have gone abroad
5. To follow their domestic customers who have gone international
6. To explore new markets through the expertise of their foreign licensing partners

Licensing allows companies to achieve these "multinational" objectives and to expand considerably their strategic horizons. The key to the success of a company's strategy to become a multinational through licensing is to start small with a clear understanding of direction and ultimate purpose. Used this way, licensing can become a highly flexible multinational strategy for survival.

Licensing is a strategic investment decision of time and resources in foreign market growth. The foreign licensee has to be viewed as a partner in market development, and the licensing strategy has to be seen as a strategic decision that will extend a long way into the future and eventually impact the very nature of the business.

Licensing as a Source of Incremental Profits

One of the more common ways in which licensing is used is as a source of incremental profits. At the beginning of the chapter we referred to the concept of "licensing in and licensing out." What that means in practice is that trading in technology is a sensible business technique with a wide variety of options and opportunities.

Licensing out is done for two equally important business reasons. First, licensing out may be necessary to obtain technology that the company needs, and thus it can function as a barter or trade agreement in technology. Second, licensing is a way to commercialize technologies that the company has developed over time that they are now unable to use properly. Sometimes this happens because of a change in the overall strategic direction of the company. If these technologies can be licensed to another company, they may serve another useful purpose while generating incremental income.

Licensing in generates incremental income while making the strategy happen. As a result of access to what generally is much needed new technology, the company's overall business improves and incremental profits naturally accrue.

THE FUTURE OF LICENSING

Someone in some part of the world is constantly building a better mousetrap. The cyclical nature of business constantly creates new business opportunities for the have's and the have-not's. What is old to those at the leading edge of technology can be very new to someone else with fewer resources and capabilities. Licensing is at the core of worldwide technology transfer.

A Viable Alternative to Stimulating World Trade

With worldwide markets shrinking and the balance of power constantly shifting, political and economic stability is becoming more and more the exception rather than the rule. It stands to reason that the only way that businesses can survive is to become more global in scope. It is already very obvious that the automobile manufacturers have to adopt a "world car" planning mentality.

In the constant give and take of a "you've got what I need" environment, worldwide mergers and acquisitions will probably accelerate to heighten competition. Protectionism will increase as a natural backlash to the big foreign company phenomenon. Licensing has a role in world trade. It stimulates it, it facilitates it, and it works.

The emerging third world is starving for technology; since they do not have the experience, licensing is a very attractive way to acquire technology and grow with it. Licensing will continue to offer a solution to many business problems as businesses and products mature in their respective worldwide markets.

A Business Expansion Vehicle

A clear case has been made for licensing as a business expansion vehicle. It clearly can make for many potential marriages of the have's and have-not's for the betterment of both. In addition, it has a natural tendency to draw local businesses out of their local markets, give them a broader perspective on world business, and often present them with opportunities they otherwise would have missed.

Learning about new markets and new ways to market is only one of the ways that licensing can work as a business expansion vehicle. Frequently, as a result of exploring one licensing concept, several other mutually beneficial cooperative ventures materialize. The sharing of ideas by a cross-section of managers from different functional disciplines from two companies can be terribly creative. The range of ideas can go from cost-effective manufacturing techniques to research scientists being inspired by the marketing insight of a stimulating discussion of market requirements.

This intangible cross-pollination has created many exciting business combinations that grew out of exploring licensing possibilities and trying to make them happen. Whole new industries have been created by using licensing as a vehicle. Universities and technical research laboratories around the world are funded by companies hoping to license the products of their institutions' work. Every day new grants are being made exclusively for the rights to license any technological results of research projects.

Some venture capital groups have been formed solely for the purpose of investing in high-technology developments that eventually can be licensed. There is a tremendous market emerging in biogenetics, and the licensing possibilities are mindboggling. With the continuing proliferation of advanced computer systems, software licensing is becoming a big business. Another set of examples of how licensing is used as a business expansion vehicle includes the fantastic success of trend-setting designers like Ralph Lauren and the yet-to-be-totally-determined market for licensing of E.T. (the extra terrestrial).

From clothing, animal genetics, chemical and pharmaceutical compounds, software, toys, robotics, to advanced electronics, licensing is playing an invaluable role as the technique for expanding business opportunities around the world. It truly facilitates the process of transferring technological innovation on a global basis from the simplest to the most complex products, designs, and ideas.

Strategic Planning Imperative

Through the evolution of telecommunications via satellite, increased travel possibilities at decreased times, and the energy crisis, a world market has materialized. This world market has created unprecedented opportunities for hitherto domestic businesses to become multinationals. Licensing has proven to be one of the more effective ways for domestic companies to make that happen quickly, effectively, and with a minimum of risk.

Given that the industrialized nations and the third world are racing toward this concept of a global marketplace of products and technology, licensing certainly seems like a strategic planning imperative for any company that wants to survive. In the early 1980s, we have already seen a tremendous shift in products and technology around the world that will make for substantially different kinds and sizes of companies in many different industries. In the United States, for example, it is already obvious that a major shift is underway which not only will change the country from basically a manufacturing economy to a service economy but will also downsize the overall industrial capacity and size of the companies who survive and stay as they were. The automobile industry is a classic example—those companies that do survive will be smaller and will produce more of a world car.

In the midst of all this, many companies still are prudently planning for the future and have been able to stay at the forefront of technological innovation and their markets. All these companies have been able to position themselves to take advantage of these emerging trends through good strategic planning. Likewise, one of their key strategies has been using the concept and techniques of licensing to accomplish their strategic goals and objectives. As we continue to move to more of an international marketplace, more and more products will look the same. Those companies who will continue to grow and prosper in this global competitive environment will probably do so through advanced management information systems and good telecommunications. With systems technology outdating yesterday's new release, licensing of software will be an intelligent strategy.

Thus, for companies of all sizes, licensing represents a strategic planning imperative. It is one of the best ways yet developed to help manage a business through difficult competitive times using conceptual and intuitive strategic thinking about the future.

Appendix 9A
A Checklist for
a Licensing Agreement

The following represents a list of questions that should be answered to the satisfaction of both licensing partners, and those answers should also represent the basic content of the final licensing agreement:

1. Is it clear how this arrangement fits in with our strategic plan? Can we get that down in writing for the benefit of each partner's respective management team? Are we both sure we know *why* we are doing this?

2. Do we have a written mission statement of the overall goals, objectives, and parameters within which we plan to work together on this agreement? Have we captured those points in the "spirit" of the contract? Is each partner's share of the outcome defined?

3. What is the anticipated length of time encompassed by this agreement? What are the key time frames (strategic milestones) that require both partners' senior management to come together to make major decisions about how to reallocate resources, restructure the agreement, or terminate the agreement when it becomes no longer practical or of real business sense to continue?

4. What are the specific organizational commitments of personnel, to what tasks, for how long, and how do we measure performance? You need key performance indicators and strategic milestones to report against for management control purposes.

5. Do both partners have a respective budget established for the first year of the agreement, have they shared their respective budgets, and out of each is there a mutually agreed upon budget for the project? Is there a procedure built into the agreement for updating these budgets annually as a routine part of the overall planning cycle?

6. Have contingency plans been developed to deal with greater or less-than-planned performance, and has each partner's responsibilities in each case been clearly spelled out in the agreement?

7. Has a provision been built into the licensing contract to deal with the disposition of the agreement if something were to suddenly happen (acquisition, change in senior management, or nationalization) to substantially change the ability or desire of one of the partners to continue with the agreement? Is there an arbitration clause?

8. What is the controlling language of the agreement and what standard is to be used for currency valuation for the common moneys involved in the agreement?

9. If incremental income is involved in the form of a royalty, it has to be clearly detailed as to what the royalty is based upon, how often it is paid, and where and in what form it is paid.

10. Has the agreement been reviewed thoroughly by international lawyers and tax experts?

11. Have we established the format for the monthly management reports on the project, as well as quarterly and semi-annual meetings with senior management of both partners to review operational progress against strategic milestones?

12. Is there a secrecy provision and a clear explanation of how by-product inventions, technological breakthroughs, and anything that can result in a patent or trademark are to be shared amongst the licensing partners?

13. Are the countries, or parts of the world, where this contract is valid identified?

14. It it clearly identified who will pay for all of the fees associated with preparations for, and the research associated with (patent search, legal, accounting, taxes, etc.) entering into a licensing agreement?

15. Is there a provision discussing who is liable for what in case of an accident, death, or property damage during the life of the agreement?

16. Is there a provision, or option, for the disposition of the products expected from the licensing project by either partner during the life of the licensing agreement? Can a partner assign their rights?

17. Is there a noncompete clause built into the agreement in case one of the principals to the agreement decides to leave and become a competitor?

18. Has a mechanism been built into the agreement to deal with currency fluctuations?

19. Have the long-term research and development plans of each partner been discussed in a common forum so that each can see how the other's research and development efforts may continue to be complimentary for the future?

20. Has there been a discussion of how the products of the licensing project are to be marketed, by each partner, and how other products can also be considered for joint marketing efforts? Have these issues been addressed in the licensing agreement?

Appendix 9B
Sample
Licensing Agreement

COMPONENTS

- Intent
- Products/Markets
- Length of the agreement/Strategic milestones
- Principals/Sharing of information
- Accounting/Currency
- Licensing team/Executive committee
- Arbitration
- Right of first refusal/Termination
- Products/Patents/Trademarks
- Liabilities/Rights

AGREEMENT

This agreement dated   , to be known as a Licensing Agreement, is being entered into by (company X) and (company Y) for the purpose of sharing their respective and accumulated experience in the development of (products) for the (XYZ) markets.

Intent

The intent of the agreement is that this sharing of information about markets, research, and competitors is to be kept secret between the licensing partners, and that any sales from the products that come from their joint efforts are to be shared as outlined in this agreement. Likewise, any patents, trademarks, inventions, and trade secrets that evolve out of this relationship are also to be shared as outlined below. This agreement is not intended to represent the basis for a joint sharing of markets for other products of the partners (except where specified), nor a joint venture or the beginning of establishing conditions for the acquisition of one partner by the other. However, a first right, if the potential for an acquisition arises, of refusal clause has been included to protect the rights and investment of each partner to this agreement.

Products/Markets

This agreement is designed to allow the partners to explore how their respective strengths can be used in a complimentary fashion to enhance their accumulated research on (products) in order to develop better (products) for (markets). These are the only products covered by this agreement, but there is a provision to incorporate by-products that may evolve out of this agreement.

Company X currently markets their products in (countries) and Company Y currently markets their products in (countries). This agreement specifically covers efforts to enhance products that will be marketed in (countries). A provision has been included to allow for the number of these countries to be expanded or contracted under certain conditions.

Length of the Agreement/Strategic Milestones

This agreement is being entered into this day for a period of (years) and provides for annual review meetings between the principals to this agreement, or those who take over their responsibilities, at which the principles may:

1. Extend, curtail, amend, or terminate the agreement.
2. Establish a budget for the next year's mutual efforts on the licensing project.
3. Reallocate resources (capital and personnel).
4. Change the make-up of the licensing team.
5. Revise key performance indicators for the project.
6. Change the parts of the world that the agreement encompasses.

Principals/Sharing of Information

The principals to this agreement are the following officers of each company:

Company X		*Company Y*	
Name	*Title*	*Name*	*Title*

In consideration of the payment of (currency/value) and to offset the costs of development thus far, Company X will acquire the exclusive rights to (products) for (countries). In addition, Company X will pay Company Y a royalty of   percent on any sales of these products during the life of this agreement.

Company X will also have access to the records of Company Y that relate to the evolution of developments and research that brought these products to their current state. Company X will be updated periodically, preferably quarterly, but at least annually, on the result of ongoing research and development on these products by Company Y. Company X will share the results of their research and development efforts with Company Y, as well.

Likewise, competitive marketing information, package design changes, and all advertising and promotional developments will be shared on at least a quarterly basis.

Accounting/Currency

(Currency) will be the prevailing currency and budgets for this project will be developed in that currency. The currency will be subject to revaluation at least annually, if necessary, and will be reviewed quarterly.

All expenditures on the project will be accounted for on a cost center basis related to the respective steps associated with accomplishing the goals and objectives of the agreement. It is agreed that the project will be audited by (auditors) and a report developed for both companies.

For royalty payments based on sales, the calculation of the royalty payment will be: (calculation). Royalty payments will be paid by Company X to Company Y at the end of each quarter. Royalty payment checks will be in (currency) and be accompanied by a remittance advice detailing every sales transaction with copies of the respective invoices available for review by Company Y, if they so desire to audit the invoices.

Monthly budget to actual performance reports will be prepared and delivered to the members of the licensing agreement executive committee. Quarterly reviews will also be prepared and made available to all the principals to this agreement.

Licensing Team/Executive Committee Responsibilities

The principals to the contract agree that (name) will be the chairperson and the following managers will make up the Licensing Agreement Executive Committee:

Company X		Company Y	
Manager	*Committee Title*	*Manager*	*Committee Title*

In addition, the following other managers represent additional members of the licensing team with specific responsibilities:

Manager	*Company*	*Specific Responsibility*

The tasks of the Executive Committee are:

1. To oversee the implementation of the licensing agreement within the parameters outlined in this contract under the overall direction of the chairperson.
2. To have quarterly review meetings to assess progress on strategic milestones, budget performance, share marketing, and research and development progress. These meetings will be held at (locations) and any expenses related to bringing this group together will have been budgeted and mutually agreed to by X and Y Companies.
3. For the chairperson to develop a quarterly status report for the principals.
4. To work together to develop annual budgets for the licensing agreement and to make recommendations related thereto as to changes that should be made:
   a. to the overall agreement.
   b. to the structure of the licensing team.
   c. to additional projects that should be considered as supplemental to the overall agreement.
5. To develop contingency plans.
6. To recommend matters that should be subject to arbitration because they cannot be resolved within the executive committee.

Arbitration

When circumstances warrant, issues that cannot be resolved by the executive committee should be presented to the principals to this agreement for:

1. The principals to resolve amicably amongst themselves; or
2. Put to a vote with each principal's vote equally weighted.

If the agreement is unacceptable to either company under either of these methods then the agreement should be equitably terminated.

Right of First Refusal/Termination

During the course of this agreement it is reasonable to assume that some changes will occur in the management of each company, their respective markets, their overall ability to continue financially, or a major technological innovation may make the basic intent and purpose of this agreement obsolete. It is also possible, though not contemplated in any way at the inception of this agreement, that one company or the other may:

1. Become acquired by another company
2. Acquire another company with advanced technology, market share, or some other attractive attribute
3. Change their strategic plan to preclude the basic intent of this agreement

In anticipation of any of these unfavorable circumstances materializing and in keeping with the spirit of this agreement, Company X grants to Company Y, and Y to X in turn, the option in the case of a potential acquisition to participate. This option, or first right of refusal, will be good for 30 days from the date one company notifies the other. For all other circumstances than an acquisition, it is agreed that an open dialogue will be maintained to ensure that adequate planning will be done sufficiently in advance to allow for an equitable and amicable resolution of values associated with the investment of each company in this agreement.

Products/Patents/Trademarks

It is the intent of this agreement that through cooperative research several new products will be developed. As Company X has put forth moneys to offset some of the early developmental work of Company Y, Company X is entitled to apply for the patent rights and trademarks of any new products developed as a result of this cooperative research agreement. In addition, Company X has the right to market these new products in the countries designated in the agreement for a period of one year prior to Company Y having the right to market these same products in their respective markets under their own brand names. Company X will make available to Company Y all of their experience in marketing these products in their markets.

Liabilities/Rights

Each partner to this agreement agrees to have adequate insurance to cover any accidents or other claims that may evolve out of actions by both parties to this agreement. In the event that products are created and marketed, the company marketing those products will have sufficient product liability insurance.

Both partners agree to equal rights in the following matters:

1. To receive information relative to all matters pertaining to this agreement when requested in writing.
2. To visit each other's place of business, laboratories, or factories involved in this agreement with thirty days written request for such a visit.
3. To call a meeting of the principals and executive committee when it appears that there are substantive issues to be discussed that cannot be resolved within.
4. To be reimbursed for any losses incurred as a result of unethical or illegal practices by the other partners, agents, or employees.
5. To transfer their rights to another organization, if approved by their partner.
6. To negotiate other licensing agreements for other products and concepts that do not interfere with this agreement.

Ten:
Financing
Foreign Trade:
Import and Export
Fund Sources

SHIVA C. VOHRA

Shiva C. Vohra is vice president and manager in the Directorate of International Corporate Finance of Algemene Bank Nederland N.V., New York. Prior to that, he was manager of the International Financial Consultancy services for Chemical Bank. His responsibilities included consulting with multinationals worldwide on a broad range of international finance and corporate treasury problems. His earlier experience includes several management positions with W. R. Grace & Co. dealing with foreign exchange, cash management, acquisitions, and financing. Mr. Vohra received an M.B.A. in finance from Columbia University, a B.Sc. (Hons.) in physics from St. Xavier's College, and an A.P.C. in international finance from New York University, and he attended the special summer program in international finance offered by the Sloan School of Management of the Massachusetts Institute of Technology. He is also a certified public accountant. Mr. Vohra has authored articles on cash management in Japan published by Business International Corporation and has frequently lectured on international finance issues.

THE ROLE OF IMPORT AND EXPORT IN INTERNATIONAL BUSINESS

Countries frequently harp about mounting trade deficits, declining current account balances, and worsening terms of trade. These macrofeatures of a country's economy are based on statistics derived by aggregating all the actual international trade transactions that occurred between the country and its trading partners during the period. This chapter describes the nuts and bolts needed to make any one of these international trade transactions work—to show which risk factors are involved, what instruments are necessary, and what financing is required. The descriptions are practical, designed for clear understanding and easy reference—the objective is to avoid unnecessary pedagogy. The approach is also somewhat broad-brush: to provide a flavoring. A reference section at the end of the chapter indicates some sources for more comprehensive treatment, and two appendixes list commonly used terms in international trade and commerce.

BASIC REQUIREMENTS OF IMPORT-EXPORT FINANCING

An international trade transaction requires that the two parties at the extremities of the transaction, the importer and the exporter, are sure that both will receive what they had contracted. This confidence fittingly rests on conventions and documents that have evolved over centuries of export-import transactions. Such documentation eliminates or reduces uncertainties in the transaction and expedites it.

Noncompletion Risk

In an international transaction, buyers and sellers have conflicting demands. Sellers would prefer to keep title over the goods until they receive assurance of the buyer's ability to pay, or some other guarantee of payment. Buyers are concerned that their payment might precede the actual receipt of the goods which, when received, do not comply with the agreed terms of trade or are delayed long enough to create cash flow problems. These differences may be a source of understated tensions.

In domestic transactions, evolved relationships between parties and the general availability of finance and business data on the buyer and seller provides a measure of security. Intermediary institutions, such as banks, are passive, and their principal role is to provide a mechanism for the passage of those funds.

In international transactions, relationships are usually new, and financial and business data are sadly lacking. The parties are within the ambit of the respective countries' courts of law. Cultural differences may convey divergent perspectives of the marketplace and the substance behind a particular transaction. Hazy cross-country communication lines and lengthy transportation periods involving many intermediaries further complicate the issues. In addition, all the many international factors addressed in this handbook— foreign exchange regulations and exposure, international law, and taxes— increase the complexity.

Both parties, to alleviate their concerns and to manifest their trust in more concrete forms, use their banks to participate in the transaction and to guarantee some measure of payment if the conditions of the transaction are not met. The mechanism that has evolved to facilitate this relies heavily on three documents—the letter of credit, the draft, and the bill of lading—to provide protection against the risk of noncompletion. As a result, during the completion of a transaction the parties involved know their position in the cycle precisely. Through clever variations, these three documents can provide both limited insulation from foreign exchange risk and financing flexibility.

Foreign Exchange Risk

As described in Chapter 3, when a transaction involves an exchange of currency and a time element, both necessary components of international trade transactions, the parties involved must bear a foreign exchange "transaction risk." Further, depending on the choice of invoicing currency, the risk is borne by the exporter, importer, or both (if a third currency, typically the dollar, is the agreed mode of exchange). Chapter 5 describes the suitable response to offset such a transaction exposure. The basic instrument, the forward cover, is effective in international trade as the coordinates of time, amount, and currency are fixed and stipulated in the three documents.

Financing of Transaction

International trade transactions require the movement of goods across countries. The process may involve great distances for transport, causing the locking up of considerable sums of money by the exporter while the goods are in transit. Although the opportunity cost of the unused funds are usually passed on to the importer, the exporter may suffer temporary illiquidity. Financial institutions at both ends of the cycle offer innovative financing alternatives that can reduce or eliminate either party's working capital needs. Banks are willing to underwrite because well-drawn trade documents may practically eliminate credit risk. Moreover, for added protection, an international transaction is viewed as two independent agreements—one covering the financial aspects for which the bank is a party and is operating well within its expertise, and a second covering the merchandise quality, specifications, and so on for which the bank is not a party and is not liable.

The principal parties in commercial trade are the exporter, importer, and two banks; other peripheral participants are the shipper, freight forwarder, and correspondent banks. The exporter or seller of the goods is technically the "beneficiary," and the importer the "buyer." (These terms will be used interchangeably.)

There are three principal documents used in a typical import-export transaction—a letter of credit, a draft, and a bill of lading, although others of lesser importance also are necessary to complete the trade.

LETTER OF CREDIT

Letters of credit, often referred to simply as L/Cs, have been described as the "crank-shaft of international commerce" because of their central role in trade. They facilitate trade by providing a bank's assurance of ready funds to sellers when they make shipments as called for in the letter of credit and assurance to the buyer that no payments will be made to the seller until the latter has performed as specified in the letter of credit. Using a letter of credit, merchants can set in motion the machinery which makes possible the shipment of goods from exporting countries, such as tobacco from Turkey, wool from Australia, or coffee from Brazil, to their importing partners in other countries.

The letter of credit may also be referred to as a "documentary letter of credit," or a "commercial letter of credit." A commercial or documentary letter of credit must be distinguished from a nondocumentary letter of credit such as a traveler's letter of credit that is used in noncommercial transactions. A traveler's letter of credit calls for payment to the exporter on a nondocumentary or "clean" draft as opposed to a commercial letter of credit where payment is made after documentary evidence. Shorn of all the embellishments, a letter of credit is basically a formal letter issued by a bank at the request of the importer that pledges to pay an exporter upon presentation of documents specified in the letter of credit. The documents show that the goods have been shipped by the exporter under the terms of the sales agreement. The relationship between the three parties—the importer, the exporter and the bank—is represented in Exhibit 10-1.

The terms of a letter of credit vary greatly, since the conditions of each credit must fit the requirements of the transaction. However, a common characteristic is that the seller of the goods is authorized to draw on the issuing bank provided that the conditions stated in the letter of credit are met. In other words, the bank substitutes its security for that of the buyer. In fact, in the most binding "irrevocable" letter of credit, this security cannot be taken away except by mutual consent of the seller, the buyer, and the bank. It is important, however, to bear in mind that the bank agrees to pay if the documentation is proper but does not vouch for the quantity or quality of the actual merchandise parlayed in the transaction.

As an example of a drawing of a typical letter of credit, assume that an importer (buyer) and an exporter (seller) enter into a sales agreement and the importer applies to a local bank for the issuance of a letter of credit. See Exhibit 10-2 for a sample application.

The importer's bank, called the "issuing" or "opening" bank in international trade jargon, will issue the letter of credit based on the importer's creditworthiness and their relationship. To protect itself, the bank may require collateral. The issuing bank would require transaction details—type, amount involved, and what documentation must accompany the draft that will be presented by the exporter.

A sample letter of credit is shown in Exhibit 10-3. It specifies precisely what documents must accompany the draft drawn against the letter of credit, in this case, a commercial invoice, a U.S. Customs invoice, and a bill of lading are required. By granting the letter of credit, the issuing bank has substituted its credit for that of the importer. A "financial contract" now exists between the bank and the designated beneficiary, the exporter. The specimen shows the beneficiary as Jose Doe & Cia. This financial contract is a separate transaction from the sale of the merchandise. Other participants in the transaction may now rely on the bank's credit and are not concerned

**Exhibit 10-1 Relationships between
Three Parties Involved in Letter of Credit**

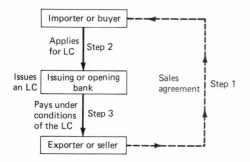

Exhibit 10-2　Sample Application, Import Letter of Credit

CHEMICALBANK
International Operations
PO Box 44, Church Street Station, New York, N.Y. 10008
Cable Address: **Chemsam**

SAMPLE Application Import Letter of Credit

Application for Commercial Letter of Credit

1 **Credit Number**
of Chemical Bank　　　　　of Advising Bank

2 **Advising Bank**

3 **For Account of** · Applicant
Name
Address
City/State　　　　Zip

4 **In favor of** · Beneficiary
Name
Address
Country

5 **Amount**
words

6 ☐ Presentation for negotiation
on or before
Date

7 ☐ Presentation at Chemical bank,
N.Y. on or before
Date

8 Please issue an irrevocable Letter of Credit substantially as set forth and forward same to your correspondent for delivery to the beneficiary by:
☐ Air Mail only
☐ Air Mail with preliminary brief details cable
Delete one: Night Letter/Full Rate
☐ full details cable
Delete one: Night Letter/Full Rate

9 Available by beneficiary's draft(s) at
10 ☐
☐ Sight on Chemical Bank, New York
for _____ % of invoice value.
for _____ % of invoice value

11 **Covering** · Merchandise must be described in the invoice as:

12 **Terms:** ☐ FAS _____ ☐ FOB _____ ☐ C&F _____ ☐ CIF _____ ☐ C&I _____

13 **Draft(s) must be accompanied by the following documents — Refer to box(es) checked below**
☐ Commercial Invoice, original and _____ copies
☐ U.S. Customs invoice in duplicate
☐ Marine Insurance policy or certificate including war risk
☐ Airway Bill · Consigned to Chemical Bank marked notify applicant as shown above
☐ On Board — Ocean Bills of Lading required if more than one original has been issued to order of Chemical Bank marked notify applicant as shown above

14

15 **Shipment from:**
To:　　16 Latest

Partial Shipment(s): ☐ Permitted ☐ Prohibited
17 Transshipment(s): ☐ Permitted ☐ Prohibited

18 ☐ Insurance effected by applicant with: _____ Insurance Company _____ under _____ Policy No

19 Documents must be presented to negotiating or drawee bank within _____ days, after shipment, but within validity of the Letter of Credit
If number of days left blank it will automatically be considered 21 days

20 ☐ Additional Instructions, if any

Unless otherwise instructed, documents may be forwarded in one airmail by negotiating or paying bank

21 **If credit is in foreign currency,** Refer to box checked:
☐ Foreign exchange is to be purchased for our account immediately
☐ Foreign exchange is not to be purchased at this time

22 **If credit is at sight in foreign currency,** Refer to box checked:
☐ We **do desire** cable advice of payment to you by paying bank
☐ We **do not desire** cable advice of payment to you by paying bank
This application is subject to the conditions on the reverse side hereof, which is an integral part of this application.

23 Our Account No. with CB

24 _____ Company or Corporation Name _____ Date

For Bank Use Only
S.V.

Authorized signature(s) on file with bank

03 0575 (3-78)

Exhibit 10-3   Sample Import Letter of Credit

CHEMICAL BANK

International Operations
PO Box 44, Church Street Station, New York, N.Y. 10008
Cable Address: **Chemsam**

SAMPLE Import Letter of Credit

Irrevocable Letter of Credit	Credit Number	
	of Chemical Bank 800,000	of Advising Bank

Advising Bank Banco de Banco Manizales, Colombia	For Account of - Applicant
	Name John Smith & Co. Address 1234 Wall Street City/State New York, N.Y. Zip

In favor of - Beneficiary	Amount
Name Jose Doe & Cia. Address Manizales, Colombia Country	Twenty Six Thousand Six Hundred Twenty Five Dollars United States Currency (U.S.) ☒ Presentation for negotiation on or before: Date September 30, 19 ☐ Presentation at Chemical bank, N.Y. on or before: Date

We hereby establish our irrevocable Letter of Credit in your favor, the required draft(s) to be marked 'Drawn under Chemical Bank, New York,' Letter of Credit number *indicated above.*

Available by beneficiary's draft(s) at   ☒ Sight on Chemical Bank New York   100 % of invoice value .
                                                ☐ _____ for _____ % of invoice value.

Covering - *Merchandise must be described in the invoice as:* 500 Bags Coffee

Terms: ☐ FAS _____   ☒ FOB Manizales   C&F _____   ☐ CIF _____   ☐ C&I _____

Draft(s) must be accompanied by the following documents — (refer to box(s) checked below:
☒ Commercial Invoice, original and 3 copies
☒ U.S. Customs invoice in duplicate
☐ Marine Insurance policy or certificate including war risk
☐ Airway Bill - Consigned to Chemical Bank marked notify applicant as shown above
☒ On Board — Ocean Bills of Lading - Full set required if more than one original has been issued to order of Chemical Bank marked notify applicant as shown above

Shipment from: Colombian Port   Partial Shipment(s): ☒ Permitted   ☐ Prohibited
To: U.S.A. Port _____ Latest _____   Transshipment(s):   ☐ Permitted   ☒ Prohibited
☒ Insurance effected by applicant with: York Insurance Company   under K123456
                                          Insurance Company   *Policy No*

Documents must be presented to negotiating or drawee bank within 5 days after shipment, but within validity of the Letter of Credit.
If number of days left blank it will automatically be considered 21 days.

All documents must be forwarded to us in one airmail.

We hereby agree with you that drafts drawn under and in compliance with the terms of this credit will be duly honored upon presentation and delivery of the documents as specified if presented at this office
Letter of Credit Department:
55 Water Street,
New York, N.Y. 10041
on or before the latest date for presentation indicated above.

Advising Bank Notification

This is an irrevocable Letter of Credit of the above mentioned issuing bank and is transmitted to you without any responsibility or engagement on our part.

Authorized Signature - Chemical Bank - Issuing Bank

Place date, name and signature of Advising Bank

This credit is subject to the Uniform Customs and Practice for Documentary Credits (1974 Revision). International Chamber of Commerce Publication No. 290.

03 4400 (4-78)

with the creditworthiness of the importer.

A letter of credit is valid only if it has the following components:

1. Fee or other consideration received by the issuing bank for the undertaking.
2. Specified expiration date and a definite term.
3. Definite amount to which the issuing bank's undertaking is limited.
4. Issuing bank is obligated to pay only on presentation of specific documents.
5. Importer must have an unqualified obligation to reimburse the issuing bank on the same conditions as the bank paid.

The next step requires the issuing bank to send the document details (or telex the terms) to a correspondent bank in the exporter's country or to the exporter's bank. This bank "advises" the exporter (seller) that a letter of credit has been opened in its name. The intermediary bank is known as the "advising" bank. The exporter is now satisfied with the financial arrangement because the importer's bank has ensured payment for the goods if the exporter can fulfill its part of the bargain.

On shipping the goods, the exporter draws a draft against the issuing bank in compliance with the terms of the letter of credit, attaches the required documents, and presents the draft to its own bank for payment. At this stage, various steps may occur. Let us follow the transaction through for the simplest case; that is, assume that the exporter's bank has not "confirmed" the credit, which means that the exporter's bank has not further guaranteed to pay in addition to such a promise already existing from the issuing bank.

The exporter's bank will forward the draft and the accompanying documents to the issuing bank. If the documents comply with the terms and conditions specified in the letter of credit, the issuing bank (i.e., the importer's bank) will honor the draft by paying the exporter's bank, who then pays the exporter.

The issuing bank collects from the importer in accordance with the original terms of the letter of credit. The importer needs the documents, including the order bill of lading, to take physical possession of the merchandise. The importer receives the documents from the bank either by paying immediately or under a trust receipt arrangement whereby the importer agrees to pay at a later date.

In the transaction, the role of the issuing bank was more important than that of the exporter's bank because it paid after inspecting the documents and noting their compliance. The exporter's bank performed only a document collection and transmission function. An oft-used variation occurs when the exporter's bank "confirms" the letter of credit. Now the exporter's bank would honor the draft presented by the exporter, pay the necessary funds, and obtain reimbursement from the issuing bank. Again, remember that the letter of credit is not a guarantee of the underlying commercial transaction but only sets the financial basis of the transaction to facilitate the crossborder payments.

Types of Letters of Credit

Commercial letters of credit usually fall under the following categories:

Documentary. Most commercial letters of credit are documentary, meaning that specified documents must be presented with the draft. Typical documents include bills of lading, commercial invoices, insurance certificates, certificates of origin, consular invoices, inspection certificates, and weight or packing lists.

Irrevocable or Revocable. An irrevocable letter of credit fastens the issuing bank's paying responsibility so that it must, without exception, honor drafts in compliance with the credit. No modification of the arrangement is permissible without the consent of all the parties. An irrevocable letter of credit must state an expiration date before which the documents are to be presented. By contrast, a revocable letter of credit can be cancelled or amended at any time before payment—its purpose is to provide a convenient means for payment, not a guarantee of payment.

Confirmed or Unconfirmed. A letter of credit issued by a bank and confirmed by another obligates both banks to honor drafts drawn in compliance with the credit. An unconfirmed letter of credit obligates the issuing bank only.

An exporter cannot evaluate the issuing bank's financial condition, and, if there are questions about the political or economic state of the foreign country, will likely insist on "confirming" the letter of credit by a domestic bank. Confirmation is frequently desired even when the letter of credit is irrevocable. In a rare instance, in 1975, the Bank of Nigeria, the central bank and also the issuing bank, refused to pay exporters of cement against irrevocable letters of credit because of problems of overpurchase by Nigerian importers. Exporters suffered major losses that would have been deflected if the letters of credit had been confirmed by banks in their home countries.

Revolving or Nonrevolving. Letters of credit are typically issued for a single transaction—one letter of credit covering one transaction. The transaction is nonrevolving. Sometimes, however, a revolving credit is issued when an importer must make frequent, known purchases. In this case, the letter of credit's duration may "revolve" weekly—in other words, the exporter/beneficiary can draw against the value of the letter of credit every week.

Most revolving credits are revocable, since the total obligation can mount up and would have to be paid by the issuing bank if the letter of credit instead was irrevocable and the goods were found not to conform when delivered several periods later.

With a "noncumulative" revolving credit, the allowed credit expires if it is not used within the prescribed period; in a "cumulative" revolving credit, the allowed credit, if not used, is tacked on to the next period's credit.

Transferrable. A transferrable letter of credit permits the beneficiary to transfer all or part of the payment to other parties. Such a transfer can only be made once.

Letter of Credit Preferences

The exporter would typically negotiate one of the following kinds of letters of credit (they are ranked in descending order of collectibility). The first two are particularly safe because collection is ensured by a domestic bank. The last arrangement is least desirable.

1. Irrevocable L/C issued by the foreign bank (importer's bank) and confirmed irrevocably by a domestic bank or a third-country foreign bank that is well regarded and has international standing
2. An irrevocable L/C issued by a domestic bank
3. An irrevocable L/C issued by a foreign bank with no intermediary bank as guarantor (the domestic, or advising, bank functions as a conduit for information and facilitates the flow of documents)
4. A revocable L/C

Letter of Credit Advantages

The many advantages of using a letter of credit all derive from the involvement of banks. Banks, being financial institutions, are obviously better movers of funds across international borders than are commercial enterprises. Large banks, with greater visibility and international experience, are well positioned to fill a role in international trade where their creditworthiness is substituted for that of commercial enterprises. Given their international portfolios, these banks are ideally suited to deal with the constantly shifting patterns of foreign exchange, trade, and regulation. In some cases, the blocked road of restrictive regulations may be bypassed. For instance, an L/C confirmed by a bank in the exporter's country eliminates problems of foreign currency collection and conversion.

An exporter who is the beneficiary of an irrevocable letter of credit may obtain domestic preexport financing. Funds are borrowed from a bank to manufacture the goods that are shipped as specified under the letter of credit, and payment is then collected from the importer. A portion of the payment is used to extinguish the preexport financing debt.

Importers view the letter of credit as a tool whose flexibility allows them to postpone payment until the documents have arrived as stipulated in the letter of credit. Additional financing may be possible if banker's acceptances are created. Preexport financing and banker's acceptances are explained later in this chapter.

Bank Liabilities

The obligations of banks are specified in the *Uniform Customs and Practice for Documentary Credits* published by the United States Council of the International Chamber of Commerce. Since documents play a major role in seeing the transaction through and the physical goods have no direct bearing on the banks, banks must exert reasonable care in examining the documents and attesting compliance with the terms of the letter of credit.

The banks do not have responsibility for the form, sufficiency, accuracy, authenticity, falsifications, or legal effect of any documents; nor for the description, quantity, weight, quality, condition, packing, delivery, value, or existence of the goods; nor for the good faith or acts and/or omissions, solvency, performance, or standing of any of the parties of the transactions, including carriers and insurers. Banks are not liable for the consequences of delays; for losses in transit of messages, letter, or documents; or for errors in transmission of information or the translation and interpretation of technical terms. Also, no liability can be ascribed to banks for losses from uncontrollable events such as strikes, riots, war, or force majeure acts.

Exporters sometimes find that drafts and documents presented for payment are "turned down" because they are not in accordance with the terms of the letter of credit. In this case, the paying bank may be willing to accept the exporter's guarantee to make the bank whole should the importer refuse to accept the documents because of such discrepancies. Exporters who offer these guarantees should be aware that final settlement rests with the importer, who may decide it advantageous not to accept the documents as presented. To prevent this, exporters may request the paying bank to cable the "opening" bank for authority to pay against the documents as submitted.

THE DRAFT

A draft, also known as a "bill of exchange," is a written order, signed by one party (the maker or drawer) requesting a second party (the drawee) to make an exact payment at a specified future date to a third party (the payee). Drafts arise in international trade where sellers (exporters) agree to transfer goods to buyers (importers), after which, the sellers (as drawer) make out a draft ordering the buyers or their bank (drawees) to pay the sellers' bank (payees) for the goods purchased.

The draft is frequently a negotiable instrument, not unlike checks, that can be traded among parties as funds. Drafts may occasionally be written to be nonnegotiable in that they will not meet all the requirements of the Uniform Negotiable Instruments Act, which states that, to be negotiable, an "instrument" must conform to the following requirements.

1. It must be in writing and signed by the maker or drawer.
2. It must contain an unconditional promise or order to pay a certain sum in money.
3. It must be payable on demand or at a fixed determinable future time.
4. It must be payable to order or to bearer.
5. Where the instrument is addressed to a drawee, the drawee must be named or otherwise indicated therein with reasonable certainty.

Instruments, such as checks, drafts, or promissory notes meeting the above requirements, may be transferred to other parties as consideration. The new holder, called the "transferee," is known as a "holder in due course" and is entitled to financial compensation regardless of any later dispute arising from the trade transaction.

Types of Drafts

Drafts are generally classified by their time component. The time period fixed for the payment is known as "tenor" or "usance." The following is a list of basic types of drafts; the first three are the most common.

1. A *sight* draft is also known as a "presentation" or "demand" draft. Here the drawee must pay immediately on presentation of the draft.
2. A *time* or "usance" draft is presented at sight, "accepted," and then paid on an agreed on date, which may be thirty, sixty, ninety days or longer after presentation or acceptance. See Exhibit 10-4 for an example of a sample time draft and collection instructions.
3. A *date* draft matures in a stipulated number of days after its date, regardless of when it is accepted.
4. An *arrival* draft is a modified sight draft which does not require payment until after the arrival of goods at the port of destination.
5. An *interest-bearing* draft is used with either U.S. dollar or pound sterling drafts, principally by exporters selling to the Far East and Africa. Such drafts require the drawee to pay interest from the date of the draft to the date that the remittance is received.

In international trade, the importer generally needs documents to collect the goods; therefore most drafts are "documentary," and the attached documents ordinarily control title to the goods shipped. A clean draft has no attached titled documents. The documents attached to the draft are passed on to the importer either on payment (sight drafts) or on acceptance (time drafts). If the documents are to be passed on to the importer on payment, it is a "D/P" draft. Alternatively, a "D/A" draft is one in which the documents are delivered on acceptance.

Clean drafts are frequently used for cross-border transactions between affiliates of a multinational when credit and risk factors are less critical.

Exhibit 10-4   Combined Collection Letter—Sample Time Draft and Collection Instructions

TO **CHEMICALBANK**

Foreign Collection Department
P.O. Box 44, New York, N.Y. 10008

Combined Collection Letter
SAMPLE Time Draft and Collection Instructions

Collecting Bank

Date __July 5, 19__

(If blank, your correspondent)

We enclose the following item for [X] Collection   and   [X] credit to our account number   000-123456
                                      [ ] an advance   [ ] remittance to us by check

Subject to uniform rules for the collection of Commercial Paper (1967 Revision) International Chamber of Commerce, Brochure No. 254 and the conditions listed on the reverse side.

Drawer's Reference No.	Date of Draft	Tenor	Amount
201	July 5, 19	90 Days Sight	$1,164.60

Drawer
Export Corporation of America
123 First Avenue
Address New York, N.Y.

Drawee
Gomez y Florencio
964 Avenida Antonio
Bogotá, Colombia

Bills of Lading Orig.	Dup.	Parcel Post Receipt	Insur. Cert's	Invoices	Consular Invoice	Packing Lists	Weight	Cert. Origin	Other Documents
3	2	—	3	6	4	2		—	

Deliver Documents Against	[X] Acceptance	Payment	Charges	[X] Drawer's Expense	[X] Drawee's Expense
Advise By Cable	Acceptance	Payment	Documents	[X] Drawee's Expense	Drawer's Expense
Remit Proceeds By Cable	Drawee's Expense		Foreign Bank Charges	[X] Drawee's Expense	Drawer's Expense
[X] Remit Proceeds By Airmail			Waive Charges If Refused		
Protest	Acceptance		[X] Do Not Waive Charges		
[X] Do Not Protest		[X] Hold For Arrival of Merchandise			

[X] IF DOLLAR EXCHANGE IS NOT IMMEDIATELY AVAILABLE ... OR ON PRESENTATION IF DRAWN AT SIGHT) AND IT IS NECESSARY TO PROVISIONALLY ACCEPT LOCAL CURRENCY PENDING AVAILABILITY OF DOLLAR EXCHANGE IT MUST ... UNDERSTOOD THAT THE DRAWEE SHALL REMAIN LIABLE FOR ALL EXCHANGE DIFFERENCES, AT TIME OF DEPOSIT OF LOCAL CURRENCY OBTAIN FROM DRAWEES ... PAYMENT IS UNDER ... TO BE RESPONSIBLE FOR ANY EXCHANGE DIFFERENCES. THE DRAFT MUST NOT BE SURRENDERED TO DRAWEES UNTIL FINAL PAYMENT FOR FACE AMOUNT ... CHANGE.

Allow a discount of ____ if paid ____

Collect interest at the rate of ____ % From ____

In case of need refer to	Francisco Mellos 234 Avenida Cinco, Bogota, Colombia	Who is empowered by us: to act fully on our behalf i.e. authorized reductions, extensions, free delivery, waiving of protests etc.	Who may assist in obtaining acceptance or payment of draft, as drawn, but is not to alter [X] its terms in any way.

Other Instructions

Authorized Signature

$ 1,164.60   Date July 5, 19   No. 201

SOLE BILL OF EXCHANGE

90 DAYS AFTER Sight   of this SOLE BILL OF EXCHANGE

Pay To The Order Of **CHEMICALBANK**

One Thousand One Hundred Sixty Four 60/100
Value received and charge the same to account of

To___ Gomez y Florencio
964 Avenida Antonio, Bogota, Colombia

Export Corporation of America
(signed)

02 0267417 75

They are also used for nontrade transactions or for collection of an outstanding debt. The creditor, to pressure or embarass the debtor, may draw a clean draft for processing through the banking channels and for presentation to the debtor by the debtor's own bank.

A documentary draft is also used when, for whatever reasons, there is no underlying letter of credit supporting the transaction. In such a case, an exporter will ship the goods to an importer and draw a documentary sight draft against the importer. The importer cannot take possession of the goods without receiving the documents, which, in turn, can be had only on payment, on sight, of the draft. This method obviously presents risks, since the importer, because of a change in market conditions, for instance, may decide not to accept the merchandise. The exporter, without the underlying letter of credit, may have little recourse against the importer and has none against the intermediary banks.

Acceptances

When exporters draw a time draft on an importer's bank, they may choose to receive immediate payment by "discounting" the draft at their bank. This is clearly possible if the exporter's bank has no fear of noncollection. The exporter's bank sends the time draft to the importer's bank, which then stamps "accepted" on the draft, which implies that it has guaranteed payment and has created an irrevocable obligation. The draft is now an "acceptance." The exporter's bank may decide on one of two steps. If it has no immediate need for cash, it will wire the importer's bank to return the draft and will then hold it to maturity as an investment, at which time it will present it to the importer's bank for payment. If it desired the funds immediately, the importer's bank would pay it a discounted amount and then either hold the acceptance or sell it to a third-party investor for eventual payment at maturity. By accepting, the bank agrees to meet the payment if the importer reneges.

Banker's acceptances generally arise out of foreign trade transactions, mostly from the trade of bulk commodities. Some may have a domestic basis. Owing to the complexity of acceptance operations, only large banks with well-staffed foreign departments act as accepting banks. Consequently the majority of all acceptances originate in New York, San Francisco, and Chicago. The big banks that create acceptances generally keep a portion of them in their portfolio of investments and sell the rest in the short-term money markets either directly or through dealers. Major investors are other banks, foreign central banks, and corporations.

Banker's acceptances resemble commercial paper in that they are short-term, non-interest-bearing notes that are sold at a discount and redeemed by the accepting bank at maturity for full face value. However, banker's acceptances are perceived to be less risky because of the somewhat more impressive backing of the instrument by the importer, the underlying goods, and the accepting bank. Commercial paper carries the guarantee of only the issuing company. The less risky perception results in slightly lower yields for acceptances. Since an acceptance is not paid off at presentation, it serves as a source of working capital. This benefit is described later in the section on Acceptance Financing.

Banker's acceptances which are time drafts that are drawn on and accepted by a bank must be distinguished from trade acceptances that are drawn on and accepted by a business enterprise. The latter are generally not marketable, but their accepting and payment process resemble those for banker's acceptances. A major difference between the two is that trade acceptances are not guaranteed by a bank and banker's acceptances are.

In the past decade foreign importers have used acceptance financing to pay for their imports; this has caused the entire domestic U.S. banker's acceptances market to rise sharply. A Dutch company, for instance, may import U.S. goods and arrange a letter of credit from a U.S. bank (the opening bank) under which the bank will accept dollar drafts drawn by the U.S. exporter against the Dutch importer. This kind of transaction increased dramatically after the 1974 oil crisis, following which many countries used the U.S. acceptance market to finance their oil imports. An interesting result was that a high percentage of outstanding banker's acceptances represented third-country trade, that is, where neither the exporter nor the importer was a U.S. party.

Banker's acceptances generally trade in round lots—$100,000 or, more typically, $500,000. Larger transactions are usually broken into multiple drafts each of $500,000. There are fourteen primary dealers who make an ongoing market in banker's acceptances, and the most common maturity periods are 30 to 180 days.

Foreign investors sometimes prefer acceptances for investment purposes despite their lower yields because the income earned on acceptances is not subject to the U.S. federal withholding tax of 30 percent that is imposed on interest earned by foreigners. Banker's acceptances may also be eligible or ineligible for federal reserve requirement purposes; rules to determine eligibility are complex. The central aspect is that if an acceptance is deemed eligible, it can be sold by member banks and will be discounted by the Federal Reserve. Banks must also maintain reserves against eligible instruments. The basic feature for eligibility requires that the acceptance have a short-term maturity date and must arise out of specific commercial transactions. Ineligible acceptances do not meet these criteria and are typically created when a borrower wants to convert a promissory note to acceptances to finance general working capital needs.

As pointed out, a banker's acceptance resembles commercial paper and is traded in the short-term money markets. An investor holding a banker's acceptance as a short-term investment may trade it in the secondary markets and does not have to hold the investment to maturity. Consider two examples that show the net proceeds received:

Example 1

An exporter ships merchandise and draws a time draft of $1,000,000 maturing in ninety days against the importer which is accepted by the importer's bank. The bank charges a fee of 1 percent per annum for the service. If the exporter holds the bank's acceptance to maturity, she or he will receive:

Face value of acceptance	$1,000,000
Less bank's acceptance fee of 1 percent/annum	(2,500)
Net value received by exporter at maturity	$ 997,500

Example 2

Assume the same situation as Example 1 except that the exporter needs liquid funds and decides to sell the acceptance paper immediately. Assume a market discount rate of 9 percent. The exporter will receive immediately:

Face value of acceptance		$1,000,000
Less: Bank's acceptance fee		
of 1 percent/annum	$ 2,500	
Discount amount for		
ninety days at 9 percent/annum	22,500	(25,000)
Discounted value received by exporter immediately		$ 975,000

If the bank decides to sell the banker's acceptance after holding it for twenty days as investment, the new investor (for example, another bank or corporation) will pay an amount equal to the face value less a discount on seventy days (the period remaining to maturity) and bank commissions. The investor would collect $1 million at maturity, that is, seventy days later.

BILL OF LADING

The bill of lading, also denoted B/L, is another key document in international trade. The bill of lading is made out to the exporter by a carrier (railroad, steamship, or other common carrier) who is transporting the merchandise. The bill of lading describes the conditions under which the goods are accepted by the carrier and provides details of the nature and quantity of the goods, name of the vessel (if shipped by sea), identifying marks and numbers, destination, etc. The person sending the goods is the "shipper" or "consigner," the company or agent transporting the goods is the "carrier," and the person to whom the goods are destined is the "consignee." A bill of lading may be negotiable (if straight) or nonnegotiable (if to order).

The bill of lading serves three functions:

1. A receipt for the goods
2. A contract to deliver the goods to a designated person or to that person's order
3. Title rights to the goods when the bill of lading is negotiable

The last function, as a title document, becomes important when the goods shipped have been financed by a bank. Upon shipping, the bill of lading is endorsed over to the bank by the exporter. The bank can make itself whole by selling off the goods if the exporter cannot clear its debt. Obviously, this is extremely rare.

The carrier, like the bank, has no responsibility for the authenticity or quantity of the goods described in the bill of lading. The goods are taken entirely at face value.

When shipping charges are prepaid, which is the common practice in international trade, the bill of lading is stamped "freight paid." If the charges are to be paid at destination, the carrier keeps a lien on the goods until freight is paid.

Types of Bills of Lading

Although there are two principle varieties of bills of lading—straight and order—the following list includes some other common types.

1. With a *straight* bill of lading, the shipment is consigned to a specific party, normally the importer. The carrier delivers the goods at the point of destination to anyone representing the party (consignee) as named in the bill of lading. Such a bill of lading does not represent title (hence is nonnegotiable) to the goods and is not required by the importer (consignee) to obtain possession. Since it is not a title document, it is not considered good collateral in international trade and is used for cash-in-advance transactions, open account shipments where no financing is involved, or in cases where the nonpayment risk is low or irrelevant such as interaffiliate transactions.

2. An *order* bill of lading directs the carrier to deliver the shipment to the order of a designated party. The carrier delivers the goods at the point of destination and only to the person to whom the document is addressed. An order bill of lading grants title over the shipment and therefore is negotiable. The usual procedure is for the bill of lading to be made to the order of the exporter who retains title until payment is received. The exporter is advanced the funds by its local bank upon submitting its documentary draft, and the bill of lading is endorsed over to the bank in blank. The local bank sends the documents to the importer's bank, who releases the documents to the importer after payment (sight draft) or acceptance (time draft).

3. A *clean* bill of lading describes the goods as having been received in "apparently good order and condition" and without qualification. The opposite, a "foul" or "unclean" B/L bears a notation made by the carrier of defects found in the goods when they were received for transporting—for example, "3 sacks torn." A foul bill of lading is generally not acceptable under a letter of credit and therefore lacks complete negotiability.

4. When a B/L has not been presented under a letter of credit to the issuing bank within a reasonable time after its date and the shipment has arrived at the port of destination before the bill of lading, it is considered to be a *stale* B/L.

5. An *on-board* bill of lading is the most commonly used form that indicates, by signature of the captain of the vessel or captain's representative, that the goods are on board. Importers can thereby control when they receive goods by stating in the sales contract that the on-board bill of lading should be no later than a certain date. On-board bills of lading are important since some insurance coverage, such as war risk, are effective only if the goods are on board the vessel. A much less common form is the *received-for-shipment* bill of lading that merely acknowledges that the carrier company has received the goods but does not guarantee that the goods have been loaded on the vessel. The received-for-shipment bill of lading is unsatisfactory when seasonal or perishable goods are involved. A received-for-shipment bill of lading can be converted to an *on-board* bill simply by stamping "on-board" and indicating the name of the vessel, the date, and the signature of an official of the vessel.

6. A freight forwarder may consolidate orders of many exporters to get a lower bulk rate from the carrier and then issues his or her own bill of lading, *forwarder's* B/L, as proof of receipt. Such a document is nonnegotiable and is little more than a receipt. The freight forwarder gets a bill of lading from the carrier for the consolidated shipment.

To pull the above variations together, the most commonly used and most desirable bill of lading from a collection and a bank's perspective is a clean, on-board, order bill of lading.

OTHER EXPORT DOCUMENTS

In addition to the three key documents—the letter of credit, the draft, and the bill of lading—other documents must usually accompany the draft as stated in the letter of credit. For instance, the letter of credit in Exhibit 10-3, required a commercial invoice, a bill of lading, and a U.S. Customs invoice. Some other commonly required documents are as follows.

Commercial Invoice

A commercial invoice describes in detail the goods shipped, has information such as unit price, grades, quality, total price, and other price and shipping features. Other information includes name and address of both exporter and importer; payment terms including currency, time, and place; detailed itemization of other expenses collectible from importer (e.g., transportation). Some commonly used abbreviations that state price under different transportation situations are:

C. & F. (Cost and Freight). "C. & F. (named point of destination)," the seller quotes a price that includes the cost of transportation to the named point of destination.

C.I.F. (Cost, Insurance, Freight). "C.I.F. (named point of destination)," the seller quotes a price that includes the cost of the goods, marine insurance, and all transportation charges to the named point of destination.

Ex (Point of Origin). "Ex Factory," "Ex Mill," "Ex Mine," "Ex Plantation," "Ex Warehouse (named point of origin)." The price quoted applies only at the point of origin, and the seller agrees to place the goods at the disposal of the buyer at the agreed place on the date or within the period fixed.

Ex Dock (Named Point of Origin). Seller quotes a price that includes the cost of the goods and all additional costs necessary to place the goods on the dock at the named port of importation, duty paid, if any.

F.O.B. (Free on Board). "F.O.B. (named inland carrier at named inland point of departure)." The price quoted applies only at inland shipping point, and the seller arranges for loading of the good on, or in, railway cars, trucks, lighters, barges, aircraft, or other conveyance furnished for transportation.

F.A.S. (Free Along Side). "F.A.S. Vessel (named port of shipment)." The seller quotes a price that includes delivery of the goods alongside overseas vessel and within reach of its loading tackle.

F.O.B. Vessel (Named Port of Shipment). The seller quotes a price that covers all expenses up to and including delivery of the goods on the overseas vessel provided by, or for, the buyer at the named port of shipment.

F.O.B. (Named Inland Point in Country of Importation). The seller quotes a price that includes the cost of the merchandise and all costs of transportation to the named inland point in the country of importation.

Insurance Policy or Certificate

Almost all shipments in international trade are insured, and the insurance document must accompany the draft. Insurance is generally arranged by the exporter, but, in some cases, it may be arranged by the importer. In the latter case, there is usually a statutory requirement in the importer's country that coverage must be arranged locally to consolidate foreign exchange reserves. The requirement also promotes the growth of the local insurance industry.

Insurance policies are generally of two kinds: "specific," where individual shipments are covered, and "open," where all goods shipped during the policy period are covered. When an open policy coverage is in effect, a draft is accompanied by an insurance certificate, not the original master policy. The certificate is drawn up by the exporter on the insurance company's stationery. Each policy specifically details who and what are covered and for what kinds of losses. The policies contain information such as parties to the insurance contract, nature and value of goods, types of conveyances (ship, air, or mail), geographical area within which coverage extends, limit of liability.

Interestingly enough, the adventurous beginnings of ocean voyages that led to marine coverage (pioneered by Lloyds) are responsible for the quaint words below that are often used to describe insurance coverage.

To understand trade insurance, one must first distinguish the four basic types of losses:

1. Total loss: Loss of entire shipment because of fire or sea perils, or some other cause.
2. Total loss of part of shipment: When the shipment consists of distinct parts, units, or packages and when coverage is arranged so that the loss of any one or more is considered a total loss.
3. Particular average loss: A partial loss.
4. General average loss: When, to save the goods, it may be necessary to destroy part of the goods—e.g., in a fire, when water is used to douse the flames and some of the surrounding goods may suffer water damage. In cases like this, all interests, including those whose property was saved, may have a general average loss claim levied against them.

A policy frequently will include the term "free of," such as in "free of particular average," which signifies that the underwriter will not pay any particular damage claims. What the underwriter will reimburse when a loss occurs depends on the insurance clauses contracted and which of the above four categories of losses they fall under as provided in the policy. Some clauses are:

Perils. Basic risks such as sea damage, fire, forced jettison, theft, deliberate negligence, etc.

All Risks. Provides much greater coverage than basic perils clause; any physical loss due to an external cause is covered

Franchise. Has something akin to a "deductible" amount so that small claims are not allowed because of the high processing costs

Other. Explosion, warehouse and forwarding, Inchmaree (serious mechanical damage of vessel), rust, leakage, breakage, etc.

Consular Invoices and Other Export Documents

A *consular invoice* is a notation on the commercial invoice by the consul of the importing country or a special form from the consul that must be completed to obtain customs clearance and to provide local customs officials with information for assessing import duties. A *packing list* identifies precise content of each package and usually speeds customs clearance. An *inspection certificate* is a document made by an independent inspection company (maybe an importer's agent) at the loading port attesting to the quality and quantity of the goods, and a *certificate of origin* is used to comply with tariff treaties which give favorable treatment to goods of certain countries. In this document the exporter certifies the place of origin (manufacture) of the goods.

SOURCES OF IMPORT-EXPORT FINANCE

All trade must be financed either from the exporter's own working capital or from an external source. The external source is generally from one of the following five categories: direct financing of exporter by importer, indirect financing of exporter by importer, other commercial bank financing, government agencies, or private agencies.

Direct Financing of Exporter by Importer

Direct financing by importer generally takes one of two forms, either the importer pays the exporter in advance or the importer opens a "red clause" letter of credit. In the first case, the exporter receives cash in advance for the goods that will be shipped. In this transaction the exporter is basically receiving a loan, and the importer bears the risk that the exporter may not deliver the goods as promised. This risk is usually unacceptable to importers. If an importer opens a red clause letter of credit, the red clause allows an exporter to draw a designated amount of funds under the letter of credit even before presenting the documents required for payment under the L/C. The importer, in effect, makes an unsecured loan to the exporter. This type of L/C provides the exporter with working capital sufficient to perform as specified by the terms of the L/C. To draw in advance, the exporter must, with each drawing, promise to use the funds to fulfill the conditions of the L/C. Further, exporters must present the documents necessary for payment under the L/C prior to its expiration. A bank advancing the funds to the exporter (the paying bank) assumes limited risks because the red clause states that the opening bank will reimburse for any money advanced to the exporter. All other risks under red clause letters of credit are assumed by the importers and to some extent by their bank (the issuing bank), since it takes on the credit risk associated with the importers. When the exporter presents the draft and documents to the paying bank for the total amount of the letter of credit, the bank deducts the aggregate advanced on the issuing bank's behalf and its fees and pays the balance to the exporter.

Indirect Financing of Exporter by Importer

Indirect financing by importer usually takes one of four forms: assignment of a letter of credit, back-to-back letters of credit, bridge letters of credit, or transferable letters of credit.

Assignment of a Letter of Credit. Here a letter of credit is opened in favor of an exporter who uses this letter to support bank borrowings. In this type of financing, exporters assign their rights and interest in the letter of credit to a bank, i.e., they pledge that the cash proceeds of the letter of credit will be used to retire the outstanding loan.

Back-to-Back Letters of Credit. The exporter has a letter of credit opened in her or his favor by the importer's bank. Then the exporter's bank opens a letter of credit in favor of the supplier. Both letters of credit must have the same basic payment terms. However, to give flexibility, differences are allowed in the amount of letter of credit, invoice, unit prices, shipping date, and validity date. The exporter may add additional terms to the supplier letter of credit. When presented with the supplier's documents, the exporter's bank will pay the supplier because it then has the documents required to be paid under the letter of credit in favor of the exporter. If back-to-back letters of credit are to work, the terms on both letters of credit must match exactly in all other respects. Also, both letters of credit should be payable by the same bank.

Bridge Letter of Credit. When a back-to-back letter of credit cannot be structured because of documentary differences between the exporter's letter of credit and the supplier's letter of credit, a bridge letter of credit may be used. Here the exporter adds the necessary documents to the documentation provided under supplier's letter of credit (i.e., "bridges the gap"). The exporter then uses this new set of documents to collect payment under the letter of credit in his or her favor. The supplier credit in this transaction is open risk to the exporter and the exporter's bank.

Transferable Letter of Credit. In a transferable letter of credit, an importer indicates that the beneficiary (exporter) may transfer right to payment under the letter of credit to one or more other beneficiaries. In essence, this feature of transferability allows the exporter to induce the bank to open letters of credit in favor of the suppliers for the account. Now the exporter's bank can open letters of credit which are transferred in favor of the exporter's suppliers—based not on the exporter's creditworthiness but on the strength of the transferable letter of credit. The documentation required for payment under the suppliers' letters of credit must be virtually identical to the documentation required for the exporters to be paid under the letter of credit in their favor. The payment terms of the letters of credit in favor of the suppliers can differ from the letter of credit in favor of the exporter in only five specific ways: invoice, amount of letter of credit, quantity, latest date for shipment, and latest date for negotiation. This type of letter of credit is particularly useful to undercapitalized exporters who do not have the financial muscle to support a financing of suppliers.

Other Commercial Bank Financing

A significant portion of international trade is financed by unsecured credit lines. Companies that are creditworthy have little difficulty in obtaining such financing without having to pledge collateral. Unsecured short-term borrowings of this nature can be drawn down from a company's credit line or may be borrowed directly for working capital needs. In either case the borrowing does not have to be for a specific international transaction, although it may be used for this purpose.

For less creditworthy companies, secured financing is available, and collateral is required. Trading companies, even the respected ones, may be forced to obtain secured financing because their business requires considerable financial leveraging. Collateral may be in the form of money market securities, real estate, metals, inventory, etc.

Three other forms of commercial bank financing available for trade transactions are forfaiting, note purchases, and acceptance financing. "Forfaiting" denotes buying, without recourse, obligations—usually trade drafts or promissory notes—arising from international trade transactions. The original French term conveys the idea of surrendering rights, which is essentially the case. In a forfaiting transaction, the buyer of the obligations explicitly forgoes the legal right to claim on any previous owner of the debt such as the seller, by use of the term "without recourse" when endorsing. The seller of forfaitable trade drafts or promissory notes is usually an exporter who has taken the obligations in full or part payment for goods supplied and who wishes to pass on all risks and responsibility for collection of the debt to the forfaiting financier and receive immediate cash.

Promissory notes or bills of exchange accepted for forfaiting will almost always be accompanied by a bank security in the form of an "aval." An aval is essentially a bank guarantee to pay the holder the face amount of the trade draft at maturity. For all practical purposes, forfait paper could be likened to bankers acceptances here in the United States.

A U.S. bank's interest in purchasing this type of paper is somewhat limited because an aval is not recognized in U.S. law. Further, unlike the banker's acceptance market in the United States, forfait paper is traded across country borders. Therefore, in the event of nonpayment, the holder in due course of such obligation would have to process it through the courts of the country in which the paper originated. This, of course, could be time consuming and expensive.

A note purchase is a form of financing where a bank purchases the receivables of an exporter and advances payment at the time of such purchase. For example, if an exporter were to sell to a foreign buyer with repayment to occur over a period of six years with twelve semiannual payments, the exporter would then, in turn, discount these notes with a bank and receive payment immediately rather than wait until the maturity of each note.

The financing of a note purchase can be on either a recourse or a nonrecourse basis. In general, the notes are sold on a nonrecourse basis because exporters want immediate cash and also want to relieve themselves of any foreign, political, or economic risks inherent in holding these notes until maturity. The notes are purchased on a recourse basis when the bank is unwilling to accept the risk of the obligor of the notes or has insufficient available credit allocated to the buyer or the buyer's country. Note purchase financing is sometimes used to allow the seller to quote "cosmetic" interest rates on the notes. Some countries or buyers, as a matter of prestige, refuse to pay market rates on the credit extended to them. In this case, the exporter includes in the "cash" price the regular profit and an additional markup to provide for discounting the notes at a higher rate with the bank. In this way, the exporter is able to quote a financing charge of, say, 9 percent, to the borrower when the appropriate rate might be higher at 12 percent.

Acceptance financing is an extremely versatile means of financing trade. It may be used by the importer or exporter. For the exporter, acceptance financing proves particularly valuable as a means of financing the buildup in short-term assets required to fulfill an export order. The exporter can also use it to provide the importer with flexible payment terms while receiving payment immediately on presentation of documents. An importer may cleverly create an acceptance that delays actual payment even though the exporter may receive payment on a cash-against-documents basis. (These methods of financing are elaborated further below.)

To recall from the section on drafts, a banker's acceptance is created when a time draft is drawn on and accepted by a bank. By accepting the draft, the bank commits to pay the face value at maturity. In this way, the bank interposes its credit between the money markets and its customer, the importer, and provides the importer with low, fixed rate financing. Banks prefer this type of financing because they can fund the advances made under banker's acceptances through the money market. Furthermore, banks book no loans—the obligation to pay is treated as a liability for accounting purposes. All earnings on banker's acceptances are tallied as fee income. Depending on competitive market conditions, banker's acceptances usually carry a commission of between 1 to 1½ percent per annum. Two practical examples illustrating the use of acceptance financing follow.

Preexport Acceptance Financing for the Exporter. This method is used by an exporter to secure fixed rate financing to build up the inventory required to fulfill an order. The exporter secures a commitment from a bank to provide acceptance financing on a preexport basis. (Exporters must necessarily be creditworthy because the bank has, in substance, made a short-term loan to them.) The exporter then executes a banker's acceptance contract and agrees to repay the full amount of the draft to the bank one day prior to the maturity date. Next, the exporter draws a draft on the bank who accepts it. The bank then advances the funds to the exporter—face value of draft less commission and discount charges. The bank can now sell (and usually does) the acceptance in the money markets and receives face value less discount charges. The bank has also collected its commission. One day prior to maturity, the exporter will deposit with the bank the full value of the draft. In fact, the exporter may have, by now, completed the export transaction and received payment from the importer. The following day, the bank pays off the bearer of the acceptance. The transaction has gone full cycle.

Acceptance Financing for the Importer When the Exporter Requires Immediate Payment. If an importer's desired payment terms are not offered by the exporter, the importer may resort to banker's acceptances. Hence the importer would request the bank to create an acceptance for the importer's account when the exporter has presented all documents required for payment. Assume that the importer's bank opened a letter of credit in favor of the exporter who wants payment "on sight." When the exporter presents the sight draft and supporting documents for payment, the importer's bank pays the exporter the face value of the draft. The exporter is out of the transaction at this point. The importer's bank would now create an acceptance for the same amount for the maturity date desired by the importer and sell the acceptance in the market and charge the account of the importer for the discount charges and the bank's commission. On maturity the importer's bank would pay the bearer of the banker's acceptance the face amount of the draft and debit the importer for a like amount. At this point, the transaction is completed.

A *trade acceptance* is created when an exporter sells a product to an importer without a letter of credit. The procedure is very similar to that under a letter of credit except that the bank's credit and backing is not interposed. When sales are made on a collection basis, the exporter presents documents to the importer's bank accompanied by a draft drawn on the importer. This may be a sight or a time draft. For a sight draft, the paying bank would inform the importer that the documents have been received and the draft is payable. When the importer pays the draft amount to the bank, the bank will release the documents to the importer and, in turn, will pay the exporter.

In the case of a time draft, the exporter presents documents to the paying bank along with a draft indicating the maturity date. Once again, the bank advises the importer of the receipt of the documents and the time draft. The importer would then stamp "accepted" across the draft, indicate where the payment will be made at maturity, and have an authorized official sign the draft. A trade acceptance has been created. There is no bank intermediary in this transaction. The credit risk of the exporter lies solely with the promise of the importer to pay when due. After the importer's acceptance, the draft is returned to the paying bank in exchange for the title documents. At the maturity of the draft, it is expected that the importer will pay the exporter the face amount of the draft.

Based on the strength of the importer who has accepted a trade draft, a bank may be willing to purchase the draft from the exporter and advance funds equal to its discounted value. Drafts may be purchased on a recourse or a nonrecourse basis. When the bank purchases on a nonrecourse basis, it has, in effect, granted a short-term unsecured loan to the importer. There-fore, the bank must be confident that the importer is an acceptable credit risk and that there are no credit limit constraints regarding the borrower (importer) or the borrower's country. When the bank purchases a trade acceptance on a nonrecourse basis, it ends the role of the exporter in the transaction. A bank may finance trade acceptances on a recourse basis when it is fully extended in the country or if the drawee represents an unaccept-able credit risk. Here, the bank would discount the trade acceptance on behalf of the exporter and advance the discounted amount. However, if later the draft is not honored, the bank will look to the exporter for payment. It is obvious that recourse financing is not favored by exporters because the foreign collection risk remains lodged with them.

Government Agencies

To promote worldwide trade, many countries offer subsidies to assist ex-porters. These may take the form of concessionary terms on loans or of insurance against various losses and credit risk. In recent years a credit war of sorts has developed, each country increasing its subsidies and menu of concessionary loans to encourage its exports. The salient features of some government agencies that assist exporters or importers are outlined below within a general operating framework. It should be noted that specific rates and provisions change frequently, and current information should be ob-tained directly from the agency.

    I. Export-Import Bank (EXIMBANK—U.S.)
      A. Description: A financially self-sustaining independent U.S. gov-ernment agency set up to promote the export of U.S. goods and services through a variety of financing programs. It is authorized to provide loans, guarantees, and insurance on deferred credit terms and basically supplements private financing sources.
      B. Eligible participants and markets
        1. U.S. exporters, commercial banks, overseas importers, and for-eign banks.
        2. All countries except where the United States has severe politi-cal or commercial disagreement.
      C. Principal benefits
        1. Covers all political risks.
        2. Reinsures certain excess commercial risks.
        3. Offers financing at rates and terms which are competitive with foreign official export credit agencies. Eximbank selectively matches the competition through such initiatives as an increase in the percentage of direct loan coverage, a reduction in interest rates, and the occasional extension of repayment terms.

D. Financing programs
  1. General conditions
    a. Must be used exclusively to support the export of goods and services of U.S. origins.
    b. Eximbank assistance must be arranged before the shipment of goods, performance of services, or the signing of commercial contracts.
    c. Repayment may be in foreign currencies under long- and medium-term guarantee programs.
    d. The exported items will not be defense products, except, in certain cases, to developed countries.
    e. Transactions should offer "reasonable assurance of repayment" and should not adversely affect the U.S. economy.
    f. A minimum down payment is required of the purchaser of 15 percent of the total U.S. export value. The down payment may be financed.
    g. When Eximbank participates as a direct lender, all U.S. goods must be shipped on vessels of U.S. registry, except when the U.S. Maritime Administration has granted a waiver.
  2. Direct loans financing and financial guarantees
    a. Under this program, long-term financing (over five years) is available. Borrowers are overseas importers. Large purchases of U.S. goods or projects are involved. In many cases, commercial banks finance the required 15 percent down payment.
    b. Loans are generally granted in U.S. dollars, although in some cases foreign currency loans are available. Financial guarantees coverage includes loans made in foreign currencies and in Eurocurrencies.
  3. Discount loans
    a. Under this facility, medium-term financing (generally up to five years) is available. Duration normally exceeds one year and repayment is in U.S. dollars. Borrowers are U.S. financial institutions.
    b. The program offers fixed rate funding to a bank at 1 percent less than the bank's rate to its customer. The funding covers 100 percent of the bank's loan. Bank cannot lend to importer at a rate greater than 1 percent over the federal discount rate, fixed at the time of authorization. There is a limit of $10 million on aggregate discount loan commitments per foreign buyer per year.
  4. Guarantees
    a. Nonrecourse medium-term financing (181 days to 5 years, but generally 1 to 5 years). Guaranteed parties may be U.S. or

non-U.S. financial institutions. Buyer may be public or private.

b. Guarantee covers commercial and political risk; commercial banks and exporters are required to retain a share of commercial risk (10 percent for exporter, 5 or 15 percent for bank). Applicant bank retains 15 percent of the fee if its participation is 5 percent and retains 25 percent if its participation is 15 percent. The guarantee fee ranges from 0.5 to 1 percent per annum, and the commitment fee for the period between its agreement to guarantee and the time the guarantee is effective is ⅛ percent per annum.

c. Bank-to-bank line of credit guarantees available. Eximbank guarantees U.S. commercial banks' revolving line of credit to foreign bank. Commercial bank retains 10 percent of the commercial risk and Eximbank retains 100 percent political risk. Repayment guidelines are:

Contract value	Terms
Up to $50,000	181 days to 2 years
$50,001 to $100,000	Up to 3 years
$100,001 to $200,000	Up to 4 years
Over $200,000	Up to 5 years

Payment is generally in semiannual installments.

5. Cooperative financing facility (CFF)

a. CFF is a medium-term direct credit program that operates in developing countries only; its primary function is to assist small foreign buyers importing from small U.S. suppliers.

b. CFF shares export financing of U.S. products and services with foreign banks; arranges U.S. dollar lines of credit with foreign banks, which, in turn, finance their customers' purchases from U.S. suppliers; and lends 50 percent of the import loan extended by the local bank. Foreign banks provide the remaining 50 percent financing. Loans from U.S. banks may be guaranteed by Eximbank.

c. Financing cost to overseas buyer is a blended interest rate: fixed rate on Eximbank funds and floating rate on foreign bank funds. Eximbank's commitment fee is ½ of 1 percent per annum on the undisbursed balance of each loan.

d. Under the CFF, the foreign bank assumes all commercial risk.

II. Overseas Private Investment Corporation (OPIC—United States)

A. Description: OPIC is wholly owned by the U.S. Treasury. It insures U.S. private investments against political risks of inconvertibility and expropriation in less developed countries and finances the investigation and development of projects of U.S. investors in those countries. It also covers losses from war, revolution, insurrection, etc. Recipient companies must be a U.S. corporation (with at least 50 percent ownership by U.S. citizens) or a foreign corporation with at least 95 percent ownership by a U.S. citizen or U.S. corporation (as defined).

B. Principle benefits

1. Proceeds of financing may be used for capital goods and services in the United States or in the less developed countries. There are almost no product restrictions.
2. OPIC is willing to commit to a substantial portion of the debt and to accept longer and more flexible maturities than other agencies. Financing is at fixed rates of interest.
3. Insurance coverage is available for conventional and some less conventional investments.
4. There is no maximum or minimum limit on loans.

C. Insurance programs

1. General conditions
    a. Investments must be made by a U.S. citizen or company and must be for a duration of at least three years.
    b. Project must assist host country's development.
    c. Host government approval of the specific project must be secured.
    d. Maximum term of OPIC insurance is twenty years. Insurance for loans may be written for the term of the loan. Minimum term is six months. OPIC insurance policies generally cover 90 percent of all political risks; the remaining 10 percent must be covered by the contractor (another institutional lender is not permitted).
    e. Premium rates vary with riskiness of the project. In general, for each six-month period, a rate of ¼ percent is applied to the amount insured during that period and a rate of ⅛ percent to any additional policy amount reserved for future coverage.
    f. OPIC issues binders committing it to issue, at a later date, insurance policies covering specific guarantees. A $1000 binder fee is refunded when the policy is issued. If the contractor does not receive the contract award, OPIC will refund $750 of the binder fee.
    g. Contractors may obtain coverage only if, prior to their bid, they register with OPIC and state their intention to bid for a contract. A registration fee of $50 is charged for investments below $100,000 and $100 for those above.
    h. Legislation prohibits the assisting of "runaway" projects, i.e., those that reduce significantly domestic employment.
    i. OPIC activities are limited to countries with a per capita gross income exceeding $1000 in 1975 dollars.

2. Specific coverages

  a. Investment insurance: Three types of political risk are covered: inconvertibility of profits, or repatriation of original investment; loss of investment due to expropriation or confiscation by foreign government; and damage to property resulting from war, revolution, or insurrection.

  b. Investment guarantees: OPIC provides coverage against all risks including business risks. Compensation in cases of business failure and liquidation is limited to 50 percent of loss.

  c. Contractor's bid, performance, and advance payment guarantees

    (1) Contractor retains full commercial risk of a drawing.

    (2) OPIC indemnifies the contractor for losses resulting from a foreign government owner's "arbitrary" drawing of a letter of credit or on demand bond (guaranty) issued as a bid, performance, or advance payment guaranty. For bid guarantees, a drawing is deemed arbitrary if it is not justified by the terms of the tender or by agreements entered into by the contractor. For advance payment or performance guarantees, a drawing is deemed arbitrary if the disputes resolution changes the underlying contract.

  d. Investigation and development of projects: OPIC offers potential investors general information on developing countries. Preinvestment assistance may be given in the form of partial financial support for feasibility studies. It assists U.S. firms in finding, planning, and developing potential investment projects.

  e. Loans: Loans are made by OPIC directly to a new or expanded foreign enterprise on a medium- to long-term basis. The loans are usually without guaranty from the sponsoring investor company and are for interest rates about 2 percentage points above prevailing U.S. Treasury borrowing rates for comparable maturities.

D. Pricing

  1. Insurance: OPIC premiums for manufacturing/services projects are:

	Current insured amount (%)	Standby amount (%)
Inconvertibility	0.30	0.25
Expropriation	0.60	0.25
War, revolution, etc.	0.60	0.25

The "Current insured amount" represents the insurance actually in force during any contract year. The difference between the current insured amount and the maximum insured amount for each coverage is known as the "standby amount."

   2. Loans

      a. Interest rates vary with OPIC's assessment of the financial and political risks involved. Interest rates depend on changes in long-term capital market rates.

      b. OPIC charges the borrower a guaranty fee which ranges from 1.75 percent to 2.5 percent per annum on the outstanding principal.

III. Export Development Corporation of Canada (EDC): The EDC is a commercially self-sustaining enterprise owned by the Canadian government and set up to provide export financing assistance for Canadian exports. Its programs include: a) fixed rate long-term financing, b) short-term credit insurance for political or commercial risk, c) financial guarantees, d) performance and bid bonds, e) foreign currency insurance, and f) government-to-government lines of credit. Eligible borrowers are Canadian entities operating outside Canada and all non-Canadian entities, public or private. In January 1981, Canada announced a special low-rate financing facility to be used over a three-year period. Known as *"credit mixte"* financing, it is a combination of conventional and concessionary export loans. It will be available only in cases where competitor nations offer similar packages.

IV. EXIMBANK of Japan: This organization is a department of the government of Japan established to supplement commercial banks in financing exports, imports, and overseas investments. Its programs include: fixed rate financing for credits exceeding two years, project lines of credit extended to government and private firms, credit insurance for commercial or political risk, local cost financing, exchange risk insurance, aid financing, and performance bond guarantees. Eligible borrowers are Japanese entities operating outside Japan and all non-Japanese entities, public or private.

V. Export insurance division of the Ministry for International Trade and Investment (Japan): This agency of the Japanese government offers export insurance coverage. Its programs include coverage for: general export, export proceeds, export bill, exchange risk, and export bonds (bid and performance).

VI. Sezione per L'Assicurazione del Credito allo Esportazione (SACE) (Italy): SACE is an Italian government agency which provides insurance and guarantees for medium- and long-term financing; it also provides reinsurance coverage for short-term transactions. Its programs include: reinsurance to commercial banks, political and commercial risk cover for medium- and long-term financing, performance bond guarantees, and inflation and exchange risk insurance.

VII. Instituto per il Credito a Medio Termine (Mediocredito Centrale) (Italy): This is an Italian government institution whose purpose is the refinancing of loans granted by commercial banks and financial institutions on behalf of Italian exporters; it specializes in refinancing or discounting of medium- and long-term export credits.

VIII. Export Credits Guarantee Department (ECGD) (United Kingdom): The ECGD is a department of the U.K. government created to provide adequate financial support to stimulate U.K. exports. Unlike COFACE and Hermes (see page 10-33) or EDC whose repayment must be made in local currency, ECGD accepts all hard currencies. Its programs include: comprehensive short-term guarantees, medium- and long-term buyer and supplier credit and financial guarantees, inflation risk insurance, exchange risk insurance, refinancing and interest rate subsidy for medium- and long-term credit, direct funding when all other options for long-term credits are exhausted, lines of credit, and short-term loan insurance. Eligible borrowers are British entities operating outside the United Kingdom and all non-British entities, public or private.

Private Agencies

Like government agencies, many private associations exist in several countries, and their stated objective is export promotion. Many of these organizations work closely with government agencies in their home countries and offer similar facilities. Therefore, the line dividing private and government entities is often unclear. Brief descriptions of the agencies and their services follow.

I. Foreign Credit Insurance Association (FCIA) (United States): The FCIA is an association of some of the nation's leading marine, property, and casualty insurance and reinsurance companies. It insures U.S. exporters and financial institutions against the risk of nonpayment by foreign buyers for commercial and political reasons. FCIA works in coordination with the Eximbank of the U.S. FCIA operates under a competitive disadvantage in that comparable foreign institutions generally offer both a wider range of guarantees (such as foreign exchange risk coverage) and subsidize interest rates.

    A. Principal benefits

        1. Protection typically against the riskiest portion of a company's asset portfolio foreign receivables; also protects against overseas events beyond the U.S. seller's control—commercial or political risk.

        2. The program encourages the exporter to offer competitive terms of payment to foreign buyers and provides flexibility for the exporter to match foreign competitors who may be subsidized or have other backing.

        3. The program provides the exporter with greater financial liquidity and flexibility in administering foreign receivables portfolio and permits discounting of receivables.

B. Specific coverages

1. Bank policy

   a. FCIA offers bank insurance protection against potential default of a foreign receivable and provides 90 percent commercial coverage and 100 percent political coverage. No deductibles are mandated for either form of coverage, and 15 percent down payment is required.

   b. Short- and medium-term repayment periods are available.

   c. Rate schedule varies on a case-by-case basis.

2. Medium-term policy

   a. Insurance on export sales of capital goods.

   b. Offers 100 percent political risk coverage. In addition, comprehensive coverage is offered which covers 90 percent of commercial and 100 percent of political risk; 15 percent down payment required.

   c. Coverage offered for periods between 181 days and 5 years, depending on the contract price and repayment terms.

   d. Insurance fees based on whether a buyer is a public or private entity and the tenor of the transaction.

3. Combination policy

   a. Policy provides inventory and receivables financing. Policy can be designed to cover short- and medium-term periods.

   b. Political and commercial coverage available; 15 percent down payment required.

4. Master policy: Offers blanket insurance covering all short- and medium-term exports. Commercial coverage of 90 percent is provided, and the first loss is deductible. Political coverage offered is 100 percent with no deductible; 15 percent down payment required on medium-term portion only.

II. Private Export Funding Corporation (PEFCO) (United States): PEFCO is a private corporation owned by fifty-four commercial banks, seven industrial corporations, and one investment banking firm. It lends to public and private borrowers located outside the United States who require medium- and long-term financing for the purchase of U.S. goods and services such as aircrafts, power plants, and other big ticket items. PEFCO competes with foreign export credit organizations and is frequently at a disadvantage because foreign organizations appear to receive greater government support and can offer lower interest rates. There is no maximum limit on loans, although a minimum of $1 million exists. PEFCO does not make loans for the purchase of military equipment nor does it lend in countries with which the United States has trade restrictions. Usually a commercial bank submits a PEFCO application, although occasionally an exporter may approach PEFCO directly.

A. Principal benefits: PEFCO will offer maturities which are unattractive to commercial banks. Although Eximbank is usually willing to finance the later maturities and commercial banks the earlier ones, PEFCO tends to pick up the intermediate maturities. The loans are quoted on a fixed rate basis, but floating rates are possible. In agreements where commercial banks and PEFCO are co-lenders, PEFCO is the junior creditor.

B. General conditions

    1. Original maturities of loans usually extend to fifteen years. However, there is no upper limit.

    2. PEFCO normally participates in loans in which a commercial bank and Eximbank are co-lenders. Eximbank is a full guarantor of all PEFCO loans, principal, and interest. Therefore, Eximbank's guarantee must be obtained before all lending.

    3. Prepayment by the borrower of outstanding loans is prohibited except with approval from PEFCO.

    4. Most of PEFCO's loans are at fixed rates of interest. PEFCO lending rates are based on its estimated cost of money plus a nominal spread for profit and administrative cost and a factor reflecting the exposure to interest rate fluctuations over the period of the loan. A commitment fee of 0.5 percent per annum commencing from the borrower's acceptance date is also levied.

    5. All repayments must be in U.S. dollars.

    6. A minimum down payment by the purchasers of 15 percent of the total U.S. export value is required.

III. Compagnie Française d'Assurance pour le Commerce Exterieur (COFACE) (France): COFACE is a publically owned organization established to issue, on its behalf or on behalf of the government, guarantees to support French exports. Programs include: exchange rate fluctuation; inflation risk; contractor's guarantees, performance, and bid bonds; short-term credit insurance against commercial or political risk; local cost exchange rate fluctuation; and medium- or long-term loan guarantees at fixed rates. Eligible borrowers are French entities operating outside France and all non-French entities, public or private.

IV. Hermes/AKA (Germany): This is also a public stock company set up to act as an agent of the West German government for issuing guarantees to support West Germany's exports. Its programs include: short-term credit insurance for political or commercial risk, exchange risk insurance, performance and bid bond insurance, and local cost or preshipment coverage. Eligible borrowers are German entities operating outside Germany and all non-German entities, public or private.

Appendix 10A:
Common Abbreviations
and Terms
Used by Foreign Firms

Abbreviations	Foreign	English Equivalents
	Abogado (Spanish)	Lawyer
A/B	*Aktiebolaget* (Swedish)	Joint stock company
A. en P.	*Asociación en Participación* (Spanish)	Association in participation
A.G. (Akt. Ges.)	*Aktiengesellschaft* (German)	Joint stock company
A/S	*Aktieselskabet* (Danish)	Joint stock company
A/S	*Aktieselskapet* (Norwegian)	Joint stock company
Br.	*Bröderna* (Swedish)	Brothers
Br.	*Brödrene* (Danish, Norwegian)	Brothers
	Bussan (Japanese)	Products
Ca.	*Compagnia* (Italian)	Company
Cia.	*Companhia* (Portuguese)	Company
Cia.	*Compañia* (Spanish)	Company
Cie.	*Compagnie* (French)	Company
Com.	*Comanditario* (Spanish)	Partner (silent)
Com.	*Comisionista* (Spanish)	Commission merchant
C. por A.	*Compañia por Acciones* (Spanish)	Stock company
	de (French, Spanish)	of
	di (Italian)	of
	do (Portuguese)	of
	e (Spanish, Portuguese)	and
	Ehemals (German)	Formerly
	et (French)	and
	Contador (Spanish)	Accountant
Etabs.	*Etablissements* (French)	Establishments
Eftf.	*Efterfölger* (Norwegian)	Successor
Eftr.	*Efterträdare* (Swedish)	Successor
	Fréres (French)	Brothers

	Figlio, Figli (Italian)	Son, sons
	Filho (Portuguese)	Son
	Fils (French)	Son, sons
F-lli.	*Fratelli* (Italian)	Brothers
F-llo.	*Fratello* (Italian)	Brother
	Gerente (Spanish)	Manager
Ges.	*Gesellschaft* (German)	Company
G.m.b.H.	*Gesellschaft mit beschränkter Haftung* (German)	Limited liability company
G.K.	*Gomei Kaisha* (Japanese)	Unlimited partnership
Gebr.	*Gebrüder* (German)	Brothers
Hers.	*Héritiers* (French)	Heirs
H/B	*Handelsbolaget* (Swedish)	Trading company
H.mij.	*Handelmaatschappij* (Dutch)	Trading company
Handelsges.	*Handelsgesellschaft* (German)	Trading company
H.ver.	*Handelsvereeniging* (Dutch)	Commercial association
Handels A/B	*Handelsaktiebolaget* (Swedish)	Commercial corporation
Hno.	*Hermano* (Spanish)	Brother
Hnos.	*Hermanos* (Spanish)	Brothers
Hers.	*Herdeiros* (Portuguese)	Heirs
Hereds.	*Herederos* (Spanish)	Heirs
Hnos. en Liq.	*Hermanos en Liquidación* (Spanish)	Brothers in liquidation
	Hijos (Spanish)	Sons
Inh.	*Inhaber* (German)	Proprietor
Ing.	*Ingenieur* (German)	Engineer
	Irmaos (Portuguese)	Brothers
	Jefe (Spanish)	Head of department
K.G.	*Kommanditgesellschaft* (German)	Limited silent partnership
K.B.	*Kommanditbolaget* (Swedish)	Limited silent partnership
K.S.	*Kommanditselskabet* (Danish)	Limited silent partnership
K.K.	*Kabushiki Kaisha* (Japanese)	Joint stock company
K.G.K.	*Kabushiki Goshi Kaisha* (Japanese)	Joint stock limited partnership
K.	*Kaisha* (Japanese)	Company
K.	*Kompaniet* (Danish)	Company
	Kokeisha (Japanese)	Successors

	Kyodai (Japanese)	Brothers
Ltd.	(English)	Limited
Ltda.	*Limitada* (Spanish)	Limited
Lda.	*Limitada* (Portuguese)	Limited
	Musuko (Japanese)	Sons
Mij.	*Maatschappij* (Dutch)	Company
	Maison (French)	House (or store)
Nachf.	*Nachfolger* (German)	Successor
N/V	*Naamlooze Vennootschap* (Dutch)	Stock company
	og (Norwegian)	and
O/Y	*Osakeyhtio* (Finnish)	Stock company
Pty.	(English)	Proprietary
Pty. Ltd.	(English)	Proprietary limited
Prop.	(English)	Proprietor (owner)
S.A. (Soc. Anon.)	*Sociedad Anónima* (Spanish)	Corporation
S.A.	*Sociedade Anonima* (Portuguese)	Corporation
S.A.	*Societa Anonima* (Italian)	Corporation
S.A.	*Société Anonyme* (French)	Corporation
S.Acc.	*Società Accomandita* (Italian)	Limited partnership
S.A. de C.V.	*Sociedad Anónima de Capital Variable* (Spanish)	Stock company of variable capital
S.A.R.L.	*Société à Responsabilité Limité* (French)	Limited liability company
S. de R.L.	*Sociedad de Responsabilidad Limitada* (Spanish)	Partnership of limited liability
S. en C.	*Sociedad en Comandita* (Spanish)	Limited silent partnership
S. en C.	*Sociedade en Commandita* (Portuguese)	Limited silent partnership
S. en C.	*Société en Commandite* (French)	Limited silent partnership
S. en C. por A.	*Sociedad en Comandita por Acciones* (Spanish)	Limited partnership by shares
S. en N.C.	*Sociedad en Nombre Colectivo* (Spanish)	Collective partnership
S. en N.C.	*Société en Nom Colectif* (French)	Joint stock company
S. en P. de R.L.	*Sociedad en Participación de Responsabilidad Limitada* (Spanish)	Firm in participation with limited liability
	Shoyuken (Japanese)	Proprietorship

S.p.A.	*Società per Azioni* (Italian)	Stock company
S. por A.	*Sociedad por Acciones* (Spanish)	Stock company
Soc.	*Sociedad* (Spanish)	Partnership or company
Soc.	*Sociedade* (Portuguese)	Partnership or company
Soc.	*Société* (French)	Partnership or company
Sn.	*Sohn* (German)	Son
Sucs.	*Sucesores* (Spanish)	Successors
Sucs.	*Sucessores* (Portuguese)	Successors
Succs.	*Successeurs* (French)	Successors
Suc.	*Sucursal* (Spanish)	Branch
Test. de	*Testamentaria de* (Spanish)	Estate of
Ver.	*Vereeniging* (Dutch)	Association
Vda.	*Viuda* (Spanish)	Widow
V/h	*Vorheen* (Dutch)	Formerly
Vva.	*Viuva* (Portuguese)	Widow
Vve.	*Veuve* (French)	Widow
Wwe.	*Witwe* (German)	Widow
	y (Spanish)	and
Zn.	*Zoon* (Dutch)	Son
Znen.	*Zoonen* (Dutch)	Sons

Appendix 10B: Common International Trade Abbreviations

A.A.R.	Against all risks
A/P	Authority to purchase or authority to pay
B/E	Bill of exchange
B.M.	Board measure
C.A.D.	Cash against documents
C. & D.	Collection and delivery
C. & F.	Cost and freight
C.F. & I.	Cost, freight, and insurance
C.I.F.	Cost, insurance, freight
C.I.F. & C.	Cost, insurance, freight, and commission (or charges)
C.I.F. & E.	Cost, insurance, freight, and exchange
C.I.F. & I.	Cost, insurance, freight, commission (or charges), and interest
C. & I.	Cost and insurance
cwt	Hundredweight
D/A	Documents against acceptance
D/D	Days after date
D.F.	Dead freight
D.N.	Debit note
D/P	Documents against payment
D/S	Days after sight
D/TR	Documents against trust receipt
E. & O.E.	Errors and omissions expected
E.O.M.	End of month
F.A.F.	Fly away field
F.A.Q.	Free at quay
F.A.S.	Free alongside
F.C. & S.	Free from capture and seizure
F.I.	Free in (all expenses for loading into the hold of the vessel are for the account of the consignee)
F.O.B.	Free on board
F.O.	Free out (all expenses covering unloading from the hold of the vessel are for the account of the consignee)
F.O.R.	Free on rails
F.P.A.	Free of particular average

F.P.A.A.C.	Free of particular average American conditions
F.P.A.E.C.	Free of particular average English conditions
G.A.	General average
G.T.	Gross ton
Inc.	Incorporated
Kd	Knocked down
L/C	Letter of credit
M.E.C.	Marine extension clause
m.n.	*moneda nacional* (Spanish); any local currency
M/R	Mate's receipt
M/V	Motor vessel
N.O.E.	Not otherwise enumerated
n.s.f.	not sufficient funds
O/A	Open account
O.C.P.	Overland common points
O.R.L.	Owner's risk of leakage
P/N	Promissory note
R.R.	Railroad
S/D	Sight draft
S/D-B/L	Sight draft, bill of lading attached
S/D-D/P	Sight draft, documents against payment
S.L. & C.	Shipper's load and count
S.R. & C.C.	Strikes, riots, and civil commotion
S.S.	Steamship
T/A	Trade acceptance
T.T.	Telegraphic transfer
W.A.	With average
W.R.	War risk
W/R	Warehouse receipt

REFERENCES

Business International Corporation: "Financing Foreign Operations," updated on an ongoing basis, Business International Publications, New York.

Chemical Bank: "Financing Imports & Exports. A Guide for the Use of World Wide Banking Services on International Trade," New York, 1980.

———: "International Services for the Middle Market," Worldwide Trade Services and Finance Group, New York, August 1981.

Eitman, David K. and Arthur I. Stonehill: *Multinational Business Enterprise*, 2d ed., Addison-Wesley, Reading, Mass., 1979.

Euromoney Publications: *Trade Financing*, coordinated by Charles J. Gmür, Euromoney Publications Limited, London, 1981.

Schneider, Gerhard W.: *Export-Import Financing: A Practical Guide*, Ronald, New York, 1974.
Stigum, Marcia: *The Money Market: Myth, Reality, and Practice*, Dow Jones-Irwin, Homewood, Ill., 1978.
———: *Money Market Calculations: Yields, Break-Evens, and Arbitrage*, Dow Jones-Irwin, Homewood, Ill., 1981.

Eleven: Financing Foreign Investments— The International Capital Markets

GEORGE T. CASSIDY

George T. Cassidy is treasurer of the international operations group for the St. Regis Corporation. He has extensive experience with such companies in international finance as Esso International Inc. and American Standard Inc. He earned a B.A. degree from St. John's University and attended the Graduate School of Business Administration at New York University.

T he decision by a multinational company to make an investment in new foreign operations or to expand existing foreign operations requires a "sourcing of funds" program for the investment project. The proper funding decision, because of several considerations which affect it, may be significantly more difficult than the comparable decision in domestic operations.

The *choice of an investment vehicle* is the first question when a company funds an international investment. Allocation of investment capital involves the following alternatives.

- Equity contributions from the investor, in exchange for shares of common or other classes of stock of the new foreign company
- Intercompany loans from the investor to complement the equity contribution
- Third-party borrowings from the public, banks, other financial institutions, and/or government agencies to complete the investment financing package

How investment capital is allocated may significantly affect the liquidity and profitability of the overseas unit and, therefore, its value to the investor. Funding of the project will influence such critical factors as the remittability of profits from the project and the cumulative tax rate on these profits (in the host country of the investment and the home country of the investor).

For either of the alternatives involving investor funding (equity or intercompany debt), the company must also consider and recommend whether to finance them from the parent company or from a sister company within the group.

It is highly probable that third-party borrowings in various markets will provide at least partial funding for any overseas investment project. When selecting the optimum borrowing market (domestic or offshore) and borrowing instrument for project purposes, the company must consider such diverse factors as:

- Desired term and currency of the borrowing, after considering the timing, currency and amount of projected income flows from the new overseas project, the acceptable payback and cash return to the investor, and so on
- Financial market conditions in the host country, including the depth and sophistication of these markets in light of the project's funding requirements
- Local restrictions and exchange controls applicable to the project's host country, including withholding taxes on dividends and interest, restrictions on the amounts and repayment terms of any external financing, requirements for registration of investment capital, and repatriation restrictions on equity capital and earnings attributable to it
- Assessed political and currency risk for the overseas investment project, affecting the investors' attitude toward granting of guarantees to third-party creditors and acceptance of foreign exchange risks from cross-currency financing arrangements
- Relative borrowing costs for available alternatives, involving an analysis of trade-offs between the relative interest rates for various alternatives and the possible effects of foreign exchange *P/(L) Exposure* (exposure to reportable profit [or loss] arising from exchange rate fluctuations in the case of foreign currency debt)—primarily a function of the investors' tolerance for risk in the foreign exchange area

THE INTERNATIONAL FINANCE COMMITTEE

There is as much need for an integrated, team approach to a financing decision for an overseas investment project as there is for any major decision affecting allocation of investors' funds. Many of the aforementioned factors affecting an international sourcing-of-funds decision have important tax, legal, accounting, as well as financial implications. For these reasons, an international financing decision requires the involvement of general (as well as international) management in the areas of treasury, taxation, law, and accounting. Representatives from each of these functions should be involved to ensure that all pertinent aspects of the proposed financing have been thoroughly and properly reviewed.

The *international finance committee* (IFC) represents a convenient and positive method to ensure the necessary team approach to major international financing decisions. The goal of the IFC should be development of a consensus among the general and international management experts regarding proper handling of international finances.

Such a committee might be permanently composed of the corporate controller and treasurer and their counterparts, as applicable, from international operations; the corporate tax manager; and a designated representative from the corporate legal department. Each of these individuals could designate members of their staffs to attend meetings of the IFC and to assist with IFC business.

The IFC should work across departmental and functional lines. This provides it with the means not only to expedite proper international financing decisions but also to carry out special projects in international finance and tax areas (reviews of exposure management, dividend policy, and so forth) by designation of ad hoc members and subcommittees for these purposes.

Once established, the IFC should meet at regularly specified periods to review the overall status of international financial arrangements. The IFC would direct its attention particularly to projected major developments (large overseas capital investments, acquisitions, and divestments) to incorporate all aspects of these into a coordinated accounting, tax, legal, and financial "picture."

EQUITY INVESTMENT

The traditional and most common means of providing funds for a new overseas investment project is an equity investment in common or other classes of stock of an overseas company. Every newly established foreign company will require a certain amount of equity to satisfy both authorities in the host country and outside creditors concerning its solvency.

Occasionally a company will decide to provide expansion funds to an existing operation by way of an equity investment. Such a recapitalization would provide the expanded operation with an increased capital base for financing its projected larger operations.

Equity investments are generally subordinated to the claims of all creditors in the event of liquidation, and thus an equity investment is simultaneously *least flexible for the investor* and *most acceptable to the host country authorities and potential outside creditors.*

Considerations of Dividend Taxation

Dividends, which are the profit remittances derived from equity investments, generally are relatively heavily taxed when compared with investments derived from other funding alternatives. In general, dividends from most countries to foreign shareholders are subject both to local income taxes and to withholding taxes. The latter are for the account of the foreign shareholder and are incurred when local earnings are distributed abroad, as dividends.

The problems of the heavy tax burden on dividend distributions have been somewhat mitigated by "unitary" tax code arrangements among various economic blocs and a much broader network of tax treaties, reducing withholding taxes on payments to foreign shareholders. Despite these measures, the cumulative tax burden on dividend distributions is generally much higher than on other types of international profit transfers such as interest and royalty payments.

Finally, equity investments frequently are subject to local stamp taxes and duties on capital importation into the host country. This category of expense is peculiar to equity, since no such taxes or duties are presently charged in connection with either intercompany or third-party loans.

Special Considerations for U.S. Parent Companies

The situation regarding dividend taxation is even more complex for multinational groups based in the United States because of the complex U.S. Tax Code provisions affecting the "foreign source income" which U.S. parent companies receive from their overseas investments. In most cases, the combined local income and withholding taxes on dividends paid to a U.S. parent company will exceed the ordinary, incremental U.S. tax rate on these dividends. Under these conditions, income and withholding taxes paid in respect of project income distributed to the U.S. investor will not be fully creditable against the investors' U.S. income taxes on a current basis. This results in (1) an effective tax rate that exceeds the U.S. rate, since the foreign taxes paid will not be completely relieved by offsetting credits against U.S. income taxes, and (2) an accumulation of excess foreign tax credits, which have to be applied against U.S. taxes within five years or their status will be reduced to that of deductions, thus effectively halving their value to the investor.

Strategic Sourcing of Equity Investments

Financial and tax savings can be effected through strategic sourcing of equity investments. For example, sourcing equity from a sister company, rather than directly from the parent, may be advantageous under certain circumstances. If the network of tax treaties is advantageous between the country in which the sister company is located, the parent company's home country, and the host country in which the proposed investment project will be established, the cumulative tax burden for repatriation of funds to the parent company (using the sister company as an intermediary) can be reduced by reduction or elimination of withholding taxes. If excess overseas cash can be reinvested in operations without the tax consequences which would result from repatriation to the parent company, sourcing equity from a sister company is a good strategy. For instance, the excess cash of subsidiary A of the group could be used to make an equity investment in subsidiary B, rather than being distributed as a tax-creating dividend to the parent company.

Foreign Exchange Exposure Considerations

An equity contribution effectively converts the capital of the investor from its own currency into the currency of the overseas investment project. This conversion can sometimes be used to some advantage, if an equity contribution is sourced between sister companies of the same multinational group.

Thus, if an overseas unit of a multinational group has excess available cash or relatively low-cost borrowing capacity, it can be used to fund the operations of a sister company. At the same time the group's net asset position is increased in the operating currency of the unit receiving the investment, since the investment is used either to purchase assets or retire existing liabilities, and the net liability position of the group in the operating currency of the investing unit is increased, since its own resources have been converted into foreign currency assets via the equity contribution.

This mechanism for shifting exchange exposures can be used for managing foreign exchange profit and loss to minimize their effects on corporate profits. Such investments also can be used to create net asset or liability positions in overseas units in expectation of currency value changes. For instance, a liquid overseas unit doing business in a currency which is expected to drop in value might be advised to make investments in a cash-poor sister company which is doing business in a stronger currency.

INTERCOMPANY LOANS

Instead of investing equity, a multinational company may elect to provide investment funds to its overseas operations by way of intercompany loans. The intercompany loan provides a specified repayment period for the funds invested (loan principal) and produces interest income which is taxed relatively lightly. This compares favorably with an open-ended equity commitment, which produces profits in the form of heavily taxed dividends. Thus, from the investor's point of view, an intercompany loan has certain inherent advantages over an equity investment as a vehicle for funding of overseas investment projects.

Improved Repatriation Flexibility for the Investor

In general, investments structured as intercompany loans are more readily repatriated than equity investments. To repatriate an equity investment, a formal decrease of share capital by the investor is generally required. This measure is likely to hamper good relations with host country authorities, outside creditors, and other shareholders (if any) in the foreign operation. Also, immediate repatriation of capital may be prevented, in the case of a capital decrease, by exchange control regulations in the host country. However, funds invested in the form of loan principal generally can be repatriated easily and conveniently, according to a specified repayment schedule in the intercompany loan agreement.

Tax Advantages for Profit Remittances

Profit remittances resulting from an intercompany loan investment are characterized as interest rather than dividends, and interest remittances are exempt from local income taxes. These payments to foreign creditors attract only a local withholding tax for the creditor's account. Thus interest is usually more lightly taxed than dividends when it is repatriated to the investor, provided that the rate charged is in line with going money market rates for similar advances (an "arm's-length" transaction).

If the intercompany loan is transacted under terms and conditions which artificially favor one of the parties (i.e., on other than an arm's-length basis), the loan may be designated as a disguised equity contribution by tax authorities. As a practical matter, this transaction will generally be thus designated by the authorities of the country in which the disadvantaged party, debtor or creditor, is located.

Designation of the loan transaction as a disguised equity contribution will cause the interest payments to be taxed as dividends by either or both of the countries involved. In this case, the tax advantage of an intercompany loan versus equity will be lost; thus *all* terms and conditions of an intercompany loan agreement (interest rate, term of repayment) should be executed on strictly an arm's-length basis.

Special Considerations for U.S. Parent Companies

When properly executed, investment via an intercompany loan may provide certain tax planning advantages for companies based in the United States. These derive from the reduced tax burden on interest payments to the investor as opposed to the relatively heavy tax on dividends.

The lightly taxed foreign source income represented by foreign interest receipts does not bring substantial foreign tax credits with it, since these credits are generally associated with dividend payments. Thus, increasing the proportion of interest income in total foreign source income will generally reduce foreign tax credits to a currently usable amount. This correspondingly reduces the overall effective tax burden on U.S. taxable income.

Disadvantages of Intercompany Loan Arrangements

The principal disadvantage of an intercompany loan as an investment vehicle is the apparent lack of security which it provides for other parties with an interest in the investment. The investor has the ability to repatriate the investment represented by the principal amount of the loan according to a specified repayment schedule which is unrelated to the profitability or solvency of the local operation. The flexibility thus provided to the investor is a source of concern to other potential creditors and, frequently, to authorities in the investment project's host country. Obviously, these parties would prefer the stability and commitment to the investment project which would be represented by an equity investment.

The intercompany loan investor can provide the required security for other parties of interest by executing *subordination agreements* with regard to the intercompany loan arrangements. Under the terms of such agreements, the investors commit to retain loan capital in the overseas debtor company as long as it is required to preserve that company's liquidity and/or solvency. According to these agreements, requirements for subordination would usually be triggered by failure of the overseas debtor to meet certain specified minimums in terms of income, cash flow, working capital, etc.

Execution of such subordination agreements by the investor only formalizes recognition of the choice to use intercompany debt as a substitute for equity. This surrogate equity is employed to gain the benefits of improved repatriation flexibility and reduced tax costs. In practice, all capital provided by the investor in an overseas operation, whether as equity or debt, is effectively subordinated to those funds which have been advanced by third-party creditors.

Sourcing of Intercompany Loans

Additional financial benefits may be achieved from an intercompany loan transaction by arranging for a lateral loan between sister companies instead of a direct "downstream" loan from the parent company to the overseas operation.

Lateral loans can be valuable tools for managing foreign exchange exposure in a multinational group of companies as well as for shifting funds between overseas units without creation of any immediate tax consequences. In general, the relevant considerations and benefits which the investor can achieve in these areas are similar to those outlined in connection with lateral equity investments within a multinational group.

Although the economic effects of equity and intercompany loan investments are identical with regard to foreign exchange exposure, the results of these two types of transactions may have to be reported differently, depending on the relevant accounting standards in the parent company's country. The "book," or accounting, implications of the equity and debt alternatives should be determined before deciding which to use for investment purposes.

Factors Affecting the Intercompany Lending Decision

A number of significant factors have to be considered before a company decides to use an intercompany loan as a vehicle for financing overseas investment. After the decision is made, several additional points must be considered in developing the sourcing of an intercompany loan transaction within a multinational group, whether the loan is lateral from a sister company or a direct downstream loan granted from the parent.

The *aftertax effect of the transaction* should be more favorable than the effect which could be achieved through an equivalent equity investment in the overseas project. This calculation should include both the local aftertax income of the overseas project and the aftertax return to the investor on profit distributions (interest for the loan versus dividends for the equity investment).

The loan should be structured to *optimize the effects of foreign exchange fluctuations* in the case of a multinational group of companies. That the economic effects of an intercompany loan are essentially the same as those of an equity contribution has already been noted. Both increase net assets, or decrease liabilities, in the project's local currency and have the opposite effect on the group's position in the investment currency. However, the investor always bears the exchange risk in the case of an equity contribution. The intercompany loan as a vehicle for investment offers a significant advantage in this area: an option as to which of the parties to the loan should bear the exchange risk.

In general, the tax laws of the investor's and borrower's host countries will determine how the exchange risk is to be allocated. The exchange risk will be borne by the party to the loan which is likely to receive more favorable tax treatment for the resultant foreign exchange profit or loss. If it is desired that the investor (parent or a sister company) should bear the exchange risk for the loan, it has to be denominated in the local currency of the overseas borrowing company; if the borrower is to bear the foreign exchange risk, then the loan must be denominated in the currency of the investor company.

Therefore, the most favorable *situs* for the foreign exchange risk should be evaluated and the currency of the intercompany loan denominated accordingly. At a minimum, realized foreign exchange losses from debt service should be admissible as tax deductions in the host country of the unit which bears the exchange risk.

THIRD-PARTY BORROWINGS

Virtually all overseas investment projects rely for funding to some extent on capital from someone other than their shareholders to support their operations. Investors in overseas operations realize that certain advantages derive from use of funds provided by way of loans from local and/or foreign banks, governments, other institutions, or the public. These third-party borrowings supplement the investors' own equity and debt capital inputs to these operations.

Leverage from Third-Party Borrowings

Even after adjustment for currency and political risks, an overseas investment project is likely to yield a relatively high return on funds employed in the business. As a practical matter, most investors will not commit funds to such projects unless the adjusted rate of return is superior to that experienced in their domestic business.

Under these circumstances, it should be possible to improve the return on investors' funds in a high-yielding overseas project by "leveraging" the overseas operation so that third-party loans have an interest rate which is lower than the project's actual return on investment (ROI). The concept of leverage can be demonstrated as follows:

	Own Funds		Leveraged	
	$000	ROI(%)	$000	ROI(%)
Total project investment	4000	20	4000	20
Outside debt at 15%			2000	15
Investors' funds	4000	20	2000	25

When dealing with the concept of leverage in overseas operations, however, the leveraged rate of return on investors' funds can be materially affected (sometimes drastically) by exchange rate developments. Political or economic circumstances that produce local currency exchange rates for the project which are materially different from those included in the original studies and forecasts will correspondingly affect returns on a leveraged investment. Thus any decision or recommendation to funds overseas operations with foreign currency borrowings from third parties should be accompanied by a "break even" analysis. This analysis indicates the amount of currency adjustment which can be absorbed before the leverage becomes negative versus other funding options.

Partnership with Financial Institutions

Having a large multinational bank as a "partner" in an overseas investment project can be a source of some comfort for an investor. If a large bank commits funds to such a project, authorities in the host country will be less likely to exercise economic discrimination against it.

Economic discrimination in the project's host country, if it is applied, could include exchange controls, restricted access to local credit markets, or outright expropriation of the investor from the local unit. These actions represent a real threat for foreign direct investors, particularly in developing economies. However, the presence of a world class bank as a project creditor could inhibit such actions. The host country government will not be anxious to inflict economic losses on such a bank through any actions taken against the local project. The success of the government's own future financings in international markets are likely to depend on the bank's cooperation, and therefore project borrowings from a major money market bank can provide a form of insurance to the investor, in addition to any leverage benefits.

Drawbacks of Thin Capitalization

Investors should avoid overreliance on outside financing for an overseas project, even if the apparent economic results of this course of action appear favorable. The drawbacks of such a strategy (sometimes known as "thin capitalization" or an "equity drop") can more than outweigh the leverage and insurance benefits. Overreliance on outside financing for an overseas investment project may produce a situation in which the *parent company guarantees will be required for all financings* for the project. Such guarantees effectively substitute the credit of the parent company for that of the local project; such a substitution obviates many of the advantages of outside financing.

For instance, if the local loans are guaranteed, neither the host country authorities nor a creditor bank will be as concerned about the effects of interfering with, or expropriating, the operations of the local investment project, since the parent company will still be obliged to repay any outstanding loans. These circumstances greatly reduce the insurance benefits to be derived from outside financing.

Thin capitalization is also likely to produce circumstances in which the project's results are hamstrung by debt service. All cash flow generated from local operations will have to be applied to principal and interest repayments to outside creditors. Under these conditions, no capital will be available either for reinvestment in local operations or for profit repatriations to the investor. In an extreme case, if the length of start-up or the projected profits from the project have been seriously misjudged, a real liquidity crisis may result for the local unit.

Investors in an overseas project should provide adequate project capital to avoid these undesirable side effects. The investors' capital input should be sufficient to allow for both a reasonable annual return (by way of dividends and interest) and for reinvestment of funds in the local project. The latter is required to maintain existing facilities and, occasionally, to take advantage of new and interesting opportunities for expansion.

Guidelines for Adequate Capitalization

To avoid the drawbacks inherent in thin capitalization of overseas projects, consider the following guidelines (actually, rules of thumb) when developing capitalization strategies.

- The investor's own resources should be sufficient to approximately cover the project investment in fixed assets. Outside financing should support investment in net working capital of the unit.
- The ratio of outside financing to total capitalization of the project (commonly called the "debt : equity ratio") should generally be about 0.50. Thus approximately equal amounts of outside debt and investment capital will be employed in the local project.
- The forecast earnings from the overseas project should provide adequate "interest coverage" for its intended outside debt service. To ensure continuing liquidity, these earnings should be a substantial multiple of the project's annual financial costs.

Some special circumstances would be required for an overseas project to conform exactly with all these guidelines. The indicated ratios are therefore only suggestions of proper capitalization practice with regard to overseas operations. If an overseas investment project is capitalized in general accordance with these guidelines, the local project should be able to raise outside financing on its own recognizance. An adequately capitalized overseas unit should borrow without recourse to the investors for guarantees of repayment or other security.

Timing of Debt Maturities

The repayment schedule for any outside financing will have to be structured after consideration of the project's forecast cash flow. Coordination of debt service and cash flow should minimize costly unplanned refinancings that result when the resources of the local subsidiary are not sufficient to meet scheduled debt repayments.

In general, for new projects, a sufficient allowance should be made for the project's start-up operating problems and for entry into local markets before any principal repayments are required. Thereafter, the repayment schedule for outside debt should be at a level that permits a regular cash return to investors over and above outside debt service. Adequate allowance must be made for reinvestment of locally generated cash flow in the business for maintenance and expansion of operations.

Companies have a number of outside financial options from which to choose to fund an overseas investment project, including banks, government institutions, other types of financial intermediaries, and even the public sector in the host country (via bond or share capital issues). Within several of these categories, a further choice exists between external ("Euro") financing markets and similar domestic financing arrangements in the project's host country.

FINANCING IN DOMESTIC MARKETS

The depth and sophistication of financial markets available to overseas direct investors in various host countries varies tremendously. The range of available domestic options will be a significant factor in determining the choice of markets (external or domestic) for financing an investment project.

Bank Term Financing

The most widely available vehicle for funding of an investment project is generally a term loan financing arrangement, denominated in local currency, with one or more local commercial banks. The banks chosen for these financings are often indigenous to the host country. At the investor's option and/or depending on the extent of locally available banking services, such loans may also be available from the local branches or affiliates of the investor's major multinational banks.

The local bank which grants such term financing will probably expect to receive security in the form of a mortgage over the assets of the local project. The amount of the mortgage is usually sufficient to cover the principal amount of the loan plus one period's accrued interest payment. This mortgage security is in lieu of repayment guarantees or other security from the investors, permitting the local project to borrow on the strength of its own balance sheet.

Although the investor can expect to find bank term financing available in most prospective host countries, a significant exception to this rule is in hyperinflationary host country economies. Where actual and expected inflation is rampant, the rapidly declining real value of the local currency makes extension of long-term credit an unattractive proposition for the banks. Bank financing in such hyperinflationary economies is generally limited to medium-term credits (three years, at most). Interest rates on the credits are pegged sufficiently high to obtain a real return on the loan, even after adjustment for the expected inflation during its life.

Under these circumstances, investors are often inclined to search elsewhere for economically more attractive sources of outside financing.

Local Development Banks

Development banks or other government agencies in the host country may be able to offer attractive, subsidized financing for investment projects. Development bank financing is usually made available for investments in specific regions in which the host country government wants to stimulate economic development and employment. Among the various types of financial incentives available to qualifying investors are:

- Term loans, in local or various foreign currencies, at subsidized interest rates—in inflationary economies, this may be one of the few sources of otherwise hard-to-find local currency financing
- Temporary tax holidays on all or part of profits earned by the local unit—these are usually tied to perceived foreign exchange benefits to the host country in terms of export sales, reduced imports, etc.
- Outright grants for substantial amounts of the required project capital investment

The economic analysis for any proposed overseas investment project should include availability of government grants or subsidized financing from host country authorities. Once the decision has been made to proceed with the project, any available incentives and subsidies should be fully utilized. These incentives produce a favorable leverage situation by reducing the financing costs for the project, thereby increasing the investors' return.

Public Debt and Share Issues

The option to raise project capital by issuing securities to the public in the host country, in the form of debt or equity, is not available to the investor in every situation; the existence of a local stock and bond exchange is a prerequisite for public issues. This assumes some degree of development in local financial markets and the existence of a local group with funds to invest; neither condition applies to a number of developing economies.

Whenever it is a viable option, public cooperation and investment should be explored as a vehicle for raising capital for overseas operations. To tap these markets, the services of local investment, or merchant, banks and/or stockbrokers will be required. Suitable candidates can be located either through contact with the investors' local counsel or by recommendation from the major multinational banks in the parent group's home country.

In the case of public debt securities, the interest rates and maturities offered for public bonds or debentures are often significantly better than those available from other sources of local currency financing.

Broad-based public ownership of a local operation can be achieved via an issue of equity securities listed on the local stock exchange. Such public ownership is a plus for the local operation in the eyes of host country authorities. Issuance of local equity implies a continuing interest in the economic welfare of the country and its citizens. In exchange for significant local equity participation, the local company is often exempted from various economic and financial discrimination measures enacted against foreign-owned companies. In the case of a broad-based public equity issue which is distributed among a large number of local shareholders, the benefits of local ownership can often be achieved without much sacrifice of actual working control of the organization.

Private Placements

Local currency debt and local equity can be secured through private, as well as public, placements. An overseas investment project is sometimes undertaken with the cooperation of a specific local investor (e.g., as a joint venture with local interests). If this is not the case, then the services of local investment, or merchant, banks will generally be required for private placements in local markets. Private placements can be accomplished more quickly than public issues. The documentary requirements and statutory waiting periods which sometimes apply to public issues can be largely avoided via the private placement route.

Virtually all the advantages which apply to local public issues (possibility of attractive terms and conditions, good local public relations, occasional exemption from legislation affecting foreign-controlled companies) are equally applicable to private placements. However, in the case of equity issues, concentration of shares in relatively few hands may affect the investor's working control over the operation.

FINANCING IN INTERNATIONAL ("EURO") MARKETS

The Eurocurrency market represents a tremendous pool of international liquidity on which an investor may draw for operational financing. Funds are made available in U.S. and Canadian dollars, sterling, most continental European currencies and, lately, Japanese yen.

Eurocurrencies (essentially liquid assets denominated in one of the aforementioned national currencies and held by someone who is not a resident of that country) had a modest start in the 1950s as a vehicle for the financing of international trade. The dramatic growth of the market is largely traceable to the following:

- The U.S. "Foreign Direct Investment Regulations" 1968–1972 program, which, at the height of U.S.-based multinational companies' expansion abroad, required these multinationals to finance overseas activities with foreign borrowings
- The end of the Bretton Woods and Smithsonian fixed rate systems for foreign exchange, at the end of 1971—by creating short-term profit opportunities in foreign exchange markets, the new floating rate system greatly increased both the turnover of currencies and the amount of these currencies held by nonnationals
- The 1973 and 1977 OPEC crises, which, by placing a large amount of the world's currency reserves in the hands of a relatively small group of investors, provided them with resources for investment which far exceeded opportunities in their local markets

The U.S. dollar is the dominant factor in Euromarkets. However, significant volumes of financing are done on a continuing basis in sterling, deutschemarks, Swiss francs, and, occasionally, in other Eurocurrencies.

Bank Financing in Euro Markets

Multinational commercial banks offer various credit facilities for term loans and revolving credits through the Eurocurrency markets. Corporate borrowers can avail themselves of these financing opportunities directly or (as tax and financial considerations dictate) through the intermediary of an *offshore finance subsidiary* (OFS). The availability of Eurocurrency financing and OFS as a financing vehicle will occasionally provide borrowers with increased flexibility and savings in financial cost when compared with more traditional local borrowing alternatives.

In general, the *Eurocurrency term loan* is available in any of the principal Eurocurrencies, for approximately the same terms as would be available in domestic markets for these currencies. However, because of the absence of any monetary policy or other artificial constraints on Euromarkets, there may be significant differences in interest rates between Euromarket and inland facilities, the terms and conditions of which are otherwise similar.

Fixed rate loans are more common in domestic than in Euromarkets. In the latter, interest rates are frequently expressed in terms of a specified spread over the London interbank offering rate (LIBOR). LIBOR-based rates are periodically adjusted (every six to twelve months would be a representative adjustment period) to reflect developments in financial markets.

Thus the interest rates on many long-term Eurocurrency loans are tied to short-term (six to twelve months or even less) LIBOR developments. There is an obvious potential exposure inherent in such floating rates; however, flexible arrangements for the prepayment or refunding of Eurocurrency term loans can usually be negotiated to protect against these.

It may be possible to achieve substantial savings in financial costs versus long-term fixed rate financing. This would be the case in a stable economic environment in which normal yield curves for short- versus long-term rates were prevailing.

The *multicurrency revolving credit* is a popular vehicle for short- and medium-term financing of international operations. Typically, under the terms of such a revolving credit arrangement, a borrower may draw up to a specified amount of dollars or another Eurocurrency (the basic currency) or its equivalent in other Eurocurrencies for a period of from three to five years. Interest periods for the various advances drawn under the revolving credit may vary from one to twelve months. The individual advances may be repaid, "rolled over," or refinanced in another currency at the end of each interest period, at the borrower's option. A commitment fee is charged by the commercial bank which manages the revolving credit for any undrawn amounts under the facility.

A typical pattern of advances for a multinational company having a $10 million multicurrency revolving credit available for its use might be as follows:

Loan	U.S. $ Equivalent	Interest Rate	Purpose
$3 million	$ 3 million	11⅝%	General corporate borrowing
Swiss Fr10 million	4 million	4⅛%	To balance Swiss franc assets (exposure management)
Fr. Fr 7 million	1 million	18½%	Equity investment in new French company ("bridge" financing)
	2 million	½%	Commitment fee on undrawn balances.
	$10 million		

Multicurrency facilities are particularly useful for exposure management borrowings (to offset asset positions in foreign currencies when devaluation is anticipated) or to provide bridge financing for international investment projects. In the latter case, the revolving credit may be used to supply funds for the investment until an economically suitable source of long-term financing can be located.

Use of Offshore Finance Subsidiaries

Corporate borrowers in Eurocurrency markets frequently elect to use a "captive" OFS as a financial intermediary for these loans. The OFS, which is incorporated in a "tax haven" jurisdiction such as the Netherlands Antilles, is the direct creditor for Eurocurrency borrowings. It only lends funds raised in the Euromarkets to the parent company or to other international subsidiaries and affiliates of the group.

The OFS is a vehicle created for financial and tax purposes, with relatively little tangible asset base or independent commercial purpose. Therefore, the repayment guarantee of the corporate parent company is almost always required for borrowings by an OFS.

For U.S. corporations, use of an OFS for Euromarket borrowings effectively eliminates the 30 percent U.S. withholding tax on interest paid abroad as a negative factor for prospective creditors. This feature provides broader access to funds for U.S. groups, since there are no double taxation treaties (which reduce or eliminate interest withholding tax and/or make it creditable against local taxes) in force with such important potential sources of capital as the OPEC countries.

The interest income of a U.S. corporation's captive OFS, after allocated deduction of interest and certain corporate expenses, is deemed to be "subpart F" income for U.S. tax purposes. It is therefore taxed in the United States on an "undistributed" basis (that is, regardless of whether it is paid to the United States as a dividend). This subpart F feature of OFS income can be helpful in U.S. tax planning; it tends to increase foreign source income and, therefore, the ability to absorb foreign tax credits from other sources.

In general, the benefits of withholding tax elimination and subpart F income creation should be evaluated for any Eurocurrency borrowing to determine the potential value of an OFS, as a financial intermediary, to the corporate borrower.

Regional Development Bank Financing

Numerous regional (supranational) development banks have been organized to stimulate investment and trade within various blocs and regions. These institutions raise capital in Euromarkets and lend the funds to corporate investors at preferential terms and conditions. Regional development bank financing is analogous to domestic investment incentive financing and is particularly applicable to arrangements for project financing.

The identities and areas of interest of such regional development banks, as well as the range of available incentives, should be reviewed and determined in the course of arranging financing for any new overseas investment project.

Eurobond Issues

Corporate borrowers in offshore markets have the option to float public Eurobond issues as an alternative to commercial bank term loans or revolving credits. The necessary preliminary procedures and paperwork are similar to, but not so extensive as, those required for a domestic bond issue in, say, the U.S. market.

A Eurobond issue can be prepared and marketed in a relatively short time. This feature occasionally allows corporate borrowers to take advantage of temporary "windows" in the rate structure, i.e., floating bond issues under relatively favorable terms and conditions versus those available in their domestic market. The issues are underwritten by merchant/investment banks or the offshore branches of commercial banks. Because placement of the bonds is quite broadly gauged, including investors domiciled in countries without withholding tax relief via treaties, the OFS alternative is a particularly attractive financing vehicle for Eurobond issues by a U.S. borrower.

The dollar sector has historically predominated in the Eurobond market, but loans are generally also available in such principal Eurocurrencies as sterling, deutschemarks, and Swiss francs. Occasional opportunities in such secondary currencies as French francs and Canadian dollars may prove attractive to borrowers who are based in, or have extensive operations in, those currencies.

Eurobonds have occasionally been denominated, since the 1970s, in various "currency cocktail" or "market basket" currency units. The European unit of account (EUA), European currency unit (ECU) and special drawing right (SDR) are examples of these special units. They are intended to minimize, or hedge, foreign exchange risks associated with single-currency borrowings. In spite of an apparent advantage in this area, the cocktail currency units have never gained wide acceptance with Euromarket borrowers.

Private Placements

Merchant banks and offshore branches of commercial banks can arrange Euromarket private placements under about the same terms and conditions as those described in connection with the Eurobond market. The advantage of private placements lies in flexibility and speed, since the necessary loan documentation can be drafted in days or, even, hours for substantial credit arrangements. To tap important sources of loan capital which would otherwise be closed because of withholding tax limitations, private placements by U.S. borrowers are generally structured through an OFS.

CHOICE OF MARKETS—DOMESTIC OR OFFSHORE

The conventional wisdom regarding the choice of currency for borrowing is that it should be the same denomination as the currency of the revenues which will be created and the assets which will be held by the investment project to be financed, thus minimizing problems of transaction exposure to foreign exchange losses. These would otherwise arise when the projects revenues were applied to servicing of debt denominated in another currency.

Similarly, identity of currency between assets and liabilities associated with an investment project will forestall most potential translation losses. Losses of this type would otherwise arise when converting local currency project assets and foreign currency debt into the common reporting currency of the investment group.

Predominance of Domestic Markets

Under the preceding guidelines, virtually all investment financings would be undertaken in the local currency of the host country. This, except for a few currencies which have achieved status to be regularly traded in Euromarkets, would in turn indicate use of the domestic financial markets to provide investment capital. In practice, there are several potentially significant drawbacks to the use of domestic financial markets which will have a bearing on the investor's decision regarding project funding:

- The local currency *amounts and maturities required* for the project may not be available through local financial intermediaries. This is particularly true for attractively high-yielding projects which are located in host countries with undeveloped or immature financial markets.
- *Local currency will not be generated* by the investment project, which implies that a large part of the asset base will be denominated in other than local currencies. Examples of such operations would be export-intensive manufacturing plants and regional trading companies.
- The *investor expects profits from foreign exchange* as well as the expected trading and manufacturing profits to be derived from the investment project. Investors must completely understand the potential consequences of cross-currency financing which might result from a decision to use foreign currency financing as a source of potential income. These consequences have to be assessed in the context of the investors' financial appetite for risk, which may vary widely between investors.

In practice, domestic financing markets do predominate for funding of local investment projects where an adequate local currency lending base exists to provide funds in the amount and for the term required.

Conditions Affecting Use of Offshore Borrowing Markets

If the selected currency for financing is one of the regularly traded Eurocurrencies, then offshore markets may be preferable to domestic for any number of reasons (better rate, term, speed, and flexibility of financial arrangements, etc.). However, in the majority of cases, investors use the Euromarket because their needs (for multicurrency lines to support exports or trading activities, for large amounts of loan capital, or for extended repayment terms) cannot be satisfied in the host country's domestic markets.

The investor who has decided to finance an overseas project in the Euromarkets probably will encounter lending and pricing practices that are different from domestic financial alternatives. Among the more significant of these are the following.

- *Parent company guarantees* or other undertakings by the investors (e.g., "take or pay" contracts to purchase the production output from the project) are much more likely to be required by lenders in Euromarkets than by their domestic counterparts. Traditional mortgage-type security is not acceptable to creditors in offshore markets, given their strong liquidity preference.
- *Borrowings in hard currencies* such as deutschemarks and Swiss francs can produce significant savings for the investor in terms of interest costs. The historic strength of these currencies means that creditors are often willing to extend the terms of repayment, since there is no significant probability of thereby suffering significant economic losses.

Both advantages and disadvantages are inherent in both these conditions from the viewpoint of an investor in an overseas project. Issuance of guarantees or other undertakings to secure Euroloans means that the project's assets are unencumbered and can be pledged to raise capital in local markets; however, default under the Euroloan agreement will result in mandatory recapitalization of the local project by the investor. This will be the case even if the default is caused by force majeure (exchange controls, nationalization, or expropriation of the project by authorities in the host country).

The apparent savings in cash flow and financial costs which can be achieved through hard currency borrowings in Euromarkets can be offset, or converted into losses, by adverse exchange rate developments. The currency borrowed is likely to revalue (increase in value) during the life of the loan. If the project's cash generation is not denominated in the same currency, substantial exchange losses can result. These will often be large enough to eliminate the advantages of rate and term which were achieved by borrowing the hard currency in the first place.

COPING WITH CURRENCY CONTROLS

Exchange controls are increasingly becoming a fact of international business life. They are imposed by the governments of various host countries for two principal purposes:

1. Outright economic nationalism, that is, the elimination of the perceived risk that one or more groups of investors will "strip" local investment projects by excessive repatriations of profits, too-high leverage, premature repatriations of equity and loan capital, etc. Such irresponsible actions by investors, if implemented, would destroy the employment, export and earnings benefits of the project to the local economy.
2. Preservation of foreign exchange by the host country government. If the government's reserves of foreign currencies needed to pay for its energy and other essential purchases are not sufficient to cover all outflows, then returns of profit and capital to private investors will be assigned a subordinated position in the queue for authorized foreign exchange transactions.

The effects of exchange controls on the private investor are the same regardless of which motive caused the host country government to install them. Although such controls commonly are justified, in principle, on nationalistic grounds, they are, in fact, more commonly needed as preservers of slender foreign exchange reserves. In either case, the investor in foreign projects may expect to encounter controls imposed in one or more of the following forms.

Profit Repatriation Restrictions

Limitations are frequently placed on how much dividends investors may repatriate in a year, or within some other specified period. Such limitations are usually expressed as a percentage of the investor's equity capital in the investment project. For instance, the host country government may specify that no more than a 12 percent annual dividend on equity capital is payable to foreign investors, regardless of the actual profitability of the investment project.

Actual terms and conditions of such restrictions vary significantly from time to time and country to country. However, many such controls make allowances for increasing the capital base with earnings reinvested in the local business. Thus, if an investor capitalized a local project with $1 million, with allowable repatriation of 12 percent, the first year's dividend would be limited to $120,000. If excess profits of $500,000 from the first year were reinvested in the business, the next year's dividend limitation would be raised to $180,000 [12 percent × ($1,000,000 + $500,000)].

In other cases, initial equity investments and subsequent reinvestments are creditable for repatriation rights in dollars or some other internationally traded currency. This protects the investor from erosion of repatriation rights by devaluations of the project's local currency. Under these guidelines, the investor would always be allowed to repatriate enough local currency to yield 12 percent of the dollar (or other international currency) value of the investment, regardless of the current exchange rate.

Restrictions on Repatriation of Equity Capital

To protect its economic infrastructure or to preserve foreign exchange reserves, host country authorities will frequently place restrictions on repatriation of capital investment by a foreigner. This would apply whether the repatriation of the investment resulted from a decrease in the project's equity capital by the original investor or from sale of the investment by foreigners to local interests. In either case, annual repatriation rights will be limited to a percentage of the recognized capital investment. If, for instance, annual repatriation rights were 10 percent of capital, a foreign investor would be required to wait up to ten years to recover the entire investment proceeds.

During the waiting period, the "blocked" proceeds of divestment or capital decrease usually must be held in the form of relatively unattractive host country government securities. Since these are almost always denominated in the host country's local currency, there is a considerable exchange risk involved for the investor in holding these securities. In most cases, this is not coverable by either insurance or currency futures contracts.

These restrictions on repatriation of equity capital are not generally applicable to a transfer of investment ownership between foreign investors. In most such cases, transfer of ownership and the exchange of consideration therefore are accomplished outside the host country boundaries and thus are not subject to its national restrictions. Since such an ownership transfer is an indifferent transaction for host country authorities, they may be expected to recognize it for purposes of reregistration of shareholdings, contracts, etc. in the name of the new owner.

Foreign Exchange "Licenses" or Central Bank Authorizations

In the absence of formal restrictions on repatriations of profit or capital, some of the same effects can be achieved by requiring local companies to obtain licenses, or other authorities from the host country's central bank, to engage in some (or all) foreign exchange transactions. Transactions which might require authorizations for the purchase or sale of foreign exchange include taking up, or repaying, a loan denominated in foreign currency; payment of a dividend to foreign shareholders; foreign currency collections for exports from the host country; or foreign currency payments for imports from an overseas supplier.

Requirements for conversion of foreign currency receipts by the local project (export collections, loans, capital contributions) are normally accelerated under this procedure. The project may be allowed to hold these receipts in the form of foreign currency for only a short time, or not at all. However, the bureaucratic lag experienced in applying for a license to make payments abroad will provide a de facto slowdown in the outflow of the host country's foreign exchange reserves.

Restrictions on Rate and Term of Loan Capital

Restrictions on loans are analogous to profitability and capital repatriation restrictions imposed on equity investment. However, since the need for a continuing flow of debt capital from abroad is recognized as a requirement for national maintenance, restrictions on such transactions are generally much less stringent and comprehensive than are those affecting equity investors.

Profitability may be affected by interest rate "ceiling" limitations placed on borrowing in the private sector. This will curtail or eliminate access of these units to international credit markets, which function on a strictly market rate basis.

Repatriation rights for loan capital may be affected by host country requirements for an abnormally long repayment schedule for any foreign loans taken up by local operations. Once again, such restrictions will curtail the amount of international loan capital imported into the host country.

Registration of Equity and Loan Capital

The host country government may require that all new investments of equity and loan capital be registered with their central bank or other regulatory authorities. Registration of these investments does not usually assure investors and/or creditors that their capital will be freely repatriable at their option. However, failure to register will certainly result in blocking the capital from repatriation.

In most cases where profit restrictions are applied for repatriation of dividends and/or interest, only the registered capital base is allowable for calculation of repatriation rights.

Relative Flexibility of Investment Vehicles

Equity capital is the investment vehicle that is most severely affected by the various host country exchange controls involving registration of investments and subsequent repatriability of profits and capital. The equity investor, by the very nature of the investment, is expected to provide a permanent foundation of capital on which all other creditors and suppliers can build their relationships with the investment project. This inherent lack of flexibility is mirrored in the stringency of the regulations which are imposed locally to ensure retention of a reasonable equity capital base in the overseas investment project.

Although they may be significantly affected by local exchange control restrictions, loans (third-party and intercompany) preserve a greater degree of flexibility than equity contributions. Here, intercompany debtors are the beneficiaries of the specially privileged relationships existing between international financial institutions and the governments of most host countries. International credit is almost always a prerequisite for the continued viability of these economies, and thus credit arrangements are more leniently treated by their governments. At the same, third-party and intercompany loans are seldom differentiated in the exchange control codes of these countries. For this reason, the investor can extend intercompany advances under the same preferential terms and conditions as are applied to first-class bank credits.

Use of intercompany debt as a financing vehicle for overseas investment projects therefore provides greater flexibility for the investor in a controlled exchange rate environment. As previously noted, however, maintenance of a reasonable equity base in the project will always be necessary. Thin capitalization will negate many of the advantages accruing to intercompany debt and may cause the host country authorities to construe the debt as equity. The more stringent exchange control regulations affecting equity investments would then apply to intercompany debt.

Suppliers, and trade transactions in general, also benefit from more flexible regulation in an exchange-controlled environment. Imports of raw materials and/or equipment are recognized by host country authorities as necessary for the project's success. Therefore foreign exchange for international trade will usually be assigned a relatively high priority by host country authorities.

An exception may arise if the imports of raw materials and/or equipment for the project are competitive with locally supplied products. In such cases, exchange control regulations and other local legislation (e.g., tariff barriers) may actually be constructed to punish the imports rather than to expedite them. The investor should be aware of any such conflicts before arranging terms of intercompany trade with the overseas unit.

DEALING WITH BUILDUP OF BLOCKED CURRENCIES

If successful, an overseas investment project may generate cash flow in excess of the amount required for its operations and the maximum amount allowed to be repatriated by local exchange controls. In exchange-controlled environments, profitability will result in a buildup of blocked cash resources: cash in excess of local operating requirements which cannot be repatriated to the investors for their own use. This blocked cash represents a potential loss exposure for the investor. There may not be suitable investment opportunities for it in the host country of the project; if it is invested at little or no yield, return on the investment project will suffer accordingly. Also, potential devaluations of the blocked currency versus the investor's base currency (remembering that the currency would not be blocked by exchange controls if the host country were not suffering some economic difficulties) would diminish the value of locally earned profits. Therefore minimizing the buildup of blocked liquid assets abroad is highly desirable. If profitably reinvesting them in the project (required expansions of fixed assets or working capital) is impossible, certain alternative strategies for repatriation can be applied to reduce them.

Acceleration of Intercompany Trade Terms

Acceleration ("leading") of intercompany trade terms will reduce the amount receivable by the investor on account of raw materials or equipment supplied. The liquid assets of the exchange-controlled foreign operation will be correspondingly reduced.

The effect of leading is to repatriate blocked cash from an exchange-controlled foreign operation without tax or other consequences in either country. The amount which can be so repatriated will be a function of the volume of trade between parent and subsidiary and the customary arm's-length terms of trade in their industry. Host country authorities will sometimes apply the arm's-length test to intercompany transactions, to determine whether changes in terms of trade are in fact disguised distributions of blocked profits. However, there is almost always some considerable license which can be negotiated in this area, based on differing market practices, even within the same industry.

Parallel Loan Operations

Local funds can be used to support a loan operation needed in another part of the world. A local project with blocked funds in excess of its own requirements for the foreseeable future will either place a time deposit with a local branch of a multinational bank or make a direct intercorporate loan to another investment group subsidiary in the host country. In turn, another unit of the investment group in its home country or in a third country will be able to gain access to a bank or intercorporate loan at preferential terms and conditions—the loan is supported by the blocked cash operation.

Parallel loan operations for the purpose of employing blocked cash in corporate projects are an increasingly important product offering of multinational commercial and merchant banking groups. They have the ability and client base to determine which multinational groups need and can supply currencies in exchange-controlled environments. For a modest fee, they will undertake the transaction and even interpose their own credit (by way of bank guarantees of repayment) between the parties if desired.

Other Measures

Within reason, expenses can be channeled into a local operating subsidiary in an exchange-controlled environment to "sop up" excess corporate liquidity. Regional, or even corporate, administrative functions may be performed there with the local subsidiary absorbing the tax deductible costs for their own account. Along the same lines, regional or corporate conventions and meetings may be underwritten by the exchange-controlled operation as marketing or sales promotion expense (providing some relationships actually do exist, albeit occasionally, among the operations involved).

In some instances, where no possibility exists to reinvest the blocked cash productively, it can be sold outright to currency brokers. A deep discount between the exchange rate received from the broker and the official exchange rate for approved transactions through the host country central bank will almost certainly be involved. Also, the exchange loss on the broker transaction should be absorbed by the investor, since it will probably not be admissible as a tax deduction by the local, exchange-controlled investment project.

A WORD ABOUT CORPORATE CITIZENSHIP

If unwisely applied, some of the transactions described in this chapter, although successfully executed by multinational investors at other times and places, may have serious effects on the local corporate citizenship of the investor.

Maintenance of corporate citizenship in good standing in the host country should be a primary objective of all operating and financial strategies. Similarly, sharp financial practices amounting to the illegal export of profits or capital should be avoided. A shortfall in the standards of corporate citizenship in these areas can undo much goodwill which has been created through the expansion of employment opportunities and general prosperity in the host country.

Twelve: International Banking Relationship Management

RONALD J. ROGALA

Ronald J. Rogala is a senior vice president at the Central National Bank of New York with corporate lending and management responsibilities. Prior experience includes a vice presidency of the Specialized Lending Group at Bank Hapoalim B.M. Mr. Rogala was formerly with the Chase Manhattan Bank and responsible for lending to middle-market clients and short-term earnings management. He has had significant experience with industrial firms in international finance, acquisitions, treasury management, and product planning. Mr. Rogala earned his M.B.A. degree from the Wharton School at the University of Pennsylvania and his B.S. degree in electrical engineering from Penn State. He is currently an adjunct assistant professor of banking at New York University.

This chapter focuses on the relationship between the bank and the financial manager by discussing from the company's point of view some topics that have a bearing on that relationship. Those topics include both a very brief historical background and discussion of current trends; both topics illustrate the evolutionary aspect of the bank's international role. Banking regulations in the United States have forced the development of a number of different types of banking offices to handle the international role. It is hoped that this chapter will help the financial manager to better understand the bank and the banking relationship and will provide some insights on handling that relationship.

THE INTERNATIONAL BANK

History

The nature of international banking—that is, the service provided in connection with transactions that are external to the sovereign location of the bank—was formed by forces similar to those from as far back in history as the late Middle Ages. By the close of the thirteenth century, banking was dominated by the Italians, who established banking houses in the city states of Genoa, Florence, and Venice. These banking houses grew to service the international trade related both to the import of precious metals and stones, spices, and silks from the Far East by way of the Moslem countries and to subsequent export of those goods to Europe. The discovery of the New World and the control of the trade to America by Spain, Portugal, and, later, Holland, France, and England generated a shift in the trade routes causing a commercial revolution. This in turn shifted the financial centers to northern Europe, eventually to Antwerp in the late sixteenth century and then to Amsterdam in the seventeenth century.

The establishment of the Bank of England in 1694 along with the ascendency of England as the leading colonial, commercial, and naval power in the world gradually brought the focus of international finance to London. London developed into a financial center, and the British pound sterling became a standard in world trade and other international transactions. With such a standard, finance could be carried out in a currency with stability and easy convertibility. With the decline of the economic base provided by the vast British colonial system, the London financial center adjusted by allowing entry and access to operating in London to international banks, shipping firms, and insurance companies. This encouraged international business to use London as a centralized place where its special needs could be attended to. London survives today as an internationally active commercial capital because of the farsightedness of the early bankers and businesspersons. As time went on, other financial centers such as Paris, Amsterdam, Hong Kong, Switzerland, New York, and others have also become global business centers.

Up to about the twentieth century, the common force molding the nature of international banking was the growth of indigenous banks (although sometimes they were operated by foreigners) in the centers of international business, accommodating the particular service needs of the businesses operating there. A large number of choices of services and facilities were not yet developed, and therefore those needs were met with basic, tailor-made facilities. Increasingly complex transactions of a recurring nature forced the development of somewhat standard international services of transfers, drafts, etc. that we know today.

With the evolution of the multinational or transnational company which operates its business by crossing sovereign borders or by establishing operating entities in a variety of different countries, indigenous banks serving the company in its home country adapted their operations to fit their customers. Instead of relinquishing the multicountry business of these companies, many banks have extended their banking operations to other countries where there may be business or profit returns.

Trends

A trend toward the internationalization of U.S. banks began formally in 1913, when the Federal Reserve Act permitted U.S. banks to service internationally generated transactions. The growth of foreign banking operations was slow at first but later developed rapidly, as exemplified by the growth of foreign business operations by U.S.-based companies in the 1950s and 1960s. That trend was further encouraged by efforts in the United States to correct its balance-of-payments deficits in the 1960s by initiating credit-restraining programs for banks in the United States. Banks accommodated their foreign clients by establishing foreign bank operations to draw funds from foreign sources and provide those funds as loans. Even inland U.S. banks participated in such foreign operations.

Not to be outdone by this expansion of U.S. banks to foreign countries, foreign banks extended their operations to the United States in an effort to follow their traditional clients. A typical example of this is the growth record of Japanese banking operations in the United States and their close connections with Japanese companies that operate in the United States. The regulatory atmosphere of the United States allowed the establishment of such foreign banks in this country with relatively little interference.

A major trend occurring now is the revision of loan pricing attitudes in the United States. Traditionally, loans in this country were priced on an interest spread over a prime interest lending rate (prime being the rate charged by a bank on loans to its most creditworthy customers). Particularly for larger loans ($1 million and over), the trend is to price loans at an interest rate spread over the bank's cost of funds or some other nominal base rate such as LIBOR (London interbank offering rate), the federal funds rate, or the rate paid on certificates of deposit.

Banks are now recognizing some of the difficulties in obtaining loan payments from certain foreign countries. These difficulties will affect the availability of loan funds from smaller and some regional banks for the participation and syndication in such foreign loans.

The increased development of worldwide communications and other technological innovations is finding increased application in the internal operations of banks; thus services can be expanded and improved for clients. Cash transfers, accounting determinations, tracers on wayward transactions, and other problem solving and problem recognition have all benefited from communications advances.

From the Middle Ages to the present, banking has accommodated international operations. As those operations shifted from center to center in geographic terms, banks broadened the scope of their services to international businesses. With travel and communications systems advanced to where time and space are no hindrance to operating distant subsidiaries and affiliates, banks and other businesses have expanded their international efforts. In the United States, which has had a dual regulating policy—state and federal, banking operations have been molded into a number of different types of banking offices and facilities, each with specific limitations and freedoms for doing business with international companies.

Types of Banking Offices

Consulting a telephone directory in one's town to select a bank for multinational banking may yield what appear to be a large number of internationally oriented banks. Although selection of a bank would therefore seem to be an easy task, unless one is careful, a first experience in contacting that selection can result in what seems to be an endless process of referral to one phone number after another. Most often the problem is that the banking office called does not handle the type of international business which is being sought by the inquirer. Because of banking regulations, both state and federal in the United States, and because banks seek to operate in geographic areas allowed under that regulation, a number of different banking "forms" are found.

The main banking institution is a normal contact point for those wishing to obtain multinational or international banking services. Depending on its size, the nature of its local market, and its perception of its goals, the bank normally will have an international department to deal directly with the businessperson or to act as a specialist to provide international services to a generalist bank officer who in turn brings those services to the business client.

In smaller or medium-size cities there is usually no great problem, but the contact officer in the larger city may be a generalist and could be oriented toward servicing a geographic section of the city or a segment of a particular industry and may not be internationally oriented. In New York City, for example, a contact officer doing business on upper Park Avenue—traditionally high-net-worth individual or trust-related business—may not be as comfortable doing international business as an officer who is doing business in the World Trade Center area, which typically is foreign trade–oriented. The more centralized nature of the banks in smaller regional banking centers involves their international business personnel at an early point in the relationship.

The larger, multinational company may be accommodated in a larger bank by virtue of the industry in which the company participates, the geographic area of the company's home office, the foreign geographic business concentration, or the type of banking business needed (merchant banking, trade financing, etc.). Therefore the international aspect may be secondary to other segmentation factors of the bank involved. These banks' ability to bring competent personnel into the relationship as needed is a great advantage in their favor. Some of these banks have developed their company relationships on a global basis to provide for coordination and control, thus in one way or another, the main banking institution can provide international services, excepting some isolated inland banks where the bulk of such services and expertise would have to be provided by a correspondent.

In financial centers, subsidiary banks of foreign-based banks can be found operating in financial centers under state or federal charters. This type of banking operation is an entity legally separate from the foreign bank except for the ownership of its stock by a foreign parent. The subsidiary bank has the flexibility to operate in a mode equal to that of a domestic bank and is relatively free of restrictions to perform similar banking functions and take similar office and branch forms as a domestic bank. It has a lending limit to any one borrower based on the capital of the subsidiary bank. Depending on the jurisdiction of its chartering, the subsidiary bank may have restrictions regarding its minimum initial capital and residency and citizenship of its directors. If the domestic company requires a concentration of expertise in doing business in a particular foreign country, the foreign subsidiary bank may maintain contacts with its parent and thereby be provided with specialized expertise and knowledge about the foreign country where that parent is based.

Branches of U.S. domestic banks are, of course, found in proximity to their home offices (depending on domestic branching regulations), but they are also found in many foreign locations. So that these foreign branches of U.S. banks can compete effectively in those foreign markets, the Federal Reserve Board's Regulation K has allowed those branches to engage in activities other than the ones they are permitted domestically. Those activities include:

1. Issuing guaranties within certain limitations (domestic branches cannot)
2. Investing in foreign governments or private entities
3. Underwriting, distributing, and selling the obligations of foreign governments
4. Acting as an insurance agency or broker
5. Engaging in repurchase arrangements involving commodities and securities that may be considered extensions of credit
6. Lending to officers of the bank and paying employees a greater rate of interest than other depositors

Other activities may be permitted by the Federal Reserve Board if those activities are usual in the transaction of banking in its foreign location.

Although not technically found in the United States, the foreign "shell branch" evolved in the 1970s for obtaining favorable tax treatments, funding credits, interbank placings, purchase of loan shares, and to take advantage of the absence of reserve requirements on deposits. These are branches of U.S. and foreign banks typically domiciled technically in the Cayman Islands or Nassau with their operations directed from the parent bank or branch in the United States and accounted for on the shell's books.

Branches of foreign banks are commonly found in U.S. cities where they have identified a particular market to serve. Most are located in the larger cities. They can operate much the same as a domestic banking activity and can provide the same services as a domestic bank branch. Since it is a branch of the foreign-based bank, its lending limit is based on the capital of the consolidated bank, which provides the branch with the capability to lend in cases where large loans are requested.

At the present time—prior to the possible deregulation of interstate banking activities on a broad scale—an anomaly exists in which foreign banks that have existing branches in a number of U.S. cities in different states can take deposits locally and engage in a full range of banking activities that no domestic bank as yet can do. This situation occurred because a number of foreign banks established full branch activities in those cities under granted charters and licensing of individual states. The International Banking Act of 1978 (IBA) has since limited this by requiring foreign banks to declare a "home" state and to conduct expansion as a domestic bank in that state would. Those branches which were previously established were "grandfathered" and allowed to remain in existence, operating as they had before the IBA.

A popular form of banking facility has lately been receiving renewed attention. That form, referred to as an "Edge Act corporation," is increasingly found where expected international business volume would justify its operation. Edge Act corporations (Edges) are U.S. corporations (foreign- or U.S.-owned) chartered by the Federal Reserve Board to conduct only international banking activities. Edges of U.S. banks characteristically have the designator "International" or "Overseas" in their names. The advantage to the bank is that the Edge can be established in states other than that of the parent bank or the designated home state of a foreign bank. The Edge has been used by the larger banks, in particular, for two main business activities: investment and banking. Investment Edges were often colocated with the parent bank. They functioned primarily as a holding company that invested in foreign corporations that engaged in activities other than banking. The Bank Holding Company Act (BHCA) as amended in 1970 allowed the same investments by bank holding companies, and therefore the special advantage of the investment Edge was reduced and it became redundant. The banking Edge is limited to offering international and foreign business—related banking and other services. Since its lending limit to any one borrower is based on the capital and surplus of the Edge itself, a parent Edge is commonly established, and branches of the parent Edge are operated in one or more states and cities. This offers the banks the opportunity of interstate banking for international business. The Edge can finance the following.

1. The indirect or direct export or import of goods to or from the United States
2. The domestic shipment or temporary storage of goods being imported or exported
3. The assembly or repackaging of goods imported or to be exported
4. Foreign contracts, projects, or other activities
5. Production costs or services which have been identified for export

The Edge's ability to accept deposits from the following is just no less important than its financing capabilities.

1. Foreign governments, organizations, and persons
2. Persons and organizations conducting their business principally from outside the United States
3. Individuals residing abroad
4. Persons and organizations whose deposits relate to foreign transmittals, foreign collections, and—as they relate to permitted Edge corporation business—obligations, collateral, payments, credit proceeds, and compensation for credit extensions

Because of the relative freedom to branch, the Edge banks are opening Edge offices in cities which were not previously considered oriented to multinational business. This freedom allows the Edge banks to establish a presence not previously or currently allowed for domestic operations, thereby positioning themselves for when interstate banking limitations will be lifted. For businesses located in those cities, this added expertise in international banking is a bonus.

Agreement corporations are most often referred to in the same context as the Edge corporations—since they have similar objectives—or they are ignored altogether. Agreement corporations were the result of an effort to permit smaller banks to establish Edgelike state-chartered corporations without the $2 million capital requirement necessary for an Edge corporation. Since that capital requirement has been redefined for the Edge to be ". . . in an amount that is adequate in relation to the scope and character of its activities" and with liberalization of the regulation of foreign ownership of the Edge, most banks opt for the Edge corporation instead of the Agreement corporation. With most of the differences between the Edge and Agreement corporations narrowed, Edges will probably be the most likely form found.

Another form of banking facility found is the agency office. An agency of a foreign bank is an office of the foreign bank and is not normally a separate legal entity. It can be federally or state-chartered or licensed. The agency can make loans which are not regulated as to maximum amount to any one borrower, and the agency is frequently funded by borrowing in the U.S. domestic money market or from related banking operations abroad. Although the agency can be used as the initial entry to an area, preceding branch operations, they coexist with such operations to maintain the unregulated nature of the agency operations.

Loan production offices (LPOs) are offices of U.S. domestic banks established in countries or states other than their home state for the purpose of new business, cultivating existing relationships, and selling other bank-provided services. This business can include both domestic and international activities. These offices are not separate legal entities, and they function as liaisons between the bank's home office and the local client. The advantages to the bank are that a local presence is created, local credit investigations can be performed, close customer contact can be maintained, and travel time may be saved. The LPO's official purpose is to develop business—especially loan business—for its parent; however, the LPO cannot give final loan approval, cannot disburse loan proceeds, and cannot accept deposits.

Representative offices (ROs or rep offices) are similar to LPOs in limitations, advantages, and form except that the representative office designation usually refers to such offices of foreign banks in the United States and to foreign offices of U.S. banks. Because of the ease of establishing an RO and its inexpensive format, a large number of these offices operate, and therefore the multinational businessperson is likely to come in contact with one, particularly when doing business with the smaller banks of countries other than the major trading nations. No federal regulations apply to ROs, although some individual state regulations may apply.

Correspondents are the banks that have built networks of relationships with other banks to mutually exploit each other's deposits, services, local presence, lending capacities, reputation, access to large loan syndications, access to local markets, operations capabilities, etc. The correspondents look to each other for collateral benefits, which are the increased business available to the correspondents when they collaborate on transactions too big to service alone. Through such networks banks can extend their capabilities to countries where they do not have their own operations.

Banking offices operate today in the atmosphere of a changing regulatory environment. As the regulations change in the United States and in foreign countries, companies can look forward to changes in and expansions of activities handled by the offices just described.

WHAT TO CONSIDER WHEN CHOOSING A BANK

The most vital consideration in selecting a bank is whether that bank can provide the banking services necessary for the multinational business to carry out its goals. These services must be provided with an acceptable degree of expertise to avoid complications caused by a bank unable to serve at a satisfactory level.

Experience and Technical Expertise

The banker-businessperson relationship should provide benefits to both in a complementary manner, particularly where the expertise of the banker can fill in certain technical gaps that may occur. This is particularly true in multinational banking transactions—when the businessperson is exploring financial transactions in new or different international situations, the seasoned banker probably has had the necessary experience or knows who to consult and retain for the situation. Depending on the level of complication in the international business, a single bank officer with applicable experience may suffice, for example, in the case where a business has established its initial business contact and requires help with letters of credit. An internationally experienced banker with access to a minimum correspondent network would probably suffice. In cases where more complicated financial transactions are involved, including some foreign exchange and sovereign risk components, a banker and bank normally exposed to that type of transaction should be sought. In the first case, a local or regional bank probably would suffice, whereas the more complicated deal would require the services of a bank with a fully developed international department. To choose the bank on the basis of technical expertise, speak with the banker who would be handling the company or the transaction and contact other companies who have made similar transactions.

Services

Traditional cross-border trade evolved to include a number of bank service products that are now fundamental to international banking. One of these is the letter of credit, whereby the issuing bank lends its reputation and credit strength in place of its client to ensure that payment will be made to another party. The issuance of the letter of credit dictates that a credit decision is made regarding the client and the goods shipped so that advances can be made on behalf of the client through drafts drawn on the bank. Before issuing the letter of credit, the banker normally will require the same information as that needed to make a loan to the same company and would set up a line of credit for its use. As regards the operational handling of the letter of credit, the processing is a people-intensive operation, and therefore the bulk of all commercial letters of credit are processed by the larger banks where economies of scale prevail. Smaller banks may process letters of credit at the customer level and rely on the larger banks for further processing.

Other products available relate to the payment of various instruments. At times, payment is accomplished in an export-import transaction by the seller's (drawer of the draft) creating an unconditional demand for payment from a bank (the drawee) on behalf of the buyer, and the payment is made to a payee (the drawee and payee are often the same entity). A bank that stamps the draft "accepted" is honoring the draft, and a banker's acceptance is thereby created. If the draft was for payment in a fixed number of days after sight or presentation, this becomes a form of financing for the seller for the period or tenor of the draft. The facility to create and process related transactions is important to ensure the timely payment of cross-border trade payments and is a basic service offered by the internationally oriented bank.

Another type of basic bank service is to provide for the exchange of one country's currency into another's. In the United States, the principal market is in New York City, and exchanges are made on an informal basis between a small number of New York banks and the New York offices of a group of foreign banks. Other banks enter that market indirectly through a New York correspondent bank or by dealing with foreign exchange brokers, certain securities houses, or a number of other banks. Banks also provide companies with contracts to buy or sell foreign exchange in the forward market to hedge impending currency needs or excesses.

Providing international collections is another multinational service. In its simplest sense this is the collection of payments due on an item that is presented to the maker. Internationally, this is accomplished through a network of correspondents. Clients order collections according to their instructions, indicate how payment will be transmitted, agree on a fee, and set handling instructions for failure to collect. Collections include money orders, traveler's checks, other checks, drafts, and cash against documents, consignments, and shipments.

Certain banks, through their commercial finance divisions or subsidiaries, can factor foreign accounts receivable. Factoring involves the purchasing, by the factor, of a business's short-term receivables, usually without recourse to the seller. The factor assumes the credit risk, accounts receivable bookkeeping, and credit approval of the client's customers. The factor is concerned with the buyer's (client's customers) creditworthiness and the underlying product involved in generating the receivables. Exporters obtain factor approval of the foreign importer to make the receivable acceptable to the factor, after which all risks, including political ones, are assumed by the factor. Importers may use factors, adding them to the letter of credit application opened in favor of the foreign exporter. Since the shipping documents and eventually the physical control of the goods involved will then come under the control of the factor through those documents and trust receipts, she or he can monitor the generation of the accounts receivable from the importer's sales and can be in a position to purchase (factor) those receivables. Costs in the factoring arrangement run somewhat higher than traditional bank credit due to the additional risks and amount of administration assumed by the factor.

Banks may provide forfaiting, which is the discounting (without recourse to the holder) of promissory notes or drafts with maturities up to about seven years.

Banks can offer liaison and consultation regarding how a business can use government agencies of this country (or of some other countries) whose purpose is to aid exporters. Some banks can assist even more directly, for example, by using the Foreign Credit Insurance Association (FCIA), i.e., a bank may have a master policy under which major portions of foreign receivables generated by export sales from the United States can be insured against the risk of nonpayment by foreign buyers for commercial and political reasons. The FCIA insurance increases the quality and creditworthiness of the assets generated by the export sales; it also increases their desirability if they must be financed.

Fronting loans, sometimes called "link financing," happen when a company deposits funds in a bank and the bank lends a similar amount to the company's affiliate. By fronting for the company, the bank acts as an intermediary. Tax advantages are gained from such an arrangement when the depositing company is in a low-tax-rate (or often tax-free) country and the affiliate is in a country with a higher tax rate. The interest paid by the bank to the company (income) is therefore only nominally taxed, and the loan interest paid by the affiliate (expense) is deductible from the affiliate's taxable income.

Banks may assist in programs to minimize a company's exchange exposure risks by using the following.

1. Lock boxes: To accelerate the collection of funds in weak currencies and to quickly convert them to stronger currencies, customers of the client company remit their payments to post office boxes. Banks pick up the payments on a frequent schedule and credit them directly to the client's account.

2. Parallel loans: Banks may arrange, for a fee, two simultaneous loans such that two companies in different countries make loans to each other's subsidiary, which is usually located in the lender's country. No cross-border funds are moved, and subsidiaries are mutually funded in their respective currencies.

3. Back-to-back loans: Banks may arrange, for a fee, reciprocal loans between two companies in different currencies; they then transmit them across borders to subsidiary operations requiring the currency involved.

4. Currency swaps: Banks can arrange an agreement between two companies to exchange an equivalent amount of different currencies to be reversed at some future date that is fixed by agreement.

Other services that may be offered to a client include:

1. Foreign credit reports
2. Political and business climate reviews
3. Referrals to foreign law firms and accounting firms
4. Introductions to foreign persons who may be able to facilitate the types of transactions required
5. Foreign business and bank referrals
6. Letters of introduction

The services available to the business wishing to participate in international markets and finance are not limited to those discussed here. These services and others that are uniquely fitted to particular situations are available, although the right person in the right bank may be difficult to find. Again, contacting likely banks and other companies who may have done similar business is the best approach.

The Bank Officer

The relationship between the company and the bank is one of the most important considerations in the selection of a bank. It is this relationship that affects service given to the company, response obtained from the bank, initiatives received from the bank, credit extended when the company experiences difficulties, and prices a company will pay for its banking services (within limits).

The relationship may begin when a business manager accepts an appointment with one of the calling officers who are continually seeking new business. Allowing some time for these calls allows the manager to assess the bank's personnel and services on a first-impression basis. Followups can be developed for those which seem to have the right "chemistry," skills, bank support, and services. Exactly which banking person will be working with the company if the company decides to do business with a particular bank should be established. It is this person who must be evaluated for a potential working relationship. Some points to keep in mind are:

1. Can the officer (or other person) assigned to your account provide the service needed by the company?
2. Does the officer seem easy to work with on a personal basis?
3. What is the officer's experience and status at the bank?
4. Will your account be handled on a day-to-day basis by other junior or administrative persons? (This can sometimes be an advantage depending on the quality of the support personnel.)
5. How long has the officer assigned to the company been doing that particular job at that location? (A rapid turnover of people by the bank can give the company an unknown quantity for its relationship in a very short time.)
6. Does it seem that the officer has the ability to adjust to new situations and remain calm in stressful situations?
7. Does the officer appear knowledgeable regarding the capabilities and internal workings of his or her bank and where to get additional support if needed?
8. Is the officer curious about the company and make an effort to know the company's business?
9. Are there alternate officers assigned to the account? What are their characteristics?
10. Can the officer be easily reached during working hours?

Answering the above questions will help with some type of prejudgment. The optimal selection will provide the company with a pleasant working situation in normal times and a supportive force in bad times.

Location

The bank's location is an important consideration. Is the bank close to the client's facility? A bank that is close at hand will help the banker and the businessperson develop their relationship; this is important if the company is to realize the full benefits of the bank. This relationship is basic to the banker's way of doing business, since some degree of trust and rapport must be established between client and bank. A good relationship allows the banker to understand the client's business more completely, thus enabling the bank to offer additional services and expertise which may be advantageous to the company. In such an atmosphere, requests by the company can be processed more quickly.

Formerly, foreign business–oriented companies had to contact banks in large cities, such as New York, Chicago, or San Francisco, but, with the new banking regulations taking effect, offices specializing in international business are increasingly being established in many inland cities. Many regional banks have developed reasonable international departments and networks.

The primary locale of the bank is important. By virtue of repetitive operations in geographically concentrated areas, banks develop contacts and the confidence of foreign businesses and governments, and thus the bank can offer immeasurable aid to a business. Knowledge of foreign laws and regulations, practical foreign exchange operations, on-the-spot experience with foreign businesses, foreign financial statements, foreign accountants, political nuances, and indigenous methods of finance depend on the bank's primary area of operations. A bank or branch located in a foreign country with a foreign-based company can maintain close contact with and, therefore, provide information about that company to another concern.

Some foreign-based banks may have developed an expertise in a specific industry because their home offices are in an area where that industry is of primary importance. For example, certain Brazilian banks have a particular expertise in business related to coffee.

Some banks, by the nature of their home country's former colonial or political common interests, may have close relations to banks in other, more inaccessible countries. For example, banks of the United Kingdom have strong banking interests in many formerly colonial African nations; French banks have close relationships with some North African nations.

Costs

Costs for international transactions can vary widely within certain reasonable limits. These limits are dictated by competition, by alternative means for accomplishing the same ends, by the risk perceived by the bank, and by the actual costs of the transaction. Competition will dictate that the costs will probably be at their minimums, but these minimums can include the risk judgment by the bank. The risk evaluation by the bank includes the weighing of many factors that might affect successful completion of the transaction. Those factors include:

1. Financial strength of the companies involved
2. Business strength and capabilities of the companies
3. Products and goods involved
4. Countries and sovereign entities involved
5. Currencies and foreign exchange required
6. Individuals
7. Experience of the banks involved
8. How long the risk will be outstanding
9. Intricacy of the transaction
10. Size of the transaction

This list is by no means complete, and other factors peculiar to individual transactions can be included. Although the risk will be reflected in the costs of the transaction, the amount of risk which a bank will consider prudent is limited, and, in some cases, even though high rates would be justified, the high risk involved would cause the transaction to be turned down. Therefore the evaluation of risk is one of the most important for the bank.

The actual costs of the transaction include those costs the bank must incur, such as legal expenses, administrative costs, operations costs, other bank charges, and the cost of funds to the bank (plus its profit). For example, if the transaction involves a large number of individual item handlings, bookkeeping and operations expenses will be high. There may be a great deal of unseen transactions generated as a result of the client's transaction, e.g., the physical movement of documents, communications, charges and credits in accounts between banks, and legal opinions. In a loan transaction, the largest cost component in the rate charged to the client company will be the cost of money that must be funded either internally or externally. Seemingly high rates of interest levied for loans involve a correspondingly high rate that the bank pays for funds plus an interest rate spread. That interest rate spread is levied to absorb actual costs and a reasonable profit increment.

The costs involved in most other services (other than loans) provided to the foreign business client similarly include all the previously discussed factors, but the basic structure for computing the costs is somewhat different from a simple interest rate. Some of those services are strictly transaction oriented and do not require the acquisition of funds by the bank. Therefore rates based on the amount of money involved reflect only the interest-rate-spread portion with some provision for a minimum charge; thus typically they are much less than the loan rate, since the cost of funds to the bank is not included. Some examples of the pricing structures for common international service products are discussed below. No specific dollar amounts are included, nor are any rates specified. Both these items can vary, depending on the local conditions and the banks and companies involved.

Costs for letters of credit normally are based on a fraction of a per annum percentage of the value of the letter plus a minimum fee. Standby letters of credit, because of their longer time span, are considered somewhat more risky and therefore are priced with a larger minimum fee and a per annum interest rate that is much higher than the fractional rate charged for trade-related letters of credit. In cases where postage, cable, or telex are used, those charges can be passed on to the client company.

Acceptances normally have a minimum fee with a commission charge of some per annum percentage rate—usually above 1 percent—of the value of the acceptance. Refinancing commissions run about the same but with the prevailing discount charges taken into account.

Documentary collections are priced somewhat lower than letters of credit. Minimum and maximum charges may be provided for with a fractional per annum percentage charge on the amount to be collected. Clean collections normally have fixed charges for services, with a minimum and a maximum established at levels lower than those of documentary collections.

Foreign remittances for outgoing drafts, mail, and cable transfers have nominal charges most often based on the amount of the transaction involved.

The specific charges and costs for all transactions and services can be determined by polling competitive banks. Cost checking should be done occasionally, using the same transaction to determine the relative position of the banks' cost structures. If a company is exploring new areas of business, cost should not be the primary consideration, provided that it is reasonable. In addition, a bank that provides trouble-free services is worth the extra expense that it may charge. In all cases, the bank should be allowed a reasonable return for its services.

Facility Approval Process

Another consideration in choosing a bank is how that bank approves its loans and how smoothly its method operates. This is becoming less important in today's world of rapid and reliable communications systems, but some companies may require a great deal of flexibility in their banking relationship, especially with respect to credit requests. If this requirement is unpredictable and changeable, then the approval process method is important. In addition, if the company understands how a bank is approving its requests, the need for early involvement of the bank in the request for a credit facility and the need to give an adequate presentation of supporting data for the facility to the bank become obvious.

Although most approval processes are unique to the banks involved, two types operate with many variations in between. The centralized method seeks to center approval authority in a home office or regional subsidiary where basic credit information is reviewed by what the bank considers its most competent credit and management personnel. Credit information is gathered, analyzed, and packaged at the client contact level and may be screened by lower-level credit personnel or committees. Passing these, the credit is forwarded with recommendations and critical comments to the final, central approving authority. The screening and final approval may be done on a regular basis, or when quick action is paramount, the screening and final approval may take place on an "as required" basis. With the communications systems available today, this approval process, even though centralized, can sometimes be accomplished in a matter of hours or within a day, but more routine approvals can take a few days to a few weeks.

The decentralized method involves the delegation of the approval authorities to lower management and lending levels. At its ultimate, certain line lending personnel are entrusted with an approval authority of some defined magnitude within which they may approve loans. Other such methods may require two or more such persons to approve any one credit facility. The amount or limit of this authority for any one person depends on demonstrated abilities and track record, training, the market operated in, whether the facility is secured or unsecured, etc. For routine and uncomplicated credit facilities, this can be a very nimble and quick method.

Most banks have methods for handling requests for credit in a reasonably timely fashion. The methods selected depend on:

1. Ability of the lower-level or line lending officers
2. Recent experiences with the bank's loan portfolio
3. Size of the loan requested in relation to the bank's capital or overall loan portfolio size
4. Speed at which credit requests must complete the approval process
5. Type of deal or loan request proposed, its structure, price, tenor, countries involved, etc.

The main external effect of the approval process is the observed time in which an approval is accomplished. For routine lines of credit, timeliness should not be a problem for a normally operating company. The bank's ability to quickly process a loan request when the approval is time sensitive can only be determined with experience with the case and bank in real life situation.

WORKING WITH THE BANK

Monitoring and Administering the International Banking Relationship

The control of banking relationships by company management has tended toward the side of centralization, but in recent years the complexity of coordinating large numbers of units in fast-moving markets has generated a need for regional control centers. Controlling those relationships in either a centralized or decentralized system requires an analysis of historical operating financial requirements of the remote operation and a projection of these short-term requirements into the short-term future, adding to those the planned capital expenditure requirements. The derived operating and capital requirements are introduced into the company's overall financial plan. After considering the impact of remote or local financing against the factors of local banking conditions, the expertise and capabilities of the remote operations management, taxes, foreign exchange conditions, political factors, cash management strategies for various corporate levels, etc., the plan for individual banking relationships can be developed and implemented.

If deemed feasible, local financing policy may be set to limit the size of the credit facility for normal operating needs and to formally designate how and for what purpose individual banks may be used. To ensure understanding of the policy, the chief financial officer of the remote entity should report back on a periodic basis regarding the specific nature of relations with the local banks, the banks involved, planned usage of the bank facility, the actual usage, the remote entity's control procedures on bank usage, and any recommendations regarding local bank use. In addition, more frequent, regular reporting should be required regarding liquidity position, cash, expected collections, bank borrowings, and anticipated bank borrowings by means of available telecommunications. The frequency of this reporting depends on the degree of control required, the volatility of the liquidity position, and the critical nature of the entity's business.

Reports of the bank relationships should be made a regular agenda item by local managers and the local board of directors. Information regarding corporate resolutions for the purpose of using banks should be forwarded to the controlling center. This information should include any minutes of board meetings in which such resolutions were adopted and copies of the resolutions.

Financing of capital expenditure requirements can be handled on a project control basis, especially when one-time bank financing is required. If the project is of sufficient magnitude, the controlling center's financial officer may have to manage the local financing and the overall relationship with the financing bank. If not, policy can require the development of local selection of the financing bank with the appropriate degree of information regarding the financing provided to the controlling center. All actual borrowings or other relations with the bank can be reported to the controlling center together with the disposition of the borrowed funds.

The controlling center is responsible for recommending, formulating, and implementing policies and procedures for the general guidance of local use of banks and for the reporting of such use. It also is responsible for analyzing the needs for banking relationships and formulating the optimal ways to satisfy those needs. Using overall corporate policy, tax considerations, analysis of plans, past history, foreign country characteristics, local management capabilities, etc., each remote entity can be assigned specifically designed banking programs. Such programs can include the individual authorities allowed, the types of relationships to maintain, the maximum limits of the facility, the compensation structure, the types of services the banks are to provide, considerations and methods for approving banks, and the reports required to the controlling center, and these should be developed considering the characteristics unique to each entity involved. Specific techniques such as requiring countersignatures on documents in dealing with banks or limiting the liability of the parent company for obligations incurred by subsidiaries can be used.

Adequate internal audit procedures must be instituted to ensure compliance with established policies and procedures. External auditors should be aware of the existing banking relationships, and their audit attention should be directed toward control of relationships. The control function depends on determining the overall corporate goals, establishing policy and procedures, delegating for flexibility, setting up a reporting system, developing two-way communications, and implementing auditing control procedures.

Loan Negotiation Tactics

Loan-negotiating tactics seem to invoke an adversary relationship between the company and the bank, but this can be dispelled with some knowledge of how the bank officer operates. This is also valuable as a tool in the negotiating process. Knowing the way bankers look at their businesses and knowing the constraints under which they operate, the company representative will understand what is negotiable and what is not.

In normal situations the banking officer is motivated by what seem to be opposing forces: (1) the desire to obtain new or increased business and (2) the need to limit it to reasonably high quality business. The opposing nature of these forces derives from the market situation—a large amount of business is available at a lower quality, and high-quality business limitations do not allow significantly large volumes of business (assuming a competitive banking atmosphere). If the banker's initial attitude is open and receptive to additional or new business, the company will put itself in the best possible negotiating position by proving to the bank and banker that the transaction to be financed and the company involved are of high quality. If this is a new relationship or one in which an additional or new bank might be used, a second bank can be used to make its offer for the business. If each bank is aware that another bank might get the business, there may be some increase in willingness to entertain the transaction. Caution should be exercised in the use of competition and in how it is introduced, since both competitors will assume that they must produce a firm offer. That firm offer can require banks to perform detailed analyses and to run the formal approval hurdles within their own banks. Therefore the banks not selected will have some justification for ill feelings toward the company. To avoid this problem, start the process early to allow time to obtain two or more bids if one fails to deliver and to obtain initial "ballpark" or nonbinding estimates from banks regarding the amounts, rates, covenants, security, terms, etc. When the competitive situation is introduced at the initial stages of the search for a bank, the experienced banker will handle it professionally.

There is a requirement—although it is usually ignored—for the company to convince the banker that this relationship constitutes quality business. The presentation of the company as a desirable commodity is one of the most important tactics available. Obviously, desirable or prime business will command the minimum rates and charges and the maximum in service and facility size limits. By training, experience, and knowledge of the bank's objectives, the banker should be concerned with the quality of the company and the transaction. To a banker in a loan transaction, this means that the principal and interest on the loan very probably will be repaid as agreed. The evaluation considers the company's willingness and ability to fulfill its obligations. To establish the company in this light, it should be prepared to meet certain requirements which the banker may levy in an investigation and evaluation of the company's creditworthiness. One of the most common misconceptions on the part of companies is the assumption that, if there are sufficient assets in the company and they are offered for security, a credit facility is justified and should be automatically granted. Indeed such loans are granted, and many foreign bank lenders place a high degree of reliance on such collateral; however, more sophisticated bankers look to collateral as a secondary source of loan repayment or safety net that can be taken and liquidated to repay a loan if the primary source of repayment (funds generated from the business or the particular transaction financed) fails to materialize.

The banker will attempt to evaluate the willingness of the company to repay. Fundamental to the credit evaluation is an assessment of the character of the company as embodied in the owners, managers, and employees. Without satisfaction that the willingness to pay is present, the lender can proceed no further. Banks' decisions are based on investigation, reputation, intuition, and record of past performance. By providing interviews with appropriate personnel and background information, the company can speed this evaluation. The remainder of the credit evaluation centers on assessment of the particular credit request, defining the following:

1. Amount of the loan
2. Purpose of the loan
3. Source of repayment
4. Schedule of repayment

If the company provides detailed information to the bank, particularly with respect to item 3, a powerful negotiating advantage is set. The information provided also helps the banker to understand the company and its transactions in sufficient detail to explain the basis for the evaluation to whatever approval authorities are necessary within the organization.

Clearly, establishing the company as a desirable piece of business is very important. Even in established relationships the same care regarding presentation of the company and its financing needs should be maintained. At all times consideration should be given to establishing credibility with the banker. If this happens on an ongoing basis, when a particular situation arises the company can expect the bank to seriously consider any reasonable requests made by the company. On an ongoing basis the company should provide press releases, financial information, company-initiated meetings, etc. without request from the bank. Surprises, particularly adverse ones, are particularly detrimental to a banking relationship and to the credibility of the company.

In instances where company survival may be at stake, the textbook tactics of deadlines, hustle, delays, switches, situational settings, competition, etc. can be used, but the continuing relationship will suffer. It can suffer to the extent that in times of credit rationing or loan portfolio upgrading, the company might find itself either reduced or without a bank.

If the costs of a service or credit facility seem too high, the company should compare those costs with a similar bank and confront its banker with those findings. Keep in mind that a smooth relationship may be worth its weight in gold; haggling over minor cost differences is easily remembered and it will harm the relationship. In cases where terms of a facility or service are not satisfactory to the company, logical justification for the company's view should be provided. For example, if covenants in an agreement are not suitable, projections of company financial results may be submitted to show that those covenants would be violated and the underlying loan would still be paid off. If service arrangements are not satisfactory, some historical or potential situations could be drawn on to demonstrate the company's view. If a logical presentation is given, the company will have won 90 percent of the negotiating battle.

In summary, hard negotiating should not be necessary except in unusual circumstances. Most of the convincing should be effected by continually striving to maintain a relationship that nurtures a high degree of credibility and adequate presentations of the company and its operations. Continued communications should be established between the bank and the company so that in time-critical situations both parties understand and feel comfortable working with each other without the necessity of difficult negotiating. Rather, a receptive atmosphere should have been developed so that both views are understood. Armed with both the knowledge of how the banker considers a request for credit and with persuasive logic laden with presentations, the company will do well in any negotiation.

SPECIAL INSTRUMENTS

Almost any loan or credit granting by a lender will begin with the evaluation of the borrower's ability to repay the loan or credit. The lender's evaluation will center primarily on the prospective borrower's willingness to repay and on the borrower's ability to generate the necessary funds to repay within some time frame. Although the lender may be satisfied with those factors as a minimum primary source of repayment, other concerns may cause the lender to consider the transaction too risky. For example, if the borrower is highly leveraged or has a minimal capitalization; if the borrower has been in business for only a short time (essentially a "start-up"); or if an untried product or process is involved. The lender will then probably try to assess what additional protection exists for repayment of the loan should the primary source of repayment fail to materialize. Also, the international framework of global remoteness, unfamiliar political and business conditions, foreign judicial systems and laws, government exchange controls, etc. generate a great many questions to be answered in sufficient detail to allow timely completion of the credit evaluation.

The chances that a borrower's current bank or the one it selects for this particular deal has sufficient lending experience in the specific transaction and international framework to allow credit approval or a loan based solely on a minimum credit evaluation would be slim at best unless the bank was selected after an extensive search or investigation. What is needed in this case is some way to enhance the minimally evaluated borrower with a creditworthiness-strengthening device.

To accomplish this strengthening—remember that the borrower must have at least a minimum ability to repay as the primary repayment source—

another entity with sufficient financial strength and creditworthiness can be used. This other entity would be considered a support of the borrower's obligation and perhaps even a secondary source of repayment should the original borrower be unable to fulfill the borrowing arrangement for payback.

An array of techniques have been developed as practical solutions to the problem of fortifying the creditworthiness of potential borrowers when only the minimum credit standards are present. Typically these techniques include agreements in "hard copy" forms that include an assortment of letters of credit, guarantees, endorsements, indemnities, and comfort letters. (Remember that the potential lender must be satisfied about both the legal enforceability of the transaction, given the entity and the foreign jurisdiction involved and the financial strength of the second or supporting entity granting its support.)

Letter Of Credit

Aside from the typical country-to-country trade use of the commercial letter of credit, which normally involves the cross-border shipment of goods, the letter of credit can be used in a variety of ways to lend secondary support to the primary borrower. The basic characteristics of the letter of credit define it as a formal, independent agreement or contract issued by a bank under the terms of the letter of credit. Normally, these terms are very simple, involving no judgments, and typically they consist of the requirement of the presentment of a notice of default or nonperformance of the borrow for drawings to be permitted. Issued by a reputable and financially strong bank on behalf of its client for the beneficiary bank (which is the lender to the original borrower), this type of letter of credit is a powerful credit enhancement tool. Once issued, the issuing bank's financial strength is substituted for that of its client and applied to the borrower by its drawing terms. For example, when a U.S.-based subsidiary—say, U.S.B. Corp.—of a Swiss company applies for a loan from, say, American Bank, it is informed that the loan was not approved because of the U.S. subsidiary's low capital base and short operating history. A letter of credit issued by Swiss Bank in favor of American Bank to be drawn against if U.S.B. Corp. defaults on its loan obligations may be offered to strengthen the secondary sources of repayment relative to loans made by U.S.B. Corp. If Swiss Bank is reputable and sound and the terms of the letter of credit are simple and not prone or open to challenge because of technical discrepancies, American Bank in all probability will approve the loan or line of credit to U.S.B. Corp.

This type of letter of credit is often referred to as a "standby letter of credit" or, in other cases, a "guarantee letter of credit." Since these do not call for documentary evidence of the shipment of goods and instead require only a draft and most often a written statement concerning the terms of the letter to be met, they are called "clean letters of credit." The lending bank's officer will normally insist that only a notice of default be able to trigger the terms by which the letter may be drawn on. This is justifiable, since, at the time of default, delays caused by settling disputes or litigation with regard to other related agreements dilute the usefulness and strength of the letter of credit.

Another use of the letter of credit is often seen by the U.S. bank from the issuing side and by the U.S. company from the account party side, where it is used instead of a surety bond. Surety bonds have traditionally been used to provide a guarantee that a contractor would comply with certain obligations with regard to bidding, subcontracting, or other related performance. With increased need for building done by U.S. contractors or where large capital goods sales are involved (requiring some type of warranty) in the international area, letters of credit have been used to provide a basis for that function, particularly in the Middle East and Europe, where the surety industry has not developed fully. Typically, U.S. contractors request their banks to issue letters of credit in favor of banks that are local or known to the persons or businesses employing the contractors. The local banks then issue their guarantees to the contractors' employers.

The primary consideration in the use of the letter of credit is that it allows drafts to be drawn under its terms, which are usually in the form of a notice of default or statement of nonperformance. The draft is honored without condition, and the bank involved does so without any judgment regarding whether a default of nonperformance has actually occurred according to some other agreement. No provision is made for weighing the merits of any claims or reasons, and the drawing is allowed with a relatively simple attesting that the event did occur. Thus there is a relatively small risk on the beneficiary side, although there can be a credit risk on the account party side. The more complicated the terms of the letter of credit are, the more open it may be to noncompliance due to possible technical deficiencies regarding the terms, and the risk to the account party may decrease while the beneficiary's risk may increase. Therefore the beneficiary seeks to have such risk of noncompliance due to technicalities decreased by requiring the very simplest terms while still providing adequate protection.

Guaranty

The use of guaranties is another method by which the credit strength of a financially stronger entity can be transferred to a weaker one. As in the previous case where the potential borrower had only a minimum primary repayment ability but also had a willingness to repay, the lender may find the prospective borrower more attractive with a potential secondary repayment source. The guaranty influences the lender's decision, because it offers a legally enforceable instrument whereby one party (the guarantor) undertakes to answer for the default of another (the primary debtor). The guaranty is one of the most commonly used support instruments. Various descriptive terms indicate the extent of the guaranty and may be used in combination to indicate the duration covered, amount, the beneficiary, obligation, and, at times, the security. Some of the more commonly used terms with regard to guaranties are:

1. Continuing: The duration of the guaranty is not limited in time; there is no expiry date.
2. Temporary: The duration of the guaranty is limited to a time that is specified in the instrument.
3. Unlimited: This term refers to full coverage of the primary debtor for amount and/or duration.
4. Limited: A limited guaranty refers to some limitation on the duration and/or amount.
5. Absolute: In an absolute guaranty, the guarantor becomes equally liable with the debtor.
6. Conditional: A conditional guaranty is a guaranty of collection in which the guarantor is secondarily liable after the debtor.
7. Secured: With a secured guaranty, the guarantor may assign or give possession of collateral to the lender.

The most desirable guaranty for a lender would be continuing, unlimited, secured, and absolute. However, the use of guaranties commonly is tailored to fit the particular situation with limitations chiefly initiated by the guarantor to limit liability as desired and still provide adequate credit support to the primary debtor. The common use of this instrument is deceptively simple, and both creditor and guarantor should be thoroughly aware of the extent and manner of the guaranty and, more importantly, the legal enforceability of the guaranty agreement in the applicable foreign or domestic jurisdiction. Many different rules govern guaranties' form, use, and the authority of a business entity (guarantor) to issue them. In all cases where the guaranty is of great importance in the credit evaluation or where there are questions of ability on the part of the guarantor to issue the guaranty, consultation with legal counsel that is familiar with the jurisdictions involved is vital.

In cases in U.S. jurisdiction, there are basic questions of guaranty validity and the consideration of the guarantors rights and defenses. Questions of guaranty validity arise when the doctrine of "ultra vires" is considered. In general, but with some exceptions, guaranteeing the obligations of another person or corporation are ultra vires or outside the guarantor's legitimate or chartered activities. It is possible that a legitimate guaranty can be accomplished if the guarantor's business is beneficially affected by the results caused by granting the guaranty. Usually this can be demonstrated in the case of a "downstream" guaranty when the stronger parent (guarantor) guaranties a subsidiary corporation. However, where an "upstream" guaranty (the subsidiary guaranteeing the parent) is used, difficulties in establishing a valid guaranty arise if specific and definable benefits to the subsidiary do not flow from the parent as a result of the guaranty. The consideration of a clear business benefit should always be present to make the guaranty legally justifiable. This justification does not arise simply by virtue of the parent-subsidiary relationship (either parent to subsidiary or subsidiary to parent). Common ownership, authorizing provisions in the corporate charter, or the purpose of promoting sales are not ordinarily enough of a business enhancement consideration.

Even when a legitimate guaranty is entered into, the creditor who relies on the ultimate enforceability of the guaranty must consider the traditional defenses and rights of guarantors. These defenses and rights are equally important to the guarantor and are developed from the following:

1. The guarantor has the right of exoneration and can be released from the guaranty if the creditor does not exercise creditor rights when called on to do so by the guarantor if the guarantor detects that the creditor's activities are leading to nonpayment of the obligation. Therefore lenders or creditors must have the ability and the willingness to move quickly and decisively to protect their and the guarantors' interests or lose the benefits of guaranties through exoneration.

2. The underlying debt that was guaranteed must have been a legally binding agreement.

3. Particularly at the time of or before the granting of the guaranty, the lender may not have either deliberately withheld information when asked, or misled the guarantor regarding information concerning the risk involved, or the guarantor may be released.

4. If the lender and the primary debtor materially change the debtor's obligation without informing or involving the guarantor, the guarantor may be released.

5. The guaranty should be executed on or before the underlying debt is incurred or is disbursed as a demonstration of the lender's reliance on the previously executed guaranty for making the loan with adequate consideration.

6. If the lender extends the schedule of repayment of the underlying debt because the primary debtor cannot meet the original schedule and the lender receives consideration in return, the guarantor may be released.

7. If another entity purchases the claims of the lender on the underlying debt, the guarantor may be released.

Guaranty instruments may be written so that the foregoing rights and defenses are either protected or limited, and both the beneficiary (lender) and the guarantor should carefully consider the legal details of that agreement.

In an international context, guaranties given by foreign-based corporations whose purpose may be construed as circumventing a country's regulations may be invalid or open to challenge by government authorities. These guaranties can be challenged at any time or when their effects are evident, i.e., when the provisions of the guaranty are drawn on in a practical situation. Typically, this can occur if the guaranty is to be paid in a foreign currency. It may be necessary to obtain central bank or ministry of finance approval to ensure the availability of foreign exchange should it be necessary to enforce the guaranty.

Although U.S. banks cannot provide "bank guaranties" (these are considered ultra vires for U.S. banks), they are permitted to issue them at overseas branches under provisions of Regulation M of the Federal Reserve Board. Most foreign bank regulations are somewhat more liberal with regard to bank guaranties and provide for their issuance by their domestic banks. Where the geographic separation between creditor and debtor is extensive, where a certain degree of uniqueness is customary in maintaining the financial books of account, or where business customs preclude an adequate credit analysis by the prospective creditor, a high degree of reliance on the bank guaranty is commonplace. Bank guaranties may be advisable in some Eximbank (The Export-Import Bank of the United States) and FCIA transactions. Bank guaranties are expected to be from internationally respected banks of good reputation and financial strength, and a credit analysis and investigation of the guarantor bank may be necessary. In cases where foreign government buyers cannot incur debts payable in currencies other than their own, guaranties from the controlling central bank or ministry of finance may be necessary to provide the access to and freedom to obtain the necessary monetary exchange to satisfy the primary debt involved.

Guaranties from government agencies are available to exporters from some countries. Typically these exist in some form in the major trading nations. To encourage their export trade, countries have developed agencies to finance that trade directly, or indirectly through various insurance, cooperative, and guaranty schemes. These programs are covered elsewhere in this Handbook in more detail, but the following are a few of the agencies that offer some type of guaranty among their facilities to give the reader an idea of the widespread use of this type of program:

EXIMBANK—USA
EXIMBANK—Japan
EXIMBANK—Korea
EXIMBANK—Republic of China
Banque Francaise du Commerce Exterior (BFCE) (France)
Export Credits Guarantee Department (ECGD) (United Kingdom)
Mediocredito Centrale (Italy)

Exports or importers from nations with such agencies and programs will find it worthwhile to explore and take advantage of those programs for financing their transactions and mitigating their risks.

Comfort Letter

The comfort letter is another instrument commonly used when a potential debtor's creditworthiness requires a lesser degree of fortification than with a more formal and legally powerful guaranty. The comfort letter is an informal statement typically given by a parent corporation or some other financially stronger or controlling entity (grantor of the letter) to indicate its position with respect to a subsidiary or some other affiliated entity in which it has an interest (the subject company). The letter's statement of position is intended to reassure the lender, who will then grant the credit requested by the subject company. In general, most of the statements made in a comfort letter are not legally binding, but sometimes they may be somewhat open to enforcement—legally—on the basis of breach of contract. Most often they fall considerably short of a formal guaranty and should not be relied on for legally enforceability or for the strength they impart to a subject company. They are not a direct substitute for a guaranty and should never be considered as such in the evaluation of a credit situation.

The comfort letter has been referred to by a variety of colorful terms, including the following.

Letter of support	Comfort letter
Letter of moral intent	Monkey letter
Letter of recognition	Keepwell letter
Letter of responsibility	Lettre de patronage
Letter of willingness	Patronatserklarungen
Letter of awareness	

Although many have attempted to differentiate among these terms, the terminology used in any situation depends on who is involved. A monkey letter discussed at the line-lending level in a bank may be the same letter of moral intent discussed by senior management of the companies involved; bank examiners might refer to an identical letter as a comfort letter.

The use of the comfort letter has evolved through attempts to satisfy two seemingly conflicting goals: The grantor of the comfort letter is often avoiding making the letter a guaranty because of policy or legal restrictions, and the lender is seeking to get the letter and its enforceability as close to a guaranty as can be obtained. This can be a stressful situation, since the achievement of one party's goal dilutes its purpose or value to the other party.

Large multinational parent corporations commonly use the comfort letter to lend their support to the bank financing of their domestic or foreign subsidiaries or affiliates. These corporations may have complex constraints and policies that restrict the issuance of guaranties, but a carefully composed comfort letter may be allowable within those restrictions. Some reasons to use comfort letters are:

1. Existing covenants in indentures, bond, or loan agreements may restrict the parent company's ability to issue a guaranty.

2. For a bank, the addition of a strongly worded comfort letter may enhance the positive evaluation of a borderline credit which may have been weakened to the extent of possible classification as a deteriorating account by bank examining authorities.

3. A formal resolution from the parent corporation's board of directors to authorize a guaranty in a corporation would be necessary, but management may be reluctant to avail themselves of this procedure when a comfort letter can be issued without it.

4. Guaranties can be considered contingent liabilities and may be noted as such in the parent's financial statement adding to the liability load of the parent, but a comfort letter would not normally be noted in that statement.

5. Guaranties of subsidiary borrowings by parent corporations may be considered investments in the foreign subsidiaries, and the remittances of earnings based on these investments may be adversely affected.

6. The acceptance by some bankers of comfort letters in lieu of a guaranty may promote their use as a marketing device.

7. As a policy of reducing legal risk, companies may seek to downgrade contingent liabilities (guaranties) to less legally binding forms such as comfort letters.

8. Currency or exchange restrictions may prohibit or limit the use of formal guaranties, and government agency approval may be necessary.

Although the foregoing list is not exhaustive, the determination of the true reason is a very important component of the analysis of the credit strength of the subject company that is being supported. The use of the comfort letter to violate the spirit of existing regulations or other lender controls would receive critical attention from a careful lender. In addition, such tactics as consistent policies of downgrading liabilities to comfort letters can be a sign of impending financial difficulties in the issuing/parent corporation.

The composition of the comfort letter is typically brief but not limited to any single format. Most, however, will have at least a few of the following common elements.

1. The parent acknowledges the specific credit facility or loan offered by the lender to its subsidiary or affiliate.
2. The parent may indicate its opinion as to whether it is in agreement with the lending arrangement.
3. The parent indicates the degree of its support of the subsidiary or affiliate. Indications of the following items may be given:
   a. Provision to the subsidiary with the financial means to meet its obligations
   b. Description of the parent's past practice in making such advances and its intent to do so in the future
   c. Provision for payment arrangements to the lender should the subsidiary be prevented from meeting its obligations due to local conditions
4. The parent indicates the extent of its ownership or control of the subsidiary or affiliate and gives some indication of its intentions with respect to its ownership or control in the future.

5. The parent indicates the extent of management participation by the parent in the subsidiary.
6. The parent indicates the degree of influence it will exert to induce the subsidiary to meet its obligations.
7. The extent of any restrictions or policies regarding dividends from subsidiary to parent may be given.
8. Some statement regarding the comfort letter's signer's authority and power to sign such documents can be given.
9. To indicate equal treatment of subsidiary creditors, a statement of negative pledge regarding the granting of other guaranties, etc. may be made.
10. A statement that the parent or the subsidiary will endeavor to maintain a certain financial condition as indicated by certain levels of ratios, liquid assets, working capital, and/or net worth may be given.
11. The comfort letter may have a disclaimer regarding the letter's being considered a guaranty.

It would be the exception to find all the above elements addressed in any one particular comfort letter; however, the subsidiary-lender relationship statement, the parent-subsidiary statement, and the parent support statement are frequently found in the minimum letter. An example of the body of a minimum comfort letter could look like the following:

We advise you the XYZ Corp. currently has a 100 percent ownership interest in XYZ (London) Ltd. XYZ Corp. is in agreement with the financial arrangement between XYZ (London) Ltd. and your bank. XYZ Corp. will use its best efforts to encourage its subsidiary to meet the financial obligations it may incur to your bank in connection with that financial arrangement.

A more comprehensive letter would look like:

This will confirm that ETT, Inc. is the owner of 75 percent of the outstanding stock of ETT International Ltd. and that it does not intend to decrease its percentage ownership without prior notification to you. It is our intention not to permit the payment of dividends until January 1, 19xx.

The obligations of ETT International Ltd. in connection with the discount and loan facilities in Eurodollars or foreign currencies through any branch of your bank are with the full knowledge of ETT, Inc., and we agree that such facilities are in order.

In consideration of your bank making such facilities available to ETT International Ltd., we hereby agree to use our best efforts to ensure that ETT International Ltd. will fulfill its obligations to your bank at any of your offices, under all commitments undertaken before January 1, 19xx for amounts not exceeding the equivalent of U.S. $10,000,000 outstanding at anyone time, plus interest accrued thereon.

Should ETT, Inc. or its subsidiaries guaranty ETT International Ltd. to any other creditor, the obligation to you will also be guarantied.

This signatory below has been empowered and authorized to sign this letter on behalf of ETT, Inc.

As you can see, the commitments, however vague or imprecise they may be, can vary a great deal. The content of the letter is most often the compromise between the company's interests on one hand—the opinion of the auditors, legal counsel, and management—and the lender's interests on the other—who would like to have the letter contain the elements of a guaranty.

Of importance to the lender are the following:

1. That the letter be received on or before the underlying loan closing as an indication that the letter was important to the granting of the loan.
2. That the letter identify the specific facility, loan, or other credit arrangement.
3. That the true purpose for using the comfort letter instead of granting a formal guaranty be clearly determined through verbal interviews with management and any other investigation deemed necessary.
4. That the type and degree of support and the conditions under which that support would become available should be clearly defined.
5. That the letter be maintained as current and "continuing," if possible, considering the tenor and payments made on the underlying credit facility.
6. That the grantor of the letter have a good history and track record regarding its own debts and support of subsidiary obligations.
7. That the signer of the letter is authorized and empowered to sign it on behalf of the issuer. A corporate resolution giving such authority, a statement in the letter itself regarding the authority, more than one signatory (such as the typical two signature countersigning in Europe), or signature by a person known to have the authority to enter into financial or legal commitments on behalf of the company may provide some comfort in the authority of the signer.
8. That the issuer of the letter is legally able to issue such a letter considering the jurisdictions involved and legal form of the issuer and its subsidiary or affiliate.
9. That the likelihood of shareholder action to block or impede the issuer from carrying out its support be assessed.
10. That the strengths of the provisions in the letter be assessed for the value they may have in the evaluation of a credit by bank auditors or examiners.

In cases where the comfort letter is critically important to the credit facility and is heavily relied on, the lender will undoubtedly be advised to obtain a local legal opinion as to the value and enforceability of the letter's provisions and commitments.

The special instruments discussed here can be used by financially inferior subsidiaries and affiliates to draw on the strength of parent corporations and banks to provide a basis for banking relations with the subsidiaries in their remote locations.

SUMMARY

Banking has had a long history of following trade and international business to provide necessary financing, monetary operations, and other banking accommodations. Today a variety of different types of banking organizations exist in the United States and abroad. In the United States, the type of banking organization considered can greatly affect the types of service and expertise offered. Selection of the bank, however, includes the additional considerations of location, personnel, home office location, method of loan approvals, etc. Promotion of the company as a desirable piece of business for the bank is helpful.

For subsidiaries and affiliates operating away from the banking relations of the parent corporation, the use of letters of credit, guaranties, and comfort letters can fortify the financial strengths of the subsidiary so that it can establish its local banking relations.

In this chapter several of the more common methods used in establishing and maintaining a banking relationship have been presented. As a practical matter, this is a complex relationship that should be carefully planned and operated so that maximum benefits can be obtained by the company from the bank. Even experienced and sophisticated companies make simple mistakes that cost both the company and the bank time and money. This chapter can at least provide a starting point for establishing a strong and mutually beneficial banking relationship.

Thirteen: International Cash Management

FRED L. COHEN

Fred L. Cohen is a manager in the Financial Institutions Consulting Group, Peat, Marwick, Mitchell & Co.; he was previously vice president of International Cash Management Consulting Services for Chemical Bank in both New York and London. In his various capacities, Mr. Cohen has managed client engagements for Centralized Treasury Management Studies, Global Liquidity Management Studies, Cash Management Reviews, and other international cash and financial management projects. He has also been associated with the First Pennsylvania Bank, advising companies on a range of international corporate financial services. Mr. Cohen earned a B.A. degree in political science from Rutgers University and an M.B.A. degree in finance and accounting from Drexel University.

The impact of inflation and high interest rates on a company's global operations is a major factor which increases awareness of the need for good cash management practices. Cash management is that aspect of financial management that unites the operations and treasury activities. The complexity of conducting global business is apparent in three distinct areas:

1. Local operations complicated by conflicts among marketing, production, and treasury units
2. Domestic complexities existing within a single country
3. Most important, the interrelationship of subsidiaries complicated by divisional and corporate management

There are a number of exclusively international business factors that need to be dealt with as well. In each country where business is done, certain regulations, product quotas, tariffs and duties, and financial customs, practices, and regulations exist for conducting business. There are regulations for transactions from a host country and other countries; there are regulations that prohibit, in some cases, the free flow of funds into and out of that country; and there may be regulations that limit the free flow of goods into and out of a given country.

Of all of the issues, taxation is an overriding factor when reviewing business and cash management operations. The major tax burden is often on the movement of funds when there are onerous withholding taxes on interest and dividends. Companies often have an undue preoccupation with reported earnings and do not pay enough attention to their overall cash flow, but they need to challenge the environment in the broadest sense. One must question a firm's internal operation on a country-by-country basis, investigate local business regulations and customs, and learn the correct procedures for dealing with myriad external regulations. Clearly, the efficient management of funds within any organization is crucial both in the long and short terms.

THE PIVOTAL ROLE

International cash management is becoming the all-encompassing phrase for global treasury and financial management. As companies increasingly focus on transactions, rather than composite accounting categories, cash management will become the key aspect of the treasury activity, because it is comprehensive in nature. It is therefore important to use a broad definition of cash management. Typically, cash management is thought to be only the mobilization of funds, the speedy movement of money from point A to point B. It is much more. Cash management has six distinct but interrelated components.

Cash Collections. The order-taking to cash collection process resulting in the depositing of cash is key to a good cash management system. It begins when an order is taken and continues until cash is actually collected and deposited at the bank. It is important, when talking about and studying cash management, to be concerned about how a firm accepts an order, how quickly the order is prepared, when the invoice is prepared, when the invoice is mailed, and ultimately, when and how the customer makes payment. Integrated in this component are the additional aspects of credit and collection management and inventory control.

Cash Disbursements. Good cash management includes the collection of funds as quickly as possible and, equally important, the disbursement of those funds in a controlled manner. Funds should be disbursed as slowly as possible, but disbursement must be consistent with the firm's credit standing. One interesting example of controlled disbursement is how companies control cash disbursements in the U.S. banking system. In the United States there are some 14,000 banks; all offer the same type of banking services, and none currently may maintain a nationwide banking system. Some U.S. companies control disbursement by taking advantage of the check clearing and mail systems—they mail checks from distant points and draw the checks on banks from even further points. One company, for example, has twelve warehouses throughout the United States. If that company purchased a product in Florida, it would probably produce and mail the check from its warehouse in Arizona, send it to the vendor in Florida, and the check would be drawn on a bank in Oregon. That is controlled disbursement.

Cash Mobilization. The aspect of cash management by which everybody incorrectly defines cash management is cash mobilization. It is an integral part of cash management, but it should not be viewed disproportionately against the other factors. Cash mobilization is how money moves from the payer to the payee, it is hoped in the least amount of time.

Investment and Debt Management. Going beyond the collection and the disbursement of funds and the mobilization of funds, investment and debt management involves the profitability component of cash management, and it becomes important once funds are collected, since they either must be invested wisely or applied against outstanding borrowings as quickly as possible. Therefore, a good comprehensive cash management program must tie the collection and the disbursement into the investment and debt management.

Cash Forecasting. One way to anticipate investment and debt decisions is through good cash forecasting. Forecasting in general is neglected in most companies and nonexistent in many companies. Cash forecasting is a major area through which companies can improve their cash management by anticipating their cash resources and requirements.

Reporting and Control. Another area neglected by companies is comprehensive reporting and control from a cash management perspective. The failure to relate good cash management with reporting and control has reached the point that many believe that the two are mutually exclusive. This is not the case. The emergence of the computer has made it possible to obtain reliable cash forecasting and good reporting required for timely cash management. Treasurers or financial directors can now acquire cost effective equipment and software to develop the cash management tools that they need. Additional capabilities are developed through a direct interface with the computer systems of production and accounting.

OBJECTIVES OF CASH MANAGEMENT

To rationalize cash flows, certain management objectives must be set. International policies will have different priorities than domestic ones. For example, liquidity might be of paramount importance for international cash management while it is less important for domestic operations. In actual practice, the multinational firm will set a policy which represents a combination of the objectives described below.

Minimize the Cost of Funds. With interest rates averaging 10 to 12 percent or more in many countries, tremendous savings are possible when the cost of funds is minimized. One way to do so is through the improved internal generation of funds and reduced borrowings.

Improve Liquidity. Many managers have probably improved the liquidity within a given country, within the parent country where the headquarters is located or, especially, in those countries where there is an efficient nation-wide banking system. But it is difficult to improve liquidity in a global context, e.g., because regulations prohibit the free transfer of funds or because companies assume a tax burden when transferring funds outside of a country. Improving liquidity is an important objective and is directly related to reducing the cost of funds.

Maintain Risk Parameters. Conducting a global business involves business, economic, and political risks. These risks are multiplied for each country where the firm conducts its business. Therefore certain risk limits need to be set. Typically, people think of risk parameters almost exclusively in investment management and, to a degree, in the management of credit to customers. A more all-encompassing objective of managing operating and financial risk parameters is needed in all aspects of any business, especially cash management.

Improve the Return on Investment. Increasingly, multinational firms look to set selected ratios to measure performance, for instance, a return on investment or asset ratio. As an example, a major multinational company operating throughout the world changed to a return-on-assets concept in managing and monitoring the performance of its various international subsidiaries. It found that its outstanding receivables, day sales outstanding, had gone down drastically, from a fifty-day average to the point where the average is about ten days on outstanding sales in most countries. Operations in the typically slower paying countries average fourteen days. Improving financial performance at the operating level is a very important aspect of treasury management.

CASH MANAGEMENT REVIEW AND ANALYSIS

Having formulated a policy or goal for cash management, the next step is to determine a program for review and analysis leading to the successful implementation of recommendations. Companies that wish to study cash and treasury management and that expect to develop a comprehensive series of recommendations as well as a comprehensive way of implementing those recommendations can choose from two standard approaches: a bottom-up approach or a top-down approach.

The Bottom-Up Approach

The bottom-up approach begins at the local subsidiary level, where one looks at the operation of an individual subsidiary to determine whether that subsidiary is performing well in comparison to the business and banking conditions in a given country. If there are multiple subsidiaries, one will look at them on a countrywide basis to make certain that cash management within that country is collectively efficient. Once the companies within a country have been evaluated, one can consider whether cash and treasury management should be brought up to a higher level beyond the subsidiary level, to a country level, or into a regional concept. One will then be in a position to determine how to bring reporting and control into the headquarters level. The bottom-up approach is a building block program for cash management (see Exhibit 13-1).

Companies that pursue this approach have primarily indigenous cash flows and either limited or one-directional cross-border cash flows. Their operations usually are fairly well confined to a given country or a given region. In those cases, the production is done locally, and the goods are sold locally. Examples would be retailers or food processing companies which purchase the raw materials locally, package the materials, and sell them to a large extent within the country.

The Top-Down Approach

The top-down approach looks at cash management from the headquarters level and examines, typically through questionnaire or through a more superficial direct observation, what the various subsidiaries are doing worldwide; it then comes up with a comprehensive plan in which the headquarters immediately improves control of treasury operations and perhaps assumes greater responsibility for financial transactions. A company that feels it is very highly centralized is able to develop this type of approach.

EXHIBIT 13-1   The Bottom-Up Approach to Cash Management

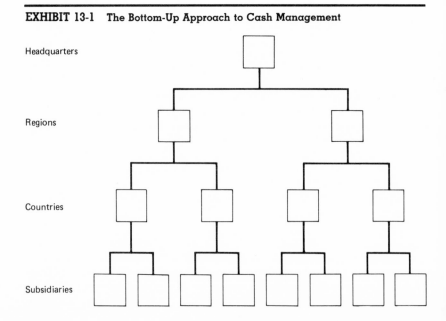

Companies that have significant cross-border flows pursue this type of approach to their cash management, and they do it because they value analyzing and improving the cross-border cash flows. The value from efficient cross-border flows is considered greater than value from the indigenous cash flows.

Companies using this approach include the high-technology companies and the component manufacturing companies that produce various components in different countries throughout the world and then assemble them at a central point. The finished product may then be shipped back and sold in the countries where the subsidiary companies have made the component parts. There is a high level of intercompany and cross-border flow that needs to be evaluated, and decisions must be made quickly, from a centralized point of view, at the headquarters level. This headquarters could be a regional headquarters; it is not necessarily the parent company (see Exhibit 13-2).

The right approach has to be tailored to suit the company's objectives; it must suit the operational style of the company, and it might be evolutionary and not necessarily revolutionary. The study also must be timely; it should not disrupt the operation. The final recommendation should be implemented promptly and in a manner that will demonstrate tangible results.

EXHIBIT 13-2   The Top-Down Approach to Cash Management

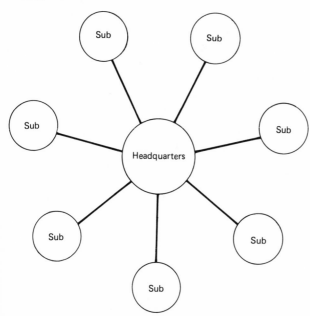

This relates to the need to be cost effective—it makes no sense to go through an elaborate analysis and to come up with very good recommendations if they cannot be cost-justified and reasonably implemented.

Of particular concern is the maintenance of performance standards with the commensurate incentives for local management. In addition, local managers must feel that their responsibilities are not diminished. In theory, multinational companies should have the same global opportunities as they do domestic ones. Some might argue that they should have more. In fact, the complications imposed by the various local environments limit some of those opportunities. There is a need, therefore, to understand the movement of indigenous and cross-border funds, what the limitations are and what the opportunities are, and to devise a structure and strategies that allow for the free movement of funds that is consistent with the company's objectives. There are several key segments of a review that need to be considered.

Collections

Before fully assessing the collection and disbursement of funds, one must understand the local banking systems. Bank clearing systems are generally little understood by people who do not deal with them on a regular basis. For effective cash management, it is important to understand how business is transacted and how the banks clear payment transactions in each country. This is often complicated in cross-border transfers, where the clearing process in all countries handling the payment must be understood. Likewise, it is important to know the clearing system for the various types of instruments used for payments and the appropriate collection procedures for a given clearing system. As an example, a lock box system will not be fully effective in a banking system that provides same-day value nationwide. Knowledge of the clearing system allows the company to select the most advantageous disbursement procedure and the manner in which it should collect payments from its customers. Equally important, knowledge about the clearing process is a major factor in preparing reliable cash forecasts; no reasoned cash forecast can be developed without specific knowledge of how long a particular item will take to clear.

The preferences in a given country for collection and mobilization differ tremendously. In the United States and the United Kingdom, for example, the check is still the predominant method of transferring funds; in other countries, other mechanisms have been developed. There are highly developed lock box and electronic transfer systems in the United States; the United Kingdom has not needed to develop the former concept.

Disbursements

It is important to consider disbursement practices rather than collection practices, because, in most cases, even though vendors collect receipts, the customers determine the method by which they will disburse the funds.

Therefore, from a cash management and a cash collection perspective, one has to first look at the disbursement preference of the customers. That preference has to be examined in conjunction with the banking system in that particular country. The U.K. system, for example, uses the check as the predominant form of payment. Other countries, in particular Germany, Holland, and Belgium, use the credit giro system, in which a customer prepares a dual or a triple voucher, depending on the country. The remittor then goes to the bank and presents the voucher; on the voucher is the name of the vendor and the bank account where the vendor wants the payment to go. That voucher is then presented through the banking system, where it ultimately reaches the vendor's account.

The reverse of the giro is the direct debit. This is not a disbursement preference but a collection preference. The vendor establishes an agreement with the customer which allows the seller's bank to charge (debit) the customer's account on a regular basis. Regular can be once a month or in accordance with the payment terms of a particular invoice. Vendors go to their banks with debit vouchers, and their banks present the vouchers to the customers' accounts. The vendors know exactly when they will receive good value. This concept is widely used in Germany, Belgium, and Holland, where vendors strongly negotiate this point with the customer. The vendor can offer the bank the job of processing its total cash collections. The value dating is negotiated based on the bank receiving all or a substantial portion of the customer's collection business. This is a valuable piece of business for the bank. The direct debit concept is growing in importance in several countries throughout the world.

Float Management and Compensation

In the United States, the banks have until recently relied heavily on the concept of compensating balances. Many European bankers will say that they do not; they deal with value dating, and their compensation is on a fee basis. Treasurers must look at their cash balances to avoid also compensating banks with balances. All these aspects of float management, the balances that are maintained with the bank and the fee compensation paid to the various banks, are part of assessing the total cost of managing the cash. In the United States, banks work on an actual value date basis which is controlled by the Federal Reserve System. In the European countries there is usually a specific value date which is assigned to each and every payment, so that one can look at the bank statement and know specifically when a particular check, or wire, or other form of payment will clear through the banking system.

In many cases, the value dating system will work to one's benefit, but in other cases it is detrimental to the operation. A company in Germany, for example, was able to negotiate a much better clearing time with its German bankers than was the standard. The business improved its cash flow tremendously by negotiating preferential terms.

Part of improving the business environment includes challenging the bankers' environment, which requires knowledge of what amount of business is given to each bank. Then one must confront the banks and negotiate a realistic price for doing business domestically and worldwide.

Bank Selection

As discussed in Chapter 12, bank selection and the overall banking network designed by the multinational company is an important topic. It is closely related to float management compensation, and successful negotiation. In any country there will be a central bank. Depending on the country, there might be a direct interface with that central bank or only an indirect association among the various commercial banks. In all countries the commercial banks will provide a complete range of financial services. There are, in addition, the savings banks. Typically, in many countries the savings banks only support the retail market, and/or support the housing market or some other specialized function. But, in countries such as Germany, the large savings banks, the *Landesbanks*, are making a major competitive thrust against the commercial banks. Thus, in certain countries, better value dating might be available at savings banks than at commercial banks.

Some countries have banking cooperatives that provide even better, or more competitive, services than some of the traditional banks. There are mortgage banks; there is the postal giro or the postal savings bank, which often provides competitive services. The post offices throughout the world have become a major factor in cash management. A study in Japan showed that the Japanese post office was an important factor in improving the company's cash flow.

Once the nature of the banks and their services is understood, one must then design the appropriate network. The successful implementation of that network and the package of services requires direct negotiation with the banks. Sound knowledge of the banking system and the company's requirements results in effective negotiations.

Cross-Border Funds Movement

The cross-border movement of funds is one of the more difficult aspects of global treasury management. There are difficulties with currency management, exchange regulations, taxation, and timing. In a foreign exchange transaction, there can be a two-day delay in the conversion to good funds. Controlling the timing of foreign exchange conversion is important; obviously, converting foreign exchange on a Thursday or Friday will tie up funds in the banking system over the weekend. The objective is to develop a structured and disciplined approach to foreign exchange remittances so that the value date occurs without a value loss over a weekend. The funds should be used efficiently and effectively within the company and not in the banking system.

Foreign exchange regulations and controls often affect a structured approach to cross-border cash movements, and these regulations must be examined on a country-by-country basis. Then one must look at the interaction of the countries, forming a matrix to come up with the optimum set of regulations, or lack of regulations, that allows for the free and timely movement of funds among all affiliated subsidiaries.

Telecommunications

Wire Transfer. For the cross-border movement of funds, the wire transfer is the old standby. It is still an efficient way to move money between two countries; however, it can be bogged down by the bureaucracy at the banks and within companies. The wire transfer system almost exclusively is a manual system in which the company prepares a manual input to the bank, the bank takes that message and types it into a telex machine, it is received by a bank, which takes the message out and types up some type of advice and possibly telephones to acknowledge receipt of funds. Clearly, this area needs further automation.

SWIFT. The SWIFT system is the automated alternative to the telex. It is a computerized information or communication system, not a payment clearing system. It enhances the clearing and payment process so that the bank inputs the transfer information in a standardized manner and the receiving bank receives the transfer information almost instantaneously. There is no multiple handling and reentry of the same payment information. Also, the banks are very aggressive in designing computer interfaces with the SWIFT system, allowing for the direct posting of an incoming payment to a customer's account. Once that manual movement of funds and documents from the bank to the customer's account is eliminated, one can expect significant cash management improvements in the cross-border transfer of funds. Companies should investigate their banks' commitment to SWIFT and the status of the automation effort. The response will provide some sign as to the aggressiveness and commitment of the bank to cash management.

Example of Savings in International Transfer

To move money across borders, payers in a given country will instruct their branch offices to initiate a transfer and to debit their accounts (Exhibit 13-3). Typically that branch office is not a major international office for that particular bank, and therefore the payment instruction is forwarded to either the headquarters or the main international branch for the region to transfer the funds out of the country. Banks deal with other banks overseas on a correspondent basis. They establish reciprocal deposit accounts and test key relationships so that the receiving bank can test the validity of a given payment instruction. Exhibit 13-3 implies that XXX Bank cannot or will not transfer funds directly to ZZZ Bank. It decided to go through its correspondent in country Y, YYY Bank who will then make payment to ZZZ Bank.

The payee typically will not have an account with the headquarters or international office but will have a branch account elsewhere with bank Z. The headquarters will then transfer the payment to the particular branch. Even with a telegraphic transfer, substantial delays can and do occur. The most obvious recommendation, resulting in immediate savings, is for the company to change its account or to ask the payer to pay from a different bank so that there is a direct relationship between box B and box D. The company can then consider moving its account from box E, the branch, to the headquarters in box D.

Finally, it might be feasible to have the payer deal directly with the head-quarter office; that would also shorten the time for the movement of funds. Vendors should not be afraid to talk to their customers about this solution. In many cases both sides are the losers in the management of cash, and one of the three banks in the process or all the three banks in the process, benefit from the current situation. A company should contact its customer and say, "You are losing value immediately, and I am not getting value for x number of days; let us share the savings and work out a more realistic manner of transferring funds between our two companies."

EXHIBIT 13-3   An International Transfer

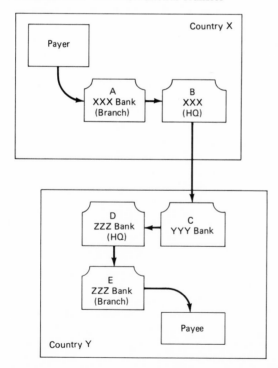

Example of Saving within a Country

Within a given country—taking the credit giro example—the payer prepares the giro. The giro voucher is presented at the payer's bank, the bank ultimately making payment to the payee's bank. Then the receiver's bank provides an advice within an appropriate time. Exhibit 13-4 illustrates the payment cycle, possibly a short route for the movement of a cash transfer. In fact, there can be numerous clearing banks in the gray area that could be involved in the clearing process. For example, suppose the payer's bank, a major German commercial bank, is the same bank as the payee's bank but a different branch. Unless the preprinted statement on the giro authorizing the German bank to use its discretion in the clearing of the giro is stricken from the voucher, the payer's bank can control the movement of that voucher through the clearing system. Since they have immediately debited the payer's account, the payment need not be expeditiously cleared to the receiver's account. It is possible that a number of intermediary branches or banks might be involved in the clearing process until payment is ultimately received by the vendor. Typically one finds, especially where there are distant payers and payees, that the banks use the clearing network to their best advantage.

EXHIBIT 13-4   Giro Processing

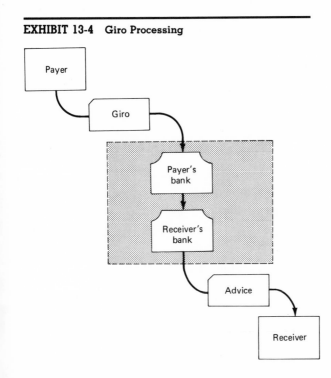

Summary: Payment Systems in Three Countries

Highlighting the collection and payment preferences in three countries will clarify differences in banking systems and payment mechanisms.

Germany. In Germany the predominant method of payment is the credit giro, the credit transfer, but increasingly the direct debit is being used (the use of checks has declined in recent years). The giro system is efficient both at the commercial and savings banks, although, as previously explained, significant discretion in the clearing process is possible. The direct debit system is inherently more efficient, because the vendor's bank is giving a specific value date and must collect the proceeds by that time. Checks are still used for large payments. The big companies know the clearing processes for checks: they know that check clearance is longer than for giros, they know the cost of paying by check, and, if there is a particularly large payment, they will send a check and not use the more efficient giro method. They control their disbursements by selecting the payment instrument with the longest clearing time.

Japan. In Japan circumstances are entirely different. There is a high use of transfer between accounts, which is comparable to a combination between a giro system and a wire transfer. Many large companies and even many consumers make payment via the direct transfer method. Japan, however, is still a cash society, and even companies pay relatively large bills with cash.

Brazil. In Brazil the check is the predominant method of payment, for three reasons: the extremely high rates of inflation, the poor postal system, and a major need for good credit and control policies. The Brazilian collection system typically involves a collector physically going to a company with an invoice and collecting the check and then driving to the nearest branch of the company's principal bank and depositing that check. Brazilian banks have moved aggressively into the area of bank listing, where a company can provide a computer to list its payments at a given bank. The list is put on computer tape and transferred to the bank in which the payment is being directed. However, even though the list is put on computer tape, the tape must be conveyed from one bank to the other by a courier and usually is not telecommunicated.

INTERNATIONAL CASH MANAGEMENT TECHNIQUES

This section describes the more sophisticated systems that multinational companies are using for their global cash management. For the most part, domestic and international cash management has been technique oriented. It is important to understand the techniques, but it is equally important to understand that these techniques are solutions and that implementation of a solution in an unstudied manner will not necessarily solve a problem. In considering a specific technique, corporate treasurers have to achieve the desired objectives and produce the expected benefits. Accordingly, this section summarizes the advantages and disadvantages of the various techniques.

Netting

Netting is a favorite technique of numerous multinational companies. This is a very simple technique principally designed for the physical offsetting of intercompany payments. The concept is to reduce the number of transactions that a multinational company would make amongst its subsidiaries and through its banks. Corresponding with that reduction in the number of transfers is a reduction in the value of those transfers and commissions paid to the banks. There are also savings in the value of the float that is flowing through the banking system. Further, savings result from centralizing the conversion of the foreign currencies at a central point and executing the transfers on a scheduled basis. Prior to initiating a netting system, a careful analysis and review of local foreign exchange control regulations must be made.

If a German subsidiary owed 6 million French francs to a French subsidiary, and the French subsidiary owed 1 million Deutsche marks to the German subsidiary, a netting system would first express those two values in either one of the currencies or in a third currency (common currency) at a spot rate. By expressing the payables in a common currency, one can identify the net payment. The net amount would be transferred in the appropriate local currency. As an example, using pounds sterling as the base currency, let us say that the German company in fact owed the equivalent of £1 million to the French company, and the French company owed the equivalent of £0.5 million to the German company; the German company would only transfer the equivalent of £0.5 million in French francs to the French company. If there were multiple invoices underlying the value of that transaction, instead of multiple payments being made, only one payment would be made with identification of all the invoices to be settled. This is an example of a bilateral net.

A multilateral netting among three or more subsidiaries is more complicated. The netting procedure takes one side of the intercompany balance sheet, either all the intercompany payables or all the intercompany receivables. A matrix is formed matching those payables or receivables against the disbursor or the recipient (Exhibit 13-5). The matrix will take all the invoices regardless of their currency and array the information expressed in a common currency. A U.K.-based multinational would probably want all the intercompany payables expressed in sterling terms regardless of the underlying currency, whereas a U.S. multinational would want a U.S. dollar–denominated matrix. The receipts are summed by each subsidiary and the aggregate payables subtracted, the payables from the receivables, to get a net payment or receipt for each subsidiary (Exhibit 13-6). Foreign exchange conversions would be centralized. In all likelihood, there would be a central treasury point that would negotiate the conversion of the currencies, thus obtaining better rates from its bank by dealing in higher volume.

Netting has two disadvantages. First, it does not significantly affect the foreign exchange exposure. One or perhaps both subsidiaries have a currency exposure, and conversions are usually on a spot basis. Depending on the firm's policy, forward exchange cover may be limited at the local subsidiary level. Second, third-party transactions often are not included in a netting program. The company with limited intercompany reciprocal trade, therefore, would not achieve optimum benefits through netting.

Pooling

Pooling is the concentration of cash at a central point. It is easily done in most countries of the world within the borders of a country, especially in those countries that have national banking systems. If the banks do not offer it freely, it is possible to negotiate with them so that either all deposits made by all subsidiaries at various branches throughout the country either are physically concentrated at a central point, or a firm is given a countrywide credit for all deposits within a particular banking institution. Thus all cash collections from subsidiaries that are generating cash would immediately offset the overdraft position from the other subsidiaries that are net borrowers. The net effect is the direct application of the cash to the outstanding debt obligations, minimizing the cost of funds for the group as a whole. A management reporting system is then needed to compensate those subsidiaries that supply funds and charge the subsidiaries that require the cash. This system is often available through the local banks.

The difficulty with pooling comes when it is organized in a multicurrency, multicountry environment. Physically concentrating funds of different currencies in a given country is almost impossible. Assume that a company has subsidiaries in the Netherlands, Germany, France, and Belgium, and all have excess cash; the company wants to concentrate those funds in Holland. But the regulatory and tax environment makes this difficult. Even

EXHIBIT 13-5 Multilateral International Payments Netting Matrix: Paying Affiliates

	United States	Belgium	France	Italy	Total receipts
United States		300	400	500	1200
Belgium	400		200	300	900
France	500	300		100	900
Italy	600	500	200		1300
Total payments	1500	1100	800	900	4300

if these issues are addressed, currency risk often makes the pooling process extremely complicated and reduces the expected benefits. If the company in our example keeps deposits in the original currencies, the purpose of pooling the funds in the first place is defeated. Taking the excess Deutsche marks and transferring them to Holland to be held in a "DM hold" account does not help—they might as well be left in Germany, since the objective is to concentrate funds in the parent's currency or appreciating currency.

Through the pooling concept, large and infrequent transfers can occur. This usually requires a multinational bank to act as an agent for the loan. As one example, if a company has excess Deutsche marks which it needs in France, it may find a bank or a group of banks where it could place the Deutsche marks on deposit and have funds borrowed in French francs by its French subsidiary, possibly minimizing the cost of funds. This is not pure pooling, but it is an offshoot of the concept. The foreign exchange risk can be covered through the interest rates and the loan contract.

Leading and Lagging

The technique of leading and lagging is typically discussed in conjunction with foreign exchange management, but it is also useful in cash management. Leading and lagging alters the sources and uses of cash within the organization. Typically, this technique is associated with intercompany accounts. The intercompany receivable and payable positions are examined worldwide. Where regulations permit leading and/or lagging, an analysis of the net cash or deficit position of the various subsidiaries, the impact of the foreign exchange rates, interest rates, and the associated tax rates is made under alternative scenarios. The company determines whether one subsidiary should pay another company in advance (lead) to take advantage of an excess cash situation at the company. Alternatively, a payment could be delayed (lagged) if the arbitrage is favorable. A payment may be lagged from one company to another when the payer company is in a deficit position and would like to forgo additional borrowings by not paying a particular invoice or group of invoices. The result of this exercise is the arbitrage of financial transactions against local and offshore interest and foreign exchange markets to the collective benefit of the company.

EXHIBIT 13-6 Multilateral International Payments Netting Matrix: Net Payments

	Payment	Receipt	Net payment	Net receipt
United States	1500	1200	300	
Belgium	1100	900	200	
France	800	900		100
Italy	900	1300		400

The dynamics of leading and lagging come into play when a sophisticated cash forecasting system is set up and leading and lagging decisions can be integrated with forecasting and exposure management. The impact of decisions can then be clearly seen on a net aftertax basis for the individual subsidiaries and for the company as a whole. As a note of warning, excessive leading and lagging, regardless of the exchange regulations, can raise potential tax problems in the jurisdictions of either the buyer or seller.

Global Liquidity Management

Global liquidity management embodies each of the techniques discussed above. Implementation of the concept requires an analysis of the firm's worldwide operations to determine where there is excess cash and where that cash can best be applied within the organization. In business jargon, the need is to find the cash "cows" and to apply that cash to the net users. In an international environment, the movement is complicated, but by first studying the tax and regulatory aspects, one can determine when the funds are available and required, the appropriate form of transfer, and how they can be transferred.

A word on the appropriate form of transfer is important. The key aspect of global liquidity management is to have all legal and tax jurisdictions treat the transactions in the same manner. By form, we mean whether the payment is a dividend, loan, interest payment, or perhaps some sort of swap, parallel, or other technique for delivery of the funds. As an example, an intercompany loan must be treated as a loan and not a capital contribution (equity), because interest and dividend payments are treated differently for tax and regulatory purposes. If a sophisticated global liquidity program is not appropriate, one can then look at the other techniques, such as netting, pooling, and leading and lagging, to see if any of these concepts further support the objectives for global liquidity management in a less complicated manner.

Global liquidity management must be consistent with the objectives of the company. Short- and long-term concerns, strategic responses that solve immediate problems, and structural solutions that solve long-term problems must be defined.

Reinvoicing Center

The reinvoicing center goes another step in sophistication. It also is usually discussed in a foreign exchange management context, and it too has direct cash management implications. A typical objective in foreign exchange management is to centralize foreign exchange exposures in one unit. Subsidiaries often buy and sell in multiple currencies and must manage the resulting exposures. Some mechanism is needed so that they operate their business exclusively on a local currency basis without the active management of currency exposures. The need is to eliminate or reduce exposure management at the operating company.

To achieve that goal, a reinvoicing company is set up that agrees to purchase on behalf of the group companies in the various foreign currencies and then to reinvoice or rebill those purchases to the operating subsidiaries in their local currencies. For example, if the French subsidiary were to purchase equipment in Germany for Deutsche marks, the reinvoicing company would purchase that equipment in the name of the French company, pay the supplier in Deutsche marks, bill the French subsidiary in French francs, and receive French francs from the buyer. The reinvoicing company would also agree to manage all intercompany and third-party receivables and payables denominated in foreign currency.

As another example, if the French subsidiary was selling into Eastern Europe and had to invoice in either Deutsche marks or dollars to be competitive in the market, the sale would be initially sold to the reinvoicing center, which would pay the French company in French francs and then reinvoice the third party in the currency that was agreed to in the contract. Again, the center has complete control over the foreign currency. To the extent that a large portion of those payments are intercompany payments, it also has complete control over the timing of the cash flows.

International Financing Vehicles

Related to the reinvoicing center is the international financing vehicle, typically referred to as the international finance company (IFC) or the offshore factoring company (OFC). This approach can have the same benefits as the reinvoicing center. For instance, where a sale is made to a third party, typically for marketing considerations, it would disrupt the buyer-seller relationship if our hypothetical French company now had an invoice prepared by an affiliated third-party (reinvoicing center) and sent to the Eastern European customer. To achieve the benefit of reinvoicing without the reinvoicing process, the French company might sell or factor the invoice, presenting the receivable to a finance company with or without recourse. An agreement would exist whereby the finance company would revalue the receivable in terms of French francs and would agree to pay the French exporter according to specified terms or actual collection from the buyer. The OFC would both provide the financing and take on the currency risk.

Although it is usually desirable to have the IFC's activities tied to trade financing, the movement and the financing of goods need not be directly interrelated. The international financing vehicle might simply be a group finance company that provides financing to various operations on a worldwide basis. The key problems with this situation are the withholding taxes on the interest paid on intercompany loans and the regulations that allow or prohibit the movement of funds between related institutions within the same company.

Both the reinvoicing center and the international financing vehicles give companies additional sophistication and an additional degree of flexibility in managing their cash.

Multicurrency Management Center

The ultimate, in terms of sophistication, is the multicurrency management center. It brings all the techniques described into a central organization. The organization might be at the headquarters level or at a regional treasury center. It might be formally constituted as a company in a specific country, or it might be a center controlling the flow of funds and, most important, the information related to that flow of funds. There are many ways to achieve an objective, but they will all fall short if the information and reporting systems are not there to support them. Decisions cannot be taken away from local management and centralized where the information is incomplete. Poor information increases the likelihood of making a wrong decision at the central entity due to incomplete data rather than poor financial skills. Fortunately, with the development of the computer this controlled information can be brought into a central point in a timely and meaningful manner.

CENTRALIZED TREASURY MANAGEMENT

In determining the appropriate techniques for a company, one must consider the stage of the firm's international development. There are four identifiable phases in the development of the multinational company. At the first level, the early development, the subsidiary is responsible for its cash management. Typically, a company decides, for various reasons, to enter a given country. It sends marketing or production people from the head office or hires locals. Because the market potential is so great, no one worries about the cash management. Reporting to headquarters is generally of a performance nature, i.e., sales and net income.

As the number of subsidiaries and production facilities grow, the company develops a division-level function for cash management. That function is typically supported by outdated reports that might not be designed specifically for the treasury function. The information includes monthly balance sheets, profit and loss statements from the subsidiaries, and maybe a listing of outstanding debt and outstanding balances of various bank accounts. By the time the information is received, either by telex or by the mail system, the situation could have changed completely, and thus not much can be done on a day-to-day management basis. Exhibit 13-7 shows, as an oversimplification, the cash flow situation that might develop in an unstructured environment. There are no central coordinating point, no organization, no rationalization of the movement of product and the cash flows. Plants are trading with each other and making payments to each other, and the sales offices are doing the same. Of greatest importance is that management only sees a month-end position and has no feel for day-to-day cash flows.

The next level of development involves a worldwide responsibility for cash management at the corporate treasurer's level. This responsibility includes the banking relationships, the mobilization of money, and funds disbursement. Many companies are just entering this phase, and very few have moved into the area of a worldwide integrated treasury system. This later phase includes not only the centralized control over cash management and integrated cash management on a global basis but also the internal systems to support this integrated treasury system. Internal systems include not only the computer support but also standardized practices and procedures for handling money globally. Thus, if a treasury manager from one subsidiary is put in charge of the treasury at another subsidiary in another country, she or he could quickly understand the procedures because they would be essentially the same.

Again as an oversimplification, the third and fourth stages of cash management will look like Exhibit 13-8. Cash management will have a center that controls at least the physical movement of funds regardless of currency.

An example of how a multinational company examined the issue of centralization follows. Do not take this cash management scheme and blindly apply the system to your company. It is not that simple. The idea is to determine on a spectrum of decentralized to centralized where a particular company is now positioned and where it should be. Then, the design of a system can be considered.

EXHIBIT 13-7   Early Stages of Multinational Company Funds Flow

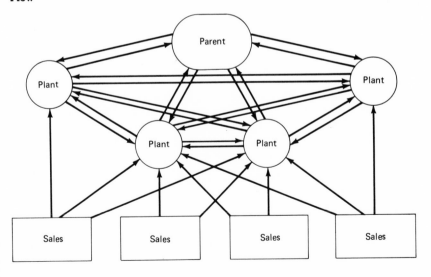

There are four basic steps. The first is to examine the need for the centralization of foreign exchange management. That might be the principal objective of the exercise. Second, if cash flows are understood as monies denominated in the various currencies, then the interrelationship between foreign exchange management and cash management can be clearly seen. One must therefore examine the centralization of cash. Third, the feasibility of integrating the two disciplines of cash management and foreign exchange management into a consistent treasury organization should then be considered with recommendations for a specific organization and policies. Finally, the desired system must be implemented, not as an "off the shelf" package that might prove to be barely satisfactory but as a desired system that the company wants and needs to tailor to its own particular requirements.

Cost. With implementation there are several areas of concern: the first is cost. It is not inexpensive to evaluate an operation and to implement recommendations. Consideration must be given to what new accounting systems, if any, might be required or what adjustments to existing accounting systems might be required. The development of an information system for the central treasury, or the group treasury, must be examined as part of a cost-benefit analysis. The number and type of staff support services required by the new central treasury organization must be considered.

Accounting. The accounting methods and systems can pose a serious problem. For example, once the financial control is taken away from the operating entities, how are the accounting entries to be collected, processed, and then transferred back to the operating companies? The recommended sys-

EXHIBIT 13-8   Multicurrency Management Center

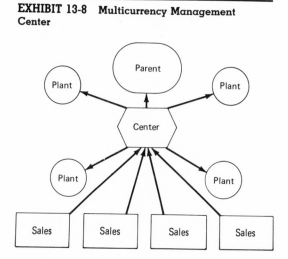

tem must coordinate with the accepted accounting practices and methods in each country of operation.

Profit Margins. Finally, profit margins have to be protected. With all the above techniques, there is no manipulation of the transfer price between subsidiaries or third parties. The central treasury function should not be developed to abuse transfer pricing within an organization. The various regulatory authorities that have to approve the new system that is under development will examine possible pricing conflicts in great detail. An arm's-length relationship should be established with profit margins maintained at the local subsidiary level.

Performance Management. Subsidiaries should not be adverse to the removal of foreign exchange risk from their purview. They need to understand the effect on their net aftertax profitability once foreign exchange and cash management is centralized, but they cannot consistently claim that the action reduces consistent operating profits. They can legitimately question whether they are being adequately compensated for their participation in a central treasury system. The management performance reporting system plays an important role in the acceptance of centralized treasury management.

Exposure Management. The most appropriate way to examine the desirability of centralized treasury management is through a phased approach as described above. Foreign exchange management policies and procedures need to be studied and examined, and they need to be evaluated from the perspective of risk rather than profitability. Centralized treasury management should not be considered a method of guaranteeing a profit on foreign exchange dealing. It should be seen as a potential for minimizing the foreign exchange risk and the gain or loss associated with the reduction of the gross foreign exchange exposure for the firm as a whole. The foreign exchange component should be clearly broken out in reviewing the formation of the central treasury company.

Cash Management. Likewise, the cash management aspect should be looked at independently. Cash flows should be examined and quantified, and what the values of those flows are and what they could be under alternative management scenarios should be analyzed. Determining what the cash management policies and procedures should be to implement the chosen cash management system is the next step. Once the cash management and the foreign exchange management have been examined, they can be brought together, and the feasibility of a central treasury organization can be looked at to determine the organization, the techniques used, and the location of that center should be. The treasury organization should be situated or associated with a major operating subsidiary rather than a tax haven. The location must make sense from an organizational and operational point of view as well as a tax point of view, and it should solve not only the short-term tax situation but a long-term one as well.

Banking. Supporting the treasury operation is a customized banking network. There is every reason to believe that the network can be built around existing relationships. It should be possible to negotiate more competitive terms with the existing banks from a central point, and there might also be a need to bring in other specialized banks. Probably, a number of banks and bank accounts will be reduced.

Benefits of Centralization

One of the major benefits of centralization is the potential reduction of exposure risk through centralizing foreign exchange exposures. It is reduced both through better management and through the matching of receivables and payables in the same currency. If one subsidiary sold only in dollars and another subsidiary purchased only in dollars and those cash flows are similar, the bringing of the two together in a central organization reduces the exposure nearly to zero.

Going through the evaluation process will throw up certain improved cash management practices that should benefit the company, and the exercises will improve liquidity. If it does not, the implementation would probably not go forward. What should be a direct benefit, but in most cases tends to be an indirect benefit, is that the information reporting from a treasury point of view is greatly improved. Treasurers or financial directors can now say that this is information they need to effectively manage the finances of their company, that they will design it the way they want it, and that they will use it how they want to use it. They need not be tied to the accounting, marketing, or production priorities of the company in their information requirements.

Fourteen: Accounting in the International Arena

J. KENNETH HICKMAN

Mr. Hickman, a certified public accountant, is a partner of Arthur Andersen & Co. and is presently director of the firm's international business practice. He received his B.S. degree from Fordham University College of Business Administration in 1951. He is a member of the American Institute of Certified Public Accountants, the New Jersey and New York State societies of certified public accountants, the National Association of Accountants, and the American Accounting Association. He is past president of the Bergen chapter of the New Jersey Society of CPAs and was a trustee of the Society. Mr. Hickman is a governor of the Foreign Policy Association and a director of the National Foreign Trade Council, the Business Council for International Understanding, and the Ireland-U.S. Council for Commerce and Industry, where he also serves as vice president. He also serves on the Advisory Board of the United Nations International Business Council and is a member of the American Council on Germany.

As chair of the E.C. Committee of the National Foreign Trade Council and an active participant in the U.S. Industry Coordinating Group on E.C. matters, he is intimately involved with developments in proposed European Community legislation that will affect trade with the ten member states.

Mr. Hickman wishes to give special recognition to Mr. Peter E. Berger, an experienced audit manager with Arthur Andersen & Co., for his invaluable assistance in preparation of this chapter.

14-1

How does one play the game when the scorekeepers cannot keep score—or worse, when each scorekeeper follows a different set of rules? The answer is, "Very carefully!" That is the way it is in the arena of international accounting. And, despite noble-sounding efforts, it will continue to be this way in to the foreseeable future.

Resignation to these circumstances is the first step for international financial executives in setting the frame for the discharge of their responsibilities for the remainder of this century. A most important next step is the maintenance of a serious monitoring of the heightened attempts to narrow the areas of accounting differences under the righteous-sounding objective of "rationalization." With this knowledge, financial managers can attempt to influence these developments in their enterprises' favor; in some companies this activity is called "issue management" and is more frequently applied to such matters as environmental controls and regulations of intellectual property. Financial executives should investigate their company's experience in these other areas and they will find that they can easily draw a parallel to their own discipline. Whether or not the issue is managed to their liking, financial executives will find sufficient time between the decision and the implementation to allow them to soften the impact of the decision for the operating benefit of their company. These matters have become important enough to warrant the establishment of a specific position within large organizations. At the least, specific responsibilities should be written into a job description within the financial department.

For decades, and particularly since World War II, businesses and governments have been figuratively wringing their hands over the diversity of accounting principles and financial reporting around the world. Many organizations are attempting to standardize, or rationalize, some principles in an attempt to make "like transactions look alike." On balance, they have met with limited success, and users of financial statements of enterprises outside their own countries are left largely to their own devices to convert these statements to their particular needs. For example, the Seventh Directive of the European Economic Community is a major step toward improving the completeness of public reporting in that it requires the preparation and publication of fully consolidated financial statements in a single currency. However, these will not be as much help to financial executives as the separate local currency financial statements of the units with which, or for which, they are contemplating a contractual relationship. In fact, these consolidated statements will have eliminated or obscured data in which executives may be greatly interested.

An area which warrants the special attention of the international financial executive is the recording of deferred income taxes so widely used in the United States and in most Commonwealth countries. To comprehend the accounting concepts, first one must understand that in these countries there are considerable differences between fair presentation of financial statements and financial reporting for tax purposes. Indeed, the existence or nonexistence of a deferred income tax account is the first clue for the financial executive in conforming accounting financial statements and in evaluating a potential investment, partner, or customer. If such an account is recorded, a thorough analysis is needed to determine present values and to predict future cash flows. If one does not exist, it is a clear indication that financial reporting is controlled and, perhaps, distorted, by tax reporting, and the financial statements are not likely to give a fair presentation in accordance with the requirements of one's home country.

This chapter provides general assistance in the conversion of local financial reports to special uses; understanding the development of accounting differences will enable the financial executive to recognize and to deal with them. Although the chapter does not make judgments about preferable standards, it does discuss two issues that will continue to occupy a great deal of attention in setting standards of public reporting and/or disclosure—accounting for inflation and for foreign currency translation. The latter may be settled in U.S. standards with the publication of Financial Accounting Standard 52, but it will continue to be a problem in other important economies of the world. International financial executives should focus on the theory as well as the pragmatic applications of these matters, because the two subjects of inflation and currency translation should continue to command attention as internal reporting requirements. In addition to attempts to assign values to each in management decision making, one cannot avoid including both factors in any equitable scheme for financial incentives to management.

Finally, this chapter provides very brief and very general comments regarding accounting for joint ventures—general because accounting standards in this regard are still emerging. However, it is clear from the trend of political developments, particularly in less developed nations, that joint ventures in a variety of legal forms, some not yet heard of, will become a much more important part of all multinational operations.

DEVELOPMENT OF INTERNATIONAL ACCOUNTING STANDARDS

Accounting data and reports are a principal facet of business information and an integral part of management decision making. Accordingly, one might expect that by now business would have achieved worldwide accounting standards—standards that are the reflection of a true and fair picture of the economic results of business decisions. However, this is not the case, as anyone who deals with financial statements prepared in accordance with the requirements of countries other than their home country can attest. Despite the conceptual appeal of worldwide standards of accounting principles, the move to "standardization" or "harmonization" is still in comparative infancy.

Accounting and reporting requirements differ considerably among the countries of the world. These differences are important to the financial executive in evaluating potential investment, in which case true and fair presentation, consistency, and future cash flow will be important. In considering customers or joint venturers, real current position and cash flow will be paramount; in preparing restatements of financial statements for consolidation, translation and consistency become more important.

The financial executive must understand the bases for these differences. Just as with tax legislation and regulations, generally accepted accounting principles in each country are based on entirely different social and economic customs and mores. Appreciation for the underlying history and concepts is frequently more important than the specific application of rules and regulations. Accounting and reporting principles in any area of the world are the result of interactions of numerous environmental forces, including social, economic, and political factors; attempts to influence all of these through tax legislation; some accounting theory; and more pragmatic accounting practices.

Colonial Traditions and Political Influences

During the period of European imperialism, nations exported more than goods and capital; they gave the world their cultures and their accounting standards. For instance, Britain's world economic position during the seventeenth and eighteenth centuries made her an ideal missionary on behalf of British accounting throughout the Empire. Meanwhile, the Germans influenced Japan, Sweden, and Czarist Russia, and the French trained most of Africa and Southeast Asia. Today, U.S. standards follow significant investments throughout the Western World, while the concept of state ownership and allocation of resources influences accounting and reporting in most of Eastern Europe and parts of Asia.

Legal Systems

In a number of countries, the requirements of company laws impede the development of sound accounting principles and practices. A number of laws sanction the use of practices that do not accord with economic reality. In Switzerland, the Code of Obligation in Acts gives "discretionary powers to the board or management of an enterprise to either carry assets at less than cost or set up hidden secret reserves; provided this is done to ensure the continued prosperity of the enterprise or to permit maintenance of the profit distribution level. Although the Company's auditors must be informed of these adjustments, no disclosure is allowed in the financial statements."[1]

In the United States, Congress specifically prohibited the accounting profession from limiting the accounting standards to be applied to the then newly enacted investment tax credit because the limitation did not suit the political purposes of the credit.

Tax Legislation

Tax legislation plays an important role in financial reporting. Of twenty-four countries surveyed in a 1975 study, nineteen reported compliance with tax laws as the primary reason for variances from accounting principles generally accepted in the United States.[2]

In a large number of countries, income and expense recognition for tax purposes must follow the reporting in the company's published results. In these countries, tax considerations significantly impact financial reporting. Expenses are frequently reported in accounts in an earlier period than the one to which they relate, and revenue is deferred.

In a publication by the Association of Authorized Public Accountants in Sweden, the impact of tax legislation is described as "having carried to the extreme the basic rule of Swedish taxation that taxable income is principally based on book income. This has been extended to the requirement that taxpayers who wish to claim several of the more important tax incentives available in Sweden must record charges in their books."[3] Accordingly, Swedish balance sheets will include a number of tax-mandated reserves, such as inventory reserves, payroll reserves, reserves for future investment, and compulsory investment reserves, that are not normally required for fair presentation. This pervasive requirement is true not only in Sweden but in a number of Latin American countries as well as other Western European countries. In Germany, to obtain the tax benefit of allowable arbitrary inventory reserves or accelerated depreciation, they must be recorded for financial reporting purposes.

In the United States, tax laws significantly impact financial reporting, although they do not generally require conformity between accounting and tax reporting. The notable exception to this nonconformity is the requirement that the LIFO (last-in, first-out) method of inventory valuation cannot be used for tax purposes unless it is also recorded for book purposes. This had a material impact on public reporting during periods of high inflation and presented a special consideration in the evaluation of U.S. companies by foreign investors who were not accustomed to this practice.

Social Legislation

Accounting is significantly affected by the economic circumstances of the nation involved—the ownership of production capacity, the average size of an enterprise, the stability of the local inflation rate, the sophistication of business management, centralization of the economy, and the stage of economic development. Accounting needs for an economy involved in agriculture or natural resources are different from those for an industrialized nation involved in high technology or financial services. Further, the same type of cost may be accounted for differently because of the social objectives of the legislation that gave rise to it. A good example is the accounting for termination indemnities. The conditions under which termination indemnities are payable vary widely from country to country. In Spain, for instance, an employer may terminate employees by either reaching agreement with the employees or obtaining government approval. Government approval will specify amounts to provide terminated employees and also allow for appeal by the affected employees. Some employers pay in excess of government requirement to avoid appeal. In general, in Italy and Peru, termination payments are required for termination, retirement, resignation, or death. In Belgium, no payment is due to resigned employees. These different economic facts require different accounting and different determinations as to when termination costs are to be accrued.

Accounting Practices around the World

To provide some insight as to the diversity of practices, the following comments briefly identify differences in accounting philosophies and principles in selected countries. Appendix 14A presents an excellent summary of significant accounting principles based on a 1982 study by F. D. S. Choi and V. B. Bayishi.[4]

United Kingdom. Accounting principles in the United Kingdom are based on "a true and fair view" of the corporation premise. In general, tax laws have little effect on accounting methods. Accounting principles are intended to protect the bondholder, creditor, and dividend-oriented investor. Accordingly, we find emphasis on such concepts as consolidated financial statements, inflation-accounting techniques, and partial allocation of deferred taxes.

Sweden. A publication by the Association of Authorized Public Accountants in Sweden states that, "The single biggest factor in distorting Swedish financial statements is the unique stranglehold which Swedish tax law and practice have on the country's accounting and reporting practices. The primary aim of Swedish financial statements is conformity with the law, in particular as regards the figure of distributable earnings. This formal approach has overshadowed the desirability of what would internationally be considered fair presentation of net income and stockholders' equity."[5]

Germany. Germany has a well-developed but highly legalistic approach to accounting. The central consideration in German reporting is compliance with the law. The underlying laws describe in detail financial reporting requirements and are strongly influenced by tax legislation. Tax incentives can be obtained only if recorded for financial reporting purposes. The principal postulate underlying German accounting principles is presentation of the corporation. As D. F. A. Davidson points out, "It is significant to note that about 70% of the equity of German companies is controlled by banks and this is the main reason why accounting is influenced by tax and auditor considerations rather than the demands of the wide-investing public."[6]

Japan. Japanese tax law requires conformity with financial statements. As Paul Aron reports, "The Japanese find it difficult to understand the meaning of two sets of books—one for the tax authorities and one for investors, let alone four sets of books that reportedly characterize some European firms—one additional for creditors and another for managers."[7] Thus the Japanese company expenses organizational, start-up, and research and development costs; rapid amortization of fixed assets and intangibles; and general purpose reserves for tax incentive purposes.

Italy. In Italy, accounting practices are governed by the civil code, which lays down certain rules as to content and the bases of valuation and is supplemented by the tax laws. Although the stated rules are clear, there is still confusion because of the way taxable income is derived; compromise is the standard. Taxes are often bookkept on a cash rather than accrual basis to avoid hampering negotiation with the tax authorities.

Brazil. Brazilian principles are significantly affected by the level of inflation. In addition to income from operations, a company's financial statements will reflect price-level restatement effects flowing through the income statement. (See section on "Accounting for Inflation.")

EFFORTS TO DEVELOP WORLDWIDE ACCOUNTING STANDARDS

This section describes the efforts of transnational organizations to standardize or harmonize worldwide accounting standards. International financial executives should heed these organizations, since they are likely to significantly impact financial reporting in the future. Even less effective organizations may provide the incubators for dramatic changes which may finally be enacted by government organizations.

Worldwide, there are uncounted bodies attempting to formulate international accounting standards. These can be divided into two categories. The first group is government or quasi-government and seeks to formulate reporting standards by political pressures, on such organizations as the United Nations, the Organization for Economic Cooperation and Development (OECD), and the European Economic Community (EEC). The second group consists of professional accounting bodies whose intent is to promulgate international accounting standards on the basis of sound theory; in the forefront is the International Accounting Standards Committee (IASC).

United Nations

The Intergovernmental Working Group of Experts on International Standards of Accounting and Reporting is the United Nations' cognizant body for the review and establishment of accounting standards. The general objective of the group is to "promote the adoption of accounting and reporting standards to improve the availability and comparability of information concerning the operations of transnationals."[8] Most of the deliberations of this group have managed to turn accounting and reporting standards into political issues between industrialized and developing nations.

The implications of the U.N. deliberations can be quite important for multinational corporations with far-flung operations extending into developing nations. The group appears intent on establishing accounting and disclosure requirements that will eventually become mandatory; that will be applied on a uniform basis to all companies irrespective of the special nature of their activities; and that will require supplementary disclosure of accounting policies used in many areas of financial reporting. These disclosures include elimination of intragroup profits; explanation of methods of accounting for investments in associated companies; segmentation of data by geographical areas, including transfers between operating units and the basis of accounting for transfers between lines of business; accounting details regarding individual member companies of the multinational group; and nonfinancial information (e.g., description of degree of centralization for decision making, description of labor relations policies in each country, employee costs, capacity utilization, and description of prospective investment projects, including their cost and effect on productive capacity). Much of the disclosure proposed by the Working Group is sensitive in one respect or another. Competitive practices and position may be revealed. Moreover, sensitive government relations may be affected by publication of some parts of the information.

The U.N. group is still in the early stages of work in this area. Corporate executives of multinationals that would be affected by these mandated disclosures should follow its progress.

Organization for Economic Cooperation and Development

The OECD began its international accounting standards efforts with its June 21, 1976 declaration by the governments of OECD member countries on international investment and multinational enterprises. Since the OECD is made up of developed countries, it represents a different view toward the multinational corporation than that of the developing world which dominates the U.N. Working Group. This is evident in the reporting standards recommended by the OECD. These standards ignore the U.N. recommendations to expand the data set contained in corporate annual reports. They tend to be distillations of national standards already used in the countries represented. Unlike the United Nations, the OECD has not really broken any new ground in its recommendations.

European Economic Community

The Treaty of Rome created the European Economic Community. Article 54(3)(g) established the goal of creating a unified business environment within the Community." To this end, the Council of Ministers of the European Communities develops directives on company law. Once directives are approved, the member nations of the EEC must incorporate them into their national laws.

The goal of EEC directives pertaining to accounting issues is "harmonization." The directives are suppose to be based on laws, accounting principles, and business practices already found within the Community. However, there is constant pressure from all sides to create new standards that have far reaching social and sometimes economic impact.

The EEC is quickly emerging as the organization most likely to have short-term effect on the development of international accounting standards. In 1978 the Council adopted the Fourth Company Law Directive, which deals with standards in the form and presentation of annual reports, valuation methods, and publication of these documents. The underlying premise is that accounts must give a true and fair view of companies' balances and financial position. The adoption of the Fourth Directive came after nearly a decade of debate on minimum standards for financial reporting. Member countries should have enacted legislation in conformity with the Fourth Directive within five years. To date only Denmark and the United Kingdom have fully enacted the appropriate legislation.

In mid-1983, the Seventh Directive was adopted. This directive is concerned with the publication of group accounts, i.e., consolidated or combined financial statements, where an entity effectively controls one or more other entities. The directive is materially different than the proposal first issued in 1976, and its enactment into national legislation may be delayed until 1990. This gives considerable opportunity to international financial executives to measure its potential impact on their enterprises and to plan accordingly.

International Accounting Standards Committee

As stated above, the most significant group of professional accounting bodies for setting international standards is the IASC. Formed in 1973, the IASC seeks to formulate and publish, in the public interest, basic standards to be observed in the presentation of audited accounts and financial statements; to secure their worldwide acceptance and observance; and to work for improvement and harmonization of regulations, accounting standards, and procedures relating to the presentation of financial statements.

The members, fifty-nine professional bodies in forty-seven countries, have agreed to support these objectives by (1) supporting the standards promulgated by the committee and (2) using their best efforts to persuade governments, securities authorities, and industrial and business communities to require financial statements that comply with the standards; to ensure that published financial statements comply with the standards or to disclose the extent to which they do not; to take appropriate actions against auditors who do not refer in their reports to situations of noncompliance with the standards; and to seek to secure similar general acceptance and observance of these standards internationally.

International accounting standards published by the IASC do not override the local regulation of the countries of each of the member bodies. The IASC pronouncements are more in the nature of recommendations, lacking direct or supranational authority. Accordingly, the degree of compliance with international accounting standards will continue to vary significantly from country to country. In countries where accounting is largely in the hands of government or quasi-government bodies rather than the accounting profession, full compliance with the standards can, in the final analysis, only be achieved if government supports the recommendations of the professional bodies and initiates the necessary legal changes.

Greater cooperation with the United Nations in the area of standards setting is being sought by the International Accounting Standards Committee. A similar overture has been made to the OECD. This development comes at a time when the IASC is seeking to improve its standing and, in particular, to increase the level of compliance with its pronouncements. Exactly what form cooperation with the other international agencies will take is not yet clear, but the IASC proposals envisage that the U.N. group would review its work on a regular basis. This could include early consideration by the United Nations of IASC exposure drafts as well as suggestions for future topics to be considered by the IASC.

Other Regional Organizations

Although the IASC dominates standards setting in the realm of private bodies, numerous regional associations are seeking to harmonize accounting principles and practices in their areas. Three significant organizations are (1) the InterAmerican Accounting Association, representing most of the national professional accounting bodies in North, Central, and South America plus the Caribbean; (2) the Confederation of Asian and Pacific Accountants; and (3) the *Union Europeannes des Experts Comptables Economiques et Financiers.*

ACCOUNTING FOR INFLATION

Although inflation has subsided from double digit-levels in some areas, it is still at significant levels in many countries in which the multinational enterprise will operate. The financial manager must be familiar with the concepts of inflation accounting to prepare and/or analyze financial statements and reporting packages that recognize the impacts of inflation. A timely and consistent system of identifying the effects of inflation provides the financial manager with better data from which to recommend a wide range of business decisions in an inflationary environment, e.g., whether and when to undertake capital expansion and how to finance it, how to develop sound wage and salary policies, and whether to revise product-pricing and dividend policies.

Numerous accounting techniques have been applied over the years either to compensate for or to recognize the impacts of inflation in published financial statements. Briefly, these approaches consist of the following.

Balance Sheet Reserves. This method entails establishing book reserves through either the income statement or equity account to cover the replacement value of fixed assets. The logic behind this approach is that depreciation of historical costs is not reflective of future cash needs. These charges should prevent inappropriate distributions in dividends or, ideally, in taxes that could result in an erosion of capital required to maintain operating capability. This method is usually quite arbitrary and accordingly does not reflect the true effect of inflation on an enterprise's resources. Further, it does not allow for a fair assessment of erosion of purchasing power or future cash flows and financial performance.

Asset Revaluations. Under this method, enterprises periodically revalue selected assets to amounts in excess of historical costs. These amounts usually are determined using appropriate price indexes and are reported as direct credits to equity. This method allows for a better assessment of future cash flows and provides information on the erosion of physical capital as well. This method is used in a number of countries, including Italy, Spain, and Greece, primarily for tax purposes, since depreciation on revalued amounts reduces the tax charge. However, the procedure provides only a partial recognition of the inflation problem, since it neither considers the effects of inflation on other nonmonetary assets (e.g., inventory) nor gives timely recognition to the gain or loss in purchasing power resulting from holding monetary assets and liabilities.

Comprehensive Price Level Accounting Systems. This method calls for adjustment to all financial statement accounts to reflect the effects of inflation. Two basic approaches can be employed under this method. One concerns general price level changes and is sometimes referred to as "constant dollar accounting." The other approach involves reporting the effects of specific price changes and is referred to as "current cost accounting."

Constant dollar financials do not change the accounting principles used to develop financial information and are analogous to translating financial statements from one currency to another. Conventional historical cost statements are based on an accumulation of dollars which had various levels of purchasing power; constant dollar statements merely adjust these dollars of varying purchasing power to dollars with equivalent purchasing power. Current cost statements, on the other hand, change the attributes being measured from historical costs to current costs. For example, the current cost of inventories is the current cost of purchasing the same goods or the current cost of resources required to produce these goods.

Very few countries, however, have provided for comprehensive inflation adjustment for both the published financial statements and the assessment of taxes. The very high inflation rates experienced by these countries, e.g., Brazil, Chile, and Argentina, have driven them to take these dramatic steps. Most countries hesitate to make such a dramatic move; more and more are turning to requirements for supplementary inflation-adjusted figures which are meant only to correct certain effects of inflation while ignoring others. However, these are not used to affect appropriate tax relief. In the United States (under FAS 33) and the United Kingdom, for example, certain types of business enterprises publish inflation-adjusted figures as a supplement to their primary reporting, which follows strictly traditional lines. In certain countries, as discussed above, primary reporting includes the restatement of fixed assets and related depreciation, because it is either allowed or obligatory.

In countries which have made quite great strides in their external reporting for inflation, the concepts and tools of inflation adjustment have not yet been integrated fully into managerial accounting (internal financial statements, cost accounting and product pricing, responsibility reporting, analysis of financial income and expense, the budgetary control system, evaluation methods of capital projects, etc.). Perhaps the reason is that managerial accounting technology has followed the leadership of the more developed countries, and these countries have had lower rates of inflation and thus less motivation to experiment with these concepts.

International financial managers should monitor the practical experiences of countries like Brazil, Argentina, and Chile, whether or not their company has operations in these countries. Pressures from owners and managers will continue to mount for practical and useful tools to cope with management decisions in an inflationary environment.

ACCOUNTING FOR FOREIGN CURRENCY TRANSLATION

For various management and investment purposes, the multinational enterprise must prepare published financial statements, budgets, and internal reports in terms of one national currency, referred to as the "reporting currency." In general, the financial statements of foreign operations are maintained in terms of local currencies, which tend to fluctuate in purchasing power when compared to the reporting currency. The foreign account balances must be translated into reporting currency following a consistent methodology to obtain meaningful results. The fundamental issues in foreign currency translation are (1) which exchange rates (current or historical) should be used and (2) how gains and losses should be treated.

Despite apparent agreement on these issues in some major industrialized nations, the international financial managers must understand the theoretical as well as pragmatic reasons for these agreements. Only then can they cope with and resolve continued differences encountered around the world.

There are four basic methods recognized for translating the accounts of a foreign subsidiary: (1) current-noncurrent, (2) monetary-nonmonetary, (3) temporal, and (4) functional currency. Exhibit 14-1 summarizes how the key balance sheet and income accounts of a foreign subsidiary are translated under each method (C = current exchange rate; H = historical exchange rate).

EXHIBIT 14-1 Translation of Key Balance Sheet and Income Accounts

	Method of translation			
	Current-noncurrent	Monetary-nonmonetary	Temporal	Functional currency
Cash	C	C	C	C
Accounts receivable	C	C	C	C
Inventory	C	H	H/C[a]	C
Property, plant, and equipment	H	H	H	C
Accounts payable	C	C	C	C
Long-term debt	H	C	C	C
Deferred income	H	H	H	C
Capital stock and surplus	H	H	H	H
Retained earnings	H	H	H	H
Sales	C[b]	C[b]	C[b]	C[b]
Cost of sales	C[b]	H	H	C[b]
Depreciation	H	H	H	C[b]

[a] For valuation at lower of cost or market
[b] Current rate in effect at transaction date

Current-Noncurrent Method

Prior to issuance of FAS 8, Chapter 12 of Accounting Research Bulletin 43 was the basic authoritative pronouncement in the United States on accounting for translation of currency. Chapter 12 called for translation following the current-noncurrent method. Under this method a foreign subsidiary's current assets and current liabilities are translated into the reporting currency at the exchange rate at the date of the balance sheet; noncurrent assets and liabilities are translated at historical rates. Income statement accounts, with the exception of depreciation and amortization, are translated at rates in effect at the date of the specific transactions or average rates throughout the period of the income statement. Depreciation and amortization are translated at historical rates. Realized gains or losses on foreign exchange transactions are recorded in the determination of net income—unrealized losses, to the extent that they exceed unrealized gains, are included in net income; net unrealized gains are deferred.

A research report published as early as 1960 described this classification scheme for translation as one that "seems to reflect the use of an established balance sheet classification for a purpose to which it is relevant."[9] In a 1972 research study, this irrelevance is aptly described as follows: "Different kinds of assets or liabilities may be measured the same way but classified differently or classified the same way but measured differently. For example, both inventory and plant and equipment are measured at historical cost, but inventory is classified as current and plant and equipment as noncurrent. Since translation is concerned with measurement and not with classification for purposes of disclosure, attributes of assets and liabilities that are not measured in financial statements but determine their classification for purposes of disclosure are irrelevant for selecting foreign exchange rates to translate."[10]

Monetary-Nonmonetary Method

The 1960 research report suggested application of the monetary-nonmonetary method developed by R. S. Hepworth. This method made a significant contribution to translation practice by suggesting that monetary assets and liabilities are more reasonably translated at the current rate rather than the historical rate, regardless of classification. Under this method, monetary assets and liabilities are translated at current rates, and nonmonetary items are translated at historical rates. Monetary assets and liabilities are claims to receive or obligations to pay a sum of money the amount of which is fixed or determinable without reference to future prices of specific goods or services. All other assets and liabilities are nonmonetary. This method is virtually identical to the temporal method (see below) when used within the historical cost accounting framework. However, if replacement cost or net realizable value methods are used, results are different, because this method calls for translation at historical rates and the latter methods require current rates.

In 1971, the Accounting Principles Board in the United States issued an exposure draft supporting a variation of this method and proposed that resulting exchange gains and losses, to the extent they did not exceed those attributable to long-term debt, be deferred and accounted for in a manner similar to debt discount. This proposal was never finalized primarily because so many assets were perceived to have both monetary and nonmonetary attributes and were not easily classified.

Temporal Method

This method was required in the United States following adoption of FAS 8 from October 1975 through December 1981, when FAS 52 (see below) was adopted. The objectives of this method are to measure and express in the reporting currency the assets, liabilities, revenues, or expenses that are measured or denominated in foreign currency. This is accomplished by translating:

1. At historical rates, asset, liability, and related revenues and expense accounts carried at prices in past exchanges
2. At current rate, asset and liability accounts carried at prices in current purchase or sale exchanges or future exchanges
3. Other revenue and expense accounts at rates in effect at the time the transaction occurred

This approach views the reporting currency (national currency of the parent) as the single unit of measure and, consequently, a foreign operation as a simple extension of the parent's domestic activities; thus the foreign operation's actions are treated as if they were conducted and measured in the parent's reporting currency. Under the temporal method, the change in net assets of a foreign subsidiary attributable to rate changes between the reporting currency and the local currency is included in the determination of net income of that period.

The temporal method created new problems and quickly became the object of widespread criticism. Its critics stated that it:

1. Created large and confusing fluctuations in reported current income by including translation gains and losses in income
2. Distorted normal relationships within the financial statements of a foreign unit
3. Resulted in reporting foreign currency exposure inconsistently with real economic exposure

After much debate, the Financial Accounting Standards Board issued FAS 52 in December 1981, supporting the functional currency method.

Functional Currency Method

The functional currency method views the parent company as having a net investment in an independent foreign business whose foreign currency earnings are generated in its local economic, legal, and political environment and accrue to the benefit of the parent company. The objectives of translations, as stated in FAS 52, are to:

(a) Provide information that is generally compatible with the expected economic effects of a rate change on an enterprise's cash flows and equity; and

(b) Reflect in consolidated statements the financial results and relationships of the individual consolidated entities as measured in their functional currencies.

Under this method, the current rate is used to translate all asset and liability accounts from the functional currency to the parent's reporting currency, and revenues and expense accounts are translated at the rate in effect at the transaction date.

The functional currency is the currency of the primary economic environment in which an entity operates, that is, where the entity normally generates and expends cash. This method preserves the relationships established in the entities' economic environments. Under this method, the translation process is viewed as having no direct effect on the foreign entity's operations or its parent's cash flow. The translation adjustment is not included in net income; instead, it is accumulated in a separate component of equity. These amounts are removed from equity and included in net income only when an investment in a foreign entity is sold or substantially or completely liquidated. This treatment is consistent with the view that functional currency assets and liabilities hedge each other and that only the net assets are exposed to exchange risk. Further, no gains or losses arise from hedged assets and liabilities.

Comparison of Temporal and Functional Currency Methods

To illustrate the differences between the temporal and functional currency methods, assume that the German operations of a U.S. enterprise started business and acquired fixed assets at the beginning of the period when the U.S. $/DM exchange rate was 0.5; the average exchange rate for the period was 0.4; the rate at the end of the period was 0.3. Inventory was acquired when the exchange rate was 0.45. See Exhibit 14-2 for the results that occur when period-end financial statements are translated from deutsche marks to dollars under the temporal and under the functional currency methods.

Its proponents see the following advantages of the functional currency method over the temporal method:

1. The functional currency approach minimizes fluctuation in the income account, not only by deferring the translation adjustment but also by using the same rate to translate both cost of sales and sales. Under the temporal approach, using historical rates for cost of sales and current rates for sales, income statement relationships and frequently used ratios are distorted.
2. By using one rate for the balance sheet, the functional currency method retains normal balance sheet relationships. Moreover, it accepts the economic fact that 100 deutsche marks are not worth more or less in dollars because they have been invested in receivables rather than inventories.

EXHIBIT 14-2. Translation from Deutsche Marks to Dollars by Two Methods

		Temporal method		Functional currency method	
	DM	Rate	U.S. $	Rate	U.S. $
Balance sheet					
Cash	25	0.3	7.5	0.3	7.5
Receivables, net	100	0.3	30.0	0.3	30.0
Inventory	150	0.45	67.5	0.3	45.0
Fixed assets	400	0.5	200.0	0.3	120.0
	675		305.0		202.5
Current liabilities	150	0.3	45.0	0.3	45.0
Long-term debt	400	0.3	120.0	0.3	120.0
Stockholder's equity:					
Common stock	110	0.5	55.0	0.5	55.0
Retained earnings	15		85.0		6.0
Cumulative translation adjustment					(23.5)
	675		305.0		202.5
Income statement					
Sales	150	0.4	60.0	0.4	60.0
Cost of sales	(100)	0.45	(45.0)	0.4	(40.0)
Depreciation	(10)	0.5	(5.0)	0.4	(4.0)
Selling and administrative expenses	(15)	0.4	(6.0)	0.4	(6.0)
Foreign exchange translation			85.0		
Income taxes	(10)	0.4	(4.0)	0.4	(4.0)
Net income	15		85.0		6.0
Ratios					
Current ratio	1.83		2.33		1.83
Debt to equity	3.20		0.86		3.20
Gross profit	0.27		0.17		0.27

3. Under the functional currency method, the immediate accounting results of a change in currency relationships are consistent with economic and business expectations.

Remeasurement of Functional Currency

In some instances a foreign operation's functional currency may not be the currency of the country in which the enterprise is located, even though that currency is used in its books. In general, this arises when a foreign operation is a direct and integral component or extension of a reporting enterprise's operations. A similar conclusion might be reached when an entity is operating in a hyperinflationary environment. In these situations, FAS 52 calls for "remeasurement" of this enterprise's accounts into the reporting currency. The remeasurement process is intended to produce the same result as if the entity's books of account had been maintained by the parent. This remeasurement process is quite similar to the translation process required under FAS 8.

Forward Exchange Contracts and Hedging

Forward exchange contracts are agreements to exchange different currencies at a specified future date and at a specified rate (the forward rate). The accounting for a forward exchange contract depends on whether the contract is (1) a hedge of a net investment in one or more foreign operations, (2) a hedge of an identifiable foreign currency commitment, or (3) a hedge of some other exposure (e.g., a contract that does not hedge any specific exposure).

Gains and losses on forward exchange contracts must be reported as follows.

1. A gain or loss on a contract that is designated as, and is effective as, an economic hedge of a net investment in a foreign operation must be included with translation adjustments in the separate component of shareholders' equity.
2. A gain or loss on a contract that meets the criteria for a hedge of an identifiable foreign currency commitment must be deferred and included in the measurement of the related foreign currency transaction. However, a loss is not to be deferred if it is estimated that deferral would lead to recognizing the loss in a later period.
3. A gain or loss on a contract that hedges some other exposure must be included in net income as it arises.
4. A gain or loss on a speculative contract must be included in net income as it arises.

A forward exchange contract or other foreign currency transaction (see below) is considered a hedge of an identifiable foreign currency commitment, provided that both the following criteria are met:

1. The forward exchange contract or other foreign currency transaction is designated as, and is effective as, a hedge of a foreign currency commitment.
2. The foreign currency commitment is firm.

The following are examples of foreign currency transactions that can be entered into in order to hedge identifiable foreign currency commitments:

1. A company committed to purchasing equipment from a German supplier for deutsche marks can buy deutsche marks and hold or invest the marks and designate them as a hedge of the commitment.
2. A contractor committed to constructing and selling a building to an English concern for sterling can borrow sterling to finance the construction and designate the borrowing as a hedge of the commitment.
3. The lessor of a computer under an operating lease denominated in Canadian dollars can obtain financing denominated in Canadian dollars and designate the debt as a hedge of the committed revenue stream under the lease.

Other Foreign Currency Transaction

A foreign currency transaction is denominated in a currency other than an entity's functional currency. Foreign currency transactions may produce receivables or payables that are fixed in terms of the amount of foreign currency that will be received or paid. A change in exchange rates between the functional currency and the currency in which the transaction is denominated increases or decreases the expected amount of functional currency cash flow when the transaction is settled. That increase or decrease is a foreign currency transaction gain or loss. Thus if a U.S. company borrows DM1000 when the U.S.$/DM exchange rate is 0.5 and then converts the proceeds to dollars, it will receive $500. If, at the time of repayment the dollar weakens against the deutsche mark to 0.6, the U.S. company will have to pay out $600 to discharge its deutsche mark obligation. Accordingly, a transaction loss has occurred. In general, such transaction gains or losses must be reported in income as they arise. FAS 52 permits the following exceptions to this rule:

1. Gains and losses attributable to a foreign currency transaction that is designated as, and is effective as, an economic hedge of a net investment in a foreign entity must be included in the separate component of share-

holders' equity in which adjustments arising from translating foreign currency financial statements are accumulated. An example of such a transaction would be the translation impact related to deutsche mark borrowing by a U.S. parent company that it designates as a hedge of its net investment in its German subsidiary.

2. Gains and losses attributable to intercompany foreign currency transactions that are of a long-term investment nature must be included in the separate component of shareholders' equity when the parties to the transaction are consolidated, combined, or accounted for by the equity method in the reporting entity's financial statements.

3. Gains and losses attributable to foreign currency transactions that hedge identifiable foreign currency commitments are to be deferred and included in the measurement of the basis of the related foreign currency transactions.

JOINT VENTURES

In the past, use of the wholly owned subsidiary was the most common approach to overseas investment. Complete ownership and control were seen as the most logical policy because the success of a worldwide strategy depended on complete control over all foreign units. However, more and more host countries, especially less developed nations, are concluding that the wholly foreign-owned enterprise does not contribute to the country's overall economic interests as much as joint ventures involving local interests do. As a necessary consequence, greater emphasis is being placed on the joint venture as a form of international business organization. This shift has created a number of financial, administrative, and accounting issues for the multinational financial executive.

Administrative Issues

The wholly owned subsidiary of a multinational corporation is a "captive customer" for the foreign parent's reporting requirements. Standardized records are maintained and reporting requirements adhered to. Personnel selection provides strong assurance in this regard.

Foreign joint ventures mitigate against this absolute control. The multinational must now educate its foreign venture partners and accounting personnel to keep records, many times supplementary records, according to its accounting principles and policies and to prepare special management reports on the basis of these records. Often this is not achieved in the early stages, and the unhappy solution is for management to report these ventures at cost rather than equity because adequate control over accounting techniques cannot be maintained.

Accounting Issues

The important questions in accounting for an investor's interest in a joint venture relate to (1) the timing of the recognition of income or loss and (2) the form of financial statement presentation.

Except for corporate joint ventures, authoritative literature is relatively quiet on these topics, and industry practice may rule. The Accounting Standards Executive Committee of the American Institute of Certified Public Accountants views joint venture accounting as requiring immediate attention, and it has sent an issue paper on this subject to the Financial Accounting Standards Board. This paper discusses the need to establish accounting standards for investments in joint ventures, regardless of legal form. The following discussion summarizes the suggested accounting.

Accounting for an investor's interest in a joint venture should be based on the substantive economic rights and obligations of the investor as set forth in the venture agreement. When more than 50 percent of the voting control in a venture is held, the venture should be consolidated and minority interest reflected. When an investor owns less than 50 percent but can exert significant influence, the venture should be accounted for under the equity method. The investment should be carried at cost when (1) control does not rest with the owners or venturers (e.g., the venture is in bankruptcy); (2) the investee is subject to restrictions or political risks in the investee's country that are so severe that they impair the investor's ability to exercise significant influence over the investee's assets and operations; or (3) the investment may be considered temporary (e.g., the investor plans to abandon the venture if certain adverse contingencies materialize). If evidence indicates a permanent loss in the carrying amount of an investment in a joint venture, the loss should be recognized no matter what method is used to account for the investment.

Income/Loss Recognition

As a general rule, the percentage of equity interest used to accrue income/loss should be based on the current ownership rights and should not consider the effects of outstanding stock rights or convertible securities held by the investor or others.

The question of what percentage to use in applying the equity method will arise when the venture agreement specifies different allocations among the investors for profits, losses, certain costs (such as depreciation), distributions from operations, and distributions on liquidation or when changes in the allocation ratios are triggered by certain events. In general, this determination should be based on how increases or decreases in the net assets of the venture are likely to affect ultimate cash payments to the investor.

Ordinarily, an investor should discontinue applying the equity method when its investment (including advances) is reduced to zero. If losses in excess of the investment are not accrued and the venture subsequently reports income, the investor should resume accruing income only after the cumulative income exceeds the unrecorded losses.

However, losses should continue to be recorded when the investor is separately liable for the obligations of the venture, is otherwise legally committed to provide additional financial support to the venture, or if any of the following conditions exist.

1. Previous support by the investor indicates that it will "make good" on the venture's obligations.
2. The investor makes public statements indicating its intention to provide such support.
3. The losses to date have resulted from expected start-up costs or material nonrecurring events, and a return to profitable operations appears certain.

When a venture is experiencing losses and a venturer is liable for more than its share of the venture's liabilities (because of guarantee or general partner status), losses up to the amount of the liability should be accrued by the venturer when the other venturers do not have the financial resources to cover their share or have indicated intent not to do so. However, when the venture's assets are carried at amounts lower than their estimated realizable value, losses may not have to be accrued to the extent of this excess.

Financial Statement Presentation of Minority Position

Joint ventures of which an investor owns 50 percent or less can be presented in an investor's financial statement in several ways.

Expanded Equity Method. Using the expanded equity method the investor's proportionate share in the accounts of the venture is presented in the venturer's statements separately under current assets, current liabilities, noncurrent assets, long-term debt, revenues, and expenses. An alternative expanded equity method would present separate noncurrent balance sheet categories, one for the investor's equity in the assets and another for its share of the liabilities of the venture. Under each category, two or more lines of detail may be presented (e.g., current assets; property, plant, and equipment; intangibles).

Proportionate Consolidation Method. Using the proportionate consolidation method, the investor combines its proportionate interest in the venturer's assets, liabilities, revenues, and expenses on a line-by-line basis with its own accounts, without distinguishing between the amounts related to the joint venture and those of the investor. This method is especially appropriate (1) when the investor, in effect, controls the venture and operates in the same industry as the venture, (2) when the venture is primarily a financing vehicle, or (3) in the unusual circumstance when the investor owns an interest in each asset and is only proportionately liable for its share of each liability.

One-Line Equity Method. This method is required by Accounting Principles Board Opinion 18 for all corporate joint ventures and for corporate investments owned 50 percent or less when the investor has significant influence over the investee (in general, the investor owns 20 to 50 percent of the companies). Further, it must be used in Securities and Exchange Commission filings unless authoritative literature or accepted industry practice permits use of other methods.

Cost Method. This method is appropriate when ability to exert significant influence over the venture does not exist or is temporary.

NOTES

1. Price Waterhouse & Co., *Doing Business in Switzerland*, New York, 1976, p. 30.
2. George C. Watt, Ed., *Guide for the Reader of Foreign Financial Statements*, Price Waterhouse & Co., New York, 1975, p. 71.
3. Association of Authorized Public Accountants in Sweden, *Key to Understanding Swedish Financial Statements 1981*, Sweden Business Report, Stockholm, Sweden, 1982, p. 1.
4. F. D. S. Choi and V. B. Bavishi, "Diversity in Multinational Accounting," *Financial Executive Magazine*, Financial Executive Institute, New York, August 1982, p. 46.
5. Association of Authorized Public Accountants in Sweden, *Key to Understanding Swedish Financial Statements 1981*, Sweden Business Report, Stockholm, Sweden, 1982, p. 1.
6. National Association of Accountants, *Management Accounting for Multinational Corporations*, New York, 1974, vol. 1, Chap. 5, p. 49.
7. Paul Aron, *Paul Aron Reports (#24)*, Daiwa Securities America, Inc., New York, April 1981, p. 1.
8. United Nations Economic and Social Council, "Report of the AdHoc Intergovernmental Working Group of Experts on International Standards of Accounting and Reporting," 1982, p. 4.
9. National Association of Accountants, "Research Report No. 36—Management Accounting Problems in Foreign Operations," New York, 1960, p. 17.
10. Leonard Lorensen, "Accounting Research Study No. 12—Reporting Foreign Operations of U.S. Companies in U.S. Dollars," American Institute of Certified Public Accountants, New York, 1972, p. 32.

Appendix 14A

Synthesis of Accounting Differences

Key

Yes—Predominant practice.
Yes*—Minor modifications, but still predominant practice.
No**—Minority practice.
No—Accounting principle in question not adhered to.
NF—Not found.
Mixed—Alternative practices followed with no majority.
B—Cost method is used.
C—Purchase method is used.

D—Long-term debt includes maturities longer than four years.
E—Current rate method of foreign currency translation.
F—Weighted average is used.
G—Cost or equity.
H—Translation gains and losses are deferred.
I—Market is used.
J—Owners' equity.
K—Equity.
L—Monetary/Nonmonetary.

Accounting principles	U.S.	Australia	Canada	France	Germany	Japan	Neth.	Sweden	Switz.	U.K.
1. Marketable securities recorded at the lower cost or market?	Yes	Yes	Yes	Yes	Yes	Yes	Yes	Yes	Yes	Yes
2. Provision for uncollectible accounts made?	Yes	Yes	Yes	No	Yes	Yes	Yes	Yes	Yes	Yes
3. Inventory costed using FIFO?	Mixed	Yes	Mixed	Mixed	Yes	Mixed	Mixed	Yes	Yes	Yes
4. Manufacturing overhead allocated to year-end inventory?	Yes	Yes	Yes	Yes	Yes	Yes	Yes	Yes	No	Yes
5. Inventory valued at the lower of cost or market?	Yes	Yes	Yes	Yes	Yes	Yes	Yes	Yes	Yes	Yes
6. Accounting for long-term investments: less than 20 percent ownership: cost method.	Yes	Yes	Yes	Yes*	Yes	Yes	No(K)	Yes	Yes	Yes
7. Accounting for long-term investments: 21–50 percent ownership: equity method	Yes	No(G)	Yes	Yes*	No(B)	No(B)	Yes	No(B)	No(B)	Yes
8. Accounting for long-term investments more than 50 percent ownership: full consolidation	Yes	Yes	Yes	Yes*	Yes	Yes	Yes	Yes	Yes	Yes
9. Both domestic and foreign subsidiaries consolidated?	Yes	Yes	Yes	Yes	No**	Yes	Yes	Yes	Yes	Yes
10. Acquisitions accounted for under the pooling of interest method?	Yes	No(C)	No(C)	No(C)	No(C)	No(C)	No(C)	No(C)	No(C)	No(C)
11. Intangible assets: goodwill amortized?	Yes	Yes	Yes	Yes	No	Yes	Mixed	Yes	No**	No**
12. Intangible assets: other than goodwill amortized?	Yes	Yes	Yes	Yes	Yes	Yes	Yes	Yes	No**	No**
13. Long-term debt includes maturities longer than one year?	Yes	Yes	Yes	Yes	No(D)	Yes	Yes	Yes	Yes	Yes
14. Discount/premium on long-term debt amortized?	Yes	Yes	Yes	No	No	Yes	Yes	No	No	No

Accounting principles	U.S.	Australia	Canada	France	Germany	Japan	Neth.	Sweden	Switz.	U.K.
15. Deferred taxes recorded when accounting income is not equal to taxable income?	Yes	Yes	Yes	Yes	Yes	Yes	Yes	No	No	Yes
16. Financial leases (long-term) capitalized?	Yes	No	Yes	No	No	No	No	No	No	No
17. Company pension fund contribution provided regularly?	Yes	Yes	Yes	Yes	Yes	Yes	Yes	Yes	Yes	Yes
18. Total pension fund assets and liabilities excluded from company's financial statement?	Yes	Yes	Yes	Yes	No	Yes	Yes	Yes	Yes	Yes
19. Research and development expensed?	Yes	Yes	Yes	Yes	Yes	Yes	Yes	Yes	Yes	Yes
20. Treasury stock deducted from owner's equity?	Yes	NF	Yes	Yes	No	Yes	Mixed	NF	NF	NF
21. Gains or losses on treasury stock taken to owner's equity?	Yes	NF	Yes	Yes	No	No**	Mixed	NF	NF	NF
22. No general purpose (purely discretionary) reserves allowed?	Yes	Yes	Yes	No	No	No	No	No	No	Yes
23. Dismissal indemnities accounted for on a pay-as-you-go basis?	Yes	Yes	Yes	Yes	Yes	Yes	NF	Yes	NF	Yes
24. Minority interest excluded from consolidated income?	Yes	Yes	Yes	Yes	No	Yes	Yes	Yes	Yes	Yes
25. Minority interest excluded from consolidated owner's equity?	Yes	Yes	Yes	Yes	No	Yes	Yes	Yes	Yes	Yes
26. Are intercompany sales/profits eliminated upon consolidation?	Yes	Yes	Yes	Yes	Yes	Yes	Yes	Yes	Yes	Yes
27. Basic financial statements reflects a historical cost valuation (no price level adjustment)?	Yes	No	Yes	No	Yes	Yes	No**	No	No	No
28. Supplementary inflation-adjusted financial statements provided?	Yes	No**	No**	No	No	No	No**	No	No**	Yes
29. Straight-line depreciation adhered to?	Yes	Yes	Yes	Mixed	Mixed	Mixed	Yes	Yes	Yes	Yes
30. No excess depreciation permitted?	Yes	No	Yes	No	Yes	Yes	No	No	No	No
31. Temporal method of foreign currency translation employed?	Yes	Mixed	Yes	No(E)	No(E)	Mixed	No(E)	No(L)	No(E)	No(E)
32. Currency translation gains or losses reflected in current income?	Yes	Mixed	Yes	Mixed	Mixed	Mixed	No(J)	Mixed	No(H)	No

SOURCE: F. D. S. Choi and V. B. Bavishi, "Diversity in Multinational Accounting," *Financial Executive Magazine*, Financial Executive Institute, New York, August 1982, p. 46.

Fifteen: Auditing in the International Arena

JOHN FRANKLIN

John Franklin is an executive office partner of Peat, Marwick, Mitchell & Co. and is in charge of the firm's "international desk." In addition to international matters, his practice specialties include real estate and insurance. Franklin was born in Winston-Salem, North Carolina, and joined Peat Marwick in Atlanta in 1962 with a B.B.A. from Wake Forest University. He distinguished himself at Wake Forest by receiving the A.M. Pullen Award for highest achievement in accounting studies and election to Beta Gamma Sigma academic honorary society. Mr. Franklin is a member of the AICPA.

Auditing in the international arena is more complicated than auditing in one country because of geographical dispersion of operations; language concerns; political, cultural, and economic differences; and the variety of government regulations. Challenges facing multinational companies in dealing with these complexities as they relate to international auditing include:

- Obtaining uniform high-quality professional audit services throughout the world
- Responding to changing corporate and foreign reporting, oversight, and auditing needs
- Implementing efficient and cost-effective approaches to coordinating international auditing services

This chapter provides information to assist financial executives of multinational corporations in meeting these challenges.

DETERMINING NEEDS

Multinational companies' needs for audit services may vary significantly from country to country. The needs are influenced by such factors as size and complexity of operations, capabilities of local personnel, government regulatory requirements, long-range plans, tax considerations, and the business and political environment. Independent auditors should be in a position to understand the effects of these factors and to assist management of multinational companies in determining needs and making priorities.

In general, multinationals require independent auditors to provide certain services, including financial reporting requirements in the parent company's country of domicile; statutory reporting requirements in countries where subsidiaries or branches are located; and requirements for special reports on such items as debt compliance, pension plans, contractual agreements, and tax compliance.

Additional services that are frequently needed (not necessarily to meet reporting requirements) include:

- Audits of subsidiaries (not required for financial or statutory reporting purposes)
- Translation of financial statements into other currencies
- Language translation of financial statements, management letters, or other documents
- Assistance in the design and completion of internal reporting packages
- Operational audits in lieu of or as a complement to internal audit efforts
- Assistance in tax matters
- Evaluations of accounting and finance-related personnel

The nature and timing of additional services can significantly affect work performed by independent auditors, deadlines established, and total audit fees. All services to be provided should be identified during the planning stages of the annual audit.

PLANNING THE AUDIT

Planning the multinational audit is more time consuming and complex than planning a single-country audit. Effective planning and coordination between home office and foreign management, independent auditors, and internal auditors is necessary to ensure responsive and cost-effective audit services.

A prerequisite for effective planning is understanding the regulatory environment in countries where operations are subject to statutory reporting and the resources of and services available from the independent auditors.

Nature and Scope of Services

To a large degree the nature and extent of audit services to be performed at various locations are determined by the independent auditors. Audit scopes are determined by the generally accepted auditing standards in the countries where audits are conducted, and auditors' reports on financial statements are issued. Audit procedures and tests are based on the auditors' judgment as to what the circumstances require. Different audit scopes are described below. The nature and extent of audit services are also influenced by additional optional services that are provided by independent auditors at the request of multinational companies (as discussed above).

Full scope audits are performed to meet corporate reporting needs, at the request of management, to fulfill statutory requirements, or to comply with external agreements such as debt instruments. In planning this type of audit, consideration should be given to any anticipated request for additional services to be provided by the auditors.

In certain situations, multinationals may request that audit services be limited to those necessary to ensure compliance with local statutory requirements (e.g., no reports issued to the home office, no deadlines other than meeting statutory filing dates, no management letters, no translated financial statements). In such cases, a clear understanding should be reached with the auditors and home office and local management as to the services to be provided with the understanding that additional services will involve additional fees. Because the auditors are already on the scene, in many cases the value of the additional services may be worth more than the savings in fees.

If a full scope audit is not required for corporate reporting or statutory purposes, the auditors' procedures may be limited to specified account balances or classes of transactions as they deem necessary to meet corporate reporting needs or to meet specific management requests. With this approach, the specific areas to be covered and the scope of additional services requested should be documented and clearly understood by home office and local management and the independent auditors.

Other factors that may affect the extent of the auditors' work and that should be evaluated during planning include the following.

- The responsibility for the review of the provision for income taxes at each location
- Intercompany transactions (corporate management should provide the auditors with enough information to understand intercompany transactions and their effect on corporate financial reporting and income tax status)
- Necessity and responsibility for currency translations of financial statements
- Additional procedures required on certain financial information such as special reserves, identified specific transactions, commitments and contingencies, inflation data, and geographical data
- The effect of consolidating entries made at the corporate level on the statutory and income tax reporting requirements of subsidiaries
- The need for separate reports on parent company or subsidiary financial statements when securities are registered on foreign exchanges or entities are incorporated in foreign countries.
- Additional services required to assist in the preparation or review of internal reporting packages

Home office and local management and the independent auditors should have a common understanding as to how each of the above items is to be handled.

Deadlines for Completion of Services

Deadlines should be responsive to reporting needs, realistic and attainable, consistent with the planning discussed above, and agreed to by all parties. Although these requirements are basic, failure to comply with them can result in deadlines that are well in advance of the dates information is actually required, deadlines that are realistic and necessary but are not viewed as such by foreign subsidiaries, inadequate allocation of resources to meet established deadlines, less than outstanding service from independent auditors due to missed deadlines, and increased audit fees due to unnecessary overtime. Certain items influence deadlines, including:

- Corporate reporting requirements
- Submission of reports to comply with statutory requirements
- Internal closing schedules at the home office and locally
- Information required to prepare special reports

Involvement of Internal Auditors

The work of the internal auditors should be coordinated with that of the independent auditors to the extent practicable to prevent duplication of effort. Coordination between the internal auditors and the independent auditors can be improved by establishing appropriate lines of communication. Communication is enhanced when independent auditors are furnished with copies of internal audit reports and management responses and internal auditors get copies of the independent auditors' management letter and company responses. Arranging for direct contact between the independent auditors serving foreign locations and corporate internal auditors is also helpful.

Close coordination is needed when internal auditor visits are scheduled at locations where the independent auditors are working. The internal auditors should provide the corporate independent auditors with sufficient information to clearly understand matters such as:

- Objectives and timing of the visit
- Scope of work to be performed
- Audit programs to be used
- Workpapers to be prepared and their availability to the local independent auditors
- Need for meetings with local independent auditors (dates and times should be furnished)
- Need to obtain access to prior year papers prepared by local independent auditors

Careful planning and coordination between the internal and independent auditors will allow maximum reliance on the work of the internal auditors, which will save on audit fees. As internal auditor visits are made closer to year-end, reliance on internal auditors generally will be greater than if work is carried out early in the year, without regard for financial reporting needs.

Engagement Letters

Ordinarily, engagement letters are required by independent auditors for the first year they are appointed auditors. They may be required in subsequent years by the auditors or by corporate management. In any event, a clear and documented understanding should be reached by all parties involved.

Engagement letters should cover services to be performed at domestic and foreign locations, including preparation of auditor reports and formal management letters, translation of financial statements into other currencies, preparation of financial statements in accordance with the home office's generally accepted accounting principles, special assistance on accounting matters, and tax planning. When the deadline for filing statutory financial statements is after the year's end, meeting year-end deadlines for group financial statements should be included. Services that will not be provided due to management request, fee arrangements, including methods of settlement, and any other matters that need to be addressed should be clearly stipulated.

Instruction Letters

Instruction materials from the home office should be tailored for each foreign location; they should be concise and understandable. Tailored instructions are especially important when small-segment locations and potential language problems are involved. Instruction letters frequently include a summary of key points, deadlines, items of interest, and the specific scope of services to be provided by the independent auditors. Other items in an instruction letter are: instructions for completing internal reporting packages or supplementary data, extent of internal auditors' involvement, identification of any known or anticipated auditing problems or unusual accounting matters, information on audit fees and billing arrangements, and acknowledgement instructions.

ADMINISTERING THE AUDIT

Communications

In addition to the routine requirements that international communications relating to the audit process be timely and understandable, other matters should be considered. The content of communications should be tailored according to the resources of the receiving location, including language capabilities and knowledge of home office technical requirements; this includes selecting the most appropriate form of communication in the circumstances. For instance, depending on the complexity or sensitivity of the situation, letters, electronic mail, telexes, or telephones may be the most effective means of communication. Certain issues can often be resolved more satisfactorily with telephone communication than by using letters or telexes. However, written communications are less likely to be misinterpreted. The possibility of delays should also be evaluated, e.g., poor postal or telephone service, labor strikes affecting mail delivery, missed shipping connections, multiple time zones, or delays caused by customs clearance. Communications should also be labeled in a manner that facilitates receipt. Also, the security of confidential transmissions must be considered.

Resolution of Issues and Problems

A primary objective in planning and administering international audits is to identify issues and potential problems early and then devote sufficient, timely attention to their appropriate resolution. The potential issues and problems that may arise in international audits are not significantly different from those encountered in multilocation audits in one country. They include accounting and auditing issues; administrative issues, e.g., ability to meet deadlines and staffing questions; and independent auditor relations involving service issues and fees. Although the issues are not unique, their resolution is sometimes more difficult for international audits because of certain potential problems:

- Distance between locations
- Language differences
- Cultural, economic, and political differences which cause problems, their potential impact, and their resolution to be viewed differently
- Lack of adequate communication between home office and local management
- Lack of adequate communication between the auditors' various offices
- Lack of understanding by home office management of statutory requirements

To obtain the most effective international audit services, the resolution of issues and problems should be prompt, effective, fair to all concerned, and executed with minimal disruption to domestic and foreign locations and to the total audit effort. Complex and sensitive issues are usually best resolved through direct meetings with the parties involved. Direct meetings allow new facts to be introduced, alternatives to be fully discussed, and resolutions to be reached in a cooperative manner without misunderstandings.

Periodic Meetings

The progress of the audit should be monitored by periodic meetings with the independent auditors to discuss the status of the audit, progress toward deadlines, and other administrative matters. Significant audit findings such as material internal control weaknesses should be reviewed, and any accounting matters which might require further research should be identified. These meetings avoid last minute surprises which could affect the release of earnings or issuance of reports.

Administrative Responsibilities of Foreign Locations

In addition to responsibilities during the planning phase of the audit, financial executives in foreign locations have certain administrative responsibilities that are necessary for the successful completion of international audits. They should provide direct input to the home office as to the progress of the audit and offer suggestions for future improvement in the audit approach and administration, promptly notifying the home office of any significant unresolved questions or any significant requirements not completed on schedule. The home office should hear about any audit and accounting matters that may have a significant effect on the subsidiary's financial statements, and subsidiaries should obtain home office concurrence for any tentative conclusions reached with the independent auditors. If it becomes apparent that items to be furnished to the auditors cannot be completed by the requested dates, the home office should be notified of the estimated date of completion and the reason for the delay. Discussion of comments contained in the auditors' management letter and any corrective action taken or planned also should take place.

The foreign offices should communicate any needs for additional services from the independent auditors beyond those contemplated by the original proposal or engagement letter. This allows home office management to discuss these matters with the corporate auditors and, if local management is not authorized to do so, to approve the additional fees involved.

MAINTAINING A RELATIONSHIP WITH THE INDEPENDENT AUDITORS

It is important for senior management, including nonfinancial senior management, of multinational companies to build and maintain good relationships with key representatives of their independent auditors. International accounting firms and firms with international affiliations or correspondents are usually in a good position to provide business advice. They understand international business and economic developments and their effects on multinational clients and are aware of industry developments. Through their meetings with senior officials of their worldwide clients, independent auditors are able to offer advice on current and anticipated conditions. They also offer an international network of resources to satisfy the needs of multinational companies.

Visits to Major Foreign Locations

One of the most effective ways for the corporate auditors to gain an understanding of conditions affecting the audits of foreign locations and to become acquainted with key foreign personnel is for them, together with home office officials, to visit major foreign locations. There are many benefits to these visits, including:

- Introducing home office officials to the auditors serving foreign locations
- Reaching an understanding with foreign officials as to the group audit process and home office needs
- Building an understanding by home office officials of the foreign location audit process and audit needs
- Expanding the knowledge and understanding of the corporate auditors
- Establishing better lines of communication
- Creating a better awareness of why certain information is needed by the home office and corporate auditors

These visits have the combined overall benefit of strengthening relationships and improving audit coordination and efficiency. If problems do arise at a foreign location, they are much easier to solve if home office management and the corporate auditors know the foreign personnel and the environment in which they work.

Usually the corporate auditors will initiate the visits to major foreign locations. Both the auditors and home office management should be involved in planning visits; before making the visit they should establish definite objectives for the visit, determine billing arrangements, decide which home office and auditor personnel should make the visit, and notify and confirm arrangements and agenda with foreign office management and auditors. Obviously, coordination of such visits between home office and local management and corporate and foreign location auditors is essential.

The content of meetings held during the visit will vary depending on the objective of the visit, the individuals involved, and the available time. Some find it useful to hold several types of meetings during a visit, e.g., joint sessions with all interested parties (i.e., home office and local management and corporate and foreign audit personnel), meetings between all audit personnel and home office management, and meetings between home office and local management. Each of these types of meetings should have planned agendas.

Audit Committee Meetings

In addition to the usual matters that auditors are asked to discuss at audit committee meetings, certain additional topics should be considered for discussion. Clearly, the overall audit plan, including an explanation of how the audit scope for foreign locations was established, is an important item. A discussion of fees is important, including efforts to control worldwide fees and monitor audit efficiency and an explanation of why fees differ from country to country. Foreign accounting and reporting requirements, internal audit coverage, special tax or legal considerations, and other special services requested should also be considered. In discussing fees, auditors should include the effects of changing inflation rates, audit scopes, currency fluctuations, and audit hours. In addition, financial statements of and management letters related to foreign operations are important topics, as are reports on visits to foreign locations.

It is often a good idea to have, on a rotating basis, the audit engagement partner of a major foreign operation attend an audit committee meeting and be available to answer any questions the audit committee might have concerning the audit of the operation or other related matters.

Other Matters

Wrap-up meetings, at which management critiques the services received and the auditors discuss company cooperation and assistance during the audit, are often useful. These meetings result in a plan to improve the efforts of both company personnel and the auditors to improve the efficiency of the audit.

Many international accounting firms sponsor client seminars and develop executive education programs on issues that relate directly to multinational companies. These seminars and programs address such topics as the regulatory environment in a particular country or region, coordination of audit efforts between the internal and external auditors, monitoring the benefit of auditor services, international taxation, and recent developments in specialized industries (e.g., banking, insurance, energy, high technology). These seminars and programs provide executives with timely information for making decisions and better managing their businesses.

In addition to accounting and auditing services provided by international auditing firms, international taxation and consulting resources are usually available to fulfill multinational business needs. Tax services of interest to multinational companies include:

- International tax diagnostic reviews
- Expatriate tax services
- Government and private sector interface
- International and industry tax studies
- Submissions to regulatory bodies
- International tax planning
- Treaty considerations
- Tax audit consultations
- Tax publications on matters of concern
- Taxpayer representations regarding tax valuations

- Representation before legislative or government authorities on pending laws or regulations

The actual services that are performed vary from country to country because of varying circumstances, but a broad range of services is usually available to assist multinational companies.

Appendix 15A is a summary of international organizations which may be of interest to multinational companies.

Appendix 15A
International Organizations

Several international organizations are important to multinational companies. This appendix briefly summarizes their background and activities.

International Federation of Accountants (IFAC). The IFAC is a private, voluntary organization composed of eighty-two accounting bodies from sixty-one countries. The IFAC concerns itself with auditing and other professional matters, such as ethics and education, that would lead to the development and enhancement of a coordinated worldwide accounting profession. The IFAC has several standing committees; one is the International Auditing Practices Committee (IAPC), which issues international auditing guidelines.

International Accounting Standards Committee (IASC). The IASC is a private voluntary organization formed by accounting bodies from various countries. In January 1983, the membership of IASC was changed to include all members of IFAC based on an agreement reached between the two organizations. The IASC issues financial accounting standards on subjects which are similar to those dealt with by the accounting standard-setting bodies of individual countries (e.g., the Financial Accounting Standards Board in the United States and the Accounting Standards Committee in the United Kingdom).

United Nations Commission on Transnational Corporations. As an arm of the United Nations, the U.N. Commission on Transnational Corporations is a quasi-government organization with worldwide participation. It reports to the U.N. Economic and Social Council, and its activities are currently directed to developing a code of conduct for transnational corporations, reviewing developments in international accounting and reporting standards and regulations, and holding hearings on multinational company involvement in certain countries.

European Economic Community (EEC). The EEC, also known as the Common Market, is a supragovernment organization. Its authority is governmental, but is restricted to the ten member countries of France, West Germany, Italy, the United Kingdom, Belgium, Denmark, Greece, Ireland, Luxembourg, and the Netherlands. EEC directives are addressed to and are binding on the member states, who must bring the directives into national laws within specified periods. Directives relating to accounting reports and related matters have been issued. The more important of these are the Fourth

Directive, which deals with the preparation, presentation, and publication of the accounts of limited liability companies throughout the EEC, and the Seventh Directive, which presents requirements for the preparation of consolidated financial statements. Other proposed directives deal with employee participation in corporate management, auditor qualifications, employee information and consultation, parent-subsidiary relationships, and corporate reorganizations.

Organization for Economic Cooperation and Development (OECD). The OECD is an intergovernment organization of twenty-four countries; it includes most of Western Europe and the Commonwealth countries, Japan, and the United States. In 1974, the OECD formed a committee on international investment and multinational enterprise; it prepares guidelines for the activities of multinational enterprises including disclosure of information, competition, financing, taxation, employment and industrial relations, and science and technology. OECD's objectives are broader than financial reporting—they include economic growth and social progress objectives, regulation of foreign enterprises entering new markets, and furtherance of world trade.

Sixteen: Budgeting for International Operations

GERALD F. LEWIS

Gerald F. Lewis is controller of Mobil Corporation. He previously held the position of controller of the Inter American Grain Corporation and senior auditing positions in both U.S. and English accounting firms. He is a frequent lecturer on topics involving planning, budgeting, analytical techniques, international accounting, and the analysis of international operations. He has also contributed to such publications as *Currency Risk and the Corporation* and *The Management of Foreign Exchange Risk* (2d edition), both published by Euromoney Publications. Mr. Lewis earned his B.S. and M.B.A. degrees from New York University. He is a C.P.A. in New York State and a fellow of the Association of Certified Accountants in the United Kingdom. His memberships include the American Institute of Certified Public Accountants, the New York State Society of CPAs, the National Association of Accountants, and the Financial Executives Institute.

SPECIAL CHARACTERISTICS OF BUDGETING FOR INTERNATIONAL OPERATIONS

The budgeting process for international operations is basically no different from that for domestic operations, except that it must recognize diverse environments and the addition of one major element—the impact of currencies. Thus the forecasting of exchange rates, exchange exposure, and anticipated gains or losses on exchange become necessary. A summary of the principal elements of exchange rate forecasting as it pertains to budgeting follows.

Forecasting Exchange Rates

The present environment of floating exchange rates has accentuated the importance of accurately forecasting exchange rates—although some would say the combination of "accurate" and "forecasting" is a contradiction in terms. Nevertheless, the forecasting process has imposed a discipline, first to identify and quantify those economic, political, and social variables which influence a currency's value and, second, to predict the direction, magnitude, and timing of a currency's change in value.

Briefly stated, forecasting techniques follow either of two basic approaches: the traditional, fundamental approach and the more recent technical, analytical approach.

Fundamental Forecasting. The fundamental approach evolved from classical economics. In applying this technique, management (usually, the treasurer) assesses certain economic and sociopolitical variables of a nation to predict the economy's performance and how such performance will affect the supply of, and demand for, that nation's currency. Economic variables include domestic monetary and fiscal policy, inflation rates, unemployment, development of natural resources, international trade competitiveness, and capital flows. Sociopolitical variables include the general attitude of government and population toward the private business sector, the system of government, its involvement in the commercial sector, labor relations, and the degree of political stability. The forecaster must also be aware of the sensitivity of each variable and its relative importance with respect to the time horizon projected. Relevant variables should be forecast for the time of interest to management in the budgeting process, e.g., one, three, or five years.

Technical Analysis. Technical analysis has developed from the study of international money market behavior in an attempt to predict cyclical trends in the demand and supply of individual currencies. This forecasting technique concentrates more on predicting the timing of exchange rate movements than on the underlying fundamentals per se. By forecasting when a shift in currency values is expected, the user of technical analysis expects to be in a position to hedge accordingly. Technical analysts often postulate that the market adjusts too swiftly to changes in fundamental variables to make a forecast based on fundamentals meaningful. They argue that it is best to observe the signals which mark a change in market mentality and climb on board before the market leaves them behind. Fundamentalists have often argued that this game plan is little better than the "school of fish" theory, which states that a fish is best protected if she or he swims with the mainstream and in the center of the school out of predators' reach.

Regardless of the forecast discipline employed, the ability to accurately predict exchange rates remains particularly important given the degree of volatility in the present floating rate system. From a practical point of view, management must decide whether it wants to forecast exchange rates on the basis of one of the aforementioned theories or whether it concludes that exchange rates cannot be forecast and that, therefore, the current exchange rate (at the time of initiating a particular budget cycle) should be used for the forward period (an exception would be made for hyperinflationary countries, where the fundamental theory would be adopted).

Forecasting Exchange Exposure

A company can be exposed to foreign currency movements in two ways. The first, transaction or economic exposure, results from intraperiod fund flows arising from transactions completed and committed in foreign currency. The second type of exposure, translation exposure, results from the translation of balance sheet assets and liabilities acquired or incurred in a foreign currency. The objective of an exchange exposure forecast is to measure a company's currency risk.

Transaction exposure is the currency risk entailed when an entity contracts for goods and services denominated in one currency but to be paid for with a different currency—for example, a company purchases goods priced in U.S. dollars and pays for them with French francs.

Forecasting the volume of goods and services involved will determine the magnitude of funds at risk. Therefore, the key to assessing transaction risk lies in the ability to predict (1) the source, price, quantity of equipment (capital investment), raw materials, or services; (2) the currency in which these will be denominated; and (3) the timing of payments.

In addition to the above parameters, establishing the time period over which the risk is being measured is also important. Forecasting short-range transaction risk for a company will require each subsidiary to report, by month, the amount of foreign currency obligations it will incur from purchases, the receipts it will generate from sales, and when remittances to the parent company are anticipated. The longer time horizon applies where fixed supply contracts of a stated number of units at a fixed price have been negotiated.

Transaction exposure related to capital project commitments can be identified from the terms of contract. However, because a project can have a lead time exceeding one to two years, the anticipated timing of payments is critical in quantifying the risk involved.

Translation exposure arises from the translation of foreign subsidiaries' balance sheets into the parent company's currency for consolidation purposes. In general, accounting, or translation, exposure can be defined as the net of exposed assets minus exposed liabilities.

Translation exposure differs under the application of Financial Accounting Standard Board statement (FAS) 52, depending on the determination of the "functional currency" of a country's operations. When a subsidiary adopts the U.S. dollar as "functional currency," balance sheet accounts considered exposed (monetary assets and liabilities) are translated at current rates of exchange. All other balance sheet accounts, such as plant and equipment and inventories, are carried at historical cost and, therefore, are not exposed. Gains and losses on exchange which result from the translation of exposed assets and liabilities at a new (for example, month-end) current exchange rate are reflected in the current profit and loss statement. When the foreign subsidiary uses its local currency as "functional currency," FAS 52 requires that all local currency assets and liabilities be converted into the parent company's currency at the current rate of exchange. Gains and losses resulting from translation differences between two periods are booked to a special shareholders' equity account instead of to the income statement. Local currency transaction gains and losses would then be reflected in the income statement, as would translation gains and losses of assets and liabilities which are denominated in a currency other than that of the local subsidiary. Under these conditions, only the results of true economic exposure show up in the income statement, and accounting exposure fluctuations are relegated to the balance sheet.

Forecasting translation exposure requires an estimate of the local currency balance sheet. This is often more difficult to predict for months between quarter-ends, since a formal financial statement is frequently not prepared for such months. One method to estimate a local currency balance sheet for a future month starts with the most recent quarterly financial statement, adjusting the largest accounts based on trade volumes, current expenses, and capital expenditures. The reporting format is uniform so that a consolidated corporate exposure, by foreign currency, can be prepared.

The objective of forecasting the above exposures is to provide a means both to measure risk and to provide management with a basis to take whatever action is deemed appropriate. Management's decision can vary from doing nothing to aggressively hedging all exposures. Determining an action plan involves weighing the cost of reducing, or hedging, the exposure against the consequences of inaction. This requires an assessment of exchange rate movements over the life of the exposure.

A hedge of foreign currency–denominated commercial transactions would be charged to the income statement, a hedge of local currency balance sheet accounts to the special shareholders' equity account, and a hedge of foreign currency–denominated capital expenditures to the cost of the investment. The object of a hedge is to gain what is expected to be lost on a future transaction (or translation) and therefore to break even or come out slightly ahead.

Forecasting Remittances—Intercompany Fund Flows

Forecasting remittances was previously mentioned as a vehicle for identifying transaction exposure. Fund flows and transaction exposure management frequently dovetail using the data from transaction exposure calculations. A remittance forecasting system must be flexible enough for each business sector to use yet uniform enough to allow corporate consolidation. A meaningful analysis of the information, and explanations of variances in forecasts versus what actually occurred, entail an in-depth understanding of each business sector. An effective remittance forecasting system should identify pertinent variables which affect cash flow and should bring them to management's attention in a timely manner. The process of implementing such a system will foster a better understanding of the company's business between line and staff management and will facilitate transaction exposure hedging if management should so desire.

ORGANIZING AND ADMINISTERING THE BUDGET PROCESS

All organizations must identify sources of income and decide how and when to disburse funds to meet the obligations of the operation and expand or otherwise improve the operation. The continuous process of forming ideas, setting strategies, and formulating detailed plans is known as the "planning cycle." Budgeting is an integral part of this cycle in any well-managed organization. (See Exhibit 16-1).

Operating budgets (the phrase "profit plans" is used interchangeably in this chapter) represent a valuable tool in the operating and financial control of a business. They tend to focus management attention on long-term strategy at regular intervals because they require the determination of alternative approaches, assessment of the general business climate, and an expression of the desired performance of the enterprise in financial terms. Properly prepared, they also provide a standard for evaluation of management performance.

As time passes, some of an organization's objectives will be met, and others will change as circumstances change. Managers, therefore, need a mechanism with which to monitor actual progress against previously laid plans and a basis from which to formulate new plans or adjust plans to comprehend changing circumstances. Budgeting provides the mechanism and the basis for these actions.

A budget is a detailed plan for a given period, consistent with the achievement of an organization's overall objectives. It reflects a planned result, derived from a series of assumptions and strategies, as distinct from a forecast, which is a prediction usually based, at least in part, on past performance.

The fundamental principles of budgeting applied to an international operation are very similar to those that pertain to a domestic operation. The key to successful budgeting is a basic understanding of the nature of the operation and the environment within which it operates. An international operation differs from a domestic operation in that it functions in diverse environments, each with its own language, viewpoint, government policies, currency, etc. As a result, the factors affecting the planning, decision making, and performance of international operations are more complex and

EXHIBIT 16-1 Planning Cycle: Operating Budget

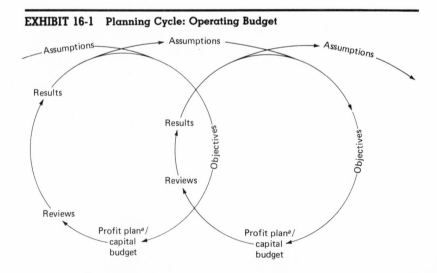

numerous than those for domestic operations, making the budget process more complex to organize and administer.

Basic Principles

Budgets are divisible in to two main categories: operating and capital. Operating budgets cover the day-to-day trading and short-term cash flow aspects of a business. They comprehend revenues, costs, and expenses for a given period and are usually expressed in the form of income and expense, profit and loss, or funds flow statements. They normally are limited to periods of one year and are frequently prepared by, or divided into, quarters or months. For longer-range objectives, operating budgets usually cover several forward years but are in a condensed format. (Since capital budgeting is discussed in Chapter 7, this section will focus on operating budgets.)

The major objective of most managements is to make the most profitable use of the resources available. When budgeting, desired levels of output are first quantified and then usually expressed in monetary terms. (Notable exceptions are workforce and time budgets, which are expressed in terms of heads and hours.) Estimated revenues, costs, and expenses are then calculated and expressed in a profit and loss format. Projected levels of output must be realistic, since unrealistic targets or assumptions lead to meaningless end products. When dealing with international operations, key industry data such as production capacities and market share of major competitors may be difficult or impossible to obtain, making it more complicated to define targets and assumptions. The experience of local personnel is often the only guide.

All costs incurred by a business may be classified as either direct or indirect. Direct costs exist solely as a result of producing a specific item or giving a particular service, for example, the material and labor that goes into the manufacture of an article. If the article is not produced, the cost does not arise. Indirect costs are simply those that are not direct, for example, light and heat for a factory or administrative staff salaries.

Certain costs vary at different levels of output, and other costs remain fixed regardless of output. The former are termed "variable" and the latter "fixed" costs. All direct costs are variable. Indirect costs may be variable or fixed. For example, the power used by machines in a factory varies with the level of production, whereas audit fees bear no relation to manufacturing output. This distinction is important for planning or interpreting the effect of changes in activity for a given period or from period to period.

Sensitivity to the local problems of an operation requires an additional dimension in planning. Both internal factors, e.g., management objectives, and external factors, e.g., government regulations or competitive forces, affect performance. Managers must quickly recognize them in order to react or adapt to them to an operation's advantage. The budget must not be regarded as a limiting factor but as a plan that needs fine tuning to a change in key assumptions. By analyzing the differences between actual and planned results, management can take the appropriate action to comprehend the change. Close comparison of actual results with the budget is, therefore, necessary from both a control and future planning viewpoint if the significant factors affecting performance are to be properly understood.

A strong link between senior management in the home country and international local managements is a basic necessity to good planning. A continuous two-way flow of information enhances this link and leads to a more effective performance at all levels. The budgeting process should be used as a tool to strengthen the link between management levels and, as a result, increase top management's understanding of local environments. In an international operation, regular visits by managers to foreign locations for budget or operations reviews are particularly useful in developing an appreciation for operational, language, and technical communication problems.

Common Problems

Common problems that arise in the budgeting process include:

- Individual objectives taking precedence over organizational objectives
- Overbudgeting
- Budgeting by precedent

An individual's objectives should not be allowed to take precedence over the organization's objectives. It is often a difficult problem, particularly when performance appraisal and incentive compensation are linked to financial results.

There are two ways of overbudgeting: "padding" and going into too much detail. When setting levels of activity, it is very easy to be overcautious. Although there is some merit in being conservative, it is essential to avoid purposely setting revenues too low and costs too high, i.e., padding the budget. Budgets that have been padded are meaningless and may lead to costly, wrong decisions. Overbudgeting by going into too much detail must also be avoided, since otherwise the cost of producing the budget is likely to exceed the benefits derived from it. There are no rules as to what depth to go to when budgeting. Basically, concentration must be placed on items which will have a material impact on performance.

Budgeting by precedent can lead to hidden inefficiency as circumstances and assumptions change. Because an expense was at a certain level one year is no reason to set it at the same or an escalated level in the following year. However, expenses that involve an individual's discretion, such as travel and entertainment, are examples where precedent may play a part.

Currency Translation

The basic steps in preparing the operating budget for an international operation include the translation of local currency revenues and costs into the reporting currency, using forecast exchange rates. The impact of currency fluctuation must be isolated from the other operating variances when comparing operating performance with other periods.

The following simplified example illustrates the impact of currency fluctuation on the marketing department expense budget of the French subsidiary of a U.S. corporation. Assume the following for the 19X3 budget:

- All expenses other than salaries, depreciation, materials, and utilities are to be escalated by 10 percent over the 19X2 projection, reflecting inflation.
- 19X3 average exchange rate is U.S. $1.00 Fr. fr6.00.
- 19X2 average exchange rate is U.S. 1.00 Fr. fr5.00.
- All expense items are to be submitted in U.S. dollars and compared with the 19X2 projection.

The subsidiary's marketing expense budget is as follows:

ABC Company (France):
19X3 Budget ($1000s)

| | | | Variance—Favorable/ (Unfavorable) | | |
Marketing expenses	19X3 Budget	19X2 Projection	Total	Currency	Other
Salaries and benefits	600	450	(150)	120	(270)
Travel and entertainment	110	120	10	22	(12)
Advertising	50	40	(10)	10	(20)
Trade exhibitions	50	50		10	(10)
Product development	29	32	3	6	(3)
Customer service	7	8	1	2	(1)
Totals	846	700	(146)	170	(316)

As can be seen, the currency impact is significant (the method of calculating the currency variance is explained in the subsection on key interfaces). Taking travel and entertainment as an example, 19X3-budgeted local currency costs show an unfavorable variance compared with 19X2 projected costs, whereas the total dollar variance is favorable. The dollar variance is favorable solely because of the movement in exchange rates between the two periods.

Organizational Considerations

Major organizational considerations include the following:

- Size and scope of operations
- Nature of the business

- Reporting structure
- Timing
- Coordination
- Communication

The size of an international business may range from a single-product private business, or operating branch marketing offices in one or two overseas locations, to a highly diversified multinational corporation. Obviously, the larger the business, the more complicated the administration process is likely to become. It follows that, as the business becomes more complex, management's information requirements increase.

Major factors determining the size and scope of budget administration include the number of profit centers, within which countries the business operates, the equity interest in each profit center, and the workforce available in each profit center.

A profit center is a decentralized unit that has its own investments on which a rate of return may be calculated. International businesses are normally divided into profit centers, which may consist of each division of the business, each subsidiary company, each factory, or each branch.

The number of countries involved is particularly important in assessing budget administration requirements, because many of the key assumptions will be unique to each country. Examples are exchange rates, growth rates, inflation rates, government legislation, and pension rights. The more foreign operations there are, the more complicated the setting of objectives and assumptions becomes.

The size of the equity interest in a particular company also has a considerable impact. Where there is a large interest and a high degree of management involvement in the running of the company, the required information is usually obtainable. However, it is often extremely difficult to obtain the planning information usually required and available when an equity interest in a foreign corporation is small.

In many instances, small interests may produce material earnings. Arrangements are frequently complicated, since they may contain a mixture of dividends, partnership shares, incentive distributions, etc. Whenever possible, the budgeting process must follow, in its buildup, all these arrangements.

Planning income in these diverse circumstances is difficult. Looking at historic performance or participating in the top management of the company as a board member, for example, are two ways of obtaining the information necessary for budgeting. Obviously, the amount of information available is likely to be more limited than it would be for a domestic operation.

The workforce available is a key to the degree of work that is put into the budget process. In a large and complex organization, a significant number of people are required simply to organize and administer budgeting. The greater the involvement of all levels of functional management the better, since data must come from all functions and key policy decisions related to those functions and the business as a whole will be made based on the data. Clearly defined duties are necessary throughout the organization, particularly as the extra workload required during the budget preparation period places a considerable strain on the organization.

Performance is affected by both internal and external factors. The nature of the business determines the information requirements regarding these factors. A commodity-type business is more influenced by supply and demand than is a specialized electronics engineering firm which depends on a high degree of technical innovation. An old and established manufacturing business with a broad product base and large market share is less susceptible to competitive pressure than a new and expanding business is. Service industries' priorities differ from manufacturing industries'. Government legislation is extensive in some industries—particularly those of a politically sensitive nature, such as energy—and not so in others, such as clothing manufacturing.

Whatever the nature of the business, the budgeting principles are the same, but the information requirements for budgeting must be tailored to suit the particular business. For illustrative purposes, consider a typical manufacturing business with a short product cycle. Information on at least some of or all the following functional areas will be required for each location:

General. Projected economic growth rates, inflation rates, exchange rates, competitive data, such as product market share

Sales. Forecast of sales volumes and sales prices by product

Supply. Forecast of raw material volumes, costs, inventory levels

Purchasing. Forecast of purchases required to meet spare parts inventory levels, critical paths for proposed capital projects, utility requirements and costs

Production. Forecast of raw material availability, production levels, maintenance requirements

Labor. Projected workforce levels, salary and wage costs, employee benefit costs

Maintenance. Forecast of maintenance downtime, spare parts availability

Marketing. Projected level of sales support, product development requirements, advertising, and promotional requirements and costs

Distribution. Projected storage levels, services required to distribute forecast sales, and related costs

Administration. Forecast of administrative costs such as accounting, audit, planning, legal, communication, and research

In a well-managed business all levels of responsibility and reporting channels are clearly defined. The structure, however, will vary depending on the nature and size of the business as well as on management information and internal control needs. The budgeting process must consider each level of responsibility, providing input at each level throughout the organization.

A large multinational corporation may be made up of profit centers by major product type, each with its own administration, accounting, planning, employee relations, marketing, etc. functions, or by major operating function, for example, manufacturing, marketing, and distribution. In the latter case, each profit center may have its own administrative, accounting, planning, and employee relations staff, as well as specialist manufacturing, marketing, or distribution staff. In either case, the profit centers are likely to be subdivided into smaller local operating units with similar structures. Businesses with widespread operations sometimes, for practical purposes, group profit centers by major geographic region, for example, European, North American, Far East, and African regions. The budgeting approach should be adapted to suit the particular organizational structure.

Budgets are normally prepared on a functional basis within each profit center, because once a budget has been completed and approved, its principal use is its later comparison with actual results for control purposes.

Most businesses adopt a two-way information flow when budgeting, since this produces the best overall blend of ideas into the budgeting process. Objectives and priorities are fed down from the top. Preliminary assumptions are set at a local unit level. Senior management reviews and agrees to the key assumptions. Budgets based on these assumptions are then built up by each function on a local unit-by-unit basis. Unit budgets are consolidated at the next management level and so on until a total consolidated budget is achieved for the whole business. At each management level the budget is thoroughly reviewed to ensure consistency with the objectives of the unit and the total business.

A timetable outlining key information deadlines is required. Concurrence with the timetable must be obtained from top management at the earliest practical date, so that executives can mesh the review requirements of the budget timetable with their other activities. Strict adherence to the timetable is imperative because delays cause serious problems that become compounded as the preparation progresses.

In most major corporations where budgeting forms part of the normal annual planning cycle (see Exhibit 16-2), some anticipation of the approximate due dates is possible. Thus, local units should consider tentative dates when setting up their schedules.

The responsibility for coordination must be placed with one group for practical purposes. Management should choose the function best suited within the overall structure of the business. Since the budget is a financial plan, it is normally coordinated by either the planning or the financial function. In some instances, the longer-range objectives are the responsibility of the planning organization, the preparation and followup of the budget the responsibility of the controller's department, and the summary of cash consequences belongs to the treasurer's department.

Many businesses have some form of budgeting or financial analysis group within the controller's portfolio, headed by a coordinator. The principal duty of this group is to set the stage of the budgeting process and, subsequently, to interpret actual financial results so that management can be provided with analyses of those results by comparison with budgets or previous periods. To provide these analyses, this group has a close interface with operating management and becomes very familiar with the factors affecting performance. Similarly, analytical groups will be found at each field profit center.

Communications on all matters related to the budget process should be through the coordinator, who is in the best position to identify potential problems quickly so that the responsible managers are alerted to avoid or remedy the problem. All instructions, timetables, and data requirements should be communicated in writing.

Electronic data processing, transmission, and storage methods using computers and word processors greatly enhance communications and considerably reduce the time, workload, and cost of budget preparation. Significant benefits are obtained in international businesses by using such methods, as delays caused by mail, time differences, and sheer distance are effectively reduced or eliminated.

Key Interfaces

Budgeting involves decision making at every level in an organization. As such, functions and divisions overlap considerably throughout the budget-

EXHIBIT 16-2   Planning Cycle: Peak Workload Periods for Large Multinational Operation

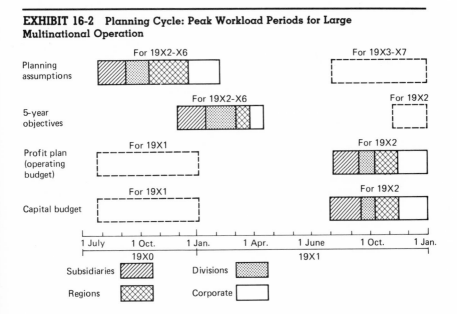

ing process. Certain interfaces, however, are key to the overall success and consistency of the end product. Key interfaces include:

- General management
- Strategic planning
- Accounting systems
- Operating statistics and other performance measurements
- Incentive compensation

The need for general management understanding and involvement in the budgeting process cannot be overemphasized. In an international business, as in a domestically widespread business, general managers provide the main link with head office management.

The budgets prepared at each local unit must be representative of, and realistic for, the unit if the resulting final product is to be meaningful. General managers provide the necessary support to all functions involved in preparing the budget. They should not be involved in the detailed work, but they must provide the channel necessary for good communication between all the functions in the unit and to the head office.

Strategic planning is an intricate process of formulating ideas and blending them into the business to the best advantage of the operation. The classic planning process involves steps as illustrated in Exhibit 16-3. Strategic planning involves setting priorities, defining strategy, and formulating detailed programs to successfully implement the programs. Budgeting involves setting out the revenues and costs required to implement the program in an orderly manner. Strategy may include:

- Acquisitions or mergers
- Expanding the geographic base of operations
- Acquiring raw material resources
- Long-range sales growth
- Product development
- Changes in product mix
- Workforce needs
- Choice of plant and equipment

In most well-run businesses, plans are evolved over a planning cycle as illustrated in Exhibit 16-4. The cycle starts with the overall business assumptions or goals, which may include:

- Anticipated economic developments
- Required return on capital employed
- Continued sales growth
- Expansion of raw material resources
- Research into new and better products

- Cost reduction programs
- Rationalization of overhead expenses

The cycle then moves into the strategy phase, when objectives are established together with projections of the capital that will be required to support them. This phase of the cycle frequently covers a five-year period. Plans for the early years of the period are often in a fairly developed stage, whereas plans for the later years are just being formed. Obviously, the further into the

---

EXHIBIT 16-3   Planning Process

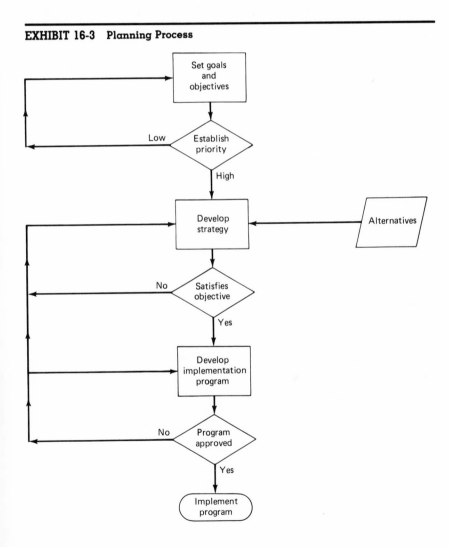

EXHIBIT 16-4 **Planning and Control: Operating Budget**

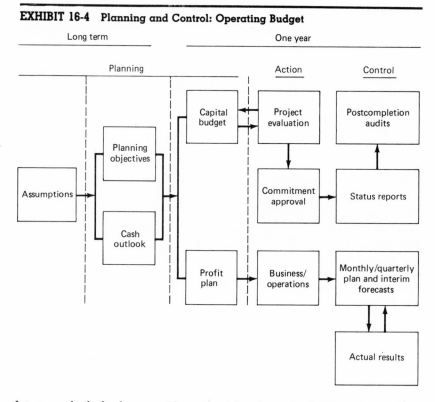

future we look the less specific we may be about the factors affecting the decision process. Some of the key items are illustrated below.

External Factors

Economic policy
Legislative policy
Exchange control policy
Environmental protection policy

Trade union policy
Workforce regulations

Inflation
Growth rates
Interest rates
Investment incentives and restrictions

Taxation
Customs and excise regulations
Trade tariffs

Internal Factors

Cost policy
Pricing policy
Financing policy
Reporting requirements

Return on capital
Sales growth
Product types
Quality control
Raw material resources

Attitude to competition
Flexibility
Attitude to customers

External Factors

Industry supply-and-demand
  forecasts
Trade federations
Raw material availability
Energy costs

Statutory reporting and audit
  requirements

Internal Factors

Employee compensation policy
Dividend policy
Capital investment policy
Competition

Financial strength
Past performance
Technical know-how
Management ability
Employee ability

In an international environment many of these factors will be unique to each particular country. However, the impact of a strike or currency devaluation, for example, in one country may be serious throughout the organization. Consideration of the impact of these factors throughout the decision-making process is therefore critical.

Many of the above items become crucial at the next stage of the planning cycle, establishing detailed plans or budgets. Just as strategies have been developed using forecasts related to the type of internal and external factors illustrated above, so must the detailed programs and budgets evolved from those strategies.

Budgets must be prepared such that they can be integrated into the accounting system for control purposes. Major aspects for consideration include the ability of the system to produce comparative information on a timely basis, accounting in multiple currencies, and following local accounting standards. In addition, the accounting system must be able to arrange revenues and expenses on a functional basis consistent with the buildup of the budget. This is fundamental to the comparison of budgeted with actual results. The accounting system must also supply functional managers with the necessary comparative information quickly enough for remedial action to be taken where variances from budget have become unacceptable.

Once the budget has been approved, it is subdivided into quarterly or monthly elements by operating unit. Budget data are then incorporated into the accounting system for comparative reporting purposes. Since most accounting systems are automated, data may be summarized at whatever level of detail is required.

Operating in a foreign location will in most instances necessitate accounting in local currencies. For budgeting and control purposes, a basic requirement is the ability to isolate and explain currency variances (briefly indicated above). When putting together the budget, forecast exchange rates are used. The exchange rate at which the actual transactions are booked will most probably be different. Assuming that transactions are accounted for in a consistent manner, it is a simple matter to isolate operating currency variances. For example, a single-product Italian subsidiary of a U.S. company has the following sales for January 19X1:

	Budget	Actual
Sales volume	200 metric tons	4500 metric tons
Sales price	It. L3000/kg	It. L2000/kg
Exchange rate It. L/U.S.$	1500	1800

	Budget	Actual	Variance
Sales realizations (Lbillions/$billions)	L6000/$4	L9000/$5	L3000/$1

Analysis of the variance shows the following:

	Total	Volume	Price	Currency
Lbillions	3000	7500	(4500)	
$billions	1	5	(3)	(1)

The sales volume and price variances are first calculated in local currency. The sales volume variance is arrived at by multiplying the change in sales volume (4500 − 2000 metric tons) by the unit selling price of the base period (L3000/kg). The base period is the period against which the comparison is being made, in this instance the budget. To get the sales price variance, take the change in selling price (L2000 − L3000/kg) and multiply it by the current period's sales volume (4500 metric tons).

The reporting currency variances related to volume and price are arrived at by translating the local currency variances at the base period exchange rate. The balance between the sum of the sales volume and price variances and the total variance represents the impact of the currency movement, namely, a $1 billion loss.

This variance can also be calculated separately by (1) translating the actual level of activity at both the actual and base period exchange rates and (2) subtracting the results of the two calculations in step 1 from one another. The difference represents the currency variance.

	Local Currency (Lbillions)	Exchange Rate (ER)	Reporting Currency ($billions)
Step 1: Actual sales realizations at actual ER	9000	1800	5
Actual sales realizations at base ER	9000	1500	6
Step 2: Currency variance by taking difference			(1)

The above illustrates the impact of a weaker local currency on the reporting currency sales realizations. If the local currency had strengthened, the currency variance would have been positive. Obviously, in either case there will be some offsetting currency impact in the cost of sales and expense sections of the profit and loss account.

Accounting standards differ in varying degrees from country to country. Areas of difference include:

• Fixed asset valuation and depreciation
• Goodwill and other intangible assets and their amortization
• Inventory valuation
• Deferred taxes
• Research and development expense
• Pension fund valuation and provisions for employee benefits
• Financial leases

Differences between countries in underlying accounting principles exist, and local budgets have to be prepared following local accounting principles, but budgets prepared for head office review and consolidation must be fully consistent with parent company accounting policies. Reliability of information produced by the accounting system is essential to its use for planning and control purposes.

The operating statistics and other performance measurements included in the budget must complement and support the other data presented. Detailed information is best included in a supplementary package which may be used for reference if required. Typical information required for the head office review of a field manufacturing unit might include some of or all the following:

• Sales volumes and prices for major product lines
• Production volumes for major product lines
• Raw material consumption and cost for major types used
• Fuel consumption volumes and costs
• Gross margins for major product lines

- Plant operating and turnaround days
- Inventory days on hand for finished products and raw materials
- Trade receivable days outstanding
- Number of employees

The data must be presented in a readily understandable and consistent manner. Displaying volume and price data in both local currency units and the home country units may be desirable.

From a budgeting viewpoint, incentive compensation is best administered at the corporate level, since the type of incentive package is not the concern of budget administration. The effect, however, that such a package may have on the attitude of managers responsible for a unit's budget and performance is of concern. Past experience with the nature of the business, the particular environment, levels of product demand, etc. is the best guide to ensuring that budgets are realistic when prepared so that incentive compensation is one of the last factors to be added to the budget. Under no circumstances should it be used to "guide" the budget results.

Since a unit's performance forms, in many incentive compensation plans, a starting point for determining the amount of compensation, the question of how profit performance versus the budget should be judged arises. Performance of controllable factors must be isolated from performance of noncontrollable factors. Some examples of noncontrollable factors are differences between local currency profits and home currency profits, nonrecurring or extraordinary profit and loss items, interest income or expense, and allocated corporate or divisional overheads. Of course, total incentive compensation requirements must be estimated and comprehended in developing the budget.

The Typical Annual Budget Cycle

Operating budgets normally cover time periods of one year. At least annually, therefore, a new budget must be prepared reflecting the detailed plans for the next period. In addition, current plans must be periodically updated to comprehend changing circumstances both for control and future planning purposes. The typical annual cycle for a large multinational operation is illustrated in Exhibit 16-5.

The basic steps to prepare an operating budget for an international operation are as follows: (1) Set assumptions, desired levels of activity, and manning levels; (2) calculate local currency revenues, costs, and expenses and express in profit and loss format; (3) translate local currency revenues, costs, and expenses into reporting currency, and express in profit and loss format; (4) review initial budget and revise where necessary to obtain an acceptable budget; (5) approve budget. Following approval, the budget is normally subdivided into monthly or quarterly periods for control purposes.

EXHIBIT 16-5   Annual Budget Cycle for Large Multinational Operation

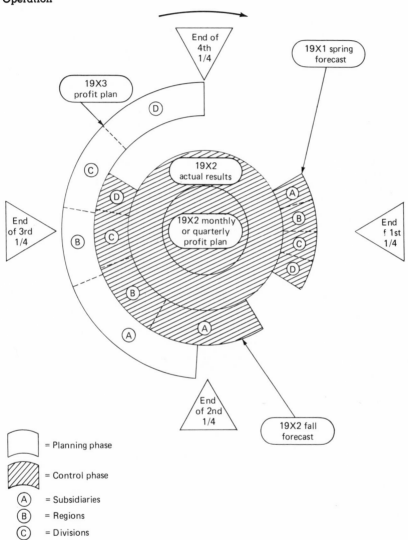

Budget Instructions

As discussed previously, the volume of information and preparation time required to develop the operating budget of an international operation are likely to be considerable. In addition, the input provided by each function, each profit center, and each group of profit centers must be prepared in a consistent manner and produced on a timely basis for the end product to be a meaningful and useful management tool. Clear and concise preparation instructions are, therefore, required at each level.

Most organizations have some form of budget manual or procedure guide outlining the basic principles of budgeting and considerations required to accomplish the budgeting objectives. These general guidelines are usually supplemented by detailed written instructions issued by each profit center or group of profit centers, outlining the specific requirements for a particular budget period. At the least, the instructions should cover the timetable, the information requirements and report format, and the review requirements. Instructions are sent out under a cover letter highlighting key items in the instructions and any special requirements. In addition, a letter announcing the budget review should be sent to all profit center general managers from the divisional or corporate chief executive officer (see Exhibit 16-6). A similar memorandum is issued by the general manager of each profit center to the unit's function managers.

The timetable itemizes the due dates of all key stages of the preparation and review process, identifying the responsibility for each item. Exhibits 16-7 and 16-8 illustrate typical division and profit center timetables.

The information requirements must be clearly defined and representative of the operation's activities. Operating budgets are normally submitted in report format; they should include as a minimum an explanatory narrative giving an overview of the significant items affecting the budget, supporting financial and other schedules, and details of the key assumptions on which the budget is based. Information requirements are summarized in Exhibit 16-9, which is a useful checklist for both the submitting and receiving units to ensure that all significant factors have been considered.

The schedule format is described by pro forma schedules (Exhibit 16-10) which, where necessary, should include brief completion instructions (Exhibit 16-11). The required schedules should be cross-referenced to the information requirement list.

The review requirements cover the procedure, data content, and timetable to be followed during senior management reviews. Since senior management will have examined the budget submission prior to the review, presentations should be limited to major aspects of the budget, sensitivities and key assumptions included in the budget, and answers to senior management's questions.

EXHIBIT 16-6   Profit Plan: Cover Letter

PROFIT PLAN - COVER LETTER

August 19, 19X2

TO: All Region General Managers
FROM: Chief Executive Officer

'A' DIVISION
<u>19X3 PROFIT PLAN</u>

We have been advised that our 19X3 Profit Plan submission is due to Corporate no later than November 15, 19X2. In order to meet this date, the division review of each operating unit's preliminary 19X3 Profit Plan has been scheduled during the week ending October 22, 19X2.

In making their presentations, operating unit executives should highlight the impact of major assumptions and operating developments on their 19X3 Profit Plan. Primary emphasis for the earnings review should be on the 19X3 Profit Plan versus 19X2 Fall Income Forecast. A brief comparison of the 19X3 Profit Plan with the 19X3 Endorsed Objectives should also be presented at the review.

The Division Controller will provide each of you with detailed guidelines for the 19X3 Profit Plan presentations. He will also work with you and your staff regarding the assumptions, specific data requirements, and timetable.

EXHIBIT 16-7   Timetable: Division

```
                        TIMETABLE - DIVISION

                          FILMS DIVISION
                          19X3 PROFIT PLAN

                         TENTATIVE TIMETABLE
```

Item	Due Date	Responsible Department
Distribute Submission Guidelines and Schedules to Regions	Aug 19	Division Financial Analysis
Review General and Administration Expense Allocations	Oct 4	Division Financial Analysis
Submit 19X3 Profit Plan to Division	Oct 8	No. American Operations, European Operations, New Markets/International Sales, Technical Operations
Submission reviews with Division President		
No. American Operations	Oct 18	No. American Operations
European Operations	Oct 19	European Operations
New Markets/International Sales	Oct 20 (AM)	New Markets/International Sales
Technical Operations	Oct 20 (PM)	Technical Operations
Division Administration	Oct 20 (PM)	Division Staff
Submit Revised 19X3 Profit Plan to Division	Nov 1	No. American Operations, European Operations, New Markets/International Sales, Technical Sales
Review Division Submission with Division President	Nov 8	Division Financial Analysis
Films Submission due to Head Office	Nov 15	Division Financial Analysis
Review Films Division Submission with Head Office Management	Nov 22	Division President and Region General Managers

EXHIBIT 16-8   Timetable: Profit Center

TIMETABLE - PROFIT CENTER

FILMS DIVISION
FILMS BELGIUM 19X3 PROFIT PLAN

TENTATIVE TIMETABLE

Date Due	Item	Responsible Department
Jul 5	Manufacturing Assumptions	Industrial Packaging Manufacturing
Jul 8	Marketing Review	Marketing
Jul 21	Direct and Indirect Labor Manning Levels Raw Material Assumptions Freight Assumptions Other Direct Manufacturing Cost Assumptions	Employee Relations Supply Distribution Manufacturing
Jul 22	Production Plan	Distribution Systems Development
Jul 23	Direct and Indirect Labor Cost	Employee Relations
Jul 26	Overhead Expense Budgets	Department Managers
Jul 30	Operating Expense Budgets	Department Managers
Aug 4	Preliminary Plan Review	Controllers
Aug 10	Preliminary Plan Review	General Management
Aug 12	Preliminary Plan due to Region	Controllers

EXHIBIT 16-9 Division Information Requirements

DIVISION INFORMATION REQUIREMENTS

FILMS DIVISION
19X3 PROFIT PLAN

INFORMATION REQUIREMENTS

for
October 8th Submission

No.	Schedule Description	U.S. Operations	Commercial Films	Design Products	European Operations	Northern Operations	Southern Operations	Canadian Operations	New Markets/Int'l Sales	Technical Operations	Division Administration
Narratives											
1	Marketing	X	X	X				X	X		
2	Manufacturing	X	X		X	X	X				
3	Distribution	X	X	X				X			
4	Operating Expenses	X	X	X				X	X	X	X
Presentation Data											
1	Key Assumptions	X			X			X	X		
2	Summary	X			X			X	X		
2A	Summary-Europe (LC)				X						
2B	Summary-Canada (LC)							X			
3	Income Var: Plan Vs. 19X2 Projection	X	X	X	X	X	X	X	X	X	X
4	Income Var: Plan Vs. 19X3 Objectives	X	X	X	X	X	X	X	X	X	X
5	Income Variance Analysis	X			X			X	X	X	
6	Sensitivities	X			X			X	X	X	
7	Cost Red./Prod. Improvement	X	X	X	X	X	X	X	X	X	
8	Employee Headcount	X			X	X	X	X	X	X	X
8A	Employee Headcount Detail										
9	Employment Costs (LC)										
Assumptions Data											
10	Market Data/Assumptions	X			X			X	X		
11	Product Data/Assumptions				X			X	X		
12	Raw Material Costs and Purchases	X			X			X			
13	Manufacturing Overhead		X	X		X	X	X			
14	Production Summary	X			X			X			
15	Inventory Reconciliation		X	X		X	X	X			
16	Inventory Summary	X	X	X		X	X	X		X	
Supplementary Data											
17	Balance Sheet										
18	Reserves & Other Adjustments										
19	Transfers/Financing Operations										
20	Investment Tax Credit										

LC = Local Currency

EXHIBIT 16-10   Division: Pro Forma Schedule

```
                          DIVISION - PRO FORMA SCHEDULE

19X3 PROFIT PLAN                                    FILMS DIVISION
SUMMARY
                          EUROPEAN OPERATIONS
                            (Profit Center)
                                            Date _____
Local Currency (LC)
```

19X1 Actual	Item	19X2 Projection	19X3 Plan	Fav. (Unfav.)	19X3 Objs.
	Sales Volumes (Metons)				
	Oriented Polypropylene (OPP)........				
	Cast Polypropylene..................				
	Polyethylene........................				
	Stretch.............................				
	Total...............................				
	Sales Prices (LC)				
	Belgian Francs				
	OPP.............................				
	Stretch.........................				
	Lire				
	OPP.............................				
	Cast Polypropylene..............				
	Polyethylene....................				
	Stretch.........................				
	Income Before Taxes (LC)				
	Belgian Francs (B Francs)				
	OPP.............................				
	Stretch.........................				
	Lire				
	OPP.............................				
	Cast Polypropylene..............				
	Polyethylene....................				
	Stretch.........................				
	Sales Before Freight				
	Belgium (M B Francs)				
	OPP.............................				
	Stretch.........................				
	Total...........................				
	Italy (MM Lire)				
	OPP.............................				
	Other...........................				
	Total...........................				
	Income Before Taxes				
	Belgium (M B Francs)				
	OPP.............................				
	Stretch.........................				
	Total...........................				
	Italy (MM Lire)				
	OPP.............................				
	Other...........................				
	Total...........................				

EXHIBIT 16-11   Division: Pro Forma Schedule with Instructions

DIVISION - PRO FORMA SCHEDULE WITH INSTRUCTIONS

19X3 PROFIT PLAN   FILMS DIVISION

INCOME VARIANCE -   SCHEDULE 3
19X3 PLAN VS. 19X2 PROJECTION

(Profit Center)

(Tenths of MM $)   Date _____

                                                                         Income

19X3 Plan
19X2 Projection
  Variance

Explanations

Note: This schedule should be used to explain with telegraphic comments, the
           income variances presented on Schedule 5, while at the same time
           bringing in the data from other schedules, e.g., Cost Reduction/
           Productivity Improvements, Employment Costs, and Manufacturing Overhead,
           Schedules 7, 9 and 13, respectively. The explanation should focus on
           the year-to-year changes in revenues and costs, as well as the "why"
           elements causing the change, such as:

           - General inflation
           - Annualization of partial year costs
           - Extraordinary income adjustments
           - Exchange rates

Seventeen: Control and Performance Evaluation of International Operations

STEPHEN A. LISTER

Stephen A. Lister is vice president of corporate budget and planning for the Colgate-Palmolive Co. He has served in many capacities at Colgate-Palmolive, including controller of the western hemisphere and vice president of finance in Mexico. Mr. Lister earned his A.B. degree at Dartmouth College and an M.B.A. degree at the Columbia Business School.

The control and evaluation of international operations is only minimally different from the normal evaluation process of reviewing any domestic operation. The major difference is the need to analyze two sets of profit and loss and balance sheet results and projections—one in local currency and the second in U.S. dollars. The primary emphasis should be on the local currency financial statements; all too often, corporate management focuses on U.S. dollar trends without fully comprehending the "real" world in local currency. Also, international operations are easier to control and evaluate because, in most cases, they can stand apart and the subsidiary can be reviewed as a total independent entity.

Performance evaluation criteria for international operations should be more remittance-oriented than domestic, and the principal emphasis should be cash flow. An investment in a foreign subsidiary must generate cash flow to the corporate/home office. Profits in a non-cash-remitting subsidiary represent an immediate cash drain to the total corporation, since most public corporations are expected to pay dividends out of reported profits to the shareholders. Attention should therefore be focused on these blocked-fund subsidiaries and on those subsidiaries that are experiencing a negative cash flow.

The basic success criteria are, first, cash flow and then standard profitability measures. Performance evaluation determines the full extent of the investment potential or lack thereof in a subsidiary's operations. Management needs to fully understand a subsidiary's performance potential to make proper investment decisions, reward the managers, and set goals and objectives. Ideally, the evaluation system should monitor and control performance on a year-to-date and quarterly basis, measured against budgeted objectives as well as prior year's results. Later in this chapter the specific performance measurements will be discussed in more detail.

Performance measurement and responsibility accounting go hand in hand. The organizational structure must conform and delegate the responsibility to those managers who are held responsible for the results being measured. There is no ideal way, organizationally, to control and manage international subsidiaries. Highly successful international operations range from the highly centralized, like Unilever, which place the worldwide category sales responsibility outside of the local general managers, to General Electric, which gives its local general managers complete sales and profit responsibility. In addition, foreign ownership and management control of the subsidiary can affect performance criteria, since business developments may well be outside the general manager's immediate control. Joint ventures present another performance measurement problem, but here the most important consideration is management control, *not* ownership. With joint ventures, accounting consolidation issues do play an important role in the ownership decision, but management control can be secured through special contracts, etc. to gain full operational control. The performance criteria must always consider the organization and responsibility structure, particularly when individual performances are being measured and rewarded.

FINANCIAL AND NONFINANCIAL MEASURES

An enormous variety of different financial measures exist to evaluate a subsidiary's performance, and this chapter will isolate those few key measures that most accurately capture a subsidiary's performance.

Financial Measures

Return on Sales. Return on sales is still the primary measure of a subsidiary's profitability: net profits ÷ sales = percent return on sales. In those countries that have royalty or licensing contracts, it is preferable to show the net profits before the royalties are deducted to receive a full appreciation of the subsidiary's profitability. The profit and loss ratios should be looked at in both local currency and U.S. dollars, and, unless there are significant currency fluctuations, the percentage relationship should be approximately the same for local currency and U.S. dollars. However, the analysis of reported net profits can be complicated by differences in tax accounting that can significantly affect reported profits. A quick calculation of tax rates should determine the tax impact on profits. As a general rule, a five-year history is a reasonably good indicator of profitability trends and will alert the reviewer to problems and opportunities. What is an appropriate return on sales? This question can be best answered from both an external and internal viewpoint. An external examination would gather comparable return-on-sales figures for competitive companies within the same industry.

This comparison is extremely helpful in determining how successfully the subsidiary is competing and what growth potential or problems the subsidiary may encounter in the future. For example, if the subsidiary's return on sales is much lower than competition, certain logical questions follow.

- Can we compete effectively in the marketplace?
- What steps can be taken to improve profitability?
- Can volume growth projections be adequately supported financially to ensure their success?

Conversely, a return on sales much higher than the competition's would generate the following.

- Are we setting "too high" a price umbrella that is permitting competitors to thrive?
- Would more aggressive pricing and pushing volume open the door to improved market-share position and reduced competition?
- Should remittances be increased to the home office if the growth opportunities do not warrant additional investment?

The real internal measure of an acceptable return-on-sales level is cash flow. The ideal return-on-sales level would generate a positive cash flow after working capital, fixed asset expenditures, and remittance requirements are funded. For example, let us examine a subsidiary with the following financial profile—sales are growing at 15 percent per year; net working capital represents 20 percent of sales; plant and equipment expenditures average 2 percent of sales; and the remittance target is 50 percent of profits. Thus the minimum return-of-sales objective would be 5.1 percent to generate a positive cash flow. This example is shown in Exhibit 17-1 as part of an abbreviated funds flow chart. If the growth projections were raised to 20 percent, using the same set of assumptions, then a return-on-sales objective of 7 percent would be required to break even on a cash flow basis. The major difference is the buildup in working capital required to support the more aggressive sales growth plan. A negative cash flow, resulting in a buildup in debt, is not all bad and should be considered in relation to the debt/equity ratios and capital structure of the subsidiary. However, a targeted return-on-sales objective should strive to generate a positive cash flow for a healthy, growing subsidiary.

Return on Capital. The second major performance criterion is return on capital. Return on capital is defined as:

$$\frac{\text{Net profit} + \text{aftertax interest}}{\text{Shareholders' equity} + \text{debt} + \text{deferred liabilities}} = \text{return on capital}$$

Return on capital measures the aftertax return of the subsidiary's use of capital, that is, its investment. Importantly, this aftertax return can screen alternative investment opportunities and should be compared to the bank deposit aftertax interest rate that is currently available in that country. Certainly, an investment should not be made whose return does not at least surpass the ordinary interest rate. This minimum rate is sometimes referred to as the "hurdle rate." In addition, each subsidiary's return on capital should be compared with the overall corporate average to determine whether the subsidiary is a positive contributor to the total corporation. Return on capital stresses the proper use of money and represents an excellent common denominator to compare a subsidiary's performance.

Remittances as a Percentage of Profits. Profits or equity accumulating in a foreign subsidiary eventually become a long-term liability to the total corporation. Countries like the Andean Pact nations (Venezuela, Colombia, Peru, Ecuador) and Brazil that impose exchange and remittance restrictions on foreign-owned subsidiaries are having trouble attracting foreign investment today. These same countries (Venezuela is an exception) are classified as hyperinflationary, and, accordingly, their equity or surplus buildup is constantly exposed to currency devaluations and the resulting exchange losses that become an aftertax charge to current-year profits. Nonremittable profits are similar to having a rich uncle whose wealth is considered as part of family but whose bank accounts are outside your control. As a general rule, the subsidiaries should be remitting to shareholders, at a minimum, the same percentage of reported profits as the parent company. Remittances include royalties and supervision charges as well as dividends, and the ratio to be used is Remittances ÷ net profits = percent. Whether net profits should be local subsidiary–reported profits or U.S.-recorded profits is an issue. U.S.-recorded profits would reflect balance sheet translation loss for hyperinflationary countries; local subsidiary profits would reflect only local

EXHIBIT 17-1   Foreign Subsidiary Cash Flow Break-even Analysis

	Dollars	Percent	Dollars	Percent
Sales (percent growth)	100.0 (+15)		105.0 (+20)	
Net profits	5.1	5.1	7.1	6.8
Depreciation	2.0	2.0	2.1	2.0
Total sources	7.1	7.1	9.2	8.8
Net working capital	2.6	2.6	3.6	3.4
Fixed assets	2.0	2.0	2.1	2.0
Remittances	2.5	2.5	3.5	3.4
Total uses	7.1	7.1	9.2	8.8
Change in net cash position	—	—	—	—

currency profits. In this case, a dual standard should be adopted which uses both profit definitions, because local subsidiary profits represent the true cash flow and remittance capability of that particular subsidiary, and the reported profits to the shareholders, which are adjusted for exchange losses, represent the final corporate test.

Debt to Capital. Debt-to-capital ratio trends will help determine whether a subsidiary's profitability level is sufficient to run the business; they also provide a clue to the subsidiary's long-term profit potential. The debt to capital ratio is defined as long- and short-term debt ÷ LTD and STD + stockholders' equity + deferred liabilities. Debt-to-capital ratios vary significantly by industry, but a general rule of thumb says that debt-to-capital ratios below 0.33 are considered acceptable; those approaching 0.50 are considered dangerous. These ratios give management a hint of future trouble because, as the ratios worsen, the interest burden will increase and dampen the subsidiary's profitability. A rising debt-to-capital ratio signals a profit downturn; conversely, a declining debt-to-capital ratio signals an upturn. Deferred liabilities are considered part of the capital base because they generally represent long-term funds which are tied up on the balance sheet and which management continues to have discretionary use of. If, for any reason, a subsidiary's deferred liability classification does not fulfill these objectives, then the deferred liabilities should be eliminated from the ratio.

Net Working Capital as a Percentage to Sales. An examination of a company's funds flow will generally reveal that working capital, particularly in high-growth subsidiaries, represents the largest use of funds. Net working capital is defined in Exhibit 17-2. Cash is not included because it is not normally related to sales, and average monthly figures should be used in addition to the normal year-end figures. Cash forecasting and performance evaluations that rely exclusively on year-end balance sheet numbers can be terribly misleading. For example, a general manager can play many different

---

EXHIBIT 17-2   Calculating Percentage to Sales

	Average	Year-end
Net accounts receivable		
Plus		
Net inventories		
Less		
Accounts payable		
Equals		
Net working capital		

sales cut-off games at year-end. Second, average calculations are a better indicator of real operating cash requirements. In addition to the percentage of sales analysis, accounts receivable should be examined from the standpoint of day's sales outstanding; inventory in terms of month's coverage; and accounts payable as a percentage of inventories, as well as day's payable outstanding. Nothing will eat up cash more quickly than a deteriorating net working capital position, particular in a growing company. Again, access to competitive company/industry net working capital data will be very helpful in evaluating a subsidiary's performance. In addition, the sales force should report competitive selling and cash discount terms, and frequent slow moving (more than six months' coverage) and obsolete (more than one year's coverage) inventory reports should be prepared to better control inventories. These trends should be analyzed quarterly to maintain timely control.

Funds Flow/Liquidity Analysis. A condensed funds flow statement is an extremely valuable method of determining what is actually happening in a subsidiary. The term "condensed" is used to connote "understandable." Detailed and lengthy funds flow statements not only confuse the basic issues but also confuse the nonfinancial executive's appreciation and understanding of the problem. The overall net change in cash position is the most important indicator of a subsidiary's health. The funds flow highlights the basic cash movements and should be presented in as simple a format as possible. (See Exhibit 17-3.)

The liquidity analysis should be performed in both local currency and in U.S. dollars. The U.S. dollars movement can be misleading due to exchange variations (particularly with fixed assets); in all cases, the local currency cash movement is a more reliable and valid funds flow indicator. Working

EXHIBIT 17-3 Funds Flow/Liquidity Analysis Statement

	Foreign subsidiary				
	19X1	19X2	19X3	19X4	19X5
Sources					
Profits					
Depreciation					
Other					
Total sources:					
Uses					
Working capital					
Fixed assets					
Remittances					
Other					
Total uses					
Net change in position					

capital should be shown as a use of cash, and a three- to five-year trend is necessary to understand the true liquidity position of the subsidiary. The subsidiary represents a parent company investment, and its performance can be evaluated only in terms of its cash return to the shareholders. A cash generating subsidiary is a profitable subsidiary, and the primary goal should be the remittance of that cash to the parent company.

Return on Investment. The return on capital analysis discussed above is principally used for total company or subsidiary evaluation. Within the subsidiary, the various business segments and categories should be subdivided into separate, identifiable entities along with the cash investment these business categories tie up. The gross investment and profit calculations are defined in Exhibit 17-4. Averages should be used rather than year-end figures. The hurdle rate to determine the viability of any business (whether it is a decision to enter, remain, or expand) is that the return on investment should be equal at a minimum to the pretax interest rate available on money deposits. Sometimes it is difficult to identify the gross fixed assets tied up with a given category, but every attempt, other than a straight sales allocation, should be used to distribute a company's fixed asset investment to the different categories. In general, accounts receivable can be allocated by sales unless different divisions or product categories have their own specific sales terms. However, inventories should be readily identifiable to the various business segments. Cash is not included here because the minimum operating cash needed is in most cases not consequential, and accounts payable are excluded because this analysis concerns just the asset side of the balance sheet and accounts payable is really supplier financing just as loans represent bank financing for either working capital or fixed assets.

The numerator—the return input—should be pretax, preinterest, and predepreciation. The pretax element is important because it will allow the parent company to compare similar-category investment performance worldwide. On the other hand, an equally strong case can be made to use aftertax profit figures to reflect the true world disparities between subsidiaries. However, your basic business should not be run by tax planning considerations, and the real long-term health of a business depends on its

---

EXHIBIT 17-4 Calculation of Return on Investment

Profit before tax, interest, and depreciation
Investment
  Gross accounts receivable
  Gross inventories
  Gross fixed assets
  Total investment
Percentage return on investment

pretax cash return on investment. Profits are shown preinterest since the investment analysis focuses on the asset side of the balance sheet and preinterest allows a more comparable worldwide analysis of investment performance and opportunities. Predepreciation is used in combination with gross assets. The use of gross assets makes all investments equal—whether the machinery and equipment are brand new or twenty years old.

NONFINANCIAL MEASURES

Volume Growth Analysis

To better understand the sales growth trends of a subsidiary one must break down the sales growth increment into its component parts. Sales increases are generated by unit volume gains; selling price increases; and, in U.S. dollar terms, by exchange variations. A subsidiary sales growth should be analyzed as shown in Exhibit 17-5. As a general rule the selling price increase at a minimum should equal the country's rate in inflation, and, to maintain a proper U.S. sales dollar perspective, should also surpass the change in exchange rate. The volume/mix gains are the real indicator of a subsidiary's performance, and, if necessary, a further separation should be calculated between volume and mix. In hyperinflationary countries, primary emphasis should be focused on selling price increases, because volume growth without the corresponding selling price increases will place a tremendous cash strain on the subsidiary for working capital and for the need to expand existing plant capacity.

Market Share

The calculation and use of market share depends on the availability of industry and competitive information, either through formal outside research organizations or inhouse/association surveys. The determination of the market size, its growth, and competitive market shares of your business categories is essential to understanding the pace of the business as well as optimizing and directing your marketing and investment efforts. (See Exhibit 17-6.) Market-share trends represent the best performance criteria and

EXHIBIT 17-5   Foreign Subsidiary Sales Growth Analysis

	Percent change	Measurement criteria
Unit volume/mix	10	Volume changes
Selling price increases	12	Average selling prices
Exchange variation	(5)	Average exchange rates
Net U.S. dollar change	17	

permit management to gauge the success or failure of its endeavors. Market-share data are the best indicators of your product health, your competitive position, and your overall performance in the marketplace. However, when dealing with these data, the information's source should be noted and its reliability checked.

Exchange Rates

As mentioned earlier, the financial statement analysis should be performed in both U.S. dollars and local currency. In particular, cash flow statements and nonvariable overhead expenses must be examined in local currency to fully appreciate what is happening on a year-to-year basis. An acceptable substitute for local currency statements is the use of constant dollars, which permits the consolidation of different subsidiary financial statements in effectively local currency terms. Constant dollars are developed by using the current or latest year-average exchange rate and converting prior years' local currency statements at the current year rate. For example, an analysis of sales increases for Subsidiary X would reveal the differences shown in Exhibit 17-7.

As Exhibit 17-7 shows, the constant dollar method restated the prior year's U.S. dollar results in terms of today's exchange rates, and the percentage changes will equal the local currency changes from year to year. Constant dollars are equivalent to the subsidiary's local currency statements and have the added advantage of allowing consolidation of the financial results of different subsidiaries.

Exchange rate forecasting is a special subject and discipline and is covered in chapters 4 and 5 of this handbook. What we should note here is that the only thing certain about exchange rates is that they will vary and, in so doing, can raise havoc with financial results as they are reported in U.S. dollars. This in turn raises the issue of how exchange rate variances should be handled in assessing the performance of an overseas subsidiary.

EXHIBIT 17-6   Market Size and Share Calculations

	\multicolumn{5}{c}{5-year trend}				
	19X1	19X2	19X3	19X4	19X5	Comment
Market size (volume)						
Percent growth						
Value						
Percent growth						
Market-share percentage						
Company						
Competition						

Major differences of opinion exist about whether a general manager should be held accountable for U.S. dollar results. One school of thought argues that since the U.S. corporation is responsible to its shareholders in terms of U.S. dollar results, then subsidiary managers' performance should also be evaluated in U.S. dollars. Particularly in hyperinflationary environments, the general manager must strive to minimize exchange losses through better working capital control, debt management, and aggressive pricing. The best way to motivate and measure this type of performance is to hold the manager responsible for results in U.S. dollars. The counterargument is that exchange rate variances are basically noncontrollable and that performance evaluation in U.S. dollars is unfair and distorted. Although the recent extreme fluctuations in exchange rates in Europe and Latin America have made the U.S. dollar responsibility argument more difficult, the two approaches will undoubtedly continue to be argued and employed by multinational corporations for many years.

Hyperinflation and Financial Accounting Standard (FAS) 52

The definition of a hyperinflationary economy set forth in FAS 52 and discussed in Chapter 14 is when the cumulative inflation in a country is in excess of approximately 100 percent over a three-year period. The 100 percent level over three years breaks down to annual rates of 26 percent compounded over three years. This hyperinflationary definition would encompass the major growth markets in South America (Venezuela is an exception) along with a few African and Middle Eastern countries.

Management's approach to hyperinflationary countries should be far more balance sheet–oriented than normal because exchange gains or losses must flow through the current year's profit and loss statement. The only effective way to minimize a subsidiary's exchange exposure is through proper balance sheet planning. Basically, it is the subsidiary's equity that is

---

EXHIBIT 17-7 Calculating Exchange Rates

	Subsidiary X's sales history ($ millions)				
	19X1	19X2	19X3	19X4	19X5
U.S. dollars	101.0	106.7	110.9	119.9	138.1
Percent increase	+11.0	+5.6	+3.9	+8.1	+15.1
Local dollars	100.0	112.0	122.1	136.7	143.6
Percent increase	+10.0	+12.0	+9.0	+12.0	+5.0
Constant dollars	96.2	107.7	117.4	131.3	138.1
Percent increase	+10.0	+12.0	+9.0	+12.0	+5.0
Exchange rate (U.S.)	1.01	1.05	1.10	1.14	1.04

exposed in a hyperinflationary country. Hyperinflation and a devaluing currency are synonomous, and the dollar value of the subsidiary's capital and undistributed profits are constantly eroding. In other words, if the subsidiary was sold or liquidated, the realizable dollar value must be reflected in today's dollars, not yesterday's or historical dollar rates. The only two assets that are protected from the ravages of inflation are fixed assets and, to a lesser degree, inventories.

The ideal balance sheet for a hyperinflationary subsidiary would incorporate the following elements.

1. Fixed assets representing a large proportion of total assets
2. Inventories rather than accounts receivable as the major component of working capital
3. Local currency rather than foreign (offshore) debt
4. A high debt-to-equity ratio to finance operations and thereby reduce the equity exposure
5. A high level of remittances to maximize the cash flow to the parent company and minimize equity exposure

Exhibit 17-8 is a very simplified example of how subsidiary's balance sheet translation loss would be calculated using the historical method of accounting. Clearly, either an increase in fixed assets or a decrease in equity will improve the subsidiary's balance sheet loss position. This balance sheet loss is an aftertax loss in the consolidated profit and loss statement. However, it is not a cash flow item, and this loss would only materialize if the subsidiary was actually sold or liquidated.

FAS 52 clearly benefits the heavy-fixed-asset investment industries, such as chemicals, who can shield their equity exposure through their fixed asset investments. A cash buildup in a hyperinflationary country must be minimized, and unfortunately, these same hyperinflationary countries generally have tight exchange and remittance controls.

EXHIBIT 17-8 Calculating Translation Losses in a Hyperinflationary Subsidiary

	Local currency	U.S. dollars (historical)
Equity	90,000	40,000
Fixed assets	(50,000)	(15,000)
Net	40,000	25,000
Year-end exchange rate	0.50	(20,000)
Net balance sheet loss		(5,000)

If the hyperinflationary countries are profitable and generate cash flow, the major options available to reduce the exchange exposure is to invest in fixed assets, increase inventories, or find innovative means to remit cash outside of the capital base/remittance restrictions.

In evaluating the profit performance of a hyperinflationary subsidiary, one must examine two levels of profitability—the subsidiary as well as the consolidated results. The following is an example.

	U.S.$
Reported profits (subsidiary)...........................	1000
Balance sheet translation adjustment—gain/(loss)	(250)
Recorded profits (consolidated)	750

The impact of exchange can effectively wipe out the reported profits of a hyperinflationary subsidiary, and only management attention to balance sheet planning or timely exchange hedging can alleviate this problem.

The establishment of two profitability levels raises the question of performance evaluation. Should subsidiary general managers be held responsible for exchange losses that are basically outside their control? In most multinational companies, the corporate head office exercises tight control over subsidiary capital expenditures, debt limits, and dividend/remittance levels. By doing so, the corporate head office is effectively controlling the exchange exposure of the subsidiary. The major exception would be a buildup in accounts receivable (the general managers' direct responsibility), and the resulting increase in balance sheet translation losses would be attributable to those actions. Obviously, any failure by the general manager to adhere to the corporate guidelines is a direct responsibility, but that could also be construed as a failure in corporate supervision.

Blocked Funds

As mentioned earlier, the primary mission of any international subsidiary of a multinational company is to remit cash back to the home office. The buildup of nonremittable cash on subsidiary balance sheets is a real operating problem. First, the consolidated balance sheet will show cash balances that are not available or discretionary for whatever corporate purpose. Certainly, smart bankers would like to know what the real manageable cash balances are of a multinational company to establish a credit rating or a lending limit. Second, blocked funds generally occur in hyperinflationary countries, where the cash is completely exposed to currency devaluations and the resulting balance sheet translation losses.

Blocked funds result from remittance or dividend restrictions, usually on a set percentage of the subsidiary's capital base. The first approach to improving the blocked funds problem is to see what steps can be taken to increase the capital base without a capital infusion from the parent company. To attract foreign investment, many countries now permit capitalization of fixed assets (for expansion and the creation of new jobs), of government bond purchases, and of newly acquired companies. The possibilities of instituting royalty contracts as well as technical assistance fees should also be explored with local governments as a remittance vehicle. A whole myriad of different approaches are available to attack the blocked funds issue depending on the country in question.

SUMMARY

The basic approach to the control and evaluation of international operations should be no different than that of a domestic business, but there will always be the complications of exchange rate variances. For this reason, it is even more important to focus control and evaluation on unit volume growth, market share, profitability ratios, sound local currency cash flows, and remittances back to the parent company.

Eighteen: International Tax Planning and Execution

CHARLES T. CRAWFORD

Charles T. Crawford is director of the Price Waterhouse Center for Transnational Taxation in New York. Mr. Crawford's prolific writings include tax articles in the Journal of Taxation, the Tax Adviser, the International Tax Institute, German-American Trade News, International Tax Journal, Euromoney, Yachting Magazine, the Golf Journal, and Amerikahandel. He has earned B.S. and LL.B. degrees from the University of Kansas and an LL.M. (taxation) degree from the University of Missouri. He is a member of the bar in New York, Kansas, and Missouri. He is also a certified public accountant in Kansas. Mr. Crawford's principal outside activity in the financial area is service as treasurer, director, and member of the Executive Committee of the United States Squash Racquets Association.

$$\mathbf{T}$$

he stakes in tax planning for a multinational corporation are enormous. Income taxes are so large in absolute terms that a relatively minor shift can be millions of dollars. This chapter considers the basic tax problems and concepts involved in international business. The discussion will help a financial executive who is not a tax expert to ask the right questions and recognize problem areas. It is not, however, a substitute for the expert advice needed before making any significant foreign investment or transaction.

This discussion is from the standpoint of a multinational company based in a major industrial country, and many of the concepts apply to a multinational based in any industrial country. The examples generally are from the standpoint of a U.S.-based multinational.

The object of tax planning is to avoid, reduce, or postpone taxes. Often this involves merely choosing the best way to structure a project that will go forward anyway (e.g., should operations in France be a branch of the U.S. parent or a French subsidiary?). In other cases, tax planning can change "no go" to "go"; e.g., sophisticated financing arrangements that eliminate U.S. withholding tax on interest payments can make a previously unattractive offshore financing viable. Lastly, foreign tax incentives can affect how and where business is done. For example, a plant may be located in Puerto Rico or Ireland to take advantage of tax holidays, without which the production would have taken place elsewhere (or perhaps not at all).

The objectives of tax planning for overseas expansion and operation include:

1. Minimizing the home country tax cost of transferring assets abroad. In some cases, transferring assets to foreign ownership is a taxable event (i.e., the excess of current value over cost basis is taxable gain).

2. Using foreign startup losses to reduce home country taxes.

3. Minimizing foreign taxes by operating in the most advantageous way in each country (e.g., branch or foreign corporation).

4. Minimizing foreign and home country taxes on intragroup money flows by taking advantage of tax treaties and tax havens. This includes using offshore finance subsidiaries to gather and redistribute, via loans, profits earned by foreign subsidiaries, without subjecting these profits to home country tax.

5. Reducing the group's overall tax burden by structuring intragroup expense/income flows (e.g., royalties) so that they are paid by high-tax-rate members of the group to low-tax-rate members.

6. Reducing the group's overall tax burden by having intragroup sales and purchases priced (to the extent practical) to allocate the maximum (realistic) profit to the low-tax-rate members.

7. Reducing home country taxes by taking fullest advantage of the foreign tax credit. In the United States this would include both making elections to reduce the amount of parent company expenses attributed to foreign source income and making elections to reduce the earnings and profits of foreign corporation subsidiaries.

8. Withdrawing from foreign operations at the least tax cost (or greatest tax benefit).

OVERSEAS EXPANSION—BRANCH VERSUS FOREIGN SUBSIDIARY

Most industrial countries tax the worldwide income of domestic corporations (i.e., corporations incorporated under the laws of the country or of a political subdivision, such as a state in the United States). Corporate "residence" also is a factor under the tax laws of some countries; a prominent example is the United Kingdom. Belgium, France, and the Netherlands are the principal countries that do not tax the foreign active business income of their domestic corporations.[1]

The United States taxes the worldwide income of U.S. corporations. Corporate residence is not a factor. The United States does not tax currently the income of foreign corporations owned by U.S. individuals or corporations unless the Subpart F (tax haven) or foreign personal holding company rules come into play. In general, these exceptions, discussed later, do not adversely affect foreign subsidiaries conducting normal commercial operations.

Typically, the profits of a foreign subsidiary are taxed only when they are brought home as dividends, when the corporation is liquidated, or when the shares of the corporation are sold. For U.S. multinationals, special rules as published in the Internal Revenue Code (IRC) make the portion of the gain on the sale or liquidation of a foreign corporation that is attributable to retained "earnings and profits" taxable as ordinary income rather than capital gain.[2]

That the income of foreign subsidiaries of U.S. multinationals is not taxed currently means that the operating losses of these subsidiaries are not recognized by the parent company until the subsidiary is sold or liquidated. Wholly owned Canadian and Mexican corporations, maintained solely to comply with rules regarding ownership of property, are the exceptions that can be included in the parent company's consolidated return [section 1504(d) IRC].

The classic way to operate overseas has been to do so as a branch of the parent company (or of another corporation included in the parent's consolidated return) as long as the activity operated at a loss. When the activity becomes profitable, it can be transferred to either a newly formed or an existing foreign subsidiary. Although still valuable in some jurisdictions, the technique has been chipped away at by the major countries that serve as bases for multinational companies.

TRANSFER OF ASSETS TO A FOREIGN CORPORATION

As a general rule, the tax laws of the industrial countries provide that corporations can transfer assets to controlled subsidiaries tax-free.[3] The theory is that only the form of ownership has changed and that the assets are still within the country's taxing jurisdiction. When assets are transferred to a foreign corporation, the home country no longer can directly tax either the gain, if the asset is sold, or the income from its exploitation, if it is retained.

The United States deals with this problem, in section 367 of the IRC, by providing that if the transferee corporation is a foreign corporation the tax-free "rollover" provisions of the tax law will not apply unless the Internal Revenue Service (IRS) determines that avoidance of U.S. tax was not a principal purpose of the transfer. In general, a taxpayer must request the ruling within 183 days of the beginning of the transfer. These rules in general also apply to transfers between two foreign subsidiaries, to the liquidation of foreign subsidiaries, and to the liquidation of U.S. subsidiaries of foreign parent corporations. Although these types of transactions do not require an IRS ruling, they must comply with the conditions stated in the regulations [section 367(b) IRC].

Guidelines issued in 1968 and temporary regulations issued subsequently state in some detail (1) the circumstances in which a favorable ruling will be given because the transaction does not involve tax avoidance and (2) the circumstances in which a favorable ruling will be issued if the taxpayer agrees to include an appropriate amount in taxable income (i.e., pay a "toll charge").[4]

The 1968 guidelines provide generally that a favorable ruling will be given if the foreign transferee is to use the transferred property in the active conduct of a trade or business. However, according to the guidelines, a favorable ruling will not be issued if transferred property includes (1) inventory or other goods held for sale to customers, (2) copyrights, patents, etc.,

(3) accounts receivable, or (4) stock or securities, unless a toll charge is paid. This generally involves the U.S. transferor picking up the unrealized gain in the transferred items as taxable income.

For many years the IRS has taken the position that a favorable section 367 ruling would not be issued for the incorporation of a foreign branch that had operated at a loss unless the U.S. taxpayer included the accumulated losses in its taxable income.[5] In 1981 this position was successfully challenged in court, but as of this writing the IRS has not dropped the requirement for a toll charge in these circumstances.[6]

FOREIGN TAX CREDIT

The countries that tax the foreign income of their citizens and domestic (or resident) corporations prevent (or mitigate) double taxation of the foreign income by providing that the foreign income taxes are a credit against the home country tax liability. In general, the foreign tax credit is limited to the amount of home country tax attributable to the foreign income. The limitation, depending on a country's rules, could be computed on a per-item, per-country, or worldwide basis.[7]

The two major problems in the foreign tax credit area are (1) determining if the foreign tax is an income tax and (2) determining foreign source taxable income.

United States law provides that credit can be taken for foreign income taxes and for taxes imposed by a foreign country (or subdivision) in lieu of an income tax.[8] Foreign sales taxes, excise taxes, and value-added taxes (VAT) are not creditable for U.S. tax purposes (although taxes based heavily on gross receipts may be deemed "in lieu of" income taxes).[9] The greatest difficulty in this area relates to the taxes on oil and gas operations in the Middle East, where, because the oil fields belong to the state, the distinction between a royalty payment (which is merely a deduction in computing taxable income) and an income tax payment (which is a credit against the home country tax liability) becomes blurred. The rules relating to the foreign tax credit of oil and gas operations are not dealt with in this chapter; they are of mind-numbing complexity, and the financial managements of the major oil companies are well aware of the problems involved in the area [sections 904(f)(4) and 907 IRC].

For U.S. tax purposes, a foreign tax that is not an income tax is still deductible in computing taxable income [section 164 IRC]. In addition, on an annual basis, a taxpayer can, by not making the credit election, deduct its foreign taxes instead of taking them as a credit. If the election is made to take foreign income taxes as a credit, it applies to all the foreign income taxes paid or accrued during the year. A deduction might be preferable to a credit where, because of the foreign tax credit limitation, the corporation's foreign income taxes far exceed the credit allowable or where the company is incurring losses and fears that the credits will expire unused. Excess foreign tax credits can only be carried back two years and forward five years [section 904(c) IRC]; but, as a general rule, net operating losses can be carried back three years and forward fifteen years [section 172(b)(1) IRC].

FOREIGN SOURCE TAXABLE INCOME

The United States limits the foreign tax credit to the portion of the U.S. tax liability attributable to foreign source taxable income [section 904(a) IRC]. This is computed by multiplying the precredit U.S. tax liability by the ratio of foreign source taxable income to worldwide taxable income. There is no downside risk in increasing foreign source income. Much of the tax planning of U.S. multinational corporations involves increasing foreign source income and thereby increasing the foreign tax credit limitation.

Determining the source of gross income generally is quite straightforward for U.S. tax purposes: As a general rule, income from foreign branch operations is foreign source, as is dividend income and interest income paid by foreign subsidiaries. Income from sales of products *purchased* in the United States and sold outside the United States is considered to be entirely from foreign sources. Income from products *manufactured* by the taxpayer in the United States and sold outside the United States is allocated between U.S. and foreign sources by a formula that takes into account where the taxpayer's property is located and where the sales take place. A sale is deemed to take place where the rights, title, and interests of the seller pass to the buyer.[10]

ALLOCATION OF DEDUCTIONS IN COMPUTING FOREIGN SOURCE TAXABLE INCOME

The United States has by far the most complicated rules for allocating deductions between U.S. source and foreign source gross income (Regulations, section 1.861-8 IRC). The regulations stating the rules were developed from the standpoint of a U.S.-based multinational company; that is, their bias often appears to be to allocate deductions generated in the United States against foreign source gross income (thus reducing the foreign tax credit limitation). The principal deductions dealt with are (1) home office management expenses, (2) research and development (R&D) expenses, and (3) interest expense. The same rules (except for interest expense incurred by foreign corporations) also apply to foreign individuals, partnerships, and corporations doing business in the United States. The bias that works against U.S.-based taxpayers by allocating U.S.-incurred expenses overseas works in favor of foreign taxpayers by allocating home office expenses and home country-incurred research and development expenses to their U.S. operations. This advantage does not affect U.S. subsidiaries of foreign multinationals, but, if they do in fact benefit from home office services and research and development, they can pay their parent corporation deductible arm's-length management fees and royalties.

If an item of home office expense can be identified with an activity, it will be allocated to that activity [Regulations, section 1.861-8(e)(4) IRC]. For example, the expense of the "international department" would normally be allocated entirely against foreign source income, and the cost of a study to determine whether to build a plant in Oregon or California normally would be allocated entirely against U.S. source income. In the case of activities that cannot be so identified, such as, perhaps, the salary of the chief executive officer, the regulations provide that any reasonable overhead allocation method will be acceptable [Regulations, section 1.861-8(b)(3) IRC]. Deductions that are not related to any item of gross income (such as charitable contributions) are allocated to foreign source gross income on the basis of the ratio of foreign source gross income to total gross income.

Research and development expenses are allocated under a complex approach that breaks R&D into 32 product categories.[11] (But note suspension period discussed in footnote.) Within each category, if 50 percent or more of the R&D expense is expended in one geographic area (e.g., the United States), then 30 percent of the total R&D expense is allocated exclusively to that geographic area. For a U.S.-based multinational, this is an incentive to do more than 50 percent of its R&D in the United States (as the provision was intended). The remaining R&D is allocated within each product category on the basis of sales, although, subject to certain limitations, the remaining R&D can be allocated on the basis of gross income.

INTEREST ALLOCATION—FUNGIBILITY APPROACH

Under the U.S. rules, interest expense for all taxpayers, except foreign corporations, is allocated between foreign source gross income and U.S. source gross income on the basis of the ratio of the tax book value (or fair market value) of assets outside the United States to those within [Regulations, section 1.861-8(e)(2) IRC]. This approach is known as the "fungibility approach" because it is based on the premise that money is fungible and that interest expense is attributable to all activities and property regardless of any specific purpose for incurring an obligation. This recognizes that management has a great deal of flexibility as to the source and use of funds and that money borrowed for a specific purpose generally will free other funds for other purposes. The regulations also permit allocation of interest on the basis of gross income, subject to certain limitations. Interest can be allocated to specific assets only when very stringent requirements are met, including that the debt be nonrecourse [Regulations, section 1.861-8(e)(2)(iv) IRC].

The interest expense of foreign corporations doing business in the United States is computed by a process that combines the fungibility approach and the separate entity approach (Regulations, section 1.882-4-5 IRC).

The complexity and importance of the allocation of expenses of a U.S.-based multinational is clear—e.g., the major U.S. multinationals use highly sophisticated computer programs to compute and plan (within designated safe havens and alternatives) how the expense allocation will be made.

DEEMED-PAID FOREIGN TAX CREDIT

Typically, the industrial countries permit their multinationals to take a foreign tax credit for taxes paid by foreign subsidiaries and, in some cases, their subsidiaries' subsidiaries.[12] The credit usually is the amount of income tax attributable to dividends paid during the year; the dividend is "grossed-up" to include the amount of the tax. For example, a foreign corporation earns $100,000 in 1983, on which it pays income tax of $30,000, and pays the remaining $70,000 as a dividend to its U.S. parent; if the U.S. parent elects to take foreign taxes as a credit (rather than a deduction), it will include the full $100,000 as dividend income and take a $30,000 foreign tax credit.[13] Such deemed-paid credits are subject to the same limitations as is a direct foreign tax credit.[14]

The deemed-paid credit generally applies only to corporate shareholders and to shareholdings that constitute at least a stated percentage of the subsidiaries' ownership (i.e., it applies to direct investment, but not to portfolio investment). The stated percentage of ownership for direct investment for Canada, the United Kingdom, and the United States is 10 percent.[15]

Foreign withholding tax on dividends is creditable directly, regardless of percentage of ownership.

PLANNING FOR DEEMED-PAID CREDIT

United States multinationals can maximize the benefit of deemed-paid (indirect) credits by timing dividends from foreign subsidiaries and making elections that reduce the earnings and profits of foreign subsidiaries because the creditable tax is deemed to equal the foreign subsidiary's income tax for the year multiplied by the ratio of the dividend paid to the subsidiary's earnings and profits for the year (determined under U.S. tax rules).[16] Thus, if earnings and profits (the denominator of the fraction) are decreased, the amount of deemed-paid tax is increased. If dividends paid during the year (including dividends paid during the first sixty days of the next taxable year) exceed the current year's earnings and profits, the excess is deemed to be paid out of prior years' earnings and profits on a last-in, first-out (LIFO) basis [section 902(c)(1) IRC].

"Earnings and profits" is a defined term for U.S. income tax purposes. To oversimplify, earnings and profits are aftertax income computed under U.S. generally accepted accounting principles, specifically using (1) accounting methods authorized by U.S. tax law, (2) inventory methods authorized by U.S. tax law, and (3) specified depreciation methods [Regulations, section 1.902-1(g) IRC].

An important tax planning point for U.S. multinationals is to elect accounting methods (e.g., LIFO inventory and accelerated depreciation) that will reduce earnings and profits of their foreign subsidiaries [Regulations, section 1.964-1(c) IRC]. These elections, in addition to increasing the deemed-paid dividend, will reduce the ordinary income the parent must pick up when the subsidiary is sold or liquidated.

An example of the deemed-paid credit computation follows.

Earnings before tax of foreign corporation for calendar year 1983.......	$1000
Foreign income tax at 30 percent	300
Earnings and profits for 1983	700
Dividend paid to U.S. parent company	700
Less foreign withholding tax at 15 percent.......................	105
Net dividend received in United States	595
Foreign creditable taxes	
Direct credit for withholding tax.............................	105
Deemed-paid credit for subsidiary's tax	
$\dfrac{700 \text{ (dividend)}}{700 \text{ (earnings and profits)}} \times 300$ (foreign tax).................	300
Total creditable taxes	405
Included in U.S. income	
Gross dividend received......................................	700
Plus foreign deemed-paid tax	300
U.S. gross dividend included..................................	1000
U.S. tax at 46 percent...	460
Less foreign tax credit	405
U.S. tax payable	55

RECAPTURE OF FOREIGN LOSSES

The U.S. tax code has a number of provisions that reduce the foreign source taxable income of U.S. taxpayers with overseas operations. If a U.S. multinational has a net foreign source taxable loss that reduces the corporation's tax on income from U.S. sources (i.e., the loss generates a tax benefit), the loss will be "recaptured" against future foreign source income in computing future years' foreign tax credit limitations [section 904(f) IRC]. The recapture in any year is limited to 50 percent of that year's foreign source taxable income. Thus if a company has $50,000 net foreign source taxable loss in 1983 (that reduces tax on income from U.S. sources) and foreign source taxable income of $80,000 in 1984, $40,000 of the $80,000 (50 percent) will be treated as U.S. source income. The remaining $10,000 ($50,000 less $40,000) remains available for recapture in later years.

The U.S. tax law also has provisions to limit the ability to generate foreign source income through profitable sales of capital assets abroad [section 904(b)(2) IRC].

INTERCOMPANY PRICING

Only a minimal degree of tax sophistication is needed to realize that the overall taxes of a group of corporations can be reduced if high-tax-rate members sell (or lease or lend or license) to low-tax-rate members at unrealistically low prices. This device also is well known to tax administrators, and the countries of the world universally reserve the right to adjust taxable income when related taxpayers (e.g., commonly controlled corporations) have not dealt with one another at arm's length.

A taxpayer's greatest danger in this area is greed. Unless the commodity being transferred has an established price in the marketplace (e.g., a specific grade of wheat) or the seller also sells the same item on identical terms to independent third parties, there is a range within which a favorable (to the taxpayer) price can be selected with little danger of attracting the IRS' attention. Moreover, in some cases the tax rules provide safe havens which will not be questioned (e.g., interest expense under the U.S. rules, discussion of which follows).

There are several factors to consider before establishing a price that is *not* within reasonable bounds:

1. If an IRS agent decides to make an adjustment, he or she will pick a price that is self-serving in the extreme to the government. The more unrealistic the price originally set by the taxpayer, the less sympathy forthcoming from the IRS (or the courts, if it comes to that).

2. Interest rates on tax deficiencies are no longer a bargain in many countries; e.g., in the United States interest is now based on the prime rate (sections 6621 and 6622 IRC).

3. The corollary of reporting an unrealistically *low* amount of income in the high-rate country is reporting an unrealistically *high* amount of income in the low-rate country. If the high-rate country makes an adjustment, the multinational group will be subject to double taxation unless the low-tax-rate country allows a "correlative adjustment" (i.e., permits an amended return or refund claim based on the revised transfer price). Most tax treaties provide "competent authority" channels to mitigate double taxation in these circumstances (discussed under "Tax Treaties"), but the procedure is slow, time consuming, expensive, and uncertain. And, particularly if the low-rate country is a less developed country or a tax haven, there often will not be a tax treaty between the countries involved.

U.S. INTERCOMPANY PRICING RULES

The regulations under section 482 of the U.S. tax code prescribe that arm's-length prices for sale of property shall be determined by the first of the following methods deemed to apply [Regulations, section 1.482-2(e)].

1. The "comparable uncontrolled price method," which must be used if there are identical or nearly identical sales to unrelated parties. To the extent the sales are not identical, adjustments will be made to compensate for the differences.

2. The "resale price method," if it applies, must be used if the comparable uncontrolled price method does not apply. Under this method, if products are sold to a related party who sells them to unrelated parties with minimal further processing, the arm's-length price will be computed by deducting a reasonable markup, for the related seller's services, from the selling price to unrelated parties.

3. The "cost plus" method must be used if neither of the above methods apply. Under this method, an arm's-length price is computed by adding an appropriate gross profit percentage to the cost of producing the item.

Very detailed rules explain when a particular method is to be used and how it is to be implemented. This guidance, however, does not keep the choice of the applicable method from being the main issue in a section 482 controversy. If none of the above methods gives a reasonable result, another method, appropriate considering of the facts and circumstances, can be used. Detailed rules in the section 482 regulations determine the arm's-length prices for performance of services, use of tangible property, transfer or use of intangible property, and use of money (interest).[17]

The Section 482 rules provide, in general, that simple interest in the range of 11 percent to 13 percent will be considered arm's length but that a taxpayer may establish that a different rate is appropriate in the circumstances. If the rate used by the taxpayer is not in the 11 percent to 13 percent range or is not otherwise determined to be arm's length, a rate of 12 percent will be used. The safe haven rates and the presumed rates are changed from time to time to reflect market rate trends.

TAX TREATIES

Taking maximum advantage of tax treaties probably is the most important area of tax planning for a multinational company. Known officially as "international double taxation conventions," tax treaties' main purpose is to eliminate double taxation. To this end, they reduce drastically the withholding rates on dividends, interest, rents, and royalties. If the often-quite-high statutory rates prevailed, there would be far less international capital flow and transfer of technology. Some of the international capital flows are facilitated by treaties between certain industrial countries and certain low-rate countries. The use of treaties with low-tax-rate countries, which is discussed below, has been attacked by the United States in its recent tax treaty negotiations.

DOUBLE TAXATION RELIEF

All the western industrial countries (including Japan) and many of the less developed countries have networks of tax treaties. Unilateral relief measures such as the foreign tax credit cannot totally relieve double taxation because, from country to country, (1) definitions of income vary, (2) treatment of similar items varies (e.g., capital gains), and (3) geographical sourcing of income varies (e.g., compensation for services rendered can be deemed earned where the services are performed, the place where they are used, the place where the contract is signed, or the place where compensation is paid).

The treaties that the western industrial countries have with each other closely follow the model income tax treaty of the Organization for Economic Cooperation and Development (OECD), which is reproduced as Appendix 18A. In general, these countries both import and export capital, so they have a common interest in (1) reducing withholding taxes on flows of investment income and royalties, (2) carefully defining and liberalizing the degree of business activity and physical presence that will subject an individual or entity to another country's taxing jurisdiction (termed a "permanent establishment"), and (3) carefully defining the income that will be deemed earned in another country and the deductions that can be taken against such income. All twenty-four OECD members have approved the model treaty, but most, including the United States, have recorded reservations to the provisions they consider unacceptable. The United States also has a model treaty of its own, which, in addition to incorporating its reservations to the OECD model, sets out special features of U.S. tax law.

Since less developed countries are the object of foreign investment and business activity, but have little outflowing foreign investment and business activity of their own, they have less incentive for tax treaties that reduce withholding rates on dividends, interest, and royalties and set a fairly high level of business activity and physical presence to constitute a permanent establishment. As a result, few of the less developed countries have tax treaties. The United Nations has developed an unofficial draft of a model tax treaty for use between developed and developing countries. The UN model treaty uses the OECD model as its base but adjusts it to reflect the circumstances and point of view of developing countries.

Permanent Establishment

Under the OECD model treaty an enterprise of one country can have fairly extensive business activity in another country without being a permanent establishment.[18] For example, under the OECD model a company can send salespersons into a country (as long as they do not independently conclude sales), advertise, display goods, store goods, purchase goods, and use independent agents (who *can* conclude sales), without creating a permanent establishment.[19] The fact that a subsidiary corporation has a permanent establishment in a country does not cause the parent corporation to be deemed to have a permanent establishment.

Industrial and Commercial Profits

The OECD model treaty provides that a permanent establishment (e.g., a branch) will be taxed as if it were a distinct and separate enterprise dealing independently with the rest of the enterprise (article 7 OECD). This means that arm's-length prices must be determined for goods and services passing between the permanent establishment and the rest of the enterprise. Deductible expenses include home office executive and general administrative expenses incurred directly for the permanent establishment and a reasonable portion of costs incurred for the benefit of the enterprise as a whole.[20]

Double Tax Relief—The Exemption Method

The OECD model treaty provides alternative methods of eliminating double taxation: (1) the credit method used by the United States (article 23B OECD), which is discussed above, and (2) the exemption method (article 23A OECD). Under the latter system, the income of a permanent establishment is not taxed by the home country. The exemption method is widely used in treaties between European countries.

To prevent taxpayers from getting the benefit of reduced tax rates in both the home country and the host country, the home country often will consider the excluded income in computing the tax on nonexempt income ("exemption with progression").[21] Thus if taxable income is 90 and nontaxable income is 10, the tax is computed on 90 but at the average rate applying to 100.

Withholding-Tax Relief

The statutory withholding rates on passive income (dividends, interest, rents, and royalties) paid abroad often are prohibitive to international investment. For example, the statutory withholding rate on passive income is 25 percent in Canada, France, and Germany, 20 percent in Japan, 30 percent in the United Kingdom (except dividends, for which special rules apply), and 30 percent in the United States.

The OECD model provides the following withholding:

1. For dividends, 5 percent withholding when the owner holds 25 percent or more of the payer's stock. If ownership is less than 25 percent, the withholding rate is 15 percent (article 10 OECD). (The U.S. model has the same rates, but the 5 percent rate applies to holdings of 10 percent or more.)
2. For interest, 10 percent withholding (article 11 OECD) (the U.S. model's rate is 0).
3. For royalties, 0 percent withholding (article 12 OECD) (the U.S. rate also is 0).

If dividends, interest, or royalties are attributable to a permanent establishment (e.g., interest earned by a branch bank) there is no withholding; these items are taxed as ordinary business income of the permanent establishment (the United States follows this rule).

Capital Gains

The OECD model permits the host country to tax capital gains on the sale of real estate and property of a permanent establishment. Other capital gains (e.g., portfolio investments) are taxable only in the seller's country of residence (article 13 OECD).

Until 1980 the United States did not tax the capital gains of foreigners on the sale of U.S. real property unless the property was connected with a trade or business of the seller in the United States.[22] The 1980 legislation changed this by allowing the United States to tax such gains; it also provides that tax treaty provisions that exempt sales of U.S. real estate from capital gains tax will not apply after 1984 (section 897 IRC).

Rental Income from Real Property

The OECD treaty provides that the host country can tax rental income from real estate (article 6 OECD). The model treaty does not distinguish between passive rental income and business rental income, and both are subject to tax at ordinary rates.

Passive rental income from U.S. sources is subject to 30 percent withholding on the gross amount,[23] and rental income from the conduct of a trade or business, net of expenses, is taxed at ordinary rates.[24] United States tax law permits foreign passive lessors to elect to be treated as if they were engaged in a trade or business so that they can be taxed on their net rental income at ordinary rates rather than at 30 percent on the gross rent received.[25] The election under U.S. tax law is permanent. The deterrent to making the election has been that it subjected the real estate to capital gains tax when it was sold (even before the 1980 change in the law discussed above). In general, foreigners owning U.S. real estate took advantage of tax treaty provisions that permitted annual (rather than permanent) elections. Capital gains tax would be avoided by not making the net income election for the year the property was sold. As noted, the 1980 change in the law provides that tax treaty provisions that exempt real estate from capital gains tax do not apply after December 31, 1984.[26]

Personal Services

Under the OECD model treaty foreign employees are not taxed in the country where services are performed if (1) they are present in that country fewer than 184 days during the taxable year, (2) their salary is not paid by an employer who is a resident of the host country, and (3) a permanent establishment or fixed base of the employer in the host country does not bear the expense of the salary (article 15 OECD). The U.S. model treaty follows this rule.[27]

The OECD model provides that payments for independent (nonemployee) personal services are not taxable in the host country unless the recipients have a fixed base regularly available for the purpose of performing their activities (and then only so much as is attributable to the fixed base) (article 14 OECD). The U.S. model has a similar provision, but some U.S. treaties provide that independent services will not be taxed if the individual is in the country fewer than 184 days in the taxable year.[28]

Competent Authority

The OECD model treaty (and the U.S. model treaty) provides that taxpayers who believe that they have not been taxed in accordance with the treaty can appeal to the "competent authority" of their own country.[29] A multinational company might resort to this procedure if there has been a transfer pricing adjustment in the home country but no correlative adjustment in the host country. If the competent authority believes the appeal has merit, it must try to resolve the matter with the competent authority of the other country.

In the United States the competent authority for this purpose is the associate commissioner of Internal Revenue (Operations) and his or her staff. The IRS has issued detailed rules on when competent authority relief is available and how application for it should be made.[30] Despite this, the procedure is slow, uncertain, expensive, and, by its nature, political. It also puts a company in the position of having the government be its advocate (lawyer). This involves a degree of disclosure that, by itself, would keep many taxpayers from going to competent authority.

Tax Sparing

To encourage foreign investment, less developed countries often give "tax holidays" for a stated number of years to business investments considered in the national interest. If the home country taxes its multinationals' world-wide income but permits a foreign tax credit, a reduction of foreign tax merely means a dollar-for-dollar increase in the home country taxes (either immediately, if the foreign operations are by a branch of the multinational, or when the profits are brought home, if the tax holiday operations are in a foreign subsidiary).

"Tax sparing" preserves the incentive value of less developed countries' tax holidays by permitting taxpayers to take a foreign tax credit "as if" the taxes forgiven had been paid. Capital-exporting countries that have at least some tax treaties with tax-sparing provisions include Germany (e.g., Malta—article 23), Switzerland (e.g., Korea—article 22), the Netherlands (e.g., Indonesia—article 24), and the United Kingdom (e.g., Bangladesh—article 22). The U.S. Senate, to date, has rejected treaties containing tax-sparing provisions. The United States does, however, permit U.S. taxpayers to exclude income earned in U.S. possessions. This lets U.S. companies take advantage of Puerto Rico's tax holidays (section 936 IRC).

Tax Havens

Multinationals primarily use tax havens (1) to accumulate foreign profits at low tax rates, (2) to serve as the base of holding companies, to take advantage of the tax havens' low tax rates and/or treaty networks, and (3) to serve as a base for international finance subsidiaries. Tax havens are also used as bases for captive insurance companies.

The qualities that make a country a tax haven for multinational companies include (1) low tax rates, (2) an extensive treaty network, (3) well-developed banking facilities, (4) modern communications and transportation facilities, (5) no currency controls, and (6) political stability. Bank and commercial secrecy, highly prized by individual taxpayers, is not as important a tax haven characteristic for multinationals conducting legitimate business.

Several of the capital-exporting countries have laws to limit tax haven abuse. The United States' Subpart F has been in force since 1962 and has been the model for other countries' anti-tax-haven legislation (sections 951–962, 964 IRC). Germany, France, Canada, and Japan have laws similar to Subpart F, and the United Kingdom is considering such legislation.[31] Several major industrial countries are beginning to limit the use of third-country treaties (referred to as "treaty shopping").[32]

SALES COMPANIES

The greatest danger in using tax haven sales subsidiaries again is greed. Intragroup sales must be at justifiable prices, and the sales subsidiary must perform substantial services. But, properly handled, the benefits are great. For example, if a U.S. manufacturer sells its products directly to customers in Germany (with no German permanent establishment), the entire profit will be taxable in the United States; and, if the products are sold to a German sales subsidiary, which in turn sells to German customers, all the profit will be taxed by either the United States or Germany.

But if the U.S. manufacturer instead sells its products to a tax haven subsidiary, which in turn sells the products either directly to the German customers or to the German sales subsidiary, a portion of the profit will be earned by the tax haven subsidiary, where it will not be taxed until brought home by the parent company (if Subpart F can be avoided). The Bahamas and Bermuda, neither of which has an income tax, often are used for this purpose.

As discussed under "Transfer Pricing," if sales prices are not arm's length, the revenue services of the countries affected can adjust them to arm's length. If the tax haven company in the above example was reselling the product to a related German company (instead of reselling to unrelated German customers), the U.S. and German adjustments might exceed the income of the tax haven company. Although, as noted, competent authority has not been a very satisfactory way out of such a situation, several countries are trying to improve the procedure.

SUBPART F

Under Subpart F of U.S. tax law, U.S. shareholders owning 10 percent or more of the voting stock of "controlled foreign corporations" (CFCs) are taxed on the following income (section 952 IRC).[33]

1. Foreign personal holding company (passive) income, including dividends, interest, royalties, capital gains, and income from personal service contracts.
2. Sales income from property purchased from or sold to a "related person" that is both (a) manufactured and (b) sold for use, outside the seller's country of incorporation. (The tax haven sales corporation discussed above would meet this test, but might escape taxation under the 10 percent threshold soon to be discussed.)
3. Income from services rendered outside the renderer's country of incorporation for a related person.
4. Certain shipping income.

These four categories are "foreign base company income" and are subject to a 10-70 rule: if combined they are less than 10 percent of the corporation's gross income, the corporation is treated as having no "foreign base company income"; if combined they exceed 70 percent of the corporation's gross income, then all its gross income is considered "foreign base company income" [section 954(b)(3) IRC].

The 10 percent threshold is an important planning tool. Substantial tax haven sales income can be sheltered from Subpart F by running the sales through a low-tax-rate corporation that has a high level of gross income from business activity not subject to these rules.

In addition to the four categories of foreign base company income, Subpart F income includes the following, which is not subject to the 10-70 rule [section 952(a) IRC].

1. Income from insurance of U.S. risks (whether or not the insured is a related person).
2. Amounts invested in U.S. property. Thus loans (and loan guarantees) by CFCs to their U.S. parent corporations generate Subpart F income to the extent that the CFC has earnings and profits.
3. International boycott income.
4. Foreign illegal payments (bribes).

Creation of Foreign Source Income

Subpart F income is foreign source income.[34] Thus, by using a tax haven sales subsidiary (as in the above example), there can be a tax advantage even though the income is taxed currently to the U.S. parent (see the earlier discussion of the foreign tax credit limitation).

Use of Holding Companies

Multinational companies often hold the shares of their foreign operating companies through foreign holding companies for two basic reasons. (1) By using a corporation incorporated in a country with a good treaty network that imposes minimal taxes on foreign dividend income (e.g., the Netherlands and Switzerland), foreign profits can be brought home at reduced tax cost. (2) If the home country does not have provisions similar to Subpart F, a holding company can accumulate funds for use offshore without subjecting them to home country taxation.

The U.S. treaty policy now is to eliminate treaty shopping, which is the practice of using third-country treaties to reduce withholding rates (e.g., a Hong Kong-based multinational forming a Netherlands Antilles corporation to own the stock of a U.S. operating subsidiary, to take advantage of the Netherlands Antilles–U.S. treaty). This, of course, is the technique now being discussed. Other countries are becoming concerned with treaty shopping but not to the same extent as is the United States.[35] Despite this cloud, the technique will be available for some years and is a key to international investment.

Foreign holding companies also are used to hold all the subsidiaries operating in a country that permits the filing of consolidated returns. Thus a German multinational might hold several U.S. operating subsidiaries through a U.S. holding company so that the U.S. group could file a consolidated return. This would permit losses in one subsidiary to offset income in another.

Foreign Personal Holding Companies (FPHC)

The United States also taxes shareholders on the undistributed personal holding company (passive) income of foreign personal holding companies (sections 551–558 IRC). These rules rarely affect U.S. multinational companies because of the individual ownership requirements (noted below). A foreign corporation is an FPHC if (1) at least 50 percent (60 percent in the first year) of its gross income is personal holding company (passive) income (defined generally the same as for Subpart F purposes) and (2) more than 50 percent in value of its outstanding stock is owned directly or indirectly by five or fewer U.S. citizens or residents [section 552(a) IRC].

If a U.S. shareholder is taxed under the FPHC rules, the individual or corporate shareholder cannot be taxed under Subpart F for the same taxable year [section 951(d) IRC]. This provision has been used to permit a foreign corporation that is both a CFC and a FPHC to lend its U.S. shareholders large sums of money which are not treated as an investment in U.S. property because in the same year the shareholders were required to report a small amount of FPHC income. (Proposed legislation would stop this.)

Use of Tax Haven Holding Companies

The golden age of the tax haven holding company is ending because of home country Subpart F-type legislation and the trend to anti-treaty-shopping provisions in tax treaties. However, holding companies still are useful devices. Even where Subpart F-type laws are in effect, worthwhile holding company uses often can be planned around them. Moreover, it should be many years before even the United States (the leader in restricting treaty shopping) renegotiates all its treaties to eliminate the use of third-country treaties.

The use of a Netherlands holding company by Canadian companies investing in the United States is a common example of holding company use to reduce withholding taxes on dividends. If a Canadian corporation owned a U.S. subsidiary directly, the Canada-U.S. treaty withholding rate of 15 percent would apply to dividends (10 percent under the signed but not yet ratified treaty).[36] However, under the U.S.-Netherlands treaty, withholding is 5 percent on dividends from the U.S. subsidiary to the Netherlands holding company,[37] which pays no income tax on such foreign income.[38] The funds then flow tax-free to the Canadian parent under the Netherlands-Canada treaty.[39] Thus total withholding is 5 percent rather than 15 percent (or 10 percent if the new U.S.-Canada treaty is ratified). As this is written, the United States is trying to renegotiate its treaty with the Netherlands to stop such third-country use.

The Netherlands treaty also can be used in conjunction with the Netherlands Antilles when the parent country does not have a tax treaty with the Netherlands. For example, if a Hong Kong company (Hong Kong has no tax treaties) decides to operate in Belgium through a Belgian subsidiary, it could form a Netherlands Antilles holding company to own the shares of a Netherlands holding company which, in turn, would own the shares of the Belgian operating subsidiary. Dividends paid by the Belgian corporation to the Netherlands holding company would bear 5 percent withholding (by treaty),[40] and there would be no withholding on dividends paid either by the Netherlands company to the Netherlands Antilles company (by treaty)[41] or by the Netherlands Antilles company to the Hong Kong parent (by Netherlands Antilles law).[42] If the Antilles company had not been inserted between the Netherlands company and the Hong Kong parent, dividends from the Netherlands would have been subject to 25 percent withholding. The only Netherlands or Netherlands Antilles tax would be Netherland Antilles income tax at a top rate of 3 percent. Netherlands Antilles holding companies also are used to channel investments from nontreaty countries into the United States.

The availability of these Netherlands and Netherlands Antilles techniques can change quickly and should never be attempted without professional advice (and in some cases advance rulings). As noted earlier, the United States is currently trying to renegotiate its treaty with the Netherlands Antilles.

International Finance Subsidiaries

Multinational companies use offshore finance subsidiaries primarily for two tax-motivated purposes: (1) to borrow funds earned by foreign subsidiaries and relend them to other foreign subsidiaries without having funds taxed by the multinational's home country and (2) to borrow funds from third parties (and related corporations) in such a way that there is zero or minimal withholding on interest payments. In both cases the following tax objectives and dangers should be considered:

1. The interest expense deduction should not be wasted. If interest expense exceeds interest income, the finance subsidiary should be part of a consolidated group so that another foreign affiliate can use the deduction.

2. Interest rates between affiliated companies must meet the arm's-length transfer pricing tests of the countries involved.

3. The thin capitalization rules of the countries involved must be considered when loans are between related parties. If debt is reclassified as equity, interest payments will be treated as nondeductible dividends and payments of principal may be treated as dividend income to the recipient. Thin capitalization rules vary from country to country. Proposed thin capitalization rules are being considered in the United States as of this writing.[43] Until rules are set, tax advisers generally are recommending that corporations maintain a debt-to-equity ratio no greater than 3 to 1.

Netherlands companies often are used as finance subsidiaries because of the extensive Dutch treaty network and because under Dutch law there is no withholding on interest payments. The Dutch require only that the subsidiary generate some taxable income (today ⅛ of 1 percent of the amount of the back-to-back loan). In other words, the interest rate on the money lent must exceed the interest rate on the money borrowed by 0.125 percent.

Intangible Property (Patent) Holding Companies

The primary use of a patent holding company is to attain treaty withholding rates (often zero) in the country of use, rather than the statutory rates, which often are quite high (e.g., 30 percent in the United States). A secondary use is to accumulate royalties offshore at low tax rates. The Subpart F rules of the United States make low-tax accumulation difficult for U.S. multinationals [the 10 percent threshold of foreign base company (Subpart F) income is a limited opportunity].

Patent holding companies are used to take advantage of host country treaty rates by patent holders from countries that do not have treaties with the host country or whose treaty with the host country has high rates. For example, a Hong Kong-based patent holder might license a wholly owned Netherlands Antilles corporation to exploit a patent; the Netherlands Antilles corporation in turn would license either a related or unrelated U.S. corporation to exploit the patent in the United States. By treaty there would be no withholding on the royalties paid by the U.S. corporation to the Netherlands Antilles corporation.[44] Under Netherlands Antilles law, there would be no withholding on the royalties paid by the Netherlands Antilles corporation to Hong King.[45] As in the case of a back-to-back financing, the Netherlands Antilles would require that the back-to-back royalty arrangement produce a small amount of taxable income.

CAPTIVE INSURANCE COMPANIES

A captive insurance company in its pure form is a wholly owned insurance company that insures only risks of its multinational group. Often it will be incorporated in Bermuda, which has special insurance laws for captives, no income tax, and good support facilities for insurance companies.

The main tax reason for using a captive insurance company (instead of self-insuring) is that insurance premiums are deductible when paid, but, in many countries (e.g., the United States), funding a contingency reserve for potential losses is not.[46]

Since 1972 the IRS has contended, with growing success, that captive insurance premiums are merely funding a self-insurance reserve and therefore are not deductible.[47]

VALUE-ADDED TAX

The value-added tax is a consumption tax borne by the final consumer. It is imposed at each stage of production at a stated percentage. At each stage the purchaser of the product (manufacturer, wholesaler, etc.) pays the full VAT rate. When the manufacturer or wholesaler sells the product, it collects the full VAT rate but deducts the amount of the VAT paid at the time of purchase when it remits the tax to the government. Only the final purchaser, the consumer, gets no credit for VAT previously paid, and thus bears the entire tax. The end result is exactly as if the consumer had paid a sales tax, with two exceptions. First, the government, by collecting tax at each stage of production, gets its money faster. Second, because the only way to get credit for VAT paid when goods are purchased is to remit VAT when they are sold, an element of self-policing is added that the sales tax lacks.

VAT has been adopted in the EEC and elsewhere.[48] The United States has not adopted VAT, but in recent years there have been serious discussions about adopting it.

VAT usually is refunded when goods are shipped abroad. Thus, exported products bear no VAT in the exporting country. If the importing country has VAT, the consumer will pay the full rate on the imported goods, and the entire VAT will go to the importing country's treasury.

LIQUIDATION OF FOREIGN INVESTMENTS

The U.S. rules regarding liquidations of foreign investments are the most sophisticated in use. The following overview of the U.S. rules will alert both U.S. and non-U.S. multinationals to the area's pitfalls.

When a U.S. domestic corporate subsidiary is liquidated by a U.S. parent, it recognizes neither gain nor loss [section 332(a) IRC] and the assets received take a carryover cost basis [section 334(b)(1) IRC]. When a U.S. parent sells the stock of a U.S. subsidiary corporation, it recognizes capital gain or loss.[49] However, when a U.S. parent either liquidates or sells the stock of a foreign subsidiary corporation, it recognizes ordinary income to the extent of the subsidiary's earnings and profits accumulated since 1962 [section 1248(a) IRC].

In addition, section 367 (discussed earlier) provides that when a foreign corporation is liquidated it will not be treated as a corporation for tax purposes unless the IRS issues a favorable ruling. Thus, absent a ruling, the U.S. parent would recognize capital gain on the assets received as well as ordinary income to the extent of earnings and profits. In general, the toll charge for a ruling is to report the accumulated earnings and profits as ordinary income. Except for pre-1962 earnings and profits, these amounts would be reported as ordinary income in any event, as noted above.

GAINS AND LOSSES ON EXCHANGE OF FOREIGN CURRENCY

The tax treatment of currency transactions varies from country to country, and many countries do not have settled rules. This complicates the goal of making (1) currency gains nontaxable (or taxable at capital gains rates) and (2) currency losses fully deductible in a high-tax jurisdiction.

Countries follow two basic approaches to tax currency gains and losses: (1) the capital/revenue concept, which treats currency transactions as capital or ordinary depending on the character of the underlying transaction (e.g., if connected with the purchase of inventory it would be revenue, if connected with the purchase of a plant site it would be capital) and (2) the net worth comparison concept, which treats all currency gains and losses as ordinary (i.e., noncapital).

The foreign currency transactions that a U.S. multinational typically faces are taxed as follows.

1. The assets (other than capital assets) of a foreign branch are converted to dollars at the end of each taxable year at the year-end exchange rate.[50] Thus currency fluctuations are reflected in income even though no funds have been remitted. Remitted funds are valued at the remittance-day exchange rate.[51]

2. Dividends, interest, royalties, etc. are valued at remittance date.[52]

3. When funds are borrowed in foreign currency, the borrower recognizes ordinary gain or loss on each repayment if there has been a change in the exchange rate since the funds were borrowed.[53]

4. Currency hedging transactions result in ordinary gain or loss if the purpose of the transaction was to hedge the effect of a devaluation on ordinary income-type assets such as inventory. If the effect of a devaluation is on the value of the stock of a subsidiary, the gain or loss on the hedge will be capital.[54]

DISC

By channeling export sales through a domestic international sales corporation (DISC), a U.S. taxpayer can defer paying tax on half of its export profits (sections 991–994 IRC). If proper elections are made and the DISC operating rules are met, half of the DISC's profits can be accumulated tax-free by the DISC (the DISC itself does not pay U.S. income tax), and the remaining profits are taxable to the DISC's shareholders as earned, whether or not they are distributed. The deferred income is taxable when distributed to the parent, when the DISC is sold, or when it no longer qualifies as a DISC. DISC dividends are treated as foreign source income, and foreign income taxes paid by the DISC qualify for deemed-paid credit in the hands of the parent corporation. The funds accumulated by the DISC must be invested in "qualified export assets," which include export property (inventory) and accounts receivables from export sales. [At this writing, legislation is proposed to replace DISC with an export incentive scheme (Foreign Sales Corporations) that eliminates a portion of the U.S. exporter's income from the U.S. tax net. The reason for the proposal is that DISC is viewed by many European countries as an illegal export incentive under the rules of the General Agreement on Tariffs and Trade (GATT).]

FINANCING DIRECT FOREIGN INVESTMENT

For tax purposes, the best way to finance direct foreign investment is to have the newly acquired or expanded foreign subsidiary borrow the money itself to the extent possible, for two reasons: (1) Typically, interest payments are deductible in the host country, but dividends are not. (2) If the funds are borrowed from the parent corporation, the interest payments will be subject to 0 percent withholding under many U.S. treaties,[55] whereas dividends bear withholding of 5 percent or more under the treaties.

If money is borrowed, the interest expense should be paid from a corporation that can deduct it currently against profits in a high-tax-rate jurisdiction. If the debt is in the new subsidiary, startup losses would mean that the interest expense would produce no immediate tax saving. If there are other profitable subsidiaries in the host country, they should be linked by a common parent holding company, as discussed earlier, so that a consolidated return can be filed.

Where the laws of the home and host countries permit, "link" companies should be considered. For example, if a U.K. multinational invests in a U.S. subsidiary and wishes the U.S. establishment to borrow to finance the purchase price, the stock of the U.S. operating company can be held by a U.S. holding company which borrows the funds in question. The U.S. holding company becomes "resident" in the United Kingdom (i.e., a U.K. corporation for U.K. tax purposes) by establishing residence there, and thus its interest expense can be deducted in the U.K. parent's return using group relief. In addition, the U.S. holding company also can file a U.S. consolidated return with the operating subsidiary, and thus when the subsidiary becomes profitable the interest expense also will reduce U.S. taxable income.[56]

SUMMARY

The preceding chapter only suggests the complexity of international tax planning. As stated at the outset, expert advice will be needed before taking action on matters involving international taxation, although this chapter provides the international financial executive with the background to recognize problem areas and ask the right questions. Another goal of this chapter is to alert the international financial executive to the stakes involved in international tax planning.

NOTES

1. See, generally, *Corporate Taxes—A Worldwide Summary*, Price Waterhouse Center for Transnational Taxation, New York, 1983.
2. Internal Revenue Code (IRC), sec. 1248.

3. For example, the United States. See IRC, sec. 351.
4. Rev. Proc. 68-23, 1968-1 CB 821; Reg. sec. 7.367, as amended December 27, 1982.
5. See, generally, Rev. Rul. 78-201, 1978-1 CB 91.
6. Hershey Foods Corp. v. Comm., 76 TC 312 (1981).
7. See *Corporate Taxes*. For more detailed rules see the information guide for the country concerned, published by the Price Waterhouse Center for Transnational Taxation, 1251 Avenue of the Americas, New York, N.Y. 10020.
8. The U.S. foreign tax credit rules are stated in IRC, secs. 901–908 and the attendant regulations.
9. IRC, sec. 903 and Reg. sec. 4.903-1(e)(3).
10. The source rules for U.S. income tax purposes are stated in IRC, secs. 861, 862, and 863 and the attendant regulations.
11. Reg. sec. 1.861-8(e)(3). These regulations have been suspended for taxpayers' first two taxable years beginning after August 13, 1981 [Act. sec. 223 of the Economic Recovery Tax Act of 1981 (P.L. 97-34).] This statutory suspension was made because of congressional concern that the regulations were causing U.S.-based multinationals to do R&D abroad rather than in the United States. During these two years all U.S.-incurred R&D will be allocated against U.S.-source income.
12. The United States permits deemed-paid credits to flow through from third-tier foreign subsidiaries. See IRC, sec. 902.
13. The gross-up is required by IRC, sec. 78.
14. IRC, sec. 172(b)(1).
15. See *Corporate Taxes*.
16. IRC, sec. 172(b)(1).
17. Reg. secs. 1.482-2(b), 1.482-2(c), 1.482-2(d), and 1.482-2(a), respectively.
18. Art. 5, OECD, *Model Convention for the Avoidance of Double Taxation with Respect to Taxes on Income and Capital*. Referred to hereafter as "OECD."
19. OECD, art. 5, para. 2.
20. Explained more fully in the OECD *Commentary* on art. 7 of the OECD. The *Commentary* is an official document which provides background and interpretive materials for the OECD model income tax treaty.
21. E.g., Switzerland. See, generally, *Corporation Taxes*.
22. In the case of foreign corporations, IRC, secs. 881, 882.
23. In the case of foreign corporations, IRC, sec. 881(a).
24. In the case of foreign corporations, IRC, sec. 882(a).
25. In the case of foreign corporations, IRC, sec. 882(d).
26. Sec. 1125 of the Foreign Investment in Real Property Tax Act, P.L. 96-499.
27. Art. 15, proposed U.S. model income tax treaty (model of June 16, 1981).
28. Art. 14, proposed U.S. model income tax treaty. For example, the U.S. income tax treaty with Belgium provides that individuals will not be taxable on income from independent services if (1) they are present in the host country fewer than 183 days in the taxable year and (2) they do not maintain a fixed base in the host country for 183 days or more during the taxable year to which the income is attributable (art. 14). Special rules apply to entertainers and athletes.
29. OECD, art. 25 and art. 25 of proposed U.S. model income tax treaty.
30. Rev. Proc. 77-16, 1977-1 CB 573.
31. For a discussion of possible anti-tax-haven legislation, see Charles T. Crawford, "Tax Havens—an Endangered Species," *The Tax Adviser*, December 1981, p. 728.
32. E.g., the United Kingdom's income tax treaty with Cyprus; art. 24A(1), added by protocol in 1980, restricts use of treaty dividend, interest, and royalty withholding rates by Cyprus offshore companies (i.e., companies fully owned by aliens and solely engaged in offshore activities).

33. A foreign corporation of which more than 50 percent of the total combined voting power of all classes of stock entitled to vote is owned (directly or indirectly) by U.S. shareholders on any day during the foreign corporation's taxable year [IRC, sec. 957(a)]. "United States shareholders" are U.S. "persons" (a term that includes U.S. corporations) that own 10 percent or more of a foreign corporation's voting stock.

34. The exception is amounts received as underwriting income derived from insurance of U.S. risks [IRC, sec. 861(a)(7)].

35. See note 32 and attendant text.

36. Art. XI(1) of the old treaty; art. X(2)(a) of the new (unratified as of this writing) U.S.-Canada income tax treaty. Commerce Clearing House, *Tax Treaties*, vol. 1.

37. United States–Netherlands income tax treaty, art. VII(1)(b). Commerce Clearing House, *Tax Treaties*, vol. 2.

38. Company Income Tax Law 1969. See *Taxation of Patent, Royalties, Dividends, Interest in Europe, Guide to European Taxation*, vol. 1, International Bureau of Fiscal Documentation.

39. Netherlands-Canada income tax treaty, Article VII(1). *Supplementary Service to European Taxation*, International Bureau of Fiscal Documentation.

40. Belgium-Netherlands income tax treaty, Article 9(2). *Supplementary Service to European Taxation*, International Bureau of Fiscal Documentation.

41. Netherlands-Netherlands Antilles income tax treaty, Article 11(1). *Supplementary Service to European Taxation*, International Bureau of Fiscal Documentation.

42. See note 38.

43. Reg. sec. 1.385-2 through Reg. sec. 1.385-10 has been "suspended" pending further amendments.

44. Art. IX of the U.S.-Netherlands treaty as modified by the Protocal (effective September 28, 1964) extending certain benefits of such treaty to the Netherlands Antilles.

45. Reg. sec. 1.461-1(a)(2). See Thriftimart, Inc. v. Comm., 59 TC 598 (1973); Acq. 1973-2 CB 4.

46. E.g., Spring Canyon Coal Co., CA-10, 43 F2d 78 (1930), *cert. denied*, 284 U.S. 654.

47. Carnation Co. v. Comm., 71 TC 400 (1978); *aff'd*, CA-9, 640 F2d 1010 (1981) and *Stearns-Roger Corp. Inc.* v. *U.S.*, no. 81-C-2046, Jan. 10, 1984, U.S. Dist. Ct. Colo.

48. All the EEC countries have a VAT. Others include Austria, Sweden, and Norway in Europe; Argentina, Brazil, Chile, and Peru in South America; plus Japan and Mexico.

49. Capital assets are defined at IRC, sec. 1221. The stock of a subsidiary is considered a capital asset unless the subsidiary was originally purchased to ensure continued supply of goods or services. See J. J. Grier Co. v. Comm., 328 F2d 163 (1964).

50. Rev. Rul. 75-106, 1975-1 CB 31 and Rev. Rul. 75-107, 1975-1 CB 32.

51. Rev. Rul. 75-107, 1975-1 CB 32.

52. Rev. Rul. 74-222, 1974-1 CB 21.

53. Rev. Rul. 78-281, 1978-2 CB 204.

54. Wool Distributing Corp., 34 TC 323 (1960); Acq. 1961-2 CB 5.

55. The U.S. model treaty (art. 11) and most of the U.S. treaties with developed countries provide 0 percent withholding for interest. The OECD (art. 11) provides 10 percent withholding.

56. This is discussed in a 1982 U.S. Treasury Department Letter Ruling (LTR 8241009).

Appendix 18A
OECD Model Convention

[¶ 151]
ORGANIZATION FOR ECONOMIC CO-OPERATION AND DEVELOPMENT MODEL CONVENTION FOR THE AVOIDANCE OF DOUBLE TAXATION WITH RESPECT TO TAXES ON INCOME AND CAPITAL

SUMMARY OF THE CONVENTION

TITLE AND PREAMBLE

TITLE

Convention between (State A) and (State B) for the avoidance of double taxation with respect to taxes on income and on capital

PREAMBLE

Note: The Preamble of the Convention shall be drafted in accordance with the constitutional procedure of both Contracting States.

CHAPTER I
SCOPE OF THE CONVENTION

Article 1
Personal Scope

This Convention shall apply to persons who are residents of one or both of the Contracting States.

Article 2
Taxes Covered

1. This Convention shall apply to taxes on income and on capital imposed on behalf of a Contracting State or of its political subdivisions or local authorities, irrespective of the manner in which they are levied.

2. There shall be regarded as taxes on income and on capital all taxes imposed on total income, on total capital, or on elements of income or of capital, including taxes on gains from the alienation of movable or immovable property, taxes on the total amounts of wages or salaries paid by enterprises, as well as taxes on capital appreciation.

3. The existing taxes to which the Convention shall apply are in particular:

(a) (in State A): ....

(b) (in State B): ....

4. The Convention shall apply also to any identical or substantially similar taxes which are imposed after the date of signature of the Convention in addition to, or in place of, the existing taxes. At the end of each year, the competent authorities of the Contracting States shall notify each other of changes which have been made in their respective taxation laws.

CHAPTER II
DEFINITIONS

Article 3
General Definitions

1. For the purposes of this Convention, unless the context otherwise requires:

(a) the term "person" includes an individual, a company and any other body of persons;

(b) the term "company" means any body corporate or any entity which is treated as a body corporate for tax purposes;

(c) the terms "enterprise of a Contracting State" and "enterprise of the other Contracting State" mean respectively an enterprise carried on by a resident of a Contracting State and an enterprise carried on by a resident of the other Contracting State;

(d) the term "international traffic" means any transport by a ship or aircraft operated by an enterprise which has its place of effective management in a Contracting State, except when the ship or aircraft is operated solely between places in the other Contracting State;

(e) the term "competent authority" means:

(i) (in State A): ....

(ii) (in State B): ....

2. As regards the application of the Convention by a Contracting State any term not defined therein shall, unless the context otherwise requires, have the meaning which it has under the law of that State concerning the taxes to which the Convention applies.

Article 4
Resident

1. For the purposes of this Convention, the term "resident of a Contracting State" means any person who, under the laws of that State, is liable to tax therein by reason of his domicile, residence, place of management or any other criterion of a similar nature. But this term does not include any person who is liable to tax in that State in respect only of income from sources in that State or capital situated therein.

2. Where by reason of the provisions of paragraph 1 an individual is a resident of both Contracting States, then his status shall be determined as follows:

(a) he shall be deemed to be a resident of the State in which he has a permanent home available to him; if he has a permanent home available to him in both States, he shall be deemed to be a resident of the State with which his personal and economic relations are closer (centre of vital interests);

(b) if the State in which he has his centre of vital interests cannot be determined, or if he has not a permanent home available to him in either State, he shall be deemed to be a resident of the State in which he has an habitual abode;

(c) if he has an habitual abode in both States or in neither of them, he shall be deemed to be a resident of the State of which he is a national;

(d) if he is a national of both States or of neither of them, the competent authorities of the Contracting States shall settle the question by mutual agreement.

3. Where by reason of the provisions of paragraph 1 a person other than an individual is a resident of both Contracting States, then it shall be deemed to be a resident of the State in which its place of effective management is situated.

Article 5
Permanent Establishment

1. For the purposes of this Convention, the term "permanent establishment" means a fixed place of business through which the business of an enterprise is wholly or partly carried on.

2. The term "permanent establishment" includes especially:

(a) a place of management;

(b) a branch;

(c) an office;

(d) a factory;

(e) a workshop; and

(f) a mine, an oil or gas well, a quarry or any other place of extraction of natural resources.

3. A building site or construction or installation project constitutes a permanent establishment only if it lasts more than twelve months.

4. Notwithstanding the preceding provisions of this Article, the term "permanent establishment" shall be deemed not to include:

(a) the use of facilities solely for the purpose of storage, display or delivery of goods or merchandise belonging to the enterprise;

(b) the maintenance of a stock of goods or merchandise belonging to the enterprise solely for the purpose of storage, display or delivery;

(c) the maintenance of a stock of goods or merchandise belonging to the enterprise solely for the purpose of processing by another enterprise;

(d) the maintenance of a fixed place of business solely for the purpose of purchasing goods or merchandise or of collecting information, for the enterprise;

(e) the maintenance of a fixed place of business solely for the purpose of carrying on, for the enterprise, any other activity of a preparatory or auxiliary character;

(f) the maintenance of a fixed place of business solely for any combination of activities mentioned in sub-paragraphs (a) to (e), provided that the overall activity of the fixed place of business resulting from this combination is of a preparatory or auxiliary character.

5. Notwithstanding the provisions of paragraphs 1 and 2, where a person—other than an agent of an independent status to whom paragraph 6 applies—is acting on behalf of an enterprise and has, and habitually exercises, in a Contracting State an authority to conclude contracts in the name of the enterprise, that enterprise shall be deemed to have a permanent establishment in that State in respect of any activities which that person undertakes for the enterprise, unless the activities of such person are limited to those mentioned in paragraph 4 which, if exercised through a fixed place of business, would not make this fixed place of business a permanent establishment under the provisions of that paragraph.

6. An enterprise shall not be deemed to have a permanent establishment in a Contracting State merely because it carries on business in that State through a broker, general commission agent or any other agent of an independent status, provided that such persons are acting in the ordinary course of their business.

7. The fact that a company which is a resident of a Contracting State controls or is controlled by a company which is a resident of the other Contracting State, or which carries on business in that other State (whether through a permanent establishment or otherwise), shall not of itself constitute either company a permanent establishment of the other.

CHAPTER III
TAXATION OF INCOME
Article 6
Income from Immovable Property

1. Income derived by a resident of a Contracting State from immovable property (including income from agriculture or forestry) situated in the other Contracting State may be taxed in that other State.

2. The term "immovable property" shall have the meaning which it has under the law of the Contracting State in which the property in question is situated. The term shall in any case include property accessory to immovable property, livestock and equipment used in agriculture and forestry, rights to which the provisions of general law respecting landed property apply, usufruct of immovable property and rights to variable or fixed payments as consideration for the working of, or the right to work, mineral deposits, sources and other natural resources; ships, boats and aircraft shall not be regarded as immovable property.

3. The provisions of paragraph 1 shall apply to income derived from the direct use, letting, or use in any other form of immovable property.

4. The provisions of paragraphs 1 and 3 shall also apply to the income from immovable property of an enterprise and to income from immovable property used for the performance of independent personal services.

Article 7
Business Profits

1. The profits of an enterprise of a Contracting State shall be taxable only in that State unless the enterprise carries on business in the other Contracting State through a permanent establishment situated therein. If the enterprise carried on business as aforesaid, the profits of the enterprise may be taxed in the other State but only so much of them as is attributable to that permanent establishment.

2. Subject to the provisions of paragraph 3, where an enterprise of a Contracting State carries on business in the other Contracting State through a permanent establishment situated therein, there shall in each Contracting State be attributed to that permanent establishment the profits which it might be expected to make if it were a distinct and separate enterprise engaged in the same or similar activities under the same or similar conditions and dealing wholly independently with the enterprise of which it is a permanent establishment.

3. In determining the profits of a permanent establishment, there shall be allowed as deductions expenses which are incurred for the purposes of the permanent establishment, including executive and general administrative expenses so incurred, whether in the State in which the permanent establishment is situated or elsewhere.

4. Insofar as it has been customary in a Contracting State to determine the profits to be attributed to a permanent establishment on the basis of an apportionment of the total profits of the enterprise to its various parts, nothing in paragraph 2 shall preclude that Contracting State from determining the profits to be taxed by such an apportionment as may be customary; the method of apportionment adopted shall, however, be such that the result shall be in accordance with the principles contained in this Article.

5. No profits shall be attributed to a permanent establishment by reason of the mere purchase by that permanent establishment of goods or merchandise for the enterprise.

6. For the purposes of the preceding paragraphs, the profits to be attributed to the permanent establishment shall be determined by the same method year by year unless there is good and sufficient reason to the contrary.

7. Where profits include items of income which are dealt with separately in other Articles of this Convention, then the provisions of those Articles shall not be affected by the provisions of this Article.

Article 8
Shipping, Inland Waterways Transport and Air Transport

1. Profits from the operation of ships or aircraft in international traffic shall be taxable only in the Contracting State in which the place of effective management of the enterprise is situated.

2. Profits from the operation of boats engaged in inland waterways transport shall be taxable only in the Contracting State in which the place of effective management of the enterprise is situated.

3. If the place of effective management of a shipping enterprise or of an inland waterways transport enterprise is aboard a ship or boat, then it shall be deemed to be situated in the Contracting State in which the home harbour of the

ship or boat is situated, or, if there is no such home harbour, in the Contracting State of which the operator of the ship or boat is a resident.

4. The provisions of paragraph 1 shall also apply to profits from the participation in a pool, a joint business or an international operating agency.

Article 9
Associated Enterprises

1. Where

(a) an enterprise of a Contracting State participates directly or indirectly in the management, control or capital of an enterprise of the other Contracting State, or

(b) the same persons participate directly or indirectly in the management, control or capital of an enterprise of a Contracting State and an enterprise of the other Contracting State,

and in either case conditions are made or imposed between the two enterprises in their commercial or financial relations which differ from those which would be made between independent enterprises, then any profits which would, but for those conditions, have accrued to one of the enterprises, but, by reason of those conditions, have not so accrued, may be included in the profits of that enterprise and taxed accordingly.

2. Where a Contracting State includes in the profits of an enterprise of that State—and taxes accordingly—profits on which an enterprise of the other Contracting State has been charged to tax in that other State and the profits so included are profits which would have accrued to the enterprise of the first-mentioned State if the conditions made between the two enterprises had been those which would have been made between independent enterprises, then that other State shall make an appropriate adjustment to the amount of the tax charged therein on those profits. In determining such adjustment, due regard shall be had to the other provisions of this Convention and the competent authorities of the Contracting States shall if necessary consult each other.

Article 10
Dividends

1. Dividends paid by a company which is a resident of a Contracting State to a resident of the other Contracting State may be taxed in that other State.

2. However, such dividends may also be taxed in the Contracting State of which the company paying the dividends is a resident and according to the laws of that State, but if the recipient is the beneficial owner of the dividends the tax so charged shall not exceed:

(a) 5 per cent of the gross amount of the dividends if the beneficial owner is a company (other than a partnership) which holds directly at least 25 per cent of the capital of the company paying the dividends.

(b) 15 per cent of the gross amount of the dividends in all other cases.

The competent authorities of the Contracting States shall by mutual agreement settle the mode of application of these limitations.

This paragraph shall not affect the taxation of the company in respect of the profits out of which the dividends are paid.

3. The term "dividends" as used in this Article means income from shares, "jouissance" shares or "jouissance" rights, mining shares, founders' shares or other rights, not being debt-claims, participating in profits, as well as income from other corporate rights which is subjected to the same taxation treatment as income from shares by the laws of the State of which the company making the distribution is a resident.

4. The provisions of paragraphs 1 and 2 shall not apply if the beneficial owner of the dividends, being a resident of a Contracting State, carries on business in the other Contracting State of which the company paying the dividends is a resident, through a permanent establishment situated therein, or performs in that other State independent personal services from a fixed base situated therein, and the holding in respect of which the dividends are paid is effectively connected with such permanent establishment or fixed base. In such case the provisions of Article 7 or Article 14, as the case may be, shall apply.

5. Where a company which is a resident of a Contracting State derives profits or income from the other Contracting State, that other State may not impose any tax on the dividends paid by the company, except insofar as such dividends are paid to a resident of that other State or insofar as the holding in respect of which the dividends are paid is effectively connected with a permanent establishment or a fixed base situated in that other State, nor subject the company's undistributed profits to a tax on the company's undistributed profits, even if the dividends paid or the undistributed profits consist wholly or partly of profits or income arising in such other State.

Article 11
Interest

1. Interest arising in a Contracting State and paid to a resident of the other Contracting State may be taxed in that other State.

2. However, such interest may also be taxed in the Contracting State in which it arises and according to the laws of that State, but if the recipient is the beneficial owner of the interest the tax so charged shall not exceed 10 per cent of the gross amount of the interest. The competent authorities of the Contracting States shall by mutual agreement settle the mode of application of this limitation.

3. The term "interest" as used in this Article means income from debt-claims of every kind, whether or not secured by mortgage and whether or not carrying a right to participate in the debtor's profits, and in particular, income from government securities and income from bonds or debentures, including premiums and prizes attaching to such securities, bonds or debentures. Penalty charges for late payment shall not be regarded as interest for the purpose of this Article.

4. The provisions of paragraphs 1 and 2 shall not apply if the beneficial owner of the interest, being a resident of a Contracting State, carries on business in the other Contracting State in which the interest arises, through a permanent establishment situated therein, or performs in that other State independent personal services from a fixed base situated therein, and the debt-claim in respect of which the interest is paid is effectively connected with such permanent estab-

lishment or fixed base. In such case the provisions of Article 7 or Article 14, as the case may be, shall apply.

5. Interest shall be deemed to arise in a Contracting State when the payer is that State itself, a political subdivision, a local authority or a resident of that State. Where, however, the person paying the interest, whether he is a resident of a Contracting State or not, has in a Contracting State a permanent establishment or a fixed base in connection with which the indebtedness on which the interest is paid was incurred, and such interest is borne by such permanent establishment or fixed base, then such interest shall be deemed to arise in the State in which the permanent establishment or fixed base is situated.

6. Where, by reason of a special relationship between the payer and the beneficial owner or between both of them and some other person, the amount of the interest, having regard to the debt-claim for which it is paid, exceeds the amount which would have been agreed upon by the payer and the beneficial owner in the absence of such relationship, the provisions of this Article shall apply only to the last-mentioned amount. In such case, the excess part of the payments shall remain taxable according to the laws of each Contracting State, due regard being had to the other provisions of this Convention.

Article 12
Royalties

1. Royalties arising in a Contracting State and paid to a resident of the other Contracting State shall be taxable only in that other State if such resident is the beneficial owner of the royalties.

2. The term "royalties" as used in this Article means payments of any kind received as a consideration for the use of, or the right to use, any copyright of literary, artistic or scientific work including cinematograph films, any patent, trade mark, design or model, plan, secret formula or process, or for the use of, or the right to use, industrial, commercial, or scientific equipment, or for information concerning industrial, commercial or scientific experience.

3. The provisions of paragraph 1 shall not apply if the beneficial owner of the royalties, being a resident of a Contracting State, carries on business in the other Contracting State in which the royalties arise, through a permanent establishment situated therein, or performs in that other State independent personal services from a fixed base situated therein, and the right or property in respect of which the royalties are paid is effectively connected with such permanent establishment or fixed base. In such case the provisions of Article 7 or Article 14, as the case may be, shall apply.

4. Where, by reason of a special relationship between the payer and the beneficial owner or between both of them and some other person, the amount of the royalties, having regard to the use, right or information for which they are paid, exceeds the amount which would have been agreed upon by the payer and the beneficial owner in the absence of such relationship, the provisions of this Article shall apply only to the last-mentioned amount. In such case, the excess part of the payments shall remain taxable according to the laws of each Contracting State, due regard being had to the other provisions of this Convention.

Article 13
Capital Gains

1. Gains derived by a resident of a Contracting State from the alienation of immovable property referred to in Article 6 and situated in the other Contracting State may be taxed in that other State.

2. Gains from the alienation of movable property forming part of the business property of a permanent establishment which an enterprise of a Contracting State has in the other Contracting State or of movable property pertaining to a fixed base available to a resident of a Contracting State in the other Contracting State for the purpose of performing independent personal services, including such gains from the alienation of such a permanent establishment (alone or with the whole enterprise) or of such fixed base, may be taxed in that other State.

3. Gains from the alienation of ships or aircraft operated in international traffic, boats engaged in inland waterways transport or movable property pertaining to the operation of such ships, aircraft or boats, shall be taxable only in the Contracting State in which the place of effective management of the enterprise is situated.

4. Gains from the alienation of any property other than that referred to in paragraphs 1, 2 and 3, shall be taxable only in the Contracting State of which the alienator is a resident.

Article 14
Independent Personal Services

1. Income derived by a resident of a Contracting State in respect of professional services or other activities of an independent character shall be taxable only in that State unless he has a fixed base regularly available to him in the other Contracting State for the purpose of performing his activities. If he has such a fixed base, the income may be taxed in the other State but only so much of it as is attributable to that fixed base.

2. The term "professional services" includes especially independent scientific, literary, artistic, educational or teaching activities as well as the independent activities of physicians, lawyers, engineers, architects, dentists and accountants.

Article 15
Dependent Personal Services

1. Subject to the provisions of Articles 16, 18 and 19, salaries, wages and other similar remuneration derived by a resident of a Contracting State in respect of an employment shall be taxable only in that State unless the employment is exercised in the other Contracting State. If the employment is so exercised, such remuneration as is derived therefrom may be taxed in that other State.

2. Notwithstanding the provisions of paragraph 1, remuneration derived by a resident of a Contracting State in respect of an employment exercised in the other Contracting State shall be taxable only in the first-mentioned State if:

(a) the recipient is present in the other State for a period or periods not exceeding in the aggregate 183 days in the fiscal year concerned, and

(b) the remuneration is paid by, or on behalf of, an employer who is not a resident of the other State, and

(c) the remuneration is not borne by a permanent establishment or a fixed base which the employer has in the other State.

3. Notwithstanding the preceding provisions of this Article, remuneration derived in respect of an employment exercised aboard a ship or aircraft operated in international traffic, or aboard a boat engaged in inland waterways transport, may be taxed in the Contracting State in which the place of effective management of the enterprise is situated.

Article 16
Directors' Fees

Directors' fees and other similar payments derived by a resident of a Contracting State in his capacity as a member of the board of directors of a company which is a resident of the other Contracting State may be taxed in that other State.

Article 17
Artistes and Athletes

1. Notwithstanding the provisions of Articles 14 and 15, income derived by a resident of a Contracting State as an entertainer, such as a theatre, motion picture, radio or television artiste, or a musician, or as an athlete, from his personal activities as such exercised in the other Contracting State, may be taxed in that other State.

2. Where income in respect of personal activities exercised by an entertainer or an athlete in his capacity as such accrues not to the entertainer or athlete himself but to another person, that income may, notwithstanding the provisions of Articles 7, 14 and 15, be taxed in the Contracting State in which the activities of the entertainer or athlete are exercised.

Article 18
Pensions

Subject to the provisions of paragraph 2 of Article 19, pensions and other similar remuneration paid to a resident of a Contracting State in consideration of past employment shall be taxable only in that State.

Article 19
Government Service

1. (a) Remuneration, other than a pension, paid by a Contracting State or a political subdivision or a local authority thereof to an individual in respect of services rendered to that State or subdivision or authority shall be taxable only in that State.

(b) However, such remuneration shall be taxable only in the other Contracting State if the services are rendered in that State and the individual is a resident of that State who:

(i) is a national of that State; or

(ii) did not become a resident of that State solely for the purpose of rendering the services.

2. (a) Any pension paid by, or out of funds created by, a Contracting State or a political subdivision or a local authority thereof to an individual in respect of services rendered to that State or subdivision or authority shall be taxable only in that State.

(b) However, such pension shall be taxable only in the other Contracting State if the individual is a resident of, and a national of, that State.

3. The provisions of Articles 15, 16 and 18 shall apply to remuneration and pensions in respect of services rendered in connection with a business carried on by a Contracting State or a political subdivision or a local authority thereof.

Article 20
Students

Payments which a student or business apprentice who is or was immediately before visiting a Contracting State a resident of the other Contracting State and who is present in the first-mentioned State solely for the purpose of his education or training receives for the purpose of his maintenance, education or training shall not be taxed in that State, provided that such payments arise from sources outside that State.

Article 21
Other Income

1. Items of income of a resident of a Contracting State, wherever arising, not dealt with in the foregoing Articles of this Convention shall be taxable only in that State.

2. The provisions of paragraph 1 shall not apply to income, other than income from immovable property as defined in paragraph 2 of Article 6, if the recipient of such income, being a resident of a Contracting State, carries on business in the other Contracting State through a permanent establishment situated therein, or performs in that other State independent personal services from a fixed base situated therein, and the right or property in respect of which the income is paid is effectively connected with such permanent establishment or fixed base. In such case the provisions of Article 7 or Article 14, as the case may be, shall apply.

CHAPTER IV
TAXATION OF CAPITAL

Article 22
Capital

1. Capital represented by immovable property referred to in Article 6, owned by a resident of a Contracting State and situated in the other Contracting State, may be taxed in that other State.

2. Capital represented by movable property forming part of the business property of a permanent establishment which an enterprise of a Contracting State has in the other Contracting State or by movable property pertaining to a fixed base available to a resident of a Contracting State in the other Contracting State for the purpose of performing independent personal services, may be taxed in that other State.

3. Capital represented by ships and aircraft operated in international traffic and by boats engaged in inland waterways transport, and by movable property pertaining to the operation of such ships, aircraft and boats, shall be taxable only in the Contracting State in which the place of effective management of the enterprise is situated.

4. All other elements of capital of a resident of a Contracting State shall be taxable only in that State.

CHAPTER V
METHODS FOR ELIMINATION OF DOUBLE TAXATION
Article 23A
Exemption Method

1. Where a resident of a Contracting State derives income or owns capital which, in accordance with the provisions of this Convention, may be taxed in the other Contracting State, the first-mentioned State shall, subject to the provisions of paragraphs 2 and 3, exempt such income or capital from tax.

2. Where a resident of a Contracting State derives items of income which, in accordance with the provisions of Articles 10 and 11, may be taxed in the other Contracting State, the first-mentioned State shall allow as a deduction from the tax on the income of that resident an amount equal to the tax paid in that other State. Such deduction shall not, however, exceed that part of the tax, as computed before the deduction is given, which is attributable to such items of income derived from that other State.

3. Where in accordance with any provision of the Convention income derived or capital owned by a resident of a Contracting State is exempt from tax in that State, such State may nevertheless, in calculating the amount of tax on the remaining income or capital of such resident, take into account the exempted income or capital.

Article 23B
Credit Method

1. Where a resident of a Contracting State derives income or owns capital which, in accordance with the provisions of this Convention, may be taxed in the other Contracting State, the first-mentioned State shall allow:

(a) as a deduction from the tax on the income of that resident, an amount equal to the income tax paid in that other State;

(b) as a deduction from the tax on the capital of that resident, an amount equal to the capital tax paid in that other State.

Such deduction in either case shall not, however, exceed that part of the income tax or capital tax, as computed before the deduction is given, which is attributable, as the case may be, to the income or the capital which may be taxed in that other State.

2. Where in accordance with any provision of the Convention income derived or capital owned by a resident of a Contracting State is exempt from tax in that State, such State may nevertheless, in calculating the amount of tax on the remaining income or capital of such resident, take into account the exempted income or capital.

CHAPTER VI
SPECIAL PROVISIONS

Article 24
Non-discrimination

1. Nationals of a Contracting State shall not be subjected in the other Contracting State to any taxation or any requirement connected therewith, which is other or more burdensome than the taxation and connected requirements to which nationals of that other State in the same circumstances are or may be subjected. This provision shall, notwithstanding the provisions of Article 1, also apply to persons who are not residents of one or both of the Contracting States.

2. The term "nationals" means:

(a) all individuals possessing the nationality of a Contracting State;

(b) all legal persons, partnerships and associations deriving their status as such from the laws in force in a Contracting State.

3. Stateless persons who are residents of a Contracting State shall not be subjected in either Contracting State to any taxation or any requirement connected therewith, which is other or more burdensome than the taxation and connected requirements to which nationals of the State concerned in the same circumstances are or may be subjected.

4. The taxation on a permanent establishment which an enterprise of a Contracting State has in the other Contracting State shall not be less favourably levied in that other State than the taxation levied on enterprises of that other State carrying on the same activities. This provision shall not be construed as obliging a Contracting State to grant to residents of the other Contracting State any personal allowances, reliefs and reductions for taxation purposes on account of civil status or family responsibilities which it grants to its own residents.

5. Except where the provisions of paragraph 1 of Article 9, paragraph 6 of Article 11, or paragraph 4 of Article 12, apply, interest, royalties and other disbursements paid by an enterprise of a Contracting State to a resident of the other Contracting State shall, for the purpose of determining the taxable profits of such enterprise, be deductible under the same conditions as if they had been paid to a resident of the first-mentioned State. Similarly, any debts of an enterprise of a Contracting State to a resident of the other Contracting State shall, for the purpose of determining the taxable capital of such enterprise, be deductible under the same conditions as if they had been contracted to a resident of the first-mentioned State.

6. Enterprises of a Contracting State, the capital of which is wholly or partly owned or controlled, directly or indirectly, by one or more residents of the other Contracting State, shall not be subjected in the first-mentioned State to any taxation or any requirement connected therewith which is other or more burdensome than the taxation and connected requirements to which other similar enterprises of the first-mentioned State are or may be subjected.

7. The provisions of this Article shall, notwithstanding the provisions of Article 2, apply to taxes of every kind and description.

Article 25
Mutual Agreement Procedure

1. Where a person considers that the actions of one or both of the Contracting States result or will result for him in taxation not in accordance with the provisions of this Convention, he may, irrespective of the remedies provided by the domestic law of those States, present his case to the competent authority of the Contracting State of which he is a resident or, if his case comes under paragraph 1 of Article 24, to that of the Contracting State of which he is a national. The case must be presented within three years from the first notification of the action resulting in taxation not in accordance with the provisions of the Convention.

2. The competent authority shall endeavour, if the objection appears to it to be justified and if it is not itself able to arrive at a satisfactory solution, to resolve the case by mutual agreement with the competent authority of the other Contracting State, with a view to the avoidance of taxation which is not in accordance with the Convention. Any agreement reached shall be implemented notwithstanding any time limits in the domestic law of the Contracting States.

3. The competent authorities of the Contracting States shall endeavour to resolve by mutual agreement any difficulties or doubts arising as to the interpretation or application of the Convention. They may also consult together for the elimination of double taxation in cases not provided for in the Convention.

4. The competent authorities of the Contracting States may communicate with each other directly for the purpose of reaching an agreement in the sense of the preceding paragraphs. When it seems advisable in order to reach agreement to have an oral exchange of opinions, such exchange may take place through a Commission consisting of representatives of the competent authorities of the Contracting States.

Article 26
Exchange of Information

1. The competent authorities of the Contracting States shall exchange such information as is necessary for carrying out the provisions of this Convention or of the domestic laws of the Contracting States concerning taxes covered by the Convention insofar as the taxation thereunder is not contrary to the Convention. The exchange of information is not restricted by Article 1. Any information received by a Contracting State shall be treated as secret in the same manner as information obtained under the domestic laws of that State and shall be disclosed only to persons or authorities (including courts and administrative bodies) involved in the assessment or collection of, the enforcement or prosecution in respect of, or the determination of appeals in relation to, the taxes covered by the Convention. Such persons or authorities shall use the information only for such purposes. They may disclose the information in public court proceedings or in judicial decisions.

2. In no case shall the provisions of paragraph 1 be construed so as to impose on a Contracting State the obligation:

(a) to carry out administrative measures at variance with the laws and administrative practice of that or of the other Contracting State;

(b) to supply information which is not obtainable under the laws or in the normal course of the administration of that or of the other Contracting State;

(c) to supply information which would disclose any trade, business, industrial, commercial or professional secret or trade process, or information, the disclosure of which would be contrary to public policy (ordre public).

Article 27
Diplomatic Agents and Consular Officers

Nothing in this Convention shall affect the fiscal privileges of diplomatic agents or consular officers under the general rules of international law or under the provisions of special agreements.

Article 28
Territorial Extension

1. This Convention may be extended, either in its entirety or with any necessary modifications [to any part of the territory of (State A) or of (State B) which is specifically excluded from the application of the Convention or], to any State or territory for whose international relations (State A) or (State B) is responsible, which imposes taxes substantially similar in character to those to which the Convention applies. Any such extension shall take effect from such date and subject to such modifications and conditions, including conditions as to termination, as may be specified and agreed between the Contracting States in notes to be exchanged through diplomatic channels or in any other manner in accordance with their constitutional procedures.

2. Unless otherwise agreed by both Contracting States, the termination of the Convention by one of them under Article 30 shall also terminate, in the manner provided for in that Article, the application of the Convention [to any part of the territory of (State A) or of (State B) or] to any State or territory to which it has been extended under this Article.

Note: The words between brackets are of relevance when, by special provision, a part of the territory of a Contracting State is excluded from the application of the Convention.

CHAPTER VII
FINAL PROVISIONS

Article 29
Entry into Force

1. This Convention shall be ratified and the instruments of ratification shall be exchanged at . . . . as soon as possible.

2. The Convention shall enter into force upon the exchange of instruments of ratification and its provisions shall have effect:

(a) (in State A): . . . .

(b) (in State B): . . . .

Article 30
Termination

This Convention shall remain in force until terminated by a Contracting State. Either Contracting State may terminate the Convention, through diplomatic channels, by giving notice of termination at least six months before the end of any calendar year after the year . . . . In such event, the Convention shall cease to have effect:

(a) (in State A): . . . .
(b) (in State B): . . . .

Terminal Clause

Note: The terminal clause concerning the signing shall be drafted in accordance with the constitutional procedure of both Contracting States.

Nineteen: International Lease Financing

TORE STEEN

Tore Steen is chief executive officer of Emery Financial Services, Inc. Mr. Steen was the founder and president of Chemco International Leasing, the international leasing arm of Chemical Bank. During his tenure as president of Chemco, this company became the largest and most truly international bank-owned leasing organization. He was also employed by Citicorp as vice president of administration and finance of the Citicorp Leasing International. Mr. Steen earned his M.B.A. degree in finance and international trade from the University of Oregon.

Leasing is today an integral part of the financial world and is often hailed by financial managers as the least expensive and most advantageous form of equipment funding. Founded on the principle that profit is produced from use of an asset, not from its ownership, it is now considered a viable (and honorable) financing alternative in most major and also many smaller capital equipment situations.

Although many forms of leasing and lease contracts exist, they all have certain common characteristics. For example, leasing separates the concept of the user and the owner (whether economic or legal) of a piece of property (whether real or personal). The lease contract will generally also stipulate how long users may use the equipment, what options they have, and what happens to the equipment at the end of the lease term.

The many alternatives available in the structuring of leases make them a flexible financing instrument. Leasing is sometimes even referred to as asset-based financing or the merchant banking for equipment. Successful people in the industry have been referred to as those with a "360 degree" financial imagination.

Perhaps it is the innovative nature of the industry and its people or the fact that the need was there—however, it is a financing concept which has spread across the world. It has been used in the specialized financing of ships, aircraft, containers, and other big ticket items across national boundaries. Such cross-border leasing is often intricate and highly sophisticated, but it can also be simple and straightforward. Many multinational companies have used leasing to promote and increase overseas sales of their products. As a matter of fact, leasing is often the only form of medium- or longer-term financing available to a customer in a foreign country.

It is difficult, and perhaps impossible, to estimate the magnitude of leasing in the world, because what is leasing to one person may not be leasing to another. Nevertheless, if one defines leasing as the hiring of equipment for medium or long terms and excludes real estate and automobiles, a guess might have the total global size of the leasing market somewhere around $250 billion. A further guess would be that approximately two-thirds of this is contained in the United States, and it is probably not far off the mark to suggest that this number is growing annually by a compound rate of 20 percent.

The beginning of modern day leasing is often attributed to the United States Leasing Corporation in the early 1950s. There are many, however, who would go back to the Sumerians and their leasing of goods several thousand years ago or to the early Roman days. Some would also point to the year of 1877 when Bell Telephone Company began to lease its telephones instead of selling them. There is no doubt that leasing has been around for a long time.

TYPES OF LEASING

In general, leasing takes one of three forms, namely, tax leasing, finance leasing, or operating leasing contracts.

A *tax lease* is a leasing contract in which the lessor (as economic owner) uses the benefits from deferral of taxes as a result of depreciation, capital allowances, and other incentives to lower the rental otherwise charged to the lessee. In some countries with high tax incentives, the implicit interest rate on the lease to the lessee can often be substantially below the normal borrowing rate. At the same time, the yield to lessors will be much higher, after including in their earnings the benefits from the tax they have deferred. In fact, both parties gain. A lease of this sort is, of course, particularly attractive to a lessee who could not have used the capital allowances anyway because of a lack of earnings and taxable income.

Under a *finance lease*, the lessor may or may not be the economic owner. However, the rental rate is set without giving any value to the tax benefits, and the lease term is long enough for the lessor to recover the investment from purchasing the equipment.

The term of an *operating lease* is generally shorter, and the lessor will most often provide services (other than purely financing), such as maintenance and insurance.

LEASING EXPANSION

There is hardly a country today where leasing is not known and practiced in some form. The 1950s saw expansion in the United States, and leasing began to flourish in Europe during the 1960s. Since the 1970s, the concept of leasing has expanded quite rapidly throughout the Far East and the rest of the world.

In its modern form, leasing is more than a contract or a transaction or a specific activity. It is indeed a concept, wide and elastic, which may take the form of many different types or methods of financing of capital equipment. It is sometimes called "equipment banking" or "asset-based financing," particularly in the international arena.

Leasing goes back many many years and some form of leasing is practiced in virtually every country of the world, developed or developing, across many national boundaries. Broadly speaking, the only true form of international leasing is that contract which goes across a national border, that is, where the lessor and the lessee are located in different countries. However, if one looks at international leasing through the eyes of a citizen of any one country, say the United States, any leasing which is performed in a foreign country is considered international leasing. It can, therefore, be said that there are two types of international leasing; in the first one of these, called "cross-border leasing," the lessee and the lessor are located in different countries. In the second type, which we shall call "foreign leasing," both the lessee and the lessor are located in the same country.

There are at least two important aspects of international leasing which must be recognized from the beginning. First, leasing is today in many different stages of development, depending on the part of the world. (See Exhibit 19-1). Second, international leasing is associated with many unique characteristics.

EXHIBIT 19-1   Comparative Leasing Characteristics

Country type	Laws/status	Accounting	Tax status	Leasing industry
Developed nation, leasing mature	Separate body of law/leasing is major industry	FAS 13 type of format	Lease rules like United States but deprecia-tion only shelters lease income; some tax leasing	Highly competitive
Developed nation, leasing not mature	Leasing clearly defined and understood	Mainly operating format	Fairly liberal lease defini-tions and applications	Profitable but competitive
Developing nation, leasing mature	Follows sale and rental laws— codification arriving	Must generally use operating format, trend toward U.S. style	Many leases are tax leases	Very profitable
Developing nation, not mature in leasing	Leasing often not recognized	No standards— many methods accepted	Tax treatment uncertain; withholding tax due on external debt payment	Some good oppor-tunities, but special risks need close evaluation

COMPLEXITIES AND UNIQUE CHARACTERISTICS

It is important to remember that the differing conditions and unique characteristics of international leasing, although often associated with problems, do in fact represent some rather exciting opportunities. This is as true for a manufacturer of leaseable products who can use leasing as a sales tool as it is for an end-user who considers leasing as a viable financing alternative for capital expenditures.

Although the complexities of international leasing are many, knowing the right questions is half way to the correct answers. The answers to many international leasing questions can only be obtained from experience, but it is possible to lay down some ground rules and to organize some of the parameters. Once a checklist is developed for one situation, it is probably fair to say that it represents 90 percent of the questions that need to be addressed for the next situation. It may still seem rather perplexing, but the second reading of a tax treaty is considerably easier than the first.

It must be remembered that international leasing will always involve geographical, social, cultural, political, and economic differences that probably will be manifested in different ways. Thus one should be aware of some of the tax treaties between various countries and that the basis for tax concepts may differ from country to country. The pricing mechanism, the documentation, and the payment methods will most likely be different than they would be for a lease between a lessor in New York City and a lessee in San Francisco.

The credit and financial aspects may be difficult, not only because of language differences but also because of different accounting treatments and principles. Different tax- and book-reporting aspects will considerably change the transaction from one country to another. One must also consider the problems involved in the translation of foreign currency financial statements for local currency purposes.

Withholding taxes, exchange control regulations, FAS 13 (or equivalent) accounting rules, value-added taxes, fixed and floating exchange rates, and foreign source income restrictions are just some of the further challenging characteristics in this exciting world of international leasing. One must cope with different national laws and government regulations, legal and tax systems, foreign languages, strange customs, and twenty-hour airplane trips. It is in many ways a different world. However, do not despair at the thought of getting involved in international leasing, whether as a lessee or as a lessor. The rewards to the persistent and successful participant are most often well worth the effort and the discomforts, from a personal as well as from a business point of view.

Some of the traditional reasons for leasing, such as off-balance-sheet and 100 percent financing, have been replaced by various other criteria such as the ability to obtain medium-term financing at fixed cost. In some of the developing countries leasing is very often the only form of medium-term financing; there may be no other capital market instruments available. Increasingly, one is faced with lessees and lessors who are looking at cash flows and discounted cash flow models and assessing potential capital expenditures with the use of the lease versus buy analysis. This indicates that the overseas leasing community is getting more and more sophisticated in their financial management.

The international leasing community has many participants. There are the end-users in various countries and the distributors of capital equipment as well as the manufacturers. There are the international banks and leasing companies. A multinational corporation about to negotiate a leasing contract through a subsidiary in a foreign country might want to ask for bids from some of the purely domestic leasing companies in that country as well as from the branches of foreign banks.

The number of leasing companies have proliferated in many countries during the last decade. Fifteen years ago there were only 10 leasing companies in Canada. This grew to about 35 leasing companies ten years ago and well over 100 today.

STATE OF THE ART AROUND THE WORLD

There are a number of countries in Europe where leasing is well defined and an important method for financing capital assets. There is a great amount of cross-border lease financing, and leasing often combines with the use of export incentive insurance and financing through the media of the Export Credit Guaranty Department (ECGD) in the United Kingdom, Hermes in Germany, and Coface in France. Using lease financing for the purchase of ships, aircraft, and large computer systems has become a trend.

The U.K. market is very sophisticated and very tax oriented. There also are, and have been for many years, many hire purchase and plant hire agreements written in this country. West Germany is very price competitive, and many leasing companies compete for a relatively small fixed rate leasing market.

France and Belgium are examples of countries which have well-defined leasing legislation. In France, leasing is defined as credit bail or location and regulated, whereas it is not regulated (by Royal Decree 55) in Belgium. Both markets have seen consistent growth over the last decade. French leasing companies are among the more sophisticated, both from a marketing and an administrative point of view. They primarily operate in the middle market, that is, where the average transaction is the equivalent of about $25,000.

The leasing industry started in Italy in the early 1960s, but it became significant only in the 1970s. There are presently around forty leasing companies operating in Italy, the majority of them owned by Italian banks or institutions with the remaining mostly affiliated with leading foreign banks. Interestingly, most of the leasing activity in Italy was done on a fixed rate basis until there were a couple of serious liquidity situations in the country. After that time, the dominant form of leasing became the floating rate transaction. This same development has since taken place in several other countries.

Leasing has been up and down in Spain and Portugal, but in general it has been on the upswing for the last ten years in the Scandinavian countries. There is also some leasing in Holland, Switzerland, Austria, and Greece. A few cross-border contracts have even been written into Eastern European countries.

On the North American continent, the leasing market has been fairly well developed and explored in Canada. However, here is a market where tax leasing used to flourish but has been legislated out. It is nevertheless a large and well-developed market, although there is not much cross-border leasing into Canada or out of the country.

The Mexican market has been well developed in the past, but it obviously has suffered from problems of a financing nature and, lately, of course, from the currency and economic problems. Most of the Latin American countries have seen some cross-border lease financing, and there are several mature domestic leasing economies, Brazil and Venezuela in particular.

There are some spotty markets for leasing on the African continent. South Africa is probably the best-developed country, although smaller countries such as Nigeria have seen an increase of lease financing. There is also some cross-border financing taking place, particularly as practiced by a few U.S. lessors that specialize on the African continent.

The biggest growth in leasing during the last decade has probably taken place in the Far East. A fair amount of cross-border leasing is taking place in this part of the world, and there are some rather mature and well-developed leasing industries. In Japan, for example, leasing is big and is similarly developing in the Philippines, Korea, Hong Kong, Taiwan, Indonesia, Malaysia, and Singapore.

WHEN IS A LEASE A LEASE?

There are many ways of defining and classifying leasing and leasing contracts. They may be called true, financing, operating, capital, full-payout, non-full-payout, net net net, service leases, and many other names. One of the important aspects, however, relates to the ownership of the equipment. In equipment financing there are generally two types of "ownership," the legal and the economic. In leasing, including conditional sales and hire purchase contracts, the lessor is virtually always the legal owner but not necessarily the economic owner of the equipment for the term of the contract. As the legal owners, the lessors are most often in a more secure position than if they merely held a lien on the equipment against a loan made to the lessee (or purchaser).

The vital question in an international leasing transaction, however, is the economic ownership question and whether the lease is a true lease for tax purposes. It is one of the challenges, and indeed one of the opportunities, in international leasing that the definition for whether a given transaction is a true lease differs from country to country. The same transaction may be considered a true tax lease in one country and not in another country. One need only allow the imagination to roll on to discover that this could provide some interesting opportunities for taking advantage of such things as special tax incentives and depreciation or capital allowances. The definition for when a lease is a true lease where the tax benefits of ownership accrue to the lessor is most often found in a country's tax code or cases.

In a true lease situation, the lessor is generally entitled to the depreciation allowances. In the United Kingdom, however, when a lease includes a purchase option given to the lessee, it requires the treatment of the lease as a conditional sales contract. In such cases, the lessee will be entitled to the depreciation or capital allowances. In Germany, the distinction between a lease and a conditional sales contract depends on how the German authorities view the economic ownership of the underlying property. In making such a determination, the following rules are applied:

1. The lessee is regarded as having the economic ownership for property if the base period of the lease contract amounts to less than 40 percent or more than 90 percent of the useful life of the property and the rent is equal to the cost of the property plus interest.

2. The lessor is regarded as having economic ownership of property if the base ownership of the lease is between 40 to 90 percent of the useful life of the property and there is an option to purchase at a price equal to no less than either the fair market value or the official depreciated value of the property.

The Dutch authorities, like the German, look at the economic ownership of each asset. In general, a lease will be considered a conditional sales contract if its term equals the useful life of the asset, if the lessee can or must purchase the asset at a price equal to its residual value at the end of the lease, or if all the economic or financial risks are borne by the lessee.

In Belgium, a royal decree provides that the lease term must equal the useful life of the equipment. A lease must contain an option to purchase the equipment, fixed in advance at an amount equal to the residual value. Any lesser or more nominal purchase option disqualifies the transaction from being a true lease.

In France, leasing is governed by article I of the law of July 1966, as amended by an ordinance passed on July 28, 1967. This article contains a full set of provisions which define finance leases. Even though the law requires the lessor to give the lessee a purchase option (as a fixed sum agreed at the outset of the lease), the lessor is entitled to depreciation deductions. Note also that only a bank or a commercial entity which is registered as a financial institution can enter into a lease as a lessor.

A royal decree specifies the requirements for leases in Spain. A firm which wants to engage in leasing in Korea must obtain a license from the minister of finance. The determination between a lease and a sale is set out on the basis of a ruling issued on July 20, 1978, in Japan. The determination of economic ownership in Luxembourg generally follows the same rules as in Germany. There are no specific regulations related to leasing in Ireland or in Hong Kong. Denmark has no special rules relating to leasing either, but they do have a Hire Purchase Act. The Central Bank of Brazil has adopted various rules and regulations related to leasing, and Decree 1.811, signed by the president of Brazil on October 27, 1980, began a change in Brazil to allow foreign-based lessors to cross the border with their leasing transactions. The Austrian leasing law is very similar to that of West Germany. Although leasing is regulated by the minister of finance in Taiwan, there is no legislation or case law in Sweden related to lease financing.

COMMERCIAL AND POLITICAL RISKS

There are obvious risks associated with the making of any contract for the financing of any equipment. However, when this contract is made in or involves another country, the risks multiply. The normal commercial risks now take on different proportions, not the least of which are those risks associated with distance, e.g., the difficulty of checking the credibility of the other party and the impracticality of sending someone around to collect a late payment.

At the same time, one must contend with the sovereign or political risks. These may take the form of potential nationalization of companies, freezing of currencies, changes in valuations of currencies, potential risks of war, and, last but not least, the great unknown of a foreign country's legal system.

Any lessor or lessee in a cross-border of foreign leasing transaction must assess the economic and political climate of the other country. Export credit agencies can be of considerable assistance, particularly because they will provide cover for political risks and in some cases also at least a portion of the commercial risks.

Some of the export credit agencies are the ECGD in the United Kingdom, Coface in France, and Hermes in Germany. In general, these offer insurance guarantees up to around 85 to 90 percent, and they generally cover the exchange of commercial and political risks. With such insurance coverage available, a lessor usually can then go to banks to negotiate advantageous fixed rate financing.

Before entering into a lease contract, either as lessee or lessor, with a party in another country, one must study the potential problems associated with exchange control. For example, permission is needed from the French government to make payments to a nonresident, although in most cases approval will be granted. In some countries, such as Nigeria, it is extremely difficult to obtain approval for a resident company to purchase foreign exchange with which to make lease payments. Also, the transfer of local earnings abroad is completely restricted—hence the term "frozen" currency.

Many major industrial countries have enacted antiavoidance provisions in their local laws. Such provisions may be applied through many means, such as fiscal legislation, exchange control restrictions, and tax regulations.

For example, the Subpart F taxation rules in the United States restrict any potential benefits of using tax havens as the incorporating country of a foreign leasing company. Belgium has put tax deductibility restrictions on lease payments to companies in tax haven countries.

It is easy to imagine the extent to which a foreign environment can affect the profitability of a lease contract for a lessor, and it is obvious that the same set of factors can affect the cost to the lessee. Whether the tax or legal environment makes leasing more or less expensive will vary from country to country or, to be more accurate, from pairs of countries to pairs of countries, since the tax and other laws are very often part of a double taxation treaty. These treaties may limit the amount of withholding tax or allow the lessor to be taxed in the foreign environment more or less the same as at home.

When comparing a cross-border lease with a similar loan, in many cases the lease will fall under different sections of the fiscal regulations. Often, the red tape needed to remit payments under lease agreements may be much less than in the case of a loan. Typically, in countries where the leasing industry is not well developed, leasing will fall under the commercial sector of both local and foreign exchange regulations as opposed to under the banking and finance sections.

STRUCTURAL ALTERNATIVES

Many lessors and lessees establish special legal structures to optimize the advantages of international leasing activities. Such structural alternatives might include the use of a home-country-incorporated company, a company in a tax haven country (for example, in the use of cross-border transactions), or a subsidiary or an affiliate located in the country where the lessee or lessor is. The decision of which type of structures to go with will depend on an analysis of all the financial, fiscal, and economic characteristics of a given transaction or set of transactions. This difficult decision will involve many tax, accounting, and legal considerations, and expert advice should be sought.

LEGAL CONSIDERATIONS

Many legal issues must be researched and analyzed in any international leasing transaction. Not only do laws and regulations differ from country to country, they also change from time to time; special rules may apply to special forms of transactions or types of lease equipment.

Necessary information includes a foreign country's laws about the rights, if any, of the various parties in an equipment financing transaction. Such important aspects as the perfection of title and security interest, the extent of enforceability of the lease contract, and the right of foreign lessees or lessors in a given country must be considered.

Whether leasing is regulated and, if so, to what extent, is an important question. Legal or statutory definitions of a lease are also important. Does the country require that the lessor, lessee, or both be registered? Import permissions or restrictions must be studied, and remember that it is not safe to assume that after checking these things for one lease that they need not be checked again for future leases. Lessors must study their repossession right in cases when they have leased a piece of equipment to a foreign lessee.

The best advice for a lessor or a lessee regarding legal considerations is that consultation with local counsel is absolutely essential.

A lease contract will undoubtedly state under what law the lease may be enforced. However, this may not comfort the foreign party a great deal. The lease may still be difficult to enforce or may be enforced in ways which would be unacceptable, particularly in countries where leasing is still relatively unfamiliar. There are cases, however, when an arbitration clause is the best safety net, particularly in transactions where the countries of both parties are signatories to the U.N. treaties about arbitrations.

CONCLUSION

The success of a venture into the world of international leasing depends on many factors. First, one must be willing to spend the time to get familiar with and study all the complexities involved. Second, one must be willing to seek expert advice when it is needed. This chapter on international leasing shows that, although the complexities are not impossible, they do need a lot of attention. Albert Einstein probably did not have leasing in mind when he said that "it may intimidate the human race into bringing order into its international affairs, which, without the pressure of fear it would not do." However, who knows?

In summary, although the factors which affect both lessor and lessee under an international lease contract are often complex and require careful evaluation, in many cases leasing clearly is a very viable financing alternative. Although statistics are not readily available, international leasing is growing rapidly, and many partnerships created between lessors and lessees are profitable for both parties.

BIBLIOGRAPHY

"Accounting for Leases," Chartered Accountant in Australia, Nov. 1980, pp. 60–65.
Alderman, J. Kenneth and C. Wayne Alderman: "Accounting for Leases," Journal of Accountancy, June 1979, pp. 74–79.
Benjamin, Robert W.: "How Tax Treaties Affect International Leasing," International Tax Journal, vol. 1, 1975, pp. 363 ff.
Berman, H. J. and C. Kaufman: "Law of International Commercial Transactions," Harvard International Law Journal, Winter 1978, pp. 221–227.

Cannaliato, Vincent J.: "What to Consider in International Leasing Transactions," in *U.S. Taxation of International Operations*, Prentice-Hall, Englewood Cliffs, N.J., 1980, pp. 7721–7736.

Choate, Alan G.: "Tax and Balance of Payment Aspects of International Financing," in: *U.S. Taxation of International Operations*, Prentice-Hall, Englewood Cliffs, N.J., 1977, pp. 5071–5084.

Clark, Gordon D.: "Foreign Tax Credits Aspects of International Leasing," *International Tax Journal*, vol. 1, 1975, pp. 235 *ff.*

Clark, T. M.: "New Ways to Boost Exports," *The Director*, July 1981, pp. 50 *ff.*

Contino, Richard M.: *Legal and Financial Aspects of Equipment Leasing Transactions*, Prentice-Hall, Englewood Cliffs, N.J., 1979.

Deming, John R.: "An Analysis of FASB No. 13," *Financial Executive*, March 1978.

"Eastern Air Lines Arranges Leverged Lease Featuring Advance Interest Payments," *Business International Money Report*, June 15, 1979, pp. 202–203.

Eigner, Richard M.: "Tax Planning under Subpart F," in Practising Law Institute, *Sixth Annual Institute on International Taxation*, New York, 1975, pp. 21–63.

Equipment Leasing 1979, Practising Law Institute, New York, 1979.

Eyer, Walter W.: "The Sale, Leasing and Financing of Aircraft," *Journal of Air Law & Commerce*, vol. 45, no. 1, 1979, pp. 217–274.

Goss, Chester C.: "Put Leasing to Work to Build Sales in Foreign Markets," *International Business*, Mar./Apr. 1979, pp. 34–47.

International Accounting Standards Committee: *Accounting for Leases*, London, Oct. 31, 1980 (Exposure Draft 19).

International Leasing, Practising Law Institute, New York, 1974.

Kramer, John L.: "Depreciation Recapture in International Liquidation," *International Tax Journal*, vol. 2, no. 4, 1976, pp. 335–353.

Machinery and Allied Products Institute: *A Handbook on Financing U.S. Exports*, 2d ed., Washington, D.C., 1976.

Pond, Jonathan D.: "Capitalizing Leased Assets," *Management Accounting*, Jan. 1977,

Power, John: "International Leasing," *Tax Planning International*, Mar. 1979, pp. 41–46.

Pritchard, Robert E. and Thomas Hindeland: *The Lease Buy Decision*, 1980.

Proctor, S.: "Leasing's Growing Pains," *International Management*, Sept. 1979, pp. 32–34.

Schachner, Leopold: "The New Accounting for Leases," *Financial Executive*, February 1978.

U.S. Domestic and International Business Administration: *A Guide to Financing Exports*, Washington, D.C., reprinted Apr. 1976.

U.S. Domestic and International Business Administration: Bureau of Domestic Commerce. *Equipment Leasing and Rental Industry Trends and Product*, Washington, D.C., 1976.

Vlieland-Boddy, Clive and Martin Vlieland-Boddy: "Tax Advantages of Equipment Leasing," *Accounting* (UK), Feb. 1980, pp. 82–84.

Wayne, Leslie: "Double Tax Breaks on Leases," *The New York Times*, April 7, 1981.

Index